THE WAILING WIND

A TALE OF LOVE AND OBSESSION

JOSEPH T. RENALDI

AUTHOR:	Joseph T. Renaldi
FRONT COVER:	Joseph T. Renaldi
BOOK LAYOUT:	H. Donald Kroitzsh
EDITOR:	H. Donald Kroitzsh

This book is a work of fiction. No character is real and no incident occurred as described in this book; no man or woman who lives within the pages of this book lives outside of it. This book depicts the social and economic environment that once existed in typical coal mining communities in the United States during the pre and post Korean War era, as well as the lives of the men and women of various ethnic groups these communities have touched and changed. The author is not writing about any specific community or individual in particular. The actions and scenes portrayed here are fictional in nature and created from the author's research and experience in the Coal Region and in the military service, not actual events.

Copyright ©1999 by Joseph T. Renaldi. All rights reserved. No part of this publication may be reproduced, stored in a retrieval system or transmitted, in any form, or by any means, electronic, mechanical, recorded, photocopied, or otherwise, without the prior written permission of the copyright owner, except by a reviewer who may quote brief passages in a review. For further information or orders contact JOREN, 400 Wallnick Drive, Frackville, PA 17931, USA, Phone: (570) 874-1431

Printed in Canada

Published by:
Five Corners Publications, Ltd.
5052 Route 100
Plymouth, Vermont 05056   USA

The Wailing Wind, A Tale of Love and Obsession
ISBN: 1-886699-17-8

Contents

Prologue
vii

Part I
Henry Shane- a Korean War Hero
1

Part II
Sinclair, Pennsylvania
1942-1953
57

Part III
A Soldier's Life in the Far East
1948-1953
253

Part IV
Immorality to Reconciliation
329

Epilogue
371

Report On Prisoners

War has been defined as a " contest of wills." A trained hand holds the weapon—but the will, the character, the spirit of the individual—these control the hand. More than ever, in the war for the minds of men moral character, will, and spirit are important.

As a service man thinketh so is he.

The Report of the Secretary of Defense's Advisory Committee on Prisoners' of War, August 1955
U.S. Government Printing Office, Washington, D. C.

This book is dedicated to my late brother, Master Sergeant Leo J. Renaldi, who served with distinction in the Combat Engineers during the Korean War, to all the veterans, especially those who endured the pain and agony of confinement in a North Korean prisoner-of-war camp.

I wish to extend a special tribute to all my friends in the Coal Region, and to all the men and women who struggled to survive under adverse conditions in an unstable environment.

Prologue

I am the son of a coal miner.

It was my misfortune to be born in Sinclair, a town located near the Stonycreek River in the Coal Region of Pennsylvania.

There I spent the first eighteen years of my life-years crowded with unhappy memories, with episodes and ventures, distressing, touching and tormenting. I intended to forget the anguish and anxiety of those experiences. I am compelled by a mysterious urge to relate as simply as I can what happened to some of the sons and daughters of coal miners, and myself, to give an elaborate account of those days and of our cumbersome life in Sinclair.

The monotonous life in Sinclair consisted of a day, a week, a month, a year, a birth, and a death. The essential requirements of survival were that each man worked in the coal mine, and bought what he needed from the company store, and ate and slept and was housed and procreated in a dwelling owned by the Coal Company.

The police force, whose members were controlled by the Coal Company, ruled the town with an iron fist. The politically oriented miner's union attempted to unravel the coal miner's problems. The physicians, who staffed the hospital, tended and healed the sick. The priests and ministers attempted to console the souls of the depressed parishioners.

During my youth, I often wondered why so many intelligent men worked in a coal mine. What moved them to spend the prime of their life in cold, treacherous confines? Yet, the fathers of Sinclair and most of their sons went to work in the coal mine, and thus it has been for several generations.

I often heard the miners speak of the perils of coal mining, yet, miners of all ages continued to go down into the depths of the earth. They knew from all the calamities that they had witnessed from boyhood observance to adult grief that coal mining is one of the most perilous methods of earning a living. They knew they would leave a family to survive and subsist in an even more uncertain position than which encompassed their own life.

Still, they would continue to toil in the mines, almost as if some spirit strapped them to their job as a coal miner. There were little incentives—only a poor salary the coal company gave them for their strenuous work.

I often thought that some evil spirit overcame their soul, binding them to the Coal Company to honor an agreement from which only death or maiming could free them from bondage.

I firmly believed that the mines had been like a mausoleum that had entombed coal miners and was made from nature's unpredictable behavior, whether it is categorically classified as environment, geography, or mountain region.

The mountains near Sinclair contained the coal, their slopes contained the people who lived in dilapidated houses who did the work of mining the coal. The region became a private and sinister haven to keep the people from moving in from other areas of the country. It was the mountainous environment that became the spiritless mausoleum, even though without fortifications or sentries, that has dominated the lives of the inhabitants so much that few of them ever learned how to leave the Coal Region.

There were many physical obstacles that had a strong influence on the minds and feelings of the people. The Stonycreek River and the Pennsylvania Railroad and the coal tipple's gigantic structure all exerted immense influences, but none, nearly as much as the high mountains near Sinclair. Mountains rear their own kind of peculiarities, developing even their own social behavior and their own dialect. They cultivate a style of ignorance too, that makes the area beyond the Coal Region a strange and prohibitive land.

After an absence of many years, I returned to the Coal Region, not as a matter of choice, but at the request of my employer to supervise the construction of a coal-fired electric power plant in a remote area near Sinclair.

Geographically, during the days of my youth, my world was the known terrain of Sinclair and the coal stripping pits and drift mines and railroad yards, which surrounded it. The history of Sinclair was my own history and the history of those whom I admired or among whom I had been born and reared.

Now I consider myself only as a face in the crowd in Sinclair. I will always be one with the belief that Sinclair is the most unique town in the Coal Region. To stroll along the old, ravaged road leading to the abandoned coal mine is to step into the realms of a history proudly lived by a people born to cope with a rigid tradition of their past.

To stroll in the dusty streets of Sinclair is to experience the memories of the past that is particular to this town and this town alone; memories with the equal parts of the majestic, the incomprehensible, and the uncertainty. There is nothing to warn you of Sinclair's melancholy background. That knowledge must be learned. No commemorative plaques hang from the sides of the coal tipple's gigantic structure or the vestibule of the town hall. No messages are on the deteriorated, weather-beaten billboards at the entrance to the town to alert visitors, except the fading remnants of block lettering on the billboards proclaiming the town's position: Sinclair—Heart of the Coal Region.

My approach to Sinclair is always silent and distracted. I returned with insurmountable energy and memories abounding around me in the form of the things in nature I loved best. Deer feeding on tender growth, the brood call of quail, squirrels chattering and leaping from tree to tree, the sweet, sharp chirping of birds in the branches of the tall oak trees. Nevertheless, my return to this grime-haunted town is filled with deep thoughts on both the sustenance and survival of the inhabitants.

The town of Sinclair in the simple, fragile modesty of its dwellings, in the ugliness of its style, in the economy and clearness of its features and the calmness of the surrounding mountain north and south of Rosemore Avenue is of historical significance. To me, Sinclair is a somber town, a mysterious town, whose history, traditions, and apparitions danced their coal pit dances and composed their evil lyrics on the blind side of the Allegheny Mountains. I scrutinized those apparitions closely once, and they were instrumental in persuading me to leave Sinclair to matriculate at an institution of higher learning.

Sinclair has a smell, a suppressing odor of sulfur, with the coal and the history of the town aging beneath the refuse, the putrid and decadent odors of a deteriorating environment. I knew what the suppressing smell of the town meant to me. During my absence I always recollected the dilapidated dwellings and the miserable living conditions which overwhelmed the town.

The majority of the houses were poorly constructed of wood, the exteriors finished with an inferior clapboard usually nailed in a shoddy manner directly to the framework. Roofs were covered with a tar-like composition material. The interior of the houses was finished off with a substandard, low-grade sheathing. The houses rested on concrete footers with poorly constructed foundations. The state of disrepair was beyond one's verbal imagination or even of pictorial description since words or pictures could not describe the scene of total negligence on the part of the Coal Company who owned the houses. Many unpainted clapboard houses, clapboard deteriorating, roofs damaged, porches drooping, steps sagging, a conglomeration of junk and rubbish and an aroma of offensive odors permeated the air.

Living near the mine often created an emotional excitement in my boyhood, and I developed an unusual obsession for it, intermingled with a genuine respect and admiration for the coal miners who challenged the mysterious and dangerous passageways below the earth. Many years later I would refer to the passageways as the catacombs of the Coal Region.

Strip mining devastated much of the rural surroundings of Sinclair. There was a time to look about the landscape and see the increase in green leaves on the live oak and maple trees, and where nature's accident of soil and moisture produced patches of luxuriant growth. Many varieties of trees such as the sturdy hemlocks were scattered in the environment along with the red and white birch, wild cherry and crabapple trees. There was an array of bright, fragrant wildflowers growing on the slopes, mountain laurel blooming late in the highlands, and the daisies with their long, white petals and yellow centers dominating the sides of the roadway. The highlands were green and succulent.

It was a dream-like contrast to the barren, trashy yards, and the dilapidated houses. They would be termed in the Coal Region as company row, but the coal miners and their families lived there then, and many of them were strange, foreign-speaking people that I knew in only a casual way.

When I traveled to Sinclair from a work assignment on the Chattahoochee River in the state of Georgia, the train meandered along the high ridge of the Allegheny Mountains, and I had a bird's eye view of the Coal Region. I gazed long and pensively at the scars and remnants of the declining coal industry: inactive mines, coal-stripping pits filled with water, and huge indescribable mounds of mine refuse. Many destitute ex-miners, unemployed and ignored by the coal companies, could be seen in mining hamlets that lay along idle railroad tracks and filthy, polluted streams as the train meandered through the lowlands and gorges near Sinclair. Unemployed and distraught, I surmised there was little they could do about their economic plight and frustration for most of the mines in the region were either closed or inactive. I envisaged that most of the men just sat on their rocking chairs on their front porches and gazed at the steep mountain slopes that had once been scenic. They were scarred by strip mining or obscured by huge mounds of mine refuse—the trademark of an industry that was responsible for much grief and suffering.

In the morning sunlight the deep, dark excavations where the coal had been stripped lay against the side of the mountain like the craters of numerous volcanoes. Before me, like the framework of a skyscraper, rose the coal tipple's gigantic structure, the weather beaten, paint starved, crumbling company houses, the polluted Stonycreek River, and most of all, the sorrowful moment of my mental disturbance.

My observations became intolerably excruciating, inexorably my thoughts immediately reflected the deplorable days of my youth and the imminent confrontation with the depressed inhabitants of Sinclair that came nearer with each passing landmark, each revolution of the locomotive's wheels.

Shortly after my arrival in Sinclair, I found myself leaning against the bar in the American Legion Post on Rosemore Avenue surrounded by a group of inebriated men from company row who were observing the anniversary of the Korean War.

These men had served in the armed forces and they had been coal miners one day, and servicemen and different the next day, and they were coal miners again, no longer uniformed, and undistinguishable from the other clientele around them. They had an enduring memory of military life, of men marching in unison, of rapturous feelings—highlighted by parades and military music. There had been a war and men of Sinclair had fought in it, and others had died in it. To these men, war was like the sound of a muffled drum, and the excitability of those who heard it, and the heartfelt emotion of watching those who marched to it. For these surviving veterans, the cessation of the war ended a chapter in their life, but not their living.

On this particular occasion, the veterans mentioned the heroic accomplishments of Henry Shane during the Korean War, and proposed a toast to him in abstention.

The inebriated veterans knew that Henry Shane was a native son, and a highly decorated soldier. His numerous heroic deeds during the Korean War had earned him countless military honors and commendations.

It was no surprise to me that Henry Shane, the soldier himself, returned to Sinclair in September of 1953, traveling out of Korea, out of a war ravaged country, out in fact of the legend encircling his past. He returned as a lame and crippled warrior to challenge the deplorable environment of the Coal Region. As far as the Coal Region and inhabitants were concerned, he was one of many who were plagued by an economic depression.

Now in the midst of these festive veterans in the American Legion Post, his name continued to drift back into myth and legend, knowledge of his reputation deeply ingrained in the minds of these military veterans to that of a folk-hero.

Later, I learned that Henry Shane was not a folk hero. It was merely that the inhabitants gave the legend meaning, order and guidance by believing without doubting all the things that afterwards were said of him.

I wondered how the days in Sinclair characterized him after he returned from the Korean War. I wondered if our characteristics were the same. I like to think of him strolling the streets of Sinclair as I had strolled them, and it pleases me to know that the people in town observed him, felt the warmth of his presence in his awkward strolls along Rosemore Avenue.

While the inebriated military veterans continued reminiscing, I indulged myself with a vision. I saw myself hiking with Henry Shane, and together we crossed the Allegheny Mountains, the war hero leading the way as we traveled westward in our great escape from the Coal Region, overjoyed with passionate freedom. It was a beautiful sight to see the Allegheny Mountains through the eyes of Henry Shane. I had one regret in this vision, I would have liked first to have shown him Sinclair through my eyes before we departed. I, too, had a living hell in Sinclair as a youth, and I, too, would have some scars to show him.

The hardened, non-persuasive smile of Henry Shane was an expression of understandable morbidity. I felt sympathy and a great admiration for this highly decorated warrior. I honor and respect the courage he did not really know he possessed.

After his discharge from the army, he felt insecure within the confines of Sinclair. Yet, he remained. The thought of his family and relatives spending a lifetime in the Coal Region denied any possibilities that he could depart from the town under any conditions other than a tarnished reputation. Once this almost happened because his name was besmirched by scandal, and later married a woman who was branded and scorned by the inhabitants as being immoral. He remembered the moment often, not because of his guilt or humiliation. It was then he had the first premonition that someday someone would tell his story, tell what it was like to live in a Coal Region town, an eyewitness report on the trials and tribulations of hard times.

Still, I learned to know what Henry Shane did for his country in time of war, and what he said, how he felt and how he survived in a prisoner of war camp, and in this pathetic town.

Amidst the cold, cruel hearts of the men and women, he felt a sense of insecurity. This is the story I will relate to you. In the Coal Region, learning to survive was somewhat of an art.

Likewise, I am a product of this Coal Region environment, and I have a strong desire to tell the world what I witnessed in Sinclair. I want to tell you how it was. I want you to understand why I dislike the town of Sinclair with all my intense emotions. Then I want you to forgive me for being a zealous supporter of the town.

Some of the inhabitants of Sinclair, who are her sons and daughters, will hate me for the rest of their life. I will not be offended. You see, I am the son of a coal miner, and Sinclair is my birthplace.

THE WAILING WIND

A TALE OF LOVE AND OBSESSION

Part One

Henry SHANE — Korean War Hero

Joseph T. Renaldi

One

The town of Sinclair, in the Coal Region of Pennsylvania, lay under a heavy covering of snow with high drift causing difficulty in walking and motoring. In a clear sky, the moon resembled an enormous distant light that cast a brilliant ray upon the white mass. The frigid air was so transparent to light that the house fronts along the street looked gray against the snow. Clumps of shrubbery and trees cast dark shadows on it and the windows of the houses sent beams of bright light far across the landscape.

I walked at a quick pace from the Wheeling Estate where I had been residing, along the deserted street, past the Eureka Store and the antiquated town hall with a statue of a coal miner near the metal gate.

Opposite the town hall, where the road fell away towards the center of town, Saint Anthony's Catholic Church reared its elaborate steeple and glowing cross.

As I strode along through the snow, many thoughts of life in Sinclair raged in my mind and mingled with the pronounced imprints caused by my quick plodding in the snow.

The night was perfectly still, and the air so dry and pure that it gave little sensation of cold. The effect produced on me was rather of an entire absence of atmosphere, as though nothing less tenuous than a trivial thought that came between the snow-covered pavement under my feet and the Star Tavern that I had seen ahead of me.

As I walked toward the Star Tavern, the partially dark front window cast a shadow on the sidewalk near the building. From the lower openings, on the side where the ground sloped steeply down Rosemore

Avenue, the neon sign cast its precise ray of light, illuminating many fresh foot prints on the sidewalk leading to the side entrance, and showing, near an adjacent parking lot, a line of snow-covered vehicles.

I paused before the darkened side of the Star Tavern. I stood there a moment, breathing quickly, and looking up and down the street, in which not another person could be seen. The silence of midnight overwhelmed the town, but some of its boisterous life was gathered behind the tavern's door, from which foul and abusive language could be heard.

Steps led down from the walk to the side entrance, and I saw several drunkards coming out at that moment leaning heavily on each other and exchanging abusive language. I barely paused before I descended the steps. I had never entered the Star Tavern, but I was anxious, and was also suffering from stress and anxiety. Seating myself in a dark and dirty corner in front of a small, filthy table, I ordered a beer, and eagerly drank it without any hesitation.

I felt instantly relieved and my brain began to clear. "How absurd I have been?" I whispered to myself. "Life must go on. Nothing should interfere with my work objectives. It was simply the stress of my job with the Keystone Power and Electric Company in Shirleysville, and the thought of a life of boredom in Sinclair."

Yet, in spite of this unworthy conclusion, my face brightened as if I had been suddenly relieved from a difficult situation, and I cast a sociable glance around the bar room. At the same time I had a contemptible suspicion that there was something artificial in this moment of cheerfulness.

Several more drunken men began to leave the tavern. A group of elated men from the Diamond Dart Club were preparing to leave on the heels of the drunken men. When they had gone, it seemed that the environment of the establishment had become peaceful and tranquil. Only a small group of men had remained. A man partly drunk, who looked like a panhandler, was sitting with a bottle of beer in front of him. A short, stout man with a long, dense beard wearing a soiled sweatshirt was nodding his head in a state of intoxication. From time to time he would come to his senses and begin to curse, rotate his short arms, and pound on his chest with his fists, though without rising from the chair on which he was sitting. These gyrations accompanied some asinine remarks, the words of which I could vaguely endeavor to recall. No one paid attention to him. His companion even received his nonsensical remarks in silence and with a matter of disturbance. The third member of the group, I surmised, looked like an unemployed, former coal miner. He sat by himself, from time to time tapping his beer mug on the table and glancing around. He, too, seemed considerably perturbed.

I was unaccustomed to crowds, and I had been shunning all social contacts with my fellows especially of late. At the present moment, however, I felt suddenly drawn to them. Thus, though this tavern was so filthy, I had a certain pleasure in being one of the customers. The proprietor of the establishment sat in another room, but appeared from time to time at the bar. He wore a wrinkled, sky-blue shirt sporadically covered with a conglomeration of food stains, and a maroon bow tie. His face seemed to glow like a light bulb. An attractive bar maid was seated on a stool near the bar, and one still younger and more vivacious was waiting on the clientele. The menu, listing the food specials of the day, was printed on a chalkboard hanging on the wall behind the counter. A moldy and nauseating odor permeated the establishment.

Occasionally I came across strangers, who interested me at first sight, even before I had exchanged a word. This was precisely the effect produced on me by the individual who looked like an unemployed coal miner. When I subsequently recalled this impression, I merely classified it as an opinion. I never took my eyes off the man, doubtless, because the latter returned his gaze and seemed anxious to engage in a conversation. He looked interested and even looked somewhat proudly upon the other men and the proprietor of the establishment; evidently he thought they were beneath him in intelligence and the social scale for him to stoop to engage in conversation with them.

He was a man of average height and appeared to be crippled. His head was sparsely covered with black and gray hair. His puffy cheeks, of a reddish hue, showed signs of intemperate habits, and under the twitching eyelids sparkled a pair of small, blood shot eyes. The most striking feature about his face was its expression of intelligence and enthusiasm, which alternated with a look of utter disgust. He wore a ragged coat sweater with several patches sewn on it. It must have been a long time since he had shaved, for his chin was covered with a growth of prickly hair. A touch of friendly seriousness was also evident in his manner, though at the present moment he seemed to be suffering from depression. He passed his hands over his head and sometimes buried his face in them on the tablemat. At length he turned to me and addressed me in a loud, decisive tone. "Shall I be imposing upon you, sir, if I venture to enter into a conversation with you? My experienced eye enables me in spite of the plainness of your apparel to perceive that you are a well-versed man, and not a frequent visitor to the bar rooms. I, myself, have always attached great importance to versatility. I am a former owner of a small coal-mine. Please allow me to introduce myself, Henry Shane, ex mine proprietor. I don't think I have seen you around here before. Are you visiting relatives in Sinclair?"

"No, I was born in Sinclair, and departed from this town several years ago to enter the army. Upon my discharge from the army, I returned to Sinclair hoping to find decent employment. The jobs were scarce, and I was fortunate to be able to matriculate at a college with the assistance of the G I Bill. Presently I am a supervisor with the Keystone Power and Electric Company in Shirleysville."

"Then you are a native son and a traveled man?" Henry Shane said promptly. "I thought as much. My instincts are unfailing, sir, and founded on considerable experience."

He touched his forehead with his finger to indicate his own estimate of his capacity and continued: "I detected in your manner of speech, sir, a Coal Region accent." I was slightly surprised by Henry Shane's courteous language, and yet annoyed at finding myself abruptly addressed by a stranger. Though I felt in a sociable mood the last half-hour, the annoyance that I usually felt when a stranger attempted to accost me was instantly revived.

"You have come a long way since your boyhood days," Henry Shane remarked in a complimentary tone. "Please allow me—." Rising, beer mug in his hand, he changed his seat to one near me. Though intoxicated, he spoke distinctly and with tolerable coherence. To see him deeply interested in my background, it might have been assumed that he, too, had not opened his lips for several days.

"Sir," Henry Shane said softly. "I think I can read trouble in your facial expression. As soon as you entered the tavern I received that impression, and that was why I addressed you. If I begin to tell you the story of my life, it isn't in order to incur the ridicule of these idlers before you, who have heard it all before, but because I seek the sympathy of a well-versed man. Allow me, out of pure curiosity, to ask you another question. Have you ever spent a night sleeping in a box car over at the railroad yard?"

"No, I never have slept in a box car. Why?"

"Well, that is where I have been sleeping the last few nights." Henry filled his beer mug, drank it off, and began to ponder. Particles of paper filler were seen adhering to his clothes, and even to his sparse hair above his ears, and he looked as if he had neither bathed nor changed his clothes for the last several days.

"You are a capricious man, Henry Shane," said Joseph Kelly the proprietor of the tavern in a loud voice. "If you proclaim to be such a concerned man, how in the hell is it that you don't work and fulfill your duties and responsibilities at home instead of coming in here and spending your money on booze?"

"Why don't I work?" responded Henry Shane, addressing himself exclusively to me, as if the question had come from me. "Isn't my inefficiency a cause of annoyance to myself? But, no, it is ridiculous to talk about it. I have never fulfilled my objectives in life; not once has anyone shown me any sympathy or compassion, but it is all in my character. I am nothing but a real ass."

"You can say that again!" Joseph Kelly said with a chuckle.

Henry Shane struck the table with his fist in anger. Realizing that he was losing his composure stopped and tried to smile, but his chin quivered. He succeeded, however, in suppressing his emotional feelings.

I didn't know what to make of this drunkard, who had left his home for several days and had been sleeping in a box car over at the railroad yard, and yet seemed to cherish some concern and attachment to his family.

"Such is my character," Henry Shane continued. "Would you believe it, sir, if I were to tell you that I have spent all of my money on booze, jeopardizing the welfare of my family? We live in a cold and drafty row house, and my wife, Edith has acute bronchitis this winter, and began to cough and spit blood. I have a stepdaughter, and my wife works her ass off from morning until night tending to the house and keeping Melissa tidy. She had been accustomed to seeing everything clean. Unfortunately, Edith is sick and frail, and it grieves me. Don't I feel it? The more I drink, the more I feel the agony. I give myself up to drink on purpose to feel and suffer the more."

I detected a sense of hopelessness and helplessness in Henry Shane, but permitted him to continue to release all of his frustrations.

"Well, I may be a drunkard, but my wife Edith, regardless of all her faults, is a lady in my opinion, and her sole pleasure in life now is to recall bygone days. Yes, she has a grand, proud sentimental soul. Her first husband, Andy Curtis, was a mine superintendent, and he was greatly attached to her. I have heard, since then, from various sources that they were not always on the best of terms. Edith began to have an extra marital affair with Robert Heim, and unfortunately, Andy Curtis became distraught and separated from Edith. Later he committed suicide while he was living in Twin Forks. Then Vito Rizzo killed her live-in companion, Robert Heim over a land dispute near the Stonycreek River. Edith always was a lonely and restless person. Although she had many previous marital problems, she still decided to marry Wayne Trent and that marriage culminated in divorce. It was a tragedy. Yet, it does not prevent her from still cherishing their memory with tears, and constantly making comparisons between them and myself, which I find by no means flattering. I am quite pleased all the same, that she should imagine her former life to have been a happy one. She found herself alone with an illegitimate child in this desolate Coal Region. It was here that I renewed a relationship with her. Then, I who had been a veteran of the Korean War, following my discharge from the army, decided to marry her if the opportunity presented itself. It was then I made a proposal of marriage to my former fiancée."

Here Henry Shane grit his teeth, and closing his eyes, leaned on the table. In another minute, however, his expression suddenly changed, and looking at me contemptuously, he continued to speak with a slight smile on his face.

"Though she had come from a respectable and hard working family, and brought up with good manners, she consented to marry me, and by that you may gauge her misery. She received my offer with tears and sobs, and twirled her thumbs, but she accepted it, for she had nowhere to go to. Can you understand, sir, what it means to have nowhere to go to? Don't realize that yet? Well, I treated her properly for a couple of years, never touching the bottle, for my feelings were honorable. I earned little money. I had to close my small mine without any fault of my own. The decline of the coal industry and strict laws governing the safety requirements led to my economic collapse, and then I took to heavy drinking to escape from all of my problems." Henry Shane paused as if his voice would serve him no longer; then he suddenly filled his beer mug again, drank the contents, and after awhile resumed:

"Oh, sir!" implored Henry Shane, "maybe like the rest of the people around here, you think all of this talk as being merely a lot of bullshit. Maybe I only bore you by relating all these foolish and pitiful details of my marital problems, but they are not as amusing in my eyes, because they penetrate my heart. Several days ago I had visions of sugar plum and illusions of grandeur. I was dreaming how I might reorganize my life, find adequate food and clothing for my family, and enable my wife to have a few luxuries, and raise my family out of the mire. How many plans I made? Well, one morning, just a few days ago—after cherishing all of these dreams—I did a stupid thing. I stole money from my wife's drawer, money that she had saved for Melissa's upkeep. How much money was there left? I can't remember. I left home a few days ago, and they don't know what has become of me. I have lost control of my predicament. Who could feel sorry for such a man?"

"Why should anyone have pity on you with all of your bullshit?" Joseph Kelly remarked sarcastically. Here Henry Shane again became overwhelmed by emotion, and he laid his head on the table with an expression of despair. He had lost all consciousness of his environment, and was overcome in a deep reverie. His words produced a certain impression on me.

Shortly, he raised his head and abruptly said, "Let us be going, sir. Please help me home. I only live a short distance from the tavern. It is time I went back to my wife and Melissa."

I had wanted to leave the tavern for sometime, and had already thought of making myself helpful to Henry Shane. His legs and voice were unsteady, and he leaned heavily on me for support. As we approached the row house, Henry Shane seemed to grow more and more uneasy.

"It isn't my wife that concerns me now," Henry stammered in his emotion. "I know she will begin to scream and curse at me, but it really doesn't matter. I do hate the thought of her heavy breathing. You never know what she might do when she is in that condition. Have you ever noticed how people breathe and snort when they are greatly agitated? I'm afraid of hearing Melissa whimper for I know, unless my wife has found her something to eat; she will have a difficult time trying to restrain her. She had little food. I don't know how they are going to survive." He continued to stammer and finally said, "Here we are at the row house where I live. There are other families that are here, too, and it isn't the most pleasant place in the world in which to live. It seems that the tenants are always raising a lot of hell at all hours of the night." We entered the row house and began to ascend to the third floor. It was close to midnight, and the higher we ascended the darker the staircase became, until it ended in complete obscurity. The door that opened on to the landing stood ajar. The rays from a low wattage lamp revealed a miserable room. It contained nothing but a cook stove, several wooden chairs and a table, bare and unpainted. There were two other adjacent rooms in sight. The door leading to the other rooms occupied by other families stood partly opened. Some of these rooms were noisy; and I assumed that the occupants were playing cards and drinking whiskey and beer. Several children were crying, and a succession of loud laughter and abusive language could be heard throughout the row house.

I recognized Henry Shane's wife at once. She was of a fair height, and had a shapely and attractive figure, but looked very ill in the face. Her black hair was still beautiful, but there were several blotches on her face apparently caused by some type of nervous disorder or allergic reaction to medication. She was walking back and forth in the small room with parched lips, pressing her hands against her breasts. Her breathing was short and very uneven. Her eyes sparkled with a feverish brilliancy, but her gaze was hard and fixed. Her diseased lungs caused a painful expression on her face, which was seen by the aid of a low wattage lamp. I judged her to be no more than thirty-five years old. She appeared to be somewhat younger than her husband. She didn't notice our arrival; she seemed to have lost all mental aptitude for sight or sound. Henry Shane stood near the entrance instead of entering the room, but signaled for me to go in. At the sight of me, the woman paused absently in front of me, and attempted for a moment to explain the apparition. So she was about to open the avenue of communication without paying any further attention to me and then a loud shrill came forth from her mouth. She had just caught sight of her husband standing near the entrance.

"So you've come back!" she cried in a voice quivering with anger. "You rotten bastard! What have you done with our money? Let me see, what have you remaining in your pockets?"

She proceeded to search his pockets. Henry Shane far from resisting at once stretched out his arms to assist her search. He hadn't a single cent on him.

"Where in the hell did all the money go?" she cried. "My God, is it possible that you have spent it all on beer and whiskey. There was at least two hundred dollars in the drawer, and that money was supposed to be saved for Melissa's upkeep. What the hell kind of man are you? What has happened to you?"

She seized her husband by the arm in a sudden rage, and dragged him into the room. Henry Shane's patience did not abandon him; he docilely followed his wife.

"It is all gone in booze, every damn cent!" the wife yelled in despair, "and you have even stayed away from us for five days!" She began to cry, and was on the verge of becoming hysterical.

"We are hungry and starving!" she said as she wrung her hands and pointed to her daughter. "And you, mister," she said suddenly turning to me, "Aren't you ashamed to come here straight from the tavern? You've been drinking with him, haven't you? Then get the hell out of here!"

I did not wait for a second command, but left without uttering a word. The outer door was rammed open, and in the doorway appeared the impudent, mocking, inquisitive faces of several of the tenants who lived in the row house. Some of them were clad in pajamas, others in undergarments, and some had a beer bottle in their hand. What amused and delighted them the most was to hear Henry Shane scream and curse at his wife when she began throwing various objects at him.

The tenants were already beginning to crowd into the room, when an annoying voice was suddenly heard; it came directly from the landlord himself, who forced his way through to restore order. He told Edith that he would have to evict her family from the premises if there ever was another disturbance. The warning was given in an insolent and contemptuous manner.

I had in my pocket the change left over from a twenty-dollar bill I had put down on the counter while at the Star Tavern. I returned to the room without attracting notice, and laid several dollar bills on the table that amounted to ten-dollars. As soon as I was descending the steps on my departure from the row house, I repented my generosity, and felt half inclined to turn back to retrieve the money. "How stupid of me? Henry Shane will probably spend the money on alcohol anyway."

After leaving the row house, I continued to work for the Keystone Power and Electric Company in Shirleysville. On weekends I enjoyed visiting the Star Tavern to drink and socialize with the clientele.

One year had elapsed since my first encounter with Henry Shane at the Star Tavern on Rosemore Avenue. Then, one cold, dreary weekend in late December, while reading a book in the Wheeling Estate, I received a notification from my employer informing me that my job as a supervisor of construction at a site near Shirleysville would terminate. The effective day was the last day of the month. I was re-assigned to another site in western North Carolina.

It delighted me when my superiors informed me that my reporting date to the new site was earmarked for the first day of the year. I had a few days remaining that would enable me to bid farewell to all the military veterans who frequented the Star Tavern on Rosemore Avenue. With this thought in mind I left the Wheeling Estate and trudged through the snow towards the Star Tavern.

A short distance from the entrance to the tavern, I heard the sound of many voices and saw a crowd beginning to gather. In the middle of the snow-covered street, I could see a large truck at a stand still, and around it flashed a number of lights.

"What could have happened?" I whispered to my self as I walked up to the crowd.

The police were there, and a number of people crowded around them. One held a flashlight, the rays of which were directed on some object lying on the street. Everyone had something to say, and, over all the confusion, I heard the truck driver endeavoring to exculpate him. I managed to push my way through the crowd to obtain, at last, a glance at the cause of the commotion. On the street a man lay unconscious with blood coming out of his mouth and trickling down the side of his face. The truck had struck him, and his face literally damaged beyond recognition.

"I was driving carefully enough," explained the driver, "but the drunken man apparently was in a stupor and didn't see the truck. I saw him standing on the curb, and before I realized it he began to stagger on to the street. I pressed on the horn to alert the man, but it was too late; he fell in front of the truck. I hit the brakes immediately and came to a gradual stop. That's how it happened."

Several men out of the crowd shouted: "That's right, we saw it happen!"

The driver did not appear to be overly worried or frightened, and it was evident by the inscription on the truck's body that it belonged to a reputable trucking firm in Jaystown. The police acted accordingly and summoned an ambulance to take the injured man to the hospital; but for some reason no one seemed to recognize the injured man lying in the street because of the extensive damage done to his face.

Meanwhile, I pushed nearer, and just then the rays from a flashlight shone on the entire body of the unfortunate man. I recognized the patches that were sewn on a ragged coat sweater that were slightly exposed beneath the dirty and shabby all weather coat which enveloped the injured man's body.

"I know this man! I know this man!" I shouted, pushing right in front. Several individuals in the crowd were flabbergasted that I recognized the bloody body lying in the street. "It is Henry Shane; he lives just a short distance from here. Where in the hell is the ambulance? Get a doctor someone! We can't let this poor man lying in the street!" I was very agitated, but the police seemed satisfied that I told them who the injured man was. I gave them his name and address and urged the police to hasten with Henry Shane to the row house.

"Yeah," one of the policemen intervened. "We know who this man is. He's nothing but a drunkard, and has a wife and a stepdaughter. Let him be taken home, so that we can get him off the street. We don't know what the hell is keeping the ambulance from getting here. Something is wrong."

Volunteers were soon found; they raised Henry Shane and put him on a stretcher. The row house was only a short distance away, and helping to carry the stretcher, I led the way.

"Here is where he lives, here it is! Be careful, don't rock the stretcher? God will reward you all for your compassion."

Edith, as usual, was feeling ill, and was walking back and forth in the room with her hands pressed against her breasts, mumbling, "the life style I had when your real father was alive and how happy I was until this drunkard forced me into poverty. Oh my God, what have I done to deserve this fate! Oh, my poor, poor child! God, what is that? What is the matter?" she cried, as she saw the door open, and people moving forward carrying a body. "What is it? What are you bringing here? Oh, God!"

"Where shall we lay him?" asked a policeman, as he looked around the room.

"On the couch, there, please be careful," I said.

"He was hit by a truck over on Rosemore Avenue," shouted someone from the entryway. "He must have been bombed out of his mind from drinking for this terrible thing to happen."

Edith stood erect, deadly pale, and breathing with difficulty. Melissa was frightened, and gave a scream and ran to her mother grasping her dress, quivering like a tree in a blustery storm. Having seeing her husband properly laid down, I turned to Edith. "Please be calm, for heaven's sake, don't be alarmed? Don't distress yourself—he will come to? I suggested that he be brought here, because the ambulance was delayed for some unknown reason. You should remember me. I assisted your husband from the tavern sometime ago in a state of intoxication, and you unjustly accused me of drinking with him, and furthermore, ordered me to leave the premises. Don't worry about the medical bills? We will try to assist you. God permitting, your husband will recover."

"He will never recover," she cried despairingly, as she ran to her husband.

I had persuaded someone to run for a doctor, who, it appeared lived, a short distance from the row house.

"Is there no water available?" I asked. Edith hastened to the other side of the room, where on a table stood a large wooden tub filled with water ready for the night's washing of her family's clothing. Edith did this several times during the week. She seized a small basin that was resting on the table along side of the tub, filled it with water, but stumbled and almost fell with the basin. I found a towel and dipping it in the water, I proceeded to wash some of the blood from Henry Shane's face, and Edith stood nearby with pain depicted on her face and grasping her throat. She looked as if she also needed medical assistance. I began to rationalize that I had perhaps done no wise deed in suggesting that the injured man is brought home. The policeman stood in doubt. During all this time the room kept filling with people, until there was not enough space to maneuver properly. The police had all departed, with the exception of one man, who tried to keep the crowd back. Edith noticed this and began to scream.

" Do you want him to die for lack of air?" she yelled at the crowd. "What have you come here to look at? This isn't a carnival! The nerve of you people to come in here with cigarettes and cigars too! Have you no respect for the dying? Get the hell out of here and leave us alone!"

A violent spell of coughing stopped her speech, but her words had been of no avail. Edith seemed to be rather feared—at any rate, the crowd began to fall back towards the door, having fulfilled that secret feeling of satisfaction at witnessing distress from which no man is free, though it may go with the most sincere feelings of sympathy and compassion. Someone in the crowd made a suggestion to take Henry Shane to the hospital, which Edith no sooner heard, and then she rushed to the door to castigate the crowd again. Here she encountered the landlord, who, hearing of the accident was making his way into the room in order to see how matters stood. He was an extremely rude and obnoxious man and sarcastically remarked, "Your drunken husband had been hit by a truck and is in serious condition. I am the landlord, and I order you to contact an ambulance to take him to the hospital."

Edith quickly responded, "You see yourself what has happened to my husband. I ask you at once to close the door and let no one enter, otherwise I swear to God that your behavior will be reported to the authorities."

At this moment Henry Shane revived and groaned in agony, and Edith ran back to him. Henry Shane opened his eyes, and stared at Edith in a lethargic way. His breath came with difficulty. Large drops of perspiration were on his forehead, and the blood still continued to ooze from his mouth. Edith watched him with a stern look, but from her eyes ran a few tears.

"My God! Look at his chest! Look at the blood, the blood!" she cried in despair. "We must take off his shirt."

Henry Shane recognized her. "A priest!" he whispered in a hoarse voice.

"Be quiet," she said to him in a gentle voice. He heard her voice, recognized it and became silent. She returned to him, and he timidly looked into her face. He did not long remain quiet, as his glance happened to fall upon his stepdaughter who was clutching her stomach, and her little eyes fixed upon her dying stepfather.

"Stomach ache!" he uttered, noticing the child holding her stomach.

"Silence!" cried Edith. "You ought to know why she is holding her stomach!"

Shortly the doctor came, an old Irishman, who, with the aid of Edith, removed Henry's bloody shirt, and bared his throat and chest. This part of his body was severely damaged, and, in addition his ribs were crushed. On his left side, near the heart, was a large black and blue spot, a contusion probably caused by the front bumper of the truck.

Sadly the doctor turned to Edith and said, "I can't do anything for him. He is dying, and it is a miracle that he has lasted this long."

"Isn't there any hope at all? Are you sure?"

"None whatsoever. He is near his last gasp. I might be able to stop the external bleeding, but it will be of no avail. There is a tremendous amount of internal damage. This is a hopeless case, and I'm certain that the end results would have been the same even if he were confined to a hospital bed. In ten minutes, at the most, he will be dead."

Some disorder took place amongst the crowd near the entrance to the room, and the people quickly made way for an old-gray haired priest, who entered the room carrying a black case which contained religious articles and other essentials for Henry Shane's last rights. The doctor moved away at once, permitting the priest to get near the body. I asked the doctor to remain, even though it was in vain. He merely shrugged his shoulders and consented to do so. All stepped back. The ceremony for the last rights took only a few minutes, and it was doubtful whether Henry understood a word and occasionally he would make a vain attempt to utter defined sounds. Edith motioned for her daughter to come forward, placing her in front, and fell upon her knees. She grit her teeth to prevent her tears, and as she prayed, sought to arrange the clothing of her shabbily dressed daughter. Only one dim candle that was placed on the table by the priest illuminated the room.

After the last rights had been administered, Edith went up to her dying husband. The priest prepared to leave the room, and, before leaving, turned to say a few words of consolation to her.

"What will become of my daughter?" Edith asked the priest directly as she pointed in the direction where she was standing.

"The Lord is merciful, my dear woman. Trust in him and thou shall have eternal salvation," commenced the priest.

"He is not merciful to us," Edith remarked with bitterness in her voice.

"You are entirely wrong, my dear woman, very wrong not to trust in the Lord," replied the priest, shaking his head in disbelief at the remarks that were being uttered by the bereaved woman.

"Am I wrong? Look there on the couch!" she said, pointing to her husband.

"What am I to say to you, my dear woman? No doubt those who were the involuntary cause of the accident will indemnify you for the loss of your husband's support, and render assistance to you."

"You do not understand me!" cried Edith, waving her arms. "Indemnify me for him? He was a drunkard who was hit by a truck. I wouldn't be surprised if he deliberately stepped in the path of the moving truck to rid himself of all of his miseries. As far as his financial support, he never did anything but cause us heartaches. He drank everything away. He robbed us to satisfy his craving for alcohol and my life and my daughter's have been ruined in the bar rooms. Maybe it is a blessing in disguise he is dying. The loss is little."

"You should be ashamed of yourself, woman. You should forgive in the hour of death. It is terrible, a mortal sin, to have such wicked thoughts," the priest said disgustingly.

Edith then turned again to her dying husband, and wiped the perspiration, and the blood from his brow, dabbed his lips with a moist cloth and straightened his pillow.

"Yes, Father, it is easy for you to speak in terms of fancy words only. Forgive you say?" Edith exclaimed. "Had he come home drunk as usual, and not seriously injured, I and Melissa would have had to cope with his mean behavior and abusive language. Such were my days and nights. You speak to me about forgiveness. What a joke, Father?"

A sudden coughing spell stopped further words from flowing freely from her mouth, and she was forced once again as a result of a habit to hold her throat with one hand, while with the other she put a handkerchief to her mouth. She withdrew it as soon as the coughing spell subsided, and held it out to the priest. It was covered with blood and sputum. The priest turned his head away, and said nothing.

Henry Shane seemed in great pain, and his eyes were rigidly staring at his wife, who was now bending over him again. He was evidently endeavoring to say something to her; his lips moved, and an indistinct sound came forth from them. Edith assumed that he wished to ask her pardon, and at once cried harshly to him:

"Keep quiet! There is no need. I know exactly what you want to say."

The dying husband refrained from further efforts, but at the same moment his now wandering eyes fell upon his stepdaughter standing in the middle of the room. "Who's that?" he asked, in a thick, rasping voice, as his face assumed an aspect of terror, and his eyes glaring wildly to where his stepdaughter stood.

"Lie still! Will you?" cried Edith.

He struggled with all his strength to raise himself, and kept his eyes immovably fixed upon his stepdaughter. Suddenly he knew her, as she stood with an expression of intense grief on her face, waiting her turn to say farewell to her dying stepfather. "My child! Forgive me!" he cried, as he attempted to seize her hand, but his strength failed him completely, and he fell back heavily, his head hanging over the couch and touching the floor. They raised him, and placed him on the couch again, but the end had come. His stepdaughter, with a feeble cry, ran and embraced him. He died in her arms.

"He is gone!" cried Edith gazing at the corpse of her husband. "What shall I do now? How am I to bury him? How shall I feed and clothe my daughter?"

I walked up to her and attempted to comfort her during this moment of bereavement.

"Sometime ago, your deceased husband imparted to me the history of his life and all his circumstances which had driven him to drink. Be assured that he spoke of you with the highest respect. That same night when I learned how devoted he was to you all, and how he lived and esteemed you especially, in spite of his unhappy weakness, that moment saw us as friends. If there is anything that I may do to assist you and Melissa, please feel free to call on me."

I rapidly passed out of the room, and made my way through the crowd to the stairs, where I came face to face with Joseph Kelly, the proprietor of the Star Tavern on Rosemore Avenue, who having heard of the misfortune, was hastening up the staircase. I had not spoken to him for some time. Joseph Kelly recognized me immediately. "You here?" he asked.

"He is dead. A doctor has been here and also a priest. All is in order. Please don't disturb the poor widow, she is despondent and is in a state of turmoil at the present time. Comfort her, if possible. You are a kind and gentle man, I know." I finished with a feeling of relief, as I looked straight into Joseph Kelly's eyes.

"You are covered with blood," said Joseph Kelly, noticing by the rays of the light some fresh blood stains upon my clothes.

"Yes, I am all over blood," I answered in a melancholy tone.

Joseph Kelly reached into his pocket for a handkerchief and casually wiped the tears from his eyes. Nodding his head from side to side he softly remarked, "What a terrible tragedy for a highly decorated Korean War veteran? He survived the pain and agony of the war and confinement in a North Korean prisoner of war camp, but unfortunately he became careless and succumbed to the abusive use of alcohol."

Joseph Kelly drew a deep breath, and though his memory was eased of its entangled thoughts, and he had no more to say; but suddenly an unexpected thought seized him.

"Well, it may be a mortal sin to say, but it is a pity that Henry Shane didn't die sooner. I said it right to our parish priest once, and he was utterly shocked that I being a Christian had the audacity to make such a statement. Only he wasn't present on many occasions when Henry was nothing but a helpless drunkard who had to be transported to his home; and to this fateful day— a helpless drunkard."

Joseph Kelly looked directly into my eyes and emphatically pointed his finger at me as if he was attempting to stress a major point and continued to talk in a forceful tone.

"I still say, and may the good Lord forgive me, if Henry Shane would have died sooner, Edith and Melissa may have lived. The way they are now, I don't see much difference between the Shanes living in Sinclair or the Shanes lying in a burial plot in Saint Anthony's Cemetery. There is one exception, that up on the highlands the Shanes can be quite, peaceful and free—free of the wailing wind."

I descended the steps quietly. A new life seemed to be emerging within me, a feeling akin to that of an imprisoned man upon being suddenly receiving his freedom.

It was that bitter, cold night in the desolate Coal Region that I found the clue to Henry Shane, and began to put together this vision of his story.

Two

I heard the details of the Henry Shane story bit by bit from various people and what generally happens in such cases each time it was a different story.

If you know Sinclair, Pennsylvania, you know the Eureka Store. If you know the Eureka Store you must have seen Henry Shane drive up to it and park his dingy pickup truck on the macadam parking lot and walk slowly into the store: and you must have asked who he was.

It was there in Sinclair that I began to observe his daily movements and the sight of him moved me deeply. Even then he was the most noticeable individual in Sinclair for he was lame and crippled as a result of wounds inflicted upon him during the Korean War and from his confinement in a North Korean prisoner of war camp. It was not so much his physical stature that distinguished him, but it was the careless, powerful look he had in spite of lameness checking each step like the jerk of an iron ball and chain.

His complexion was of a dark hue and tanned by long exposure to the elements. His blue denim jacket and trousers and his military styled hat did not distinguish him from the others, and neither did the army brogans that he wore on his feet. It was his lameness and the gait of his walk that attracted me. With this handicap, I imagined he was always and everywhere a stranger, with the reservation, the impersonal and doubtfulness of the man who can mingle in any environment but feels he belongs to none.

There was something cold and mysterious in the expression on his face, and he looked so decrepit and stiffened that I had mistaken him for an old man, and was surprised to learn that he was much younger than his general appearance displayed. I heard this from Richard Rand, who had been a former employee at one of the smaller coal mining operations in the vicinity of Sinclair, and at one time his best friend.

"He has looked that way ever since he returned from the Korean War, and many years have passed since he was discharged from the army," Richard Rand said between hesitating pauses.

The calamity of war—I gathered from the same informant—had so shortened and warped his left side that it required a determined effort to take the few steps from his pickup truck to the revolving door of the Eureka Store.

He used to drive in from his home everyday at about noon, and as that, on many occasions was the time I had available to pick up my provisions. I often passed him in the aisle or stood behind him while we waited to be checked out by the counter clerk. I noticed that though he came so punctually, he seldom bought anything but a copy of THE JAYSTOWN TRIBUNE, that he rolled and put without hesitation into his drooping back pocket. At intervals, however, he did buy milk, bread and canned goods.

I seldom paid any attention to Henry Shane's physical features when I first met him at the Star Tavern, but in the Eureka Store he once turned fully to me and nodded his head, and a cold chill suddenly dashed through me. A long, twisting scar ran down the side of his face that had been away from me, from ear to chin.

I stared at the scar—stared and wondered what terrible incident of war had so disfigured him. I could almost hear him scream of pain as I envisaged the thrust of a bayonet slashing into the living flesh—hear him scream and see the blood spurt out. Everyone in Sinclair knew him and acknowledged his presence depending on his disposition, but his unwillingness to engage in a conversation was respected, and it was only on rare occasions that one of the army veterans in town detained him for a word. On occasions when this would happen, he would listen attentively. His dark, brown eyes focused on the speaker's face, and responded in a low, rasping tone that his words seldom reached me. Then he would climb awkwardly into his pickup truck, grasping the steering wheel firmly with both hands and drive slowly away in the direction of the row house.

"What a terrible experience he must have had in Korea?" I questioned Richard Rand, looking after Henry Shane's figure and thinking how boldly his head sat on his shoulders before they were twisted out of shape.

"It was deplorable," my informant responded. "The pain and agony of the war were more than enough to kill most men. The Shanes' were a tough breed. Henry will more than likely live to be an old man, if he refrains from extensive consumption of alcohol."

I was astonished to hear this remark, for it appeared to me that Henry Shane was incapacitated and nearing death now.

Meanwhile Richard Rand pushed his hat to the back of his head and, taking out a cigarette, placed it between his lips. Then his hand moved out slowly and scraped a match on the surface of a building. He drew upon the cigarette, inhaling the smoke deep into his lungs, then exhaling the gray puffs from his nostrils. They moved upward, concealing his face. He removed the cigarette from his lips, cleared his throat and sadly remarked, "Guess he has resided in Sinclair too many years. Most of the smart people leave this town."

"Why did he come back after the war?" I asked

"Rumors have it that he felt guilty over the deplorable life style of Edith Miller. They were long time lovers, you know. Yet, others say that this town was his birthplace and he just came home to die after his ordeal in the war."

"I see. Since then who had to take care of him?" Richard Rand thoughtfully removed the cigarette from his lips. "Oh, as to that: I assume it was always Henry who took care of himself."

Though Richard Rand expressed his opinions as far as his mental and moral scope permitted, there were inconsistencies between his facts, and I had the sense that the deeper meaning of the story was in the inconsistencies. One point stood out in my memory and served as a basis by which I formulated my opinion of Henry Shane: "Guess he has lived in Sinclair too many years."

Before my mission in the vicinity of Sinclair was completed, I had learned to know what that meant, Yet, I had come in the modern day of trains, automobiles and buses when traveling was relatively easy between the smaller mountain towns and the larger communities in the valley.

When the dismal, gloomy winter season overwhelmed Sinclair and the town and adjacent mounds of mine refuse lay under a white blanket, and the snow continued to fall from the heavy sky, I began to see what life there—or its prohibitive environment—must have been during Henry Shane's formative years.

My employer, The Keystone Power and Electric Company assigned me to supervise the construction of a coal-fired electric power plant near Shirleysville, Pennsylvania. A lengthy union strike had so delayed the work that I found myself quartered in Sinclair—the nearest habitable spot—for the greater part of the winter. At first I despised it, and then, under the abnormal mentality of routine and boredom, I gradually began to find a personal and rewarding satisfaction in the life of the region. During the early part of my stay, I had been overwhelmed by the contrast between the vigorousness of the climate and the deadness of the town. I had known something of Pennsylvania Coal Region life and its climate long before my return to Sinclair, but after a lapse of many years the general feeling and memory of this type of climate had been somewhat vague.

For many days, after the December snows were over, a clear, blue sky poured down an overwhelming amount of frigid air and sunshine, which cast a light on the white landscape, that gave them back in a strong brilliancy. One would have believed that such an atmosphere would rouse the emotions as well as the blood. It seemed to produce no effect except that of impeding still more the dull and depressing disposition of Sinclair. When I had been there a little longer, I had seen this phase of crystal clearness followed by long periods of sunless cold. The storms of January and February had deposited their white drifts about the gloomy town and, the blustery winds of March had rendered support to the white mass; I began to understand why Sinclair emerged from its four-month's siege like a garrison capitulating without rations. Many years earlier the means of resistance to the blustery winter storms must have been fewer when the snow drifts paralyzed almost all the roads of access between the besieged towns.

Considering these things, I felt the real meaning of Richard Rand's remark: "Most of the smart people leave this town." If that were the case, I thought, how could any combination of events or barriers enable a man like Henry Shane to remain in such a depressing environment?

During my stay in Sinclair, I lodged with a prominent and highly respected family in the Wheeling Estate. Doctor George Wheeling had been a physician in Sinclair for many years and was forced to retire from his practice because of failing eyesight. The Wheeling Estate, where my landlord lived with his wife, Rebecca, was the most pretentious dwelling in Sinclair. It stood at one end of Highland Avenue. Its classic porch and large paned windows faced in the direction of a wide, long driveway lined with maple trees leading to a metal gate. It was evident to any observer that the Wheeling family was wealthy. They did what they could to portray a modest dignity.

In an elaborate family room illuminated by the warm rays of a sparkling fire from an enormous stone fireplace, I listened every evening to another and more highly sensitive and suspicious version of the tales of Sinclair. It was not that George and Rebecca Wheeling felt any social superiority to the other people around them; it was only the air of a sophisticated upbringing and education had just put enough distance between them and their associates to enable them to evaluate others with discretion. They were not unwilling to exercise this natural function. I had great hopes of getting from them the missing facts of the Henry Shane story, or rather a key to his character to coordinate the facts I knew.

Mrs. Wheeling had an excellent memory and was well versed. Any question about her acquaintances brought forth a volume of detail;

but on the subject of Henry Shane I found her unexpectedly silent. I merely found in her an insurmountable reluctance to speak of him or his affairs, a low, "yes, I knew them both—Henry Shane and Edith Miller—it was a disgrace," seeming to be the greatest admission that her distress could make to my curiosity.

So devious was the change in her demeanor, such a mode of suspicion it implied, that, with some doubts, I presented the case once again to my town acquaintance, Richard Rand; but got for my efforts only an uncomprehending flare of words such as:

"Mrs. Wheeling was always as nervous as a cat on a hot tin roof; and come to think of it, she was a friend of Edith Miller in her earlier years. She was one of those individuals that began to spread many of those damn rumors about Henry and Edith's immoral conduct. It all started about the time prior to Henry re-enlisting in the army. The young folks at that time were all friends, and I guess she just couldn't bear to talk about it, Now she has enough problems of her own to worry about."

All the residents in Sinclair as well as in the other Coal Region communities had troubles enough of their own to make them comparatively indifferent to those of their neighbors. Many were in agreement that Henry Shane had been an extraordinary person. Yet, no one gave me an explanation as to the carved, haggard expression on his face which, as I had persisted in thinking, neither poverty nor physical suffering could have put there. Nevertheless, I might have convinced myself with the story pieced together from these hints had it not been for the arousal of Mrs. Wheeling.

On my arrival in Sinclair, Frank Whalley, the proprietor of The Sinclair Motor Company had entered into an agreement to rent a car to me. I was able to make the daily trip to Reel's Corner where I had to board a train for Shirleysville. About the middle of the winter, I had a major disagreement with Frank Whalley over the rental charges, and this dispute left me without transportation. I found myself in a bind to find another means of transportation. Then Richard Rand suggested that Henry Shane had a pickup truck and that he might be glad to accommodate me. I disapproved of the suggestion. "Henry Shane! He is a very heavy drinker and I won't be able to rely on him. Why in the hell should he go out of his way to help me."

"I disagree with you wholeheartedly," Richard Rand responded quickly. "He is a responsible and dependable man if he stays away from the bottle."

Richard Rand's answer surprised me even more when he said, "I don't know if he will; but I know he wouldn't object to the opportunity to earn some money."

I knew from my encounters with Henry Shane at the Star Tavern and at the Eureka Store that he was poor, and that his small coal mine had been closed, and there was scarcely enough to keep his household through the winter.

"Many things haven't gone too well for him," Richard Rand said. "When a man has been sitting around, drinking heavily, and living like a recluse, and feeling sorry for himself all these years and things not working out for him, it eats his heart out, and he loses his spark. You know what one of those coal holes is worth nowadays. When Henry could bust his balls over at the mine from sun up to sun down he kind of earned a decent living, but his family ate most of the profit, even then, and I don't see how he and his family survive now. His wife, Edith has been in and out of the hospital for years. Sickness and trouble: that's what Henry has been cursed with ever since he returned from that damn Korean War."

After Richard Rand's supportive comments of Henry Shane, I felt sorry for him, and decided that he was a favorable risk. Therefore I contacted Henry Shane, and he agreed to transport me to and from Reel's Corner on a daily basis. The next morning when I looked out of a window of the Wheeling Estate, I saw the old pickup truck parked near the metal gate. It appeared as if Henry was browsing through a magazine while he was sitting on the front seat. After that, for a week, he drove me to Reel's Corner every morning, and drove me back through the icy evening to Sinclair. Under normal circumstances, the trip took approximately twenty-five minutes, but the old pickup truck's progress was slow, and even with firm snow under the tires we were nearly forty-five minutes on the roadway. Henry Shane drove in silence, holding the steering wheel firmly with both of his hands, and the profile of his head, underneath the military-like peak of his hat, reminded me of the bronze image of a hero. He never turned his face toward me, or answered, except in a low, indistinct tone, the questions I put before him. He seemed a part of the silent and morbid environment, an embodiment of its congealing sorrow, with all that was warm and firmly fixed in him fast bound below the surface.

I simply felt that he lived in an agonizing depth of moral isolation too deeply rooted for casual access. I had a sincere inward feeling that his loneliness was not merely the result of his personal plight, tragic, as it may have seemed to be, but had in it, as Richard Rand had hinted, the profound accumulated gloom and misery of Sinclair's economic environment.

Only once or twice was I able to comprehend the specific reasons for his economic plight, and impressions thus formulated confirmed my desire to know more. Once I happened to speak of an assignment I had been on the previous year near the Chattahoochee River in the state of Georgia, and the contrast between the bleak, Coal Region landscape about us and that in which I had found myself the year before. To my surprise, Henry said suddenly: "Yes, I was stationed down there many years a go. I attended the parachute school at Fort George, and for a good while afterwards I could remember how it was there during the winter season. Now it is just a faint memory."

He said no more, and I had to guess the rest from the tone of his voice and his withdrawal into silence. Another day, on boarding the train at Reel's Corner, I realized that I had misplaced my book titled, THE HISTORY OF THE KOREAN WAR that I had carried with me to read on the way. I thought no more about it until I got into the pickup truck again that evening, and saw the book in Henry Shane's hand.

"I found it on the seat after you were gone," he said as he handed the book to me.

I put the book into my brief case and we settled back into our usual silence; but as we began to drive up the steep hill from Scalp Level to the Sinclair Ridge, I became aware that he had turned his face to mine.

"There are significant facts in that book that I didn't realize ever happened," he said sheepishly. "To think, I was all over that God forsaken country."

I wondered less at his words than at the strange sound of resentment in his voice. He was evidently surprised and slightly embarrassed at his own ignorance.

"Does that sort of subject interest you?"

"Yes, it used to at one time," he replied.

I hesitated for a moment and said, "There are some interesting accounts of the Korean War in the book, events that the average person isn't aware of." I waited for a response that did not come; then I broke the silence and remarked: "If you would like to read the book further I will be glad to leave it with you."

He looked at me, and I had the impression that he felt delighted that I had made such a thoughtful suggestion.

"Thank you. I'll take you up on that offer," He answered shortly.

I hoped that this incident might improve the avenue of communication between us. Henry Shane was so simple and straightforward that I was sure his curiosity about the book was based on a genuine interest in accounts of the Korean War. Such sincere interests in a man of his condition made the contrast more piercing between his outer situation and his deep, inner feelings, and I hoped that the chance of giving expression to the latter might at least unseal his lips about his past life. Something in his past history, or in his present way of life, had apparently driven him too deeply into a shell for any casual impulse to bring him back to reality. At our next encounter he made no mention of the book, and our relationship seemed destined to remain as cold and one-sided with little hope of ever breaking the ice.

Henry Shane had been driving me over to Reel's Corner in his pickup for about a week. Then one morning I had arisen from a deep sleep and gazed out of my bedroom window into a thick snowfall, Weather forecasters on the radio had been warning people for several days of an impending snowstorm that was to strike the Coal Region. The height of the white mass on the driveway and near the metal gate showed that the storm must have been going on all night, and I feared that the drifts were likely to be heavy in the open remote areas. More than likely I assumed that my train would be delayed; but I had to be at the electric power plant that afternoon. I decided that if Henry showed up, to drive me to Reel's Corner and wait there until my train returned from Shirleysville, then I would chance it. I don't know why I put it in that perspective, however, for I never doubted that Henry Shane would not appear. He was not the type of man who would shun his responsibilities by any disruption of the weather elements. At the appointed moment his pickup truck managed to maneuver through the snow to the front of the metal gate.

I was getting to know him too well to express either wonder or gratitude at his keeping his appointment; but I was overwhelmed with emotion as I saw him turn his pickup truck in a direction opposite than we normally had traveled before.

"The main road is blocked by a tractor-trailer and got stuck in a snow drift," he explained, as we drove off into the whiteness.

"Where in the hell are we going?"

"Straight to Reel's Corner, by the shortest way," he answered promptly, pointing up Rosemore Avenue with his finger.

"To Reel's Corner on this kind of road—in this storm. You must be raving mad!"

"This jalopy will make it, don't worry? You said that you had to be at the electric power plant, I'll see that you get there."

He said it so quietly and appeared to be so unconcerned that I could only answer, "You're doing me a damn, big favor, Henry."

"That's all right," he quietly responded.

Joseph T. Renaldi

At the top of Rosemore Avenue the road forked, and we drove down a roadway to the left between large tree branches drooping to the roadway due to the weight of the snow.

I had often hiked that way on pleasant weekends, and knew the definite shapes showing through the snow-covered branches near the bottom of the hill were that of Henry Shane's coal operation. It looked tranquil with its idle equipment covered with snow, and the dilapidated storage sheds sagging from the white mass on their roofs. Henry Shane did not even turn his head as we drove by, and still in silence he managed to shift gears as we began to approach the next hill. About a mile farther, on a road I never knew existed, we came to a coal stripping pit where the area looked starved and withered among outcroppings of slate that protruded in the snow like sinners in hell begging for God's mercy. Beyond this frozen and scarred area was a hillside and above the snow covered hillside, one of those drab, rural Coal Region dwellings that made the environment appear gloomier.

"That's my former house," Henry said with a gesture of his hand. "I bought that house when I returned from the Korean War, and we lived there a few years until we had to move into a row house." Henry continued. "We were kind of out of the way from everything then, but there was considerable traffic before the Skytop Coal Company decided to strip the coal on the other side of the road."

I stared in disbelief, and in the distress and oppression of the scene I did not know what to say. The snow had ceased, and a ray of sunlight exposed the house on the hillside above us in all its ugliness. The swaying branches of a large oak tree flapped against the fading, and flimsy clapboard walls, under their peeling drab-coated paint seemed to quiver in the wind that had risen now with the ceasing of the snow.

He shifted gears with a jerky motion; then as if the mere sight of the house would prompt me to bombard him with a volume of personal questions. It caused me to hear a sorrowful note in Henry's words, and to see in the deteriorating dwelling the image of his own sorrowful body.

As we turned on to the Weaver Road headed for Reel's Corner, the snow began to fall again, cutting off our last glimpse of the dismal house; and Henry Shane fell with it and letting down between us the curtain of silence. This time the wind did not cease with the return of the snow. Instead it sprang up into squalls which now and then tossed the snow around to obscure our vision. The old pickup truck was as good as Henry's word, and we drove on to Reel's Corner through the wild, scene.

Later in the afternoon, the storm receded, and the clearness of the sky seemed to indicate the promise of a fair evening. I conducted my business at the power plant as quickly as possible and boarded the train for Reel's Corner. We headed back to Sinclair with a good chance of getting there before the darkness covered the land. I was wrong. The dark, storm clouds gathered again, bringing an earlier night which was not unusual for this region at this time of the year. The snow began to fall straight and steadily from the sky in a soft pattern that was just as troublesome as the gusts we experienced earlier in the day. The rays from the headlights of Henry Shane's pickup truck appeared to be obscured in this blustering storm, in which even his sense of familiarity ceased to assist us. On several occasions it appeared that we were going astray; and when we finally regained our sense of direction, the old pickup truck began to sputter and displayed signs of a malfunction, and then came to a complete halt in a remote and desolate area. I felt myself to blame for permitting Henry to drive in such adverse conditions.

For a moment we sat there in silence. Henry reached for his flashlight that was lying near his side on the seat and broke the silence and remarked, "We can't stay here all night."

After a brief discussion, we decided to get out of the pickup truck and walk arm in arm through the snow towards Sinclair. In this way we struggled for several miles, and at last reached a point where Henry, staring at what seemed to me to be a definite outline of a structure. Henry paused a moment and said, "That's the row house where I live."

The latter part of our walk had been the most difficult part of the way. The bitter cold and the heavy going with Henry hanging on to my body drained the energy out of me, and I could feel my heart ticking like a time bomb in my chest—ready to explode at any minute.

Suddenly Henry said, "This is enough of this bullshit for anybody."

In his own little way, I surmised that he was offering me shelter for the night, and without answering I turned into the drifted lane at his side.

Ahead of us, a ray of light radiated through the falling snow. Staggering along we headed toward the origin of the light, and stumbled into one of the deep drifts against the front of the row house. We managed to recover our footing, and eventually edged our way up the slippery steps to the porch, clearing the way through the snow with our booted feet. Then Henry pointed his flashlight, found the doorknob, and led the way into a narrow hallway. I followed him up three flights of stairs to the entrance of his room. Behind the closed door I heard a woman's rasping voice.

Henry stamped on the old, worn rug to shake the snow from his boots, and placed his flashlight on a small table which was the only piece of furniture in the narrow hallway. Then he opened the door.

"Come in," he said, and as he spoke the woman's rasping voice grew still.

I stood hesitatingly behind him as he advanced; then he turned and looked at me and said, "Do you remember my wife Edith?"

I smiled and remarked, "Yes, I remember Edith, but it was under different circumstances." She did not respond, and merely went about her business. After a short pause, Henry added pointing to a figure sitting near the table, "This is my stepdaughter, Melissa."

We had gotten very cold struggling in the snow and the heat coming from the stove gave me a mighty sense of comfort as I stepped towards it.

"I sort of expected this storm and bought a few provisions," Henry said as he took off his coat and hung it on the back of the door. He turned and reached for my coat.

Although Edith continued to remain silent, she did manage to prepare a pot of hot coffee for us to drink. Later Henry went into an adjacent room and returned with many photographs that he spread out on the table before me. I noticed immediately that the photographs were of military people and of places where he had been stationed while in the army. His comments were brief regarding each photograph, but as I glanced at my watch, I had noticed that considerable time had elapsed in the viewing process.

Then we went into the adjacent room and sat on the couch near the potbelly stove that now was roaring like a furnace in the middle of the room. I listened to the wind howling above the roof and the bitter stories of Henry Shane's life. The eerie sound of the branches of the old oak tree flapping against the exterior clapboard siding grew louder and louder, and prompted Henry to say, "I guess the storm is at its peak."

The winter storm that came roaring out of the northwest and, of a night, after rapping at the windows and howling in the chimney and whining in the woods, took possession of the Coal Region. That was the night when Henry Shane's words flowed freely from his mouth and recollecting and talking of his agonizing life seemed to ease his soul.

I fell asleep on the couch. I remembered that he stopped in the middle of a story pertaining to a Japanese girl named Keiko. Seeing that I was getting sleepy, he pushed the couch away from the potbelly stove and covered me with a blanket. It had been a mighty struggle between sleep and stories, and sleep had won.

I roused myself later and noticed that Henry was awake. I begged him to continue with the story of Keiko, but he only replied, "No, I'd rather not, it will only bring back painful memories," He put out the light and sat in a reclining chair in the far corner of the room.

I woke once or twice in the middle of the night and saw him putting coal on the fire. He did not put on the light and the gleam of the fire shone on his haggard face when he opened the door of the stove.

"Getting a little cool in here," I heard him whisper to himself as he returned to the reclining chair. He leaned back slowly, adjusting the lever of the chair. "All right," he said. "I know you're not sleeping, so quit pretending that you are."

I chuckled briefly and then sarcastically replied, "Since you also have insomnia, then why in the hell don't you just occupy your time by telling me about some of your experiences in the Korean War and your confinement in a prisoner of war camp?"

Henry Shane did not respond to my question immediately. I heard the stirring of his body as he covered himself with a blanket, and quietly and fluently from years of military service and living in the Coal Region, he began to curse. "The Goddamn war can go to hell. I had enough of that bullshit to last me a lifetime. Look at me! I'm nothing but a ruin of a man. All I got for my sufferings in the war were a few fucking medals that aren't worth an ounce of shit. And believe me, you can't eat shit. Truthfully, I want to forget about being in the army, being in the war. I'm through with the whole Goddamn mess."

Finished, he lay back and let the drowsy warmth of the blanket climb over him.

I remained awake for the greater part of the night thinking how to re-construct the events and circumstances that led to the downfall of Henry Shane.

Three

Henry Shane's military unit left Seoul, Korea in an impressive and exulting splendor. The roads were lined with crowds now accustomed to the rumble of tanks, trucks and marching feet. He had a proud and intense feeling in his heart that eventually wore away in the discomfort of travel.

For hours after the convoy started, the soldiers told a variety of stories, occasionally hummed songs, ate chocolate candy bars and jokingly punched at each other in an atmosphere clouded with cigarette smoke.

The convoy was detained here and there and moved at a slow pace. The youthful and inexperienced soldiers with no sense of pride, as it appeared to him, of the dreadful and sad business that lie ahead, went about interchanging seats while sipping on canned soda that they had concealed in their packs.

These revelers became quiet as the night wore on. They were tired and weary and began to lie back to rest. Some lay in the aisle of the truck bed, and their heads upon their packs. The air grew chilly and soon Henry could hear them snoring all about him. He closed his eyes and welcomed sleep, but a great sadness had taken a hold of him. He already had sacrificed several years of his life in the form of military service. When and where would his life be taken? He could not help wondering. The fear had mostly left him in days and nights of serious thinking. The feeling he had, with the flavor of religion, is what has made him the courageous, mighty soldier—the captain of his ship and the master of his soul.

In his sacrifice there was but one reservation—he often prayed that he would not be blown up by a hand grenade or gutted by a bayonet.

He had written a long letter to his brother, Lee, in Sinclair, Pennsylvania. He wondered if his brother would care what became of him. He had a sense of comfort thinking he would prove to his brother that he was not a coward, with all of his other faults.

He had not been able to write to his Japanese girlfriend, Keiko, or to his former love, Edith Miller, in any serious tone of his feeling in this predicament. He had treated it as kind of a meager excursion, from which he should return shortly to embrace them.

All about him the youthful soldiers seemed to be sleeping—some of them were mumbling in their sleep. As dawn approached, one after another rose and stretched, rousing their seat companion. The truck halted. A non-commissioned officer in a deep, authoritarian voice yelled, "Drop your cocks and grab your socks! Get your fat asses off this truck!" It was uttered in the same tone as he often had heard elsewhere while serving in the army.

Shortly, they were jumping out of the truck to bivouac in a wide clearing at the edge of the dirt road. So began his life as a soldier many miles beyond the 38th parallel, and how it ended with him, many have read it in a better narrative than this, but his story is here and only here in Korea.

The American soldiers were to remain in bivouac there on that lonely clearing of North Korea for three days awaiting further orders, but it ended in a two-week stay. In the long delay Henry Shane's way traversed the dead levels of boredom—the same routine day in and day out. Earlier in the month some fifty thousand of them crossed the Han River and 38thparallel into North Korea, where for the past two-weeks the American soldiers tore up the landscape, reinforcing the hillside, adjacent to the roadway with bunkers.

Everyday the soldiers in his unit heard of rumors of a large North Korean force camping above Unsan, some fifteen miles to the north of their position. Almost every night nervous sentries caused a tumult in the American ranks by exhibiting optical illusions. They were always on pins and needles.

Since the enemy appeared to be in hibernation and would not presently engage in battle, the American soldiers wanted to be on the move and have it out with them. Many of the soldiers were tired of the delay. The cry of "attack" was ringing throughout the ranks. They wanted to attack and be through with all the suspense.

Well, one night the order came from division headquarters and they were instructed to move north in the morning—fifty thousand of them, and help to put an end to the war. The American forces did not advance until mid-afternoon—it was the 21st of November 1950 when they were off, with vehicles and by foot, which enabled Henry Shane to see columns of the olive-green forces before and behind him. He had a feeling of regret for the misinformed North Koreans.

Several days later on the 25th of November the American forces were on both sides of the valley near Unsan. Henry knew the enemy was near and began to feel a tightening of his nerves. He wrote another letter to his brother, Lee, but this time for post mortem delivery, and put it into the wide pocket of his field jacket.

A few American units entered Unsan to search for the enemy, but Henry's unit was instructed to wait in reserve until further orders. His unit waited for two days and nights. Some soldiers called it a crock of shit, some cursed, and some talked of deserting. Henry went about quietly minding his own business—meditating and praying thinking about what was in store for him. On the second day an order came from the field commander. They were to assemble and attack the enemy at 0200 hours. In the dead of the night the command was given. He rose, half asleep, and heard the words far and near. He shivered in the bone-chilling night air as he made his preparations and the other soldiers near him put on their gear, shouldered their weapons and fell in line. Muffled in the darkness there was an odd silence in the great column forming rapidly and waiting for the word to move out. At each command to move forward Henry could hear the rub of the webbing, the clicking sound of weapons, and the tramping of feet. When they had hiked for an hour or so—he could hear the faint rumble of tanks in the rear. As he walked to the top of a hill, sporadic flashes from artillery could be seen in the remote distance—a splendid sight, fading into darkness and mystery.

At dawn's early light, Henry's unit passed a road junction and halted for a ten-minute break. At the conclusion of the break, they left the rough roadway, with their column bearing eastward on a crossroad that led them into an area of low, stunted trees and brush. As the sunlight sank in the thicket the first great encounter with the North Koreans began. Away to the right of them an artillery shell shook the earth hurling its boom into the still air. The sound rushed over them, rattling the thicket like the after shock of an earthquake. Suddenly Henry Shane was overcome with fear.

It seemed as if his internal organs had gone into a big lump of shit that quivered with each step he took. He hastened his pace, he was frightened, he complained, he cursed. His legs became weary, he wanted to run. Ahead of him and behind him officers were shouting wildly, "Run men! Run!"

The artillery roar was now continuous. He could feel the quake of it. When he came over a low ridge, in the open, he could see the smoke of battle in the valley. Flashes of gunfire and enormous puffs of smoke leaped out of the far thicket as artillery roared. Moving at double time he began checking his ammunition belt and grenade pack and throwing excessive items into a heap along the way without halting.

In a half-hour his unit stood waiting, the right flank of the enemy in front of them. They were given the order to attack on the run. "Forward!" was the cry, and they were off, yelling as they ran. It was an inspired group of fighting men who charged the enemy. Their entire front moved like an olive-green wave on a white immeasurable wasteland. Out of the thicket ahead of them came many flashes, apparently from concealed artillery. Rings of smoke reeled upward. Then came the deafening crash of thunders—one after the other and the screaming and whistling of projectiles overhead. Something fell into their position near him. Many cringed, crying out as the fire of the enemy mowed

The Wailing Wind

them down. Suddenly, they realized that they were attacking a superior force.

A command was give by the captain. They halted and dropped to the ground and fired volley after volley at the dark silhouettes at the edge of the thicket. A bullet struck the ground ahead of him, throwing bits of gravel and snow into his face. Another bullet brushed his helmet and he heard a wailing death scream behind him. The captain stood up and ran waving a pistol and shouting, "Get the fuck up! Get up and charge!" On they charged, screaming loudly, firing at random as they ran. Bullets went by Henry whining in his ears and thinking that his number will be soon up. Henry and his fellow soldiers dropped to the ground again flat on their stomachs. Hordes of North Korean infantrymen came rushing out of the thicket at them, yelling as they charged toward their position. Fortunately, he did not have time to rise. A soldier near him tried to get up. "Get the hell down." Henry shouted. Of the many that had started there was only a ragged remnant near him. His unit had fired many volleys at the enemy while lying there on the snow covered ground. The soldier on his left rolled upon him, squirming like a snake in the pits of hell. "We shall all be killed!" a young soldier shouted. "Where in the fuck is the captain?" One soldier questioned. "They shot him," said another. "We better get the hell out of here," said a third soldier. "Charge!" Henry Shane shouted as loudly as ever, jumping to his feet, raising his rifle above his head as he rushed forward. "Move your fat asses," he continued to shout. It was the one inspiring spark the soldiers needed—they followed him. In a brief moment the American soldiers had hurled themselves upon the enemy line thrusting with rifles and bayonets. The enemy broke before them—some retreating, some fighting like savages for their cause that God only knew.

A North Korean soldier thrust a bayonet toward Henry's stomach. Instinctively he grabbed the weapon, and in doing so he dropped his own. The North Korean came at him fiercely clubbing his rifle—a rawboned, slant eyed son of a bitch, strong as an ox. Henry caught the barrel of the rifle as it came down. The North Korean tried to pull it away, but Henry held on to it firmly. The North Korean tried to push up to him. Henry let him come and in a moment they were struggling. The North Korean was a powerful man, and Henry had all he could handle. It gave him great comfort when he caught the North Korean in a hip lock and the North Korean fell helplessly to the ground. Henry's fellow soldiers came to his support then, and they captured the North Korean along with twenty-five other enemy soldiers.

Henry's fellow Americans gathered around him, cheering and shaking his hand, but he had no idea of what they meant. He thought it was merely a tribute to his prowess.

After the skirmish with the North Koreans, the American casualties were placed in neat rows on the ground—some dead, others were begging faintly for help. The sight of dead comrades was unbearable. The red, frozen puddles of blood near them reminded him of a slaughterhouse. He felt kind of a sickness overcoming him and turned and vomited. What was left of his outfit, they regrouped and joined the advancing column. Projectiles continued to fly overhead and were ricocheting over the level valley, throwing turf and snow into the air, tossing the dead and wounded that lay there helplessly about.

Some soldiers were mangled like a shredded rag, as if the pain of death had mutilated them in their clothes. Some bent backward, with arms out stretching like one begging for mercy. Some lay as if listening, an ear close to the ground. Some as if they were sleeping—their head upon their arms. Some wept and prayed loudly, gesturing with bloody, torn hands and faintly uttering the words of a prayer.

Henry Shane suddenly realized that he was in a country where the lives of men were cheaper than blind dogs. He became a strange creature, and not giving a damn of what came about, careless of all he saw and heard.

A lieutenant approached him as they joined the main column. "You have been wounded, soldier," The lieutenant said pointing to his left arm. Before the lieutenant could utter another word, Henry felt a rush of air and saw the lieutenant splattered into bits and pieces some of which struck him as he fell backward from the blast, He did not know what had happened. He knows not more than he has told me. He remembered feeling something limp against him like an object pressing against his left side. He attempted to remove the object, but somehow it was fastened to him and kept hurting. He placed his right hand over his left side and he felt it there against him—his own arm. The arm was like that of a corpse—cold and rubbery. He pulled at it, but the arm returned helplessly against his body. It would not move. Then he realized that he too, had become one of the bloody horrors of the battle. Slowly he struggled to his feet, weak and trembling, and sick to his stomach. He must have been lying there a long time.

The firing was now at a distance. The medics were picking up the wounded on the near-by ridge. A young soldier stood staring at Henry. "Oh my God!" he shouted and then moved away from him as if afraid. There were a great number of American soldiers behind Henry some three hundred yards away. He staggered toward them, with his legs quivering. "I will never make it," he heard himself whisper.

Henry thought of his packet of painkillers and with his teeth, tore open the packet and managed to insert a few tablets into his mouth. Some time had elapsed and it enabled him to make some headway. Suddenly he heard the excited voices of his fellow countrymen as he neared them. "My God! Look out there!" He heard many saying. "Lord have mercy! Look at them on the hill!" The words went quickly from mouth to mouth. He turned to see what they were looking at. Across the valley, there was a long ridge and back of it the main position of the North Korean Army. A dark shadow was cast over them—hundreds upon hundreds—in close order, moving into the valley. A large force of American soldiers lay between them and the North Korean Army. The shrill sound of bugles, the jeering and shouting of men, and the rumbling of artillery could be heard in the distance. An officer ran by Henry and halted, lifting his binoculars to his eyes. Then he walked back hurriedly. "Hell has broken loose!" he shouted as he passed by.

The brown-coated soldiers were rushing toward the American position like a tornado—infantrymen, mobile artillery, tanks. There was a mighty uproar in the soldiers behind him—a quick movement of feet. Terror and fear spread over them like the plague. It rattled their internal organs. The force of green, inexperienced American forces began crumbling at the fringes and jamming at the center. Then it spread like a swarm of flies on a pile of shit. "Run! Run for your lives!" was a cry that echoed across the hillside.

"Halt you fucking cowards," an officer shouted. It was now approaching 1600 hours. The youthful and inexperienced American soldiers had been on their feet for many hours. They had been fighting hunger pains in their bodies, a nervous sickness in the stomach and a stubborn and fanatic enemy. They managed to turn the flank of the advancing North Korean army—victory was within the realms of possibility.

Wait! Low and behold, a new enemy was coming to the fray—innumerable, unwearied Chinese hordes from across the Yalu River—eager for battle. The long slopes bristled with their bayonets. The American soldiers looked and cursed and began to squirm. The soldiers nearest to Henry were on the brink of an awful rout. In a moment the youthful soldiers were off in retreat like male dogs in pursuit of a bitch in heat. The earth shook under them. Officers ran around like chickens with their heads cut off—cursing and threatening, but nothing could stop the Chinese.

A few soldiers had remained and stood bravely in the center of the advancing mass—the remnants of a proud band of warriors—completely annihilated. The greater and most terrifying threat now was coming—tanks.

The roar of their engines was near Henry; a cloud of death hung over the tanks and Chinese infantrymen clung to the rear of the tanks, their voices shrilling in a wild hoot of frenzy. It makes Henry tremble even now as he thinks of it, though it is muffled under the cover of many years.

Henry realized that the tanks might roll over him. Reacting as if he were inebriated, he tried to run to save himself. Staggering across the ridge, he came upon an American soldier lying in a hollow and fell headlong into his hideaway. Henry struggled madly to rise to his feet, but he couldn't. He lay his face upon the ground, weeping like a child. May God condemn, him to hell, he shall never know again the bitter pang of that moment. He thought of his hometown, Sinclair, and Edith Miller and his Japanese girlfriend in Japan; and most of all, the immoral life that he had chosen for himself.

The rout and retreat of the American forces was at hand. He could now hear the heavy tramp of hundreds of Chinese infantrymen passing him and the shrill cry of the bugle. They had no sooner passed by when he fell back and rolled half over like a log. He could feel a warm flow of blood trickling down his left arm. A shell, fired at the retreating American forces passed high above him, whining as it flew. Then his mind went free of its trouble.

A heavy sleet aroused him as it fell from the heavens, stinging the side of his face. He wondered what it might be, for he knew not where he had come from. He lifted his head and looked to see a new beginning—possibly facing the Almighty before the pearly gates of heaven. It was so dark—so dark that he felt as if he had gone blind.

Away, in the remote distance, he could once again hear the shrill cry of the bugle. It vibrated in the great silence—he had never known the likes of it. He could hear the falling and pelting of the sleet, but it seemed only to deepen the silence. He felt the cold, wet slush under his face and hand. Then he knew it was night and the battlefield where he had fallen. He was alive and might see another day—thank God.

Henry felt something move near his feet. He heard the whisper of a fellow soldier. "I thought you were dead long ago," the soldier said.

"No, No!" Henry answered. I'm alive—I know I'm alive—this is the battlefield. This is Korea."

"I'm afraid I am not going to live," the soldier moaned. "Got a terrible wound. I don't think I'll make it to daybreak."

"Dark long?" Henry asked

"For hours," the soldier answered. "I don't know how many." The soldier began to groan and utter short prayers, "Oh, my soul is at the mercy of the Lord." Henry heard him cry in a loud despairing voice.

Then there was a bit of silence in which Henry could hear the soldier whisper of his mother. Presently he began to pray again. His voice broke and trembled and sank into silence.

Henry had his own life to think about now—perhaps he had no time to lose—and he tried to remain calm. He had no strength to move and began to feel the nearing of his time. The sleet was falling faster. It chilled him to the marrow as he felt the sleet clinging to his back. He called to the soldier who lay beside him—again and again he called to him—but got no answer. Then he knew that the soldier was dead and he alone.

Long after that in the distance he heard a voice calling. It sounded very eerie in the still night. It grew plainer as he listened. He heard his own name, Henry Shane. It was certainly calling to him and he answered in a feeble cry. In a moment he could hear the tramp of someone coming. A soldier was beside him presently, who ever he might be. He could not see because of the darkness. "Who are you?" he remembered asking, but only got an indistinct answer.

At first Henry was glad, then he was overcome by a mighty horror. In a moment the soldier had picked him up and was carrying him like a bag of flour over the shoulder. The jarring and jolting steps seemed to be breaking Henry's arms at the shoulder joints. As Henry moaned and groaned, the soldier walked quickly. Henry could see nothing in the darkness, but the soldier went ahead seldom stopping except for a moment now and then to rest. Henry wondered where he was being taken and what it meant. He called again, ""Who are you?" but there was no response. "My God!" he whispered to himself. "This is no human being—this is death severing the soul from the body." Then he heard someone hailing nearby. "Help, help!" he shouted faintly. "Where are you?" Now the answer came farther away. "Can't see you." The mysterious bearer was now breathing heavily as he walked quickly, now almost in a run. "Halt! Who goes there?" an American soldier called. Then Henry could hear voices. "Did you hear that noise?" said one of the soldiers. "So dark I can't see my hand before me." "Darker than hell!" said one voice. Henry Shane continued to wonder who the mysterious bearer was that had been carrying him. "It must be Norman Wright carrying me," he murmured. "Who else would be strong enough to pick me up and carry me as if I were no bigger than a flea infested dog?"

That was what he was thinking when he passed out. From then until he regained consciousness in the field hospital near Pakchon, he remembered nothing.

While lying on a litter awaiting medical attention, he noticed the groaning men lying about him; others stood between them with portable lights. Shortly, a pretty nurse was bending over him. He felt the gentle, smooth touch of her hand upon his face and he heard her speak to him so tenderly he can not think of it, even now, without thanking God for dedicated and devoted nurses. He clung to her hand, clung desperately but only exerted the strength of a dying man while he awaited the prick of the hypodermic needle. He saw the rays of the portable lights grow pale and he fell asleep.

For several days Henry was very weak and unstable from the loss of blood and suddenly the tide turned. He was decorated for bravery and was sent to a hospital in Japan. He was in the hospital for several weeks, but he did not have any visitors—including his Japanese girlfriend, Keiko.

Following his recovery, he volunteered to return to Korea to rejoin his unit and found himself once again confronted by a horrible and fanatic enemy. His luck finally ran out. He was wounded again and captured by the Chinese, and he and other wounded prisoners were forced to march without medical attention to a prisoner of war camp near Pyongyang, North Korea.

Four

While fighting in Korea, Henry Shane had heard gruesome tales about many of the atrocious prisoner of war camps scattered throughout North Korea.

Some of the prisoner of war camps included the so called "Bean Camp" near Suan, a camp known as "Death valley" near Pukchin, another camp called the "Valley" in the vicinity of Kanggye.

Among the worst camps were the "Interrogation Center" near Pukchin and a neighboring disciplinary center called the "Caves" in the vicinity of Kanggye. It was rumored that the latter was literally composed of caverns in which the men were confined. Here they were forced to sleep without blankets. Their food was thrown at them. There were no latrine facilities. In the "Caves" the prisoners were reduced to a degree of misery and degradation almost unbelievable. Those sent to the "Caves" were prisoners accused of insubordination, breaking camp rules, attempting to escape, or committing some other crime. The crime was seldom fitted by the punishment. Some men who refused to talk to military interrogators were threatened with, or sent to the "Caves."

The first ordeal that Henry Shane, as well as the other captives had to suffer—and often the worst—was the journey to one of the prisoner of war camps.

The North Koreans frequently tied a prisoner's hands behind his back or bound his arms with wire. Wounded prisoners were jammed into trucks that jolted dripping blood, along the roads. Many of the wounded received no medical attention until they reached the camp. Some were not attended to until days thereafter.

The marching prisoners were liable to be beaten or kicked to their feet if they fell. A number of the North Korean soldiers were bullwhip barbarians and products of a semi-primitive environment. Probably some of them had never heard of the Geneva Conventions or any other code of war.

The worst of their breed were responsible for the murder of men who staggered out of line or collapsed at roadside. They were particularly brutal to South Korean captives. Many of the ROK prisoners were forced to dig their own graves before they were shot. This is an old oriental custom applied to the execution of criminals. The enemy shot some Americans, with hands tied behind their back.

So the journeys to the prison camps were death marches, especially in the winter of 1950-1951 when the trails were knee-deep in snow and polar winds thrashed the exhausted column. On the marches to the north, many men perished before they reached their destination.

When the enemy captured Henry Shane, he unfortunately was assigned as a permanent prisoner at "Pak's Palace" near Pyongyang, North Korea. He lived in a one story, wooden frame barrack near a brickyard with about fifty other Americans. He slept on the bottom level of a two-tiered, rough, boarded bunk. Rice straw stuffed into burlap bags comprised the mattress. "Pak's Palace" was as he expected in a remote corner of Asia. Prisoner rations were scanty, a basic diet of rice occasionally supplemented with some kind of foul soup.

The Chinese and North Korean authorities pointed out that this provision conformed to the rules of the Geneva Convention—the prisoner received the same food as the soldiery holding him captive. It was known that the North Koreans and Chinese soldiers were inured to a rice diet. The average American could not tolerate such a diet. Sickness broke out in the camp. Many men suffered long sieges of dysentery.

As the weeks passed, Henry Shane, like all the others had grown more starved and more haggard. Continued hunger had placed a tremendous strain on their physical and mental well being. They existed by the skin of their teeth and raw courage. Some of the prisoners lost fifty pounds in a matter of weeks.

The prisoners' clothes and flesh were filthy. The flesh had begun to recede around their cheekbones, and their eyes were glassy.

As the days passed, more and more men fainted from hunger. Those who were classified as being severely ill were put in an isolated area of the compound that the men had devised. By the disposition of the camp commandant, the medical men had received a little extra freedom and a little extra food for taking care of the sick.

The men suffered much from cold in winter and heat in summer. Water was often scarce and bathing became difficult. The barracks were foul and unsanitary. Despite the putrid conditions, some of the men tried to shave each day. This was not so much for their sake, but for the sake of keeping up appearances before the North Koreans.

Henry Shane observed, however, that a few of the men didn't care. Almost without exception they were the ones with the least education—and the least amount of discipline.

The men organized themselves into squads and platoons with a commander for each barrack. The officer in charge of all the barracks was a colonel. Nobody liked him very much. He lived with a few other officers in a separate room and was very seldom forceful in making demands of the North Koreans. Many of the prisoners felt that some officers were collaborating with the enemy.

"Pak's Palace" was one of the worst camps endured by the American prisoners of war in North Korea. It was a highly specialized interrogation center dominated by a chief interrogator, Colonel Pak, and was ably assisted by a henchman who came to be called "Dirty Pictures Wong" by the prisoners of war.

The camp was under the administration of a Colonel Lee, and there were several other interrogators on the team. Pak and Wong were symbolic of the institution. Pak was a sadist, an animal who should have been in a cave.

The team employed the usual questionnaires, the carrot-and-prod techniques to induce answers. Failing to induce them, they contrived to compel them. The "Palace" wanted military information. Coercion was used as the ultimate resort. For Pak, coercion began soon after a prisoner refused to talk. Then Pak would use violence. Threats, kicks, cigarette burns, and promises of further torture would follow abusive language. They took a terrible beating from Colonel Pak.

Some prisoners found ways to get around the beating. One way was to convince the captors that you were dumb, stupid, the low man in your class. You were awarded a contemptuous slap, and that was about all.

To the surprise of some of the prisoners at the "Palace," the interrogation team would sometimes open up with a wild political harangue. Then came the word that he enemy had established a system of indoctrination courses. The prisoner might start the hard way—and be punished by restricted rations and other privations. If he began to show the proper spirit—to cooperate with his captors—he was lectured and handed Communist literature. A docile prisoner who read the literature and listened politely to the lectures was graduated to a better class. Finally, he might be sent to "Peaceful Valley." In this lenient camp the food was relatively good. Prisoners might even have tobacco. Here they were given all sorts of Marxian propaganda.

The graduates from "Peaceful Valley" and others who accepted Communist schooling were called "Progressives." Prisoners who refused to go along with the program often remained in tougher circumstances. They were considered "Reactionaries."

The enemy followed no rigid system. Rather, his treatment of prisoners was capricious. Sometimes he showed contempt for the man who readily submitted to bullying. The prisoner who stood up to the bluster, threats, and blows of an interrogator might be dismissed with a shrug and sent to quarters as mild as any—if any prison barracks in North Korea could be described as mild.

All in all, the docile prisoner did not gain much by his docility— and sometimes he gained nothing. The prisoner who defied Pak and his breed might take a beating, but again he might not. The ordeal was never easy. The conditions weren't easy either for the combat troops out there on the front lines.

The prisoner of war political schools in North Korea were patterned after the Soviet-Russian design. They were part of a mass program to spread Marxian ideology and gain converts for international communism.

The "Progressives" were called upon to deliver lectures, write pamphlets, and make propaganda broadcasts. "Progressive leaders were sent among the "Reactionary" groups to harangue the men. They wrote speeches condemning capitalism and American aggression in Korea. They organized a group known as the "Peace Fighters."

Fortunately, only a few officers were "Progressives." However, their influence was unfortunately strong on the enlisted men. If the captain or colonel signs a peace petition and orders the rest of us to do it, we have to follow orders. Altogether the enlisted men were on a spot. That much of them refused to join the "Progressives" and rejected a promise, sometimes unfulfilled, of better food, minor luxuries, and mail call, says something for the spirit of privates and non-commissioned officers. The men who gave the "Progressives" a difficult time were the rugged "Reactionaries."

Breakdown of leadership was exactly what the enemy desired. Officers were usually segregated. Then as soon as a natural leader stepped forward in a camp, he was removed. By design and because some officers refused to assume leadership responsibility, organization in some of the camps deteriorated to an every man for himself situation.

Some of the barracks became indescribably filthy. The men scuffed for their food. Hoarders grappled all the tobacco. Morale decayed to the vanishing point. Each man mistrusted the next. Bullies persecuted the weak and the sick. Filth bred disease and contagion swept the camp. So men suffered or died for lack of leadership and discipline.

Fortunately for Henry Shane, he was confined to the same barrack as his best friend, Norman Wright. They attended most of the lectures together and rendered assistance to one another in time of need. The friendship enabled them to cope with and to endure the difficulties and hardships at "Pak's Palace."

Occasionally a few Red Cross packages got through. However, the enemy consistently refused to permit the International Red Cross to inspect the prisoner of war camps. There was good reason.

The North Koreans usually allotted a half of a Red Cross package to each man. This contained a ration of cigarettes, powdered coffee, sugar and canned meat. Heating the coffee on a hibachi at night the men talked hopefully of the progress of the war. They felt almost cheerful despite their condition. If they could only resist their own slow starvation and misery, they were sure their fellow Americans would rescue them sooner or later. When a group of recently captured Americans arrived from the south, one of the newcomers bluntly informed them that the United Nations' forces had to retreat to the vicinity of the 38th parallel.

The ray of hope had diminished to the lowest ebb. As the days and weeks merged into months of gloom and misery, the dream of repatriation faded into a dismal and melancholy state of hopelessness and helplessness.

This type of environment set the stage that led to the disgruntled disposition of Henry Shane. He began to have many negative thoughts regarding his participation in the war. He was led to believe that the American cause in Korea was simple and just, but the objectives of the Korean War were frequently confused in his mind as well as in the minds of his fellow Americans.

He was fully aware the Korean War had three aspects, for they were deeply ingrained in him because of redundant explanations by his superior officers.

There was the Civil War aspect—North Koreans fighting South Koreans for control of a divided country. There was the collective aspect—the first United Nation's attempt to stop a treaty-breaking aggressor. There was the cold war aspect—the western powers blocking the expansion of Communist imperialism. All these things he knew, but—

The causes of the war, the United Nation's objectives and the need for American intervention were not clearly delineated in his mind or in the minds of his comrades. This lack of understanding not only prevailed among other fighting men, but also among many Americans on the home front.

The North Korean and Chinese Communists attempted to exploit to the fullest this condition in both international propaganda and in dealing with the American prisoners of war. At times, the communists were successful in fulfilling their objectives.

POW
Report by the Secretary of Defense's Advisory Committee on Prisoners' of War, August 1955
U. S. Government Printing Office, Washington, D. C.

Part II

Sinclair, Pennsylvania

1942-1953

Five

Henry Shane had a severe pain in his stomach again—the same type of pain that had been prevalent in his fellow Americans prior their passing away. He had it for a long time now, and his experience in combat and the prisoner of war camp made him come to the conclusion that he was suffering from some type of dysentery. All he knew was that he had it, and now finally, the effects it had on his mind. By this time, he had learned to accept the fact that his sufferings were no greater than the sufferings of his countrymen who were held in captivity by the Chinese and North Koreans. They were all victims of war.

He and his friend, Norman Wright, came out of the corner of the compound where their comrades were lying in the midst of death. The two of them staggered slowly to the western end of the barbed wire enclosure, where they observed a North Korean military contingent drilling under the spring sun. They sat on their haunches, and neither of them said anything—not for a long time. The stench of death swarmed over them and armies of flies and other insects darted about them. When they began to talk they did not say much for their hearts were filled with compassion. This was "Pak's Palace," a prisoner of war camp near Pyongyang, North Korea, their home now. This was the living hell that the Chinese had forced upon them. "Well," Norman said. "It looks like we are going to rot in this prisoner of war camp."

"Yeah, I know and many of our buddies are going to die," Henry said faintly. He clutched his stomach with both of his hands.

"It's a hell of a thing to be confined in this prisoner of war camp," Norman replied.

The North Koreans moved back and forth outside the enclosure, and the thought was in Henry Shane now, stronger than ever. "I'm going to die in this God forsaken country! Why? Why do I have to die here, oh, Lord?" His eyes began to sting and tears flowed in a steady stream down his cheeks. He wept as he shaped the hopeless thought of reparation in his mind. He had not been a religious man, but in recent months he prayed constantly to his Supreme Maker for strength and courage. It wasn't death itself he feared, but the fear of dying in a prison camp in a remote corner of the world.

"I don't know what we had done to deserve this fate," Norman said chokingly.

"This is one of the penalties of war," Henry responded. "Still—still, someone must die for their country." The pain in his stomach was greater than ever, and now the need, the desire, the urge to live came upon him. He never knew what his true ambition in live was, but he knew it wasn't to become rich. What it was, what he was looking for, he really didn't know? It was a dismal and dark thought that moved before him, and getting between him and the barbed wire enclosure. A pain in him so severe it had the effects of death. A pain that had put a feeling in him so deep, that although he heard what his friend was saying, he did so as if in a stupor.

"We have always been close friends since we came to Korea," Norman said. "Probably closer than most men ever are. Perhaps you know that, Henry."

"Yes," Henry said again, but his mind had already begun to wander ahead of his friend.

"Go ahead and say it!" Norman shouted. "Why does it have to be us? Why are we here in the first place? I know I'll never see America again."

Henry did not respond, for he knew that he was going to die. Now, as when he was a youth, he felt excluded from the world, caught between a life of despair and the unknown destiny. He knew he was not the same person. He was one who had learned over the years to live with fear, and for the first time in his life he was happy of solitude. After the bitterness of his immoral life, the ordeal of love and war, the pain he had lived with for months seemed like a welcomed relief, and so did his present state which promised death.

Then the noise of his environment was silent, a cold sweat came forth from his body, and his breathing became more difficult. He knew the hand of death was strangling him. His entire life seemed to pass before him briefly remembering the days of his youth in Sinclair, Pennsylvania, his deceased parents, his participation in the agony of two wars, his Japanese girlfriend, Keiko, and his illicit relationship with Edith Miller.

It was difficult for him to remember what he had thought about and felt in those terrible days of the tortuous march to the North Korean POW camp. Those bleak winter days and the difficult task of survival seemed afterwards to be dismissed behind the glorious blaze of combat and love for his country, and love for Edith Miller. Later he understood the fear of death and turned to God in constant prayer. After his departure from Seoul into North Korea, when the gray winter days succeeded each other without change, and when the snow appeared to fall from the heavens forever, he lived always with the fear of the unknown. The future was but a blank in his mind. The past he recalled as having its pleasant moments and bad moments, but he always lived with tension. Something was going to happen that he could not control.

It had not been a matter of getting up out of a rice paddy and going forward into the fire of the enemy that he had already experienced. It wasn't the fear of struggling up a snow-covered mountain; it was not the jeering and screaming of fanatic Chinese and North Korean soldiers; but that of departing into the inexperienced realms of the world beyond. On the surface, his life was merely an existence. Sadness lay deep in his heart and soul. Now he no longer feared the shrill cry of the bugle, but the powerful hand of "The Almighty" beckoning him. During his early years, he walked the path of life as a carefree youth. Henry Shane thought and remembered many things, as do all men at the brink of death. His past was like a book he reviewed over and over, always finding something different he overlooked, stirring old frustrations, reliving glorious moments.

When he remembered, he always pictured himself, as he must have looked. So in this despairing moment he envisioned a dark haired boy, somewhat mature for his age, sitting on a curb in Sinclair, Pennsylvania.

Here in this town located in the heart of the coal country, were drab structures where several generations had lived and died, carving their livelihood from the depths of the earth. It was a town of foreign customs, foreign superstitions, foreign songs and tales, feuds, hatreds, fellowship, love, and a town where the elderly citizens ruled relationships. This town comprised mainly of foreign stock was resistant to change. So the development of Sinclair had been slow, but hearty foreign elements continued to trickle into this valley of "black gold."

He remembered the black faced miners returning from the mines, bending over to pat him on the head with dirty hands. The rattle of the coal cars was a noise so constant that he never became fully aware of it until he left Sinclair. He heard other boys shouting up and down the street, and women laughing and chatting in their foreign tongue from window to window and yard to yard. Noise and laughter were always prevalent in this Coal Region community.

All during his youth he was enclosed by people joined together in mutual dependence. Little by little, this friendly, comfortable community came to seem to him a place in which he had no future.

His father had taught him to believe that one does not control his destiny, but that one is free to move upon his own intuition and discretion. Beginning when he was fourteen years old, this idea became familiar to him. His father was always talking about it. It became a part of his philosophy, because it came to him when he was a youth, and because he accepted it without challenge. Still, Henry lived and wandered about Sinclair day after day, captivated but also troubled, wondering what future was in store for him. There was just one thing he could do here. He could get a job in the mine. He feared the thought of working in the mine, and the thought of going down into the depths of the earth, the possibilities of being buried under tons of earth.

Although he feared the future, he cherished the wilderness of the mountains that surrounded Sinclair. He loved the mountains, and he felt that that the mountains were his salvation. He felt best sitting in a secluded spot on bright mornings, watching far below, the hustle and bustle of Sinclair.The sky overhead, the sweet smelling air, mixed with an aroma of pine, the sun's rays seemed to reach down at him and hug him with loving arms. All these things he enjoyed. He wanted forever to remain outdoors. He wanted to be a free and happy wanderer. It was this comfortable, protective refuge into which Henry Shane escaped, and perhaps he would have remained in it all of his life if the coming of World War II had not invaded and changed his philosophy.

His thoughts also carried him back to the hearty and succulent growth of the spring season in the mountains near Sinclair. The springs past, wild with the silvery pussy willow, bright blooming dogwood, and orchid honey suckle and the petal blossoming fruit trees. The ever hanging weeping willow and water birch, and huge sycamores, that lined the banks of the Stonycreek River which looped from one side of the valley to the other.

There were the summers too, with a greenish hue covering the mountains and rolling countryside and farmland further to the east, ingrained in his never forgetting memory, and there would always be the soft, sweet smell of the good, clear mountain water in his nostrils. How subtle and amazing were those nights when sleep came beneath the twinkling of the stars.

Through many other days of his formative years, he remembered the liberal quantities of large, dark-red cherries, blackberries, raspberries, and huckleberries, had almost only for the shaking of bushes and trees. In hiking he had often seen the aroused and swift flush of coveys of quail and pheasant, new each year with life, being frightened constantly by his passing. Young fawn and deer in a herd, wandering aimlessly and suddenly disturbed by the presence of a human, scampering quickly through the brush back to safety.

Then there was the autumn season, the time of nippy, tranquil

The Wailing Wind

days and nights when the moon cast a brilliant light on the earth. The power of "The Almighty" changed the environment overnight to a yellow, red, and orange transformation that could be remembered and seen along the highlands overlooking Sinclair.

It was a way of life for Henry Shane, this panorama, of youth and animals in concert with nature, belonging now to the ages as it slipped past him forever beyond the dark and unknown world beyond.

Belonging only to memory, as he looked back over the time, were the bell-tingling mules of smaller mining operations, walking wearily, exerting great effort in their attempt to pull the little cars laden with coal, or trampling over boarded trestles from the mine to the lofty chutes. Gone forever were the calls of the miners directing the obstinate mules, dying slowly away in their own reverberations through the valley and over the farmland against the shrill sound of the whistle of the approaching locomotive.

This dying soldier, thought too, how his mother, being quiet and hard working, had the shrewd instinct of buying the family's needs, thinking of little else but their good being and welfare. His father being a stern and dedicated family man, struggling to earn a meager livelihood from the depths of the earth.

He knew that his final fate would be forever lost and forgotten in the realm of life, as all men in the scheme of their living forget the past to see only the future.

In Sinclair, Pennsylvania, on warm summer evenings, Henry Shane used to sit on a wooden bench in front of the drugstore. Across the street there was a bandstand. Every Saturday night during the summer the Sinclair Community Band treated the town's people to a concert, and this was appreciated more than anything else the town had to offer. People would come from far and nearby places. The older men and women sat on benches while the majority of the younger people danced to the beat of the music. Occasionally a couple could be seen wandering away from the scene of the dance, and disappear into the wooded area beyond the bandstand.

Saturday night in Sinclair was a night of flirtation, dining, wining and dancing, for all the fashionable, young and eligible women were there, in hope of meeting some well to do handsome stranger. The air was always filled with the squeal and laughter of excitement, with an aroma of perfume hanging low overhead.

Henry sitting alone, or at times with his friend, Richard Rand, felt as though this type of life was a big spectacle in which he had no part. For one thing, the dating of girls cost money, and he was from a poor family where they had a difficult time to make ends meet. By the time his parents purchased the necessities of life, there was nothing left to squander away. Cash was very scarce in the Shane household. The money that Henry did earn from odd jobs had to be turned over to his parents.

He never joined the dance around the bandstand because he felt strange and shabby, and for a long time no girl gave him so much as a glance, but one girl did repeatedly capture his eye. She was a well-developed young girl, with long, black hair and dark eyes. She had a feline walk and the bearing of one who was well bred. At a glance, her face was that of an angel, but her tight blouse and skirt set her apart. So, even more, did her strange behavior, for she never appeared to be interested in other boys, seldom smiled, and never greeted anyone. Proud and self centered, she moved through the crowd, as if it had not been there. Henry had watched her every time she passed with intense interest, and also with the hope of meeting her. Like him, she seemed to have no interest in the excitement of the crowd. Then one Saturday night, she turned her head in his direction and looked him full in the eye. She did not smile, but gave him a warm stare and went her way. Henry had a feeling that he had been chosen, for he had never seen her in the company of local boys.

The following Saturday he saw her again, but this time he was sitting with his friend, Richard Rand, and she did not give him a glance.

"Who is that girl that just went by?" Henry asked. "Don't you know? That girl is Edith Miller. She is new around here. Just moved to

Sinclair from Pellersville a couple of months ago. She isn't a bad looking girl at that. The guys were saying that she is sort of stuck on herself."

"She seems like a nice girl," Henry said softly.

He thought she must have an interest in him, and he knew very well that if she ever looked at him again, he was going to rise and follow her.

It happened the very next Saturday night as he sat on the bench. She passed him once without looking, but the next time she gave him that quick come on stare, and when she turned away, a smile came upon her face. He followed her at a distance, and it appeared she was heading toward her home on the outskirts of town. Henry followed her and stayed near enough to be sure he would not lose her in the dark. When she had gone a little way along Pine Street, she stopped and looked back at him, apparently to make sure he was still following. Then she left the main street and disappeared in the shadows of a side road. He thought her house must be somewhere nearby. Where she had turned, he stopped and asked himself if it was wise to pursue the adventure. He believed her to be a harmless girl, and was not afraid of her, yet he hesitated on the edge of darkness, as he hesitated on many other occasions at school and at the bandstand.

Then he heard a voice calling in the darkness of the night.

"Aren't you coming up Henry Shane? I know you followed me. Don't be afraid, there's no one at home?"

Henry felt the pounding of his heart, and a mysterious feeling crept over his body. Then he saw a light come forth through the window and that prompted him to proceed. He made his way slowly up a dark, narrow walk and knocked on the door.

"Come in!" she called, and her voice was calm and wanting.

He pushed open the door and found himself in an elaborate, clean living room with beautiful pictures on the wall. Edith was sitting on the couch, toying with her necklace. She threw him a smile and motioned for him to close the door.

"Sit down," she said. "Can I get you something to drink? A soda perhaps." For a girl that was conceited she had very pleasant manners, he thought. She went into the kitchen and re-entered the room with a bottle of soda and two glasses. "Thank you," Henry said. "How did you know I was going to follow you?"

"I always know about everyone," she said. "I knew about you." She smiled at him. "I don't just let anyone come into my house. They have to be someone extra special. You probably heard that I do."

"Yes," Henry replied. "You are very popular for only living in Sinclair for a couple of months."

"The boys tell many lies about me," she said calmly. "You must not believe everything you hear. The only reason why they spread so many lies about me is because I don't give them a chance to get intimate with me. I am a good girl. I go to school and church regularly, and I have never harmed anyone."

Henry nodded. "When I looked at you, I had to follow you. I had this deep urge to want to know you."

"I knew you would follow me," she said. "I'm glad you did. We both are loners. We ought to be friends. Besides, there aren't many boys I can trust, but for some unknown reason I feel I can trust you."

"How can you be sure?" Henry said

"I really don't know. I merely feel that way about you."

"What else can you tell me yourself, Edith?"

She laughed. "I knew you would ask me that question. Everyone does. Well, I'm sixteen years old, I have black hair and dark eyes. What else do you want to know?"

"Seriously, Edith. Tell me more about yourself."

"Well, I'll tell you when I get to know you better."

"Maybe you are interested in another boy. Anyway, I'm sure you're pretty enough to attract other boys if you really wanted to. I'm so sure of it that I'm willing to put a wager on it."

"I have nothing to bet," she said.

For a long time they sat looking at each other in an embarrassed

The Wailing Wind

silence, filled with tension. Henry was aware of her pretty face and well developed breasts. He wanted to put his arms around her, but somehow his inferiority complex was a barrier he could not overcome. He smiled, feeling a little foolish. After a long and meaningless conversation, Henry remarked, "I guess I'll hustle along now, It's getting late."

She smiled at him and bent over and kissed him on the cheek. Henry's face reddened with embarrassment and quickly stood. She shook her head in bewilderment staring into his eyes.

"Please come here next Saturday evening, just after dark," she said. "My mother will be gone for the weekend and won't be back until Sunday night."

"Okay," Henry said. "If you want me to."

"Oh, but I do want you to come and visit me again."

Henry was restless all week. He went about his chores in the same usual manner, but waiting to go to Edith's house seemed like eternity.

On Saturday night, as soon as it was dark, he set out for Edith Miller's house forcing him to hurry. He had felt sure that there was a reason for her asking him to come back to her house. Doubt and desire had been with him all week long. It seemed to him now that it was important for him to rid himself of the inferiority complex that had dominated his life. Now a girl has given him an opportunity, raised his hopes, and he was going to take advantage of the situation. He longed for this girl, but was still confused over the approach she had used to lure him. He remembered that she was puzzled when he didn't react to her kiss. He wondered after all whether she was only making a fool out of him.

Well, he thought, I'll soon find out if she was just a teaser. It was a dark night and Pine Street was deserted. He came to the railroad tracks that ran through this part of town from Mine 35. He found the side road she had entered just a week ago. He went up the narrow walk and came to her house. It appeared as if no one was at home. There was no light. He had stopped, feeling dejected. A wave of anger entered his mind against this girl who had given him a big line.

"Just as I thought," he mumbled. "She made an ass out of me." He was about to leave, but on second thought he went up on to the porch. He decided to knock on the door, just to make sure. Hoping and praying by chance that she may have fallen asleep on the couch.

He knocked on the door and stood there listening, but heard no sound except the faint music coming from the bandstand in the far distance. He tried the doorknob, and to his surprise he found the door to be unlocked. He stepped into darkness, and a cold sweat came forth from his forehead. Frightened, he could hear his own breathing in the deep silence of the room. Then he heard her voice calling to him from the vicinity of the couch. Startled he staggered towards her in the darkness.

"What the hell is the big idea?" Henry said.

"I knew you were out there," she said. "If you would have turned to leave, I'd have called you."

"The hell with all of this suspense," Henry said. "I'm going to put on the light."

"No, Henry, please don't! Just sit down near me."

As he sat down, he realized that she had converted the couch into a bed and lay there naked. "I have been waiting for you, Henry," she uttered. "Don't be afraid? Take off your clothes and lay with me."

Henry trembling slowly put his hand upon her breast. He could not begin to believe this thing that was about to happen could possibly be true. His inferiority complex vanished completely and he was overcome instead with a passionate desire for her body.

He quickly stripped the clothes from his body and mounted her. A continuous moaning came from the depths of her throat. It sounded strange and did not have in it the usual softness of her normal voice. When Henry had stopped, she pulled his head toward her face and began to kiss him as if she were in a wild rage. "Don't stop?" She cried out. "Please, don't stop?"

When they were finished, they lay there in deep silence, occasionally embracing one another. "Now I know why you wanted me to come to your house," Henry said. "I'm grateful that you permitted me to have your beautiful body."

"Put on your clothes. Don't put on the light? No boy has ever seen me naked."

When he put on the light she was completely dressed, but her long black hair hung wildly upon her shoulder. Her lips were swollen from the passionate kissing but to Henry she looked beautiful.

She sat down and began to comb her hair, and then covered her swollen lips with lipstick. She smiled at him. "You see," she said. "Just as I told you, there was nothing to be afraid of. Now do you feel better?"

"Thank you," Henry said with a smile.

He did not feel embarrassed, but weak and immensely relieved that he had overcome his inferiority complex through this girl, but most of all, he was aware that he had discovered in himself a potential that he was unaware of in the past. When he was about to depart, he pulled her body into his arms and kissed her. She was still warm and becoming. "When you want to," she said, "you can come out to see me. Saturday nights would be the best time."

Six

Now the days passed, and these were the days of Henry Shane's daring youth. It was the first time that he had been happy. He studied little at Sinclair High School, and devoted much of his time to the football program and to Edith Miller. Each day he gained more courage and soon approached Edith boldly. Best of all, he enjoyed lingering outside the school building. There he would meet Edith, sometimes laughing casually without being conscious of the teachers or the other students. They could be seen swinging arm in arm in the corridors of the school glancing wide eyed at one another. At night they could be seen together in company of other couples at the Rainbow Grill, a combination restaurant and dance hall that catered to the youthful citizenry of Sinclair.

In this fashion, in the space of a few months, a few years, the pleasure, the excitement, the companionship of Edith, a way of living that enabled him to become independent.

He passed from an inferior youth to an uncertain man. He gained confidence, and he discovered he was well accepted by other people. He became a live wire. Other girls began to show an interest in him, and they tried to lure him away from the affections of Edith. His attitude changed and he became cock-sure and proud, but Edith being love sick, could not detect the gradual change that was transpiring. Nevertheless, other people, including his best friend, Richard Rand, noticed the change in Henry Shane's behavior.

On the way home from football practice one evening in late October, Henry Shane walked along, slowly, thoughtfully thinking of Edith Miller, when as if from a great distance he heard someone calling his name. He turned and waited. While he waited, he thought of his relationship with Edith. Somehow, for some reason somewhere deep inside of him, the thought of Edith getting pregnant frightened him. He couldn't figure out why. He just couldn't. Then he forgot about Edith.

The voice was now near him, friendly and familiar. It was the voice of his best friend, Richard Rand. "How are you, Henry? Do you mind if I tag along with you?"

"Come along," Henry replied.

They crossed Rosemore Avenue and then went through the railroad yard in the twilight, and through Delaney Park near the Stonycreek River. The noise of a rumbling train dimmed behind them and then died completely.

"Care for a cigarette?" Richard asked.

"No," Henry emphatically replied. "You know damn well I don't smoke."

"I don't either," Richard said laughingly, putting the pack of cigarettes into his shirt pocket.

"If the coach knew you smoked cigarettes, he'd kick your ass and bounce you off the team," Henry said forcefully.

"Yeah, I know. Cigarettes are bad for ones health, yet I go ahead and smoke anyway. If my father knew I wasted money on cigarettes, he'd be pissed off. I shouldn't, you know. My father works hard for his money over at the mine, and comes home covered with coal dust and his body all tired out, and I-I." He shook his head and softly said, "It just doesn't make sense." They walked along quietly. A slight breeze had come up and was rustling the leaves on the ground. High in the sky, the first stars were out, glistening and sparkling. A hush was over the river. Suddenly Richard Rand turned to Henry and broke the silence.

"Gee, Henry, you and I have been good buddies for a hell of a long time, but you certainly have changed since you met up with Edith Miller. I liked you better the way you used to be. Why in the hell did you get so involved with her? I personally feel that all dames are the same, get you in trouble if you're not careful."

"What'll I do?" I've got Edith in love with me, and I've got to show my affection, and besides I like her. What the hell is wrong with that?"

"I'm going to warn you, Henry, it's better to stay away from all dames that get too serious."

"Lay off," Henry replied. They walked a short distance in silence. Richard suddenly spoke.

"Henry, you know what girls really want; love, affection, take them to a dance, show them a hell of a good time and a lot of crap like that. Getting married someday, that's what they talk about. To hear them talk, wow, they could go on and shoot the bullshit for hours and hours if they think you're interested."

"And is that so damn bad," Henry responded quickly.

"Oh Christ, Henry. What the hell is the matter with you? Don't stand there and act like an angel? Did you try with Edith? You know what I mean."

"Yeah, I know what you mean. What about that dame you were trying to make out with?"

"You mean Betty Harper," Richard said sharply. "Well I took her out a couple of times, spent a few dollars on her feeding her half ass face. Then my father said he wasn't going to give me any more money to waste on silly girls, and if I wanted to do that I'd have to earn my own money. You know, my father was right. So, I take this dame out, and got the urge to feel her big tits. She was shocked that I would even think of doing such a thing. I should have punched her right in the puss. I told that Goddamned Betty Harper off. She pretends she doesn't even know me anymore. Can you imagine, she's running around with that fruity kid, Jim Heeler."

"Jim Heeler," Henry said.

"Yeah, Jim Heeler. You know, the kid with the long hair that plays the tuba in the band."

"Now I know who you mean. His father is the manager over at the Eureka Store."

"Give me one of those country girls from over at Haysville, anytime," Richard said. "I want a girl that knows the score. A country girl—why man, a country girl is the best piece of ass you can get. Country girls first then city girls."

"They're not all that way," Henry remarked. "Some of those country girls have to be in pretty early. Their parents are usually stricter than hell."

"Oh, my God! How long do you think it takes to get a piece of ass? Here you are standing there and pretending you are cherry. Who in the hell do you think you're kidding, Henry? This is Richard Rand you're talking to. So, you're still a cherry."

"Me, hell, no," Henry said. "I didn't know about those country girls being so damn passionate."

"Come off that shit. It doesn't take long. Just take them behind the barn or up in the hay mound, and tell them to whip up their dress and then throw it to them. They're always ready. All girls are like that if they like you. Boy, you're going to have to keep your eyes open for some of those girls attending our school from Haysville."

"I sure didn't know they had so many girls like that from Haysville," Henry said.

"What else have they got to do? Haven't you noticed how many of them are hanging around the Rainbow Grill lately? Man, those two Rockingham twins, Mary Ann and Shirley, they have what it takes. And they're not just coming into town for the hell of it either. They're looking for something."

"Yeah, I noticed that," Henry said.

The next morning Henry left for school earlier than usual. He didn't wait outside for Edith as he normally had done. "Here so early," Mary Ann said. "Where is your girl friend this morning?" Henry glanced around the room. "I think she had to see Mrs. Hunter about some assignment."

"Well that's nice," Mary Ann said. "Now we can talk for a change and get better acquainted."

"You better leave him alone," Shirley muttered. "You're going to have a battle on your hands with Edith Miller if she hears about this. I've heard about her stories before, and she thinks she still owns Henry Shane."

"Is it true you love Edith Miller?" Mary Ann said.

Henry's face reddened as he looked from one girl to the other.

"I'm sorry I embarrassed you, Henry," Mary Ann said. "I just wanted to know. Well—you understand. You had that funny look in your eyes when we came into the room."

Mary Ann moved the seat closer to him, "Richard Rand has been talking to you about us. Hasn't he? What did he say?"

"Don't ask him silly questions?" Shirley protested.

"He didn't say much, Mary Ann, only that you and your sister were cute."

"Oh, did he really?" Shirley intervened. "I wonder what he really has on his mind."

"You can't help feeling sorry for Richard," Mary Ann said. "Especially the way Betty Harper treated him."

"I'd sooner feel sorry for a dog," Shirley uttered.

Henry stood there speechless in the presence of the Rockingham sisters. Then the bell rang.

There were other days now. He embraced them waiting patiently for the attentions of Mary Ann Rockingham while going steady with Edith Miller. He acquired new courage, new thrills, and made them his own.

"Have you noticed?" Mary Ann said directly to her sister one day as they were sitting in the cafeteria eating lunch. "Henry Shane has begun to look at me in the most thrilling way lately—you know what I mean—he's so cute—I wouldn't want him to get the wrong idea."

"Baloney!" Shirley remarked. "What harm is there? What are you worrying about?"

"I'm getting fond of him, and he seems so nice," Mary Ann sighed.

"I think it would be better if you didn't get involved, Mary Ann," Shirley said in a warning manner. "It's none of my business, but you do what you want to do."

"I suppose you're right. Yeah, I only wish that it were true," Mary Ann responded.

For a few weeks Mary Ann tried to avoid Henry Shane, but she was wise enough to know that her feelings were hurt rather than comforted by doing so. She also knew it was practically impossible to avoid him completely, for Henry was persistent, and continued to arrive at school earlier than he normally had done in the past. When Mary Ann was in the room, he spoke to her and she merely responded with a good morning and continued to leave the impression that she was always busy working on a minor detail of her school work which she had overlooked. He sensed that his daring attempts to lure her into a deep conversation were getting him no where, so one afternoon during a study period he risked approaching her boldly.

"Mary Ann, would you be kind enough to help me with an English lesson? It seems as if I'm having a terrible time understanding the nature of the assignment. We are to make a list of popular terms alluding to mental weakness or aberration, and then work the material into a short essay."

"Can't Edith Miller help you?" Mary Ann said smartly.

"No," Henry replied. "Besides she isn't in school today."

"Well, okay, I'll help you with the assignment."

Henry knew he could have very well asked his teacher to provide him with additional information regarding the nature of the assignment, but he felt that this was an excellent opportunity to have a few words with Mary Ann.

"What don't you understand?" she asked.

He looked at her with a puzzled look on his face. "You know, I couldn't quite understand how to go about acquiring all the terms that are necessary in writing the essay."

"Mrs. James explained it to us in class," Mary Ann said. "Where were you?"

He had the uncomfortable feeling that she saw through his plan and quickly said, "I was there in class, but I'm not as smart and clever as you are."

"Come on, Henry, you're smart too, if you really want to be. Your problem is that you don't have the discipline to study and work things out for yourself."

"Suppose you are right," he remarked.

"You try to work it out by yourself first, and if you can't manage, then I'll help you."

"Okay, I'll try," he said sheepishly.

Mary Ann rose from her seat and approached Mrs. Smith, the teacher in charge of the study group, and requested a library slip. She left the room, leaving Henry sitting at his desk struggling over his assignment. He was well aware of the fact that she was deriving some fun from his stupid approach in trying to win her affection. She was gone for ten minutes, and when she reappeared in the room, she had a confident look on her face.

"I found this book over in the library," she said with a smile on her face. "I think it will help solve some of your problems. This book is called Problems in Prose. If you decide that you want to take the book home with you, you'd better go back and see the librarian."

"Your suggestion is worth while considering, Mary Ann. Since it is a rather lengthy assignment, don't you think it would be better if I were to come to your house this evening so that you can explain the intricate details to me much better?" Then realizing his daring approach, his face turned red. He quickly took the book from her hand, looked straight into her eyes and smiled. "Thanks for getting the book for me."

"That's quite all right. If you want to, you can come to my house this evening, Henry."

"Do you really mean that?" Henry said.

"Yes, that is if you really want to come. Shirley will be there, but my mother and father won't be. They are going out to a social affair, and probably will be gone by the time you get there."

"I'll return the book to the library when the bell rings, and then I'll check it out in my name. I'll see you at six o'clock."

Early that evening, Henry Shane arrived at Mary Ann's house in Haysville, which was located approximately two miles from Sinclair. After she greeted him at the door, they proceeded into the dining room and sat down beside the table and discussed the English assignment that still appeared to be complicated to Henry. They worked diligently to complete the lesson. Upon its completion, Henry uttered a sigh of relief, pushed back his chair, and stretched his arms.

At that moment Shirley entered the room carrying her sweater.

"Where are you going?" Mary Ann said with surprise.

"Over to Jake's grill," Shirley replied. "Why? Is there something you want me to get?"

"No, I guess not," Mary Ann said. "Why don't we all go over together?"

"Just sit down and don't you worry?" Shirley said bluntly. "I won't be gone long." The door closed behind her.

"Oh dear," Mary Ann said while looking at Henry. "It seems so strange to be in a house alone with a boy. Don't you think it would be better to go to Jake's grill?"

"Okay, if it will make you feel more comfortable," Henry said. He rose to help her with her sweater, and then without realizing it, he put his arms around her, he was kissing her. He was amazed at the warmth of her lips. Then she pressed her cheek against his , keeping it there so that he could not kiss her again. She stepped back awkwardly. He tried to kiss her again. She pushed him away. She begged and pleaded with him. Moments later he quit trying, but managed to rest his head upon her shoulder, his blood still throbbing wildly in his body, her hand comforting him and her fingers running gently through his hair.

"You mustn't kiss me, you know," she whispered.

"Why in the hell not?" he said disgustingly.

"Because you are a nice guy, and I like you better just the way you are now. It would be better for the both of us if you didn't carry this thing too far. After all you're going steady with Edith Miller, and I'm not going to give charity on the side. If I knew you really loved me, then it would be a different story."

He tried to reach for her lips, but she merely turned her head. "There can't be anymore of this nonsense," Mary Ann said. "I'm not the kind of girl you may think I am."

"All right then, I'm sorry," he said. He lowered his head in shame.

"Please, Henry, don't feel sorry for yourself? Just no more of this horseplay. If I only knew that you were serious about me then—I don't want to go to school tomorrow feeling embarrassed for what I may have done. Then you would not have any respect for me catering to your wishes."

"I would, honest I would."

You're just saying that Henry Shane," she remarked.

"No I'm not kidding. If I didn't like you, I wouldn't have come over to see you this evening."

"Look, Henry, it's okay. I'll just assume that nothing drastic happened here tonight."

"Damn, it isn't that something drastic happened. I only tried to kiss you."

"One thing could have led to another," she said smiling. "It probably would have if I didn't come to my senses. I just don't want anything further to happen tonight. I'm happy to know how you feel about me, and I think you're awful nice, Henry. I hope you understand how I feel."

"Yeah, I guess I do," Henry said. "But I only wish I could make love to you."

"If you wish then, you're going to have to take me out to prove that you like me," she said boldly.

"But," Henry stuttered.

"No buts about it. I know, all of a sudden you're thinking about Edith Miller, wondering what she may do if she finds out about you're two-timing."

"The hell with Edith Miller. Okay, I'll take you out. Where do you want to go?"

"A movie will be all right," she said. "I think it would be better if we would go to a movie right here in Haysville. I don't want to get involved with Edith Miller unless I 'm absolutely sure about you, Henry."

"When do you want me to take you to the movies?"

"Tomorrow night would be a good time. Then you'll pick me up at seven o'clock."

A little amazed at his courage, Henry went the following night to Mary Ann's house. He rang the doorbell and Mrs. Rockingham stood there facing him. "I'm Henry Shane. I've come over to take Mary Ann to the movies."

"Oh, yes, do come in Henry," Mrs. Rockingham said. "I've heard my daughters speak of you quite often. Mary Ann, Mary Ann, Henry Shane is here."

Mary Ann came down the stairs and entered the room. "Look who's here!" she said happily. "I really thought you would back out." She went to the closet and reached for her sweater. "Going to take me out after all."

His face reddened. Then as he looked at her his heart began to beat rapidly. He saw the anxious look in her eyes.

"Why not," he stuttered. He lowered his head so that she could not see the embarrassment in his face. Slowly he raised his head as the hot flash gradually faded away. She looked prettier than she had at school.

"Let's go," she responded. They walked hand in hand down the street.

"We have two theaters in Haysville," she said. "You pick out the one you want to go to. It makes no difference to me. There's the Park

Theater and the Opera House, but I'd prefer to go to the Opera House. They have a peanut heaven."

"What is a peanut heaven?" Henry asked.

"Oh, that's just another name for a balcony," Mary Ann said grinning. She stepped ahead of him on the dimly lighted street and turned around slowly.

"You really look sharp tonight," Henry said.

She took his arm again. "You know, Henry, you always look sharp too."

"I don't know about that," he replied. She cuddled up to him, she stopped and reached up and pulled down his head. She kissed him and quickly withdrew her lips. "Now let's go to the Opera House." She clasped her arms around his waist.

"Hold it," Henry said. He tried to halt her, but she walked on.

"Let's go to the movies, and then afterwards we'll be able to make love." They came to the Opera House, and Henry purchased the tickets. They entered and climbed the stairs to the balcony.

"Let's sit in the back," Mary Ann said.

"Good idea," Henry remarked.

The lights went out, and the movie had begun. She gave a little sigh and slouched down in the seat. Shortly thereafter, he felt her hand. It crept toward his lap, found his hand, lifted it to her lap. Slowly she pressed it gently against her breast. She turned to him in the darkness and kissed him on the cheek.

When the movie was over they walked awkwardly down the aisle, down the steps, and on to the dimly lighted street. They walked slowly up the street, eventually coming to a wooded area on the outskirts of Haysville. Though he was less anxious to carry out what he had planned the previous night, he walked cautiously through the moon lit night. Reluctantly she followed him.

"Gee, it was nice of you to take me to the movies tonight," she said. "You know there aren't many boys that I would even be seen with."

"Come off that kind of talk now. You mean to tell me that you never permitted a boy to take you to the movies."

"No, I didn't say that," Mary Ann remarked.

"Well, how many were there then? Two, Three, how many?"

"If you really want to know," she said. "I went out with Joe Walker, John Campbell and Richard Rand."

"My best friend, Richard Rand!"

"No wonder he was telling me about all the girls from Haysville." He was surprised to hear the name of his best friend, and mumbled a few curse words.

"Did you have a good time with Richard Rand?"

"Yes, that is until he started to get too fresh."

Henry laughed and said, "Fresh about what."

"About me, silly."

"What if I were to get fresh with you?" Henry asked.

"I know you are persistent, Henry, but maybe, I'd like it." She looked at him with devilishness in her eyes.

"I don't know about that," he said. "Last night you pretended you weren't interested in messing around."

"Oh, but that was last night."

They sat under a big tree. She drew up her knees, and leaned back against the trunk of the tree. Gazing at the moon she began to grow restless. She stretched her arms and changed her sitting position. Silent for a time, then she began to laugh. "Golly, what a shame, Henry?" She uttered.

"I don't quite understand what you mean," Henry said.

"A beautiful night like this going to waste," she whispered.

"Why the sudden change in your attitude?" Henry leaned closer to her and looked into her eyes. Absently she ran her fingers through his hair. The touch of her hand and her eyes gazing at him in hungry silence caused pleasant sensations to tingle up his spine. Despite the sudden drawback of the previous night, Mary Ann was a warm girl in the flesh. He looked into the stillness of the night. He watched and listened, enjoying the beautiful night and the presence of Mary Ann Rockingham. He saw a cloud sweep across the moon and gradually fade away.

"Henry," she said in a low tone. "What is it that you like about me?"

He did not answer her at once. "I guess the fact that I can trust you. You know, Mary Ann, it could be written in the book that I'd end up marrying you some day. You are a pretty girl."

"What else do you like about me?"

"I don't know, maybe I like the way you're stacked. Suppose any boy would like that, Mary Ann. What else does a guy like?"

"That's what I'm asking you, Henry? Is it true that all boys are interested in messing around with girls? Is that why you really wanted to go out with me?"

"Suppose so," Henry said.

"Then, what are you waiting for," she said anxiously. "I'd like that too"

"You, I thought you weren't interested in something like that," Henry said sarcastically.

"I could be coaxed into it, real easy, maybe," she said.

Silence fell between them and she snuggled closer. Her hand covered his mouth. "Don't say another word?" she whispered.

Then her mouth was pressing against his ear, breathing warmly, softly. He knew only that a tingling sensation was spreading through him, and that her very nearness was getting to him. She raised her head and looked down into his face. Then she was bending to him, one hand drawing his face to hers. He saw her eyelashes quiver and fold. The next instant she was kissing him with a pressing, astonishing eagerness. Henry had never imagined her like this. Then he remembered the things that his friend Richard Rand had said about the girls' from Haysville. The surge of his desire spread over him. It held him there, dominating him completely. Though he had planned it this way the previous night, he was content that he did not have to wait longer to accomplish the feat of winning her over. Thoughts darted through his mind.

He attempted to unbutton her dress, and she began to tremble. "Henry!" She tried to break away, but he held on to her tightly.

"I've changed my mind!" She cried out. "I'm afraid, I might get pregnant!"

"What the hell are you worrying about?" he shouted. "Isn't this the way you wanted it?"

"Hell, no Henry! Stop it." She struggled with all her effort to break away from his embrace. Swinging and punching him with her fists.

"What the hell do you think I am?" She screamed. She became weary and recognized that Henry was furious. She no longer struggled to break away from his hold. She seemed too frightened. Lying still and trembling, she stared at him with bewildered eyes. " Do you think you can get a guy all worked up and then brush it off with some fancy words? What the hell are you, a teaser?"

Her mouth opened, "No, Henry I'm not a teaser. I just suddenly realized that once you satisfied your lust you'd forget all about me."

"Oh, so that's it. You might as well get damn use to the idea that boys are going to want your body. You just jumped from the frying pan into the fire."

"Henry, I didn't know," she wept. "Honest, I didn't know you wanted me this way."

"Then its about time you find out what I really wanted from you," he remarked.

With her eyes wet from tears, she looked at him. "It's late, my father is going to beat me if I don't soon get home."

"Don't worry?" he said. "It won't take long."

Her body was warm and soft and her breasts firm. Her body was moist cuddled against his chest. She said everything possible to prevent him from carrying out the act.

"You've got to be true to Edith Miller," she said calmly.

"I will," he responded.

"Oh, Henry, just say that you love me and then I wouldn't mind what you would do," she uttered. "Please, Henry. Please!"

"All right, I love you. Does that make you feel any better?"

"I didn't want to, because I kept on thinking about your relationship with Edith Miller. I'm sorry I acted the way I did. You're really a nice guy, Henry. I guess I forced you to act like a beast."

"Be quite," he said. His voice was low, he tried to control his shaky body. She looked up and no longer surprised at what was going to take place. He hugged her closer. Her voice faded. She gave up in his arms. His heart was beating faster. Her voice was changing. He turned her to him. He pressed his mouth against her mouth in a long and passionate way. Her arms tightened around him. He moved, she moved in harmony to their inner feelings. Then she cried out.

"Oh, Henry, Henry!" and then, "that's wonderful, wonderful." Then she was silent. Henry was silent still wondering whether he may have carried this act too far. She sat there panting and wiping the perspiration from her forehead, and then she slowly began to put on her clothes. She got up and walked toward the road. He followed her meek and silent. Neither said anything until they reached the Rockingham house.

"I'm sorry, Mary Ann. I shouldn't have forced you."

"You needn't be sorry. I wanted you to make love to me." Her voice was revealing the truth, "I'm glad you wanted me, because I really love you. I shouldn't have been resentful. All the time I kept thinking about you and Edith Miller. What would she do if she found out about our relationship, our affair?"

Then she kissed him, walked away in the direction of the front door, leaving him standing there rubbing his chin in a state of bewilderment.

Seven

It was in the spring of their senior year at Sinclair High School that Edith Miller finally began to sense a change in Henry Shane. He became irritable and moody in her presence. She tried to tell herself, that it was due to his concern of being drafted into the army, upon graduating from high school.

Edith also had more problems than in previous years. Her mother was ill and required more attention. During this period of time, Edith's relationship with Henry grew weaker and weaker for she did not see him too often.

One Saturday afternoon in early spring Edith was in Shaffer's Drugstore in Sinclair obtaining medicine for her sick mother, and as she raised her eyes to leave, she saw Henry pause in front of the show window with Mary Ann Rockingham. The ease of their standing there struck her like a bolt out of the blue. Their association appeared to be relaxed and friendly.

Edith knew that Mary Ann was a pretty girl and possessed a charming personality. She had attractive lips, wide blue eyes and long blond hair. She smiled as she spoke to Henry. He turned to walk and Mary Ann turned with him clasping her arm around his waist. The intimacy of their relationship added another sorrowful note to Edith's broken heart. She thought, Henry has been two-timing me all the time. Now I know why he made up all kind of excuses that he couldn't be with me on certain nights. Oh, God, and I love you so Henry.

They walked up the street together, Mary Ann moving in a staggering, wavy walk, something cocky and sure in her stride. Edith, standing now on the outside of Shaffer's Drugstore, observed that Henry had his arm around Mary Ann.

Edith's mind, which had been bitterly interrupted while the two were arm in arm, began now to worry that she may have lost Henry to Mary Ann Rockingham. She was utterly shocked and confused and could not remember how she managed to make it home. Once she got home she began to formulate plans as to how she could lure Henry back into her fold. She loved Henry and no other girl was going to steal him away from her. She waited patiently until evening to call him on the telephone. He was not at home. She asked his brother, Lee to take the message.

"Lee, please tell Henry to meet me at the Rainbow Grill tonight at nine o'clock."

When Henry received Edith's message, he proceeded to the Rainbow Grill. They met at the same place they had frequented often during their school days. They were seated at their favorite spot in a corner, and she felt a relief come over her as she sat near him. She had to hold back the tears. She looked at his eyes that were dark and mysterious and she was overcome with the fear of losing him completely.

"Henry," she said sobbing. "I do love you." Her eager words surprised him. He had heard her say those kind words before. He was pleased, but felt uneasy about the other things she might say.

"Fine," he said. "Gee, I hope you do."

"Oh, I do, I do," Edith said. "I wanted to see you—be with you. Can you come home with me tonight?"

"I'm not sure whether I should tonight."

"Please, please," she said. "I want you so much. You always said you would when I thought the time was right to announce our engagement to mother."

"Engagement," Henry said surprisingly. "I'm not sure whether I should go with you tonight. Your mother might get upset. Perhaps tomorrow might be better." "Maybe you can come after church services," Edith said quickly.

"All right, I'll come tomorrow. You act as if you're afraid of something, maybe losing me."

"Don't say that Henry? Please. I love you and I want to marry you as we have always planned."

"Doesn't that frighten you?" Henry said.

"No, Henry, it doesn't frighten me."

On Sunday morning, with an inner feeling of happiness, she broke the news to her mother. "Henry Shane is the boy I'm going to marry." Her mother seemed only mildly surprised and said, "Do you really love him? Do you think you will be happy together? Remember child, there is a war going on and he will be drafted into the army. Don't be hasty?"

This was Edith Miller's little dream, the thought of being married to Henry without concern of worldly problems. This was her own world. The shutters to it were never closed and all she thought about was her love for Henry and to marry him at all costs. Here was a joy that had surpassed its meaning, the world where Edith was not required to meet problems or responsibilities. "Oh, Henry, I can not live without you."

In June of 1944, Henry Shane and Edith Miller walked through the portals of Sinclair High school for the last time. They now entered an insecure world—a world that was in a state of confusion and chaos—a world that had felt the pangs of war for five years. Still, Edith had planned with him how she would go to work and maintain the house for him while he went to a local college. They would be married and perhaps his father or mother could give them some financial assistance. Or if he wanted to, she would stay home and rear a family while he worked.

Henry was always a little uneasy about these plans. Often he said, "If I were really wise, I'd never marry you until I had my military obligation out of the way. Then we could continue our plans without interruption."

"Interruption," she despised the word.

"Yes, interruption," he said. "Don't worry, I'm not going to wait."

Somehow she felt insecure about him, uneasy, so that she even said to him that she wished they could be married soon. He laughed at this, looking at her always with bewilderment in his eyes. The more she thought about it, the more pleasant the idea seemed. She wanted to marry him before the army would take him away. Without mentioning it to her mother, without asking for permission, she wanted to run away to Maryland and get married.

The idea pondered in her mind for several days, and then one afternoon she decided to go to Henry's house and inform him of the plan she had designed.

As she walked down Pine Street, an excitement rose in her that was a new thrill. It took complete control of her, set her thoughts running in another direction, and made her feel as light as the air. The thought of forcing Henry to marry her, the thought of proving to Henry that she was daring and willing to run away and elope.

As she approached Henry Shane's house, her heart began to beat rapidly and a cold sweat came forth from her forehead. Henry was not at home. His brother, Lee was uneasy about admitting her into the house.

"I don't know whether I should tell you this, Edith," Lee said reluctantly.

"Tell me what," Edith responded.

"Henry knows he is going to be drafted into the army and feels he should not get married. With the war going on the way it is, I don't blame him for feeling the way he does."

"Are you sure he feels that way?" Edith said.

"Yes, I'm positive," Lee replied.

"That damn Mary Ann Rockingham probably put a lot of ideas into his head," Edith said bitterly.

"Maybe she did. I still think it would be wise on his part not to get married so soon. In the first place he is still wet behind the ears. You know, growing up can change a person, and if I were you I wouldn't do something that you might regret later on. If you really love Henry, you'll wait for him."

"I'm not going to sit around and twiddle my thumbs while he is gone," Edith said.

"I don't blame you, Edith. That's why I'm against you marrying him. Henry isn't ready to settle down yet. It appears to me that he has a lot of wild oats to sow. I don't have to tell you that, you should know. It's not that he doesn't love you, but he does like excitement and new adventures."

"Excitement!" Edith said. "Sure, with Mary Ann Rockingham. I thought he would forget about her after we announced our engagement, but apparently he hasn't. He is still seeing her, isn't he? Tell me the truth, Lee. Please, please!"

"I'll tell you the truth. I know it's going to break your heart, but there is such a thing as facing reality. It's better that you find out now than later on. Yes, he is seeing Mary Ann Rockingham. How serious he is about her, I don't know. I'm sorry I had to be so frank with you, Edith."

"Oh, Lee, I'm so confused," she said with tears in her eyes

"I understand. If I were you I'd sit here and wait for him. He should be home shortly. Talk to him and lay all the cards on the table. Find out how you really stand with him."

She sat very still as if in a stupor and then she began to tremble. Her body shook so violently that she had to stand up and pace the floor. I must control myself, she thought as she paced the floor. Shall I leave before he comes—leave and not see him again? Oh, what am I going to do? I loved him so, now this. Mother, Mother, you were so right. I shouldn't have been so hasty.

When she heard him enter the room she tried to be pleasant and relaxed, and rushed to him putting her arms around his neck.

"I'm surprised to see you here," Henry said. "What prompted you to visit the Shane household? You seem to be rather affectionate today, Edith." He smiled. The smile was warm, but deceiving.

"Am I!" Her voice cried out.

"What the hell is the matter with you? You're looking at me as if I've committed a crime."

"What do you mean what's the matter? I've had a good chat with your brother, Lee. He told me that you're still running around with Mary Ann. Oh, Henry, how could you be so deceitful? I should have known that you're shacking up with Mary Ann, and to think, all this time I've been planning to marry you." Edith knew that they could never return to the same love sick kids they were in the three years they had been going together. "Aren't you going to give me an explanation?" She demanded.

"No, why should I? You have all the answers." He lowered his head and sat down. "In the first place, do you make it a point to go around and stick your nose into other people's affairs? You had no damn business coming to my house to pump information out of Lee. I know, Lee is an honest person, and he wouldn't do anything to hurt anyone. I know how he felt about me marrying you."

"How can you sit there and talk to me like that?" She said. "How would you have felt if I was sleeping with another man?"

"If you felt that way, then why in the hell didn't you?" He shouted.

She began to weep. "Henry, oh Henry, how could you do this to me?"

"I think you'd better leave. Nobody invited you here in the first place, and if you hadn't been a nosey bitch all of this wouldn't have happened."

"How dare you?" She screamed. "How can you sit there and not be ashamed? You are, aren't you? You're sleeping with her! With Mary Ann, and maybe with her sister too. My God, Henry, how could you?" She wept.

He stared at Edith in a furious manner. He saw in her angry, tear filled eyes a flash of despair and grief.

"You don't know what your talking about," with fury in his voice. "You just don't know Mary Ann very well." He knew he had lied, but tried to comfort her.

"No, I don't know what I'm talking about," she said sobbing. "They're out of my class. I wouldn't understand would I? Oh, no, those girls from Haysville never think of boys. They just milk cows and pitch hay everyday. Why, why they wouldn't know what to do with a handsome son of a bitch like you. And you're going to sit there and tell me all kind of lies. You never kissed them. I suppose you're going to tell me that—Oh my God Henry. Can't you remember when I first met you—I thought you were the boy for me? I wanted you and I permitted you to have sex with me. I've been faithful to you ever since. Honest to God, Henry, there never was anyone else but you, and now I'm sorry there wasn't." She wept bitterly.

"What's the matter with you? What's happened?"

"I just don't like to be two-timed," she said shockingly.

"Well, who in the hell is two-timing you?" Henry asked sharply.

"It's all over, Henry. I don't really care anymore. I suppose you went to Haysville and just held Mary Ann's hand."

"Suppose our engagement is broken now," Henry said. "All those damn plans we made to get married before I got drafted are all washed up."

"Oh, you! That's what I came over to tell you about, but you weren't here. You probably were with that two-bit whore. Everything was all right until she interfered with our life."

"Honest, Edith," Henry protested. "Honest you're wrong." He knew he was lying again.

"Did you like her? Did she give you what you wanted?"

"Oh, sure, sure! She was all right," Henry said boldly. "That's what you want me to say. Isn't it?"

"You, you take her out! When you want a girl, you take her. I told your brother, Lee I'm not going to wait for you, and I'm telling you the same thing. I wanted to marry you before you left Sinclair. I loved you and, probably will always for the rest of my life, but it is all over now."

"All right, don't talk to me about it anymore?" Henry said angrily.

"Just get the hell out of here and go home."

His eyes were filled with tears and he knew down deep in his heart that he was wrong. He had betrayed the girl that bestowed her love upon him. A girl that was true to him from the very first time they had met at the bandstand three summers ago. The room suddenly became a den of anguish. There was no hope now of ever apologizing to Edith Miller.

She ran out of the room and out into the street, weeping and screaming that it attracted the attention of the residents in the neighborhood.

Meanwhile, Henry Shane, instead of rejoicing in his breaking up with Edith was finding it lonely and boring while awaiting his departure into the army. Living in close quarters in Sinclair, reliving the moment with Edith who had always been open to him was not a pleasant thought, as he already was beginning to find out. For a day or two after Edith's emotional outburst from the house, he was sick. As soon as he was sufficiently recovered from the episode, he made his way, feeling very confident to Haysville to call on Mary Ann Rockingham. She kept him waiting on the porch for sometime and when she finally appeared, she was not as pleasant as she had been in the past.

"I'm right in the middle of packing my suitcases," she said without asking him to come into the house. "I don't have much time to waste. What's on your mind, Henry?"

"Are you leaving?" Henry asked in surprise.

"Yes, I'm packing. My sister and I are leaving for Washington, D. C. and we are going to work for the FBI." Henry walked toward her and was about to put his arms around her.

"Don't you go and start messing around?" Mary Ann said sharply. "I'm not in the mood for a lot of nonsense. I'm not your steady girlfriend and you better remember that. At first I thought there was a chance, and all this time you were just leading me on. Why didn't you tell me that you were going to marry Edith Miller?"

"Who in the hell has been telling you stories?" Henry said bitterly.

"Never mind," she said. "Anyway I knew you were engaged to Edith Miller, but like a fool I thought you had fallen in love with me."

"I'm not going to marry Edith Miller," Henry said shortly.

"Oh, she broke up with you," Mary Ann said sarcastically. "Well, I don't blame her. I should think she would. She finally came to her senses, and if you really loved her you wouldn't have been living it up like you have been doing in the last few months. I'm certain that she can get a decent guy, and I hear that a fellow by the name of Andy Curtis that lives near her has a crush on her. Funny though, I can't figure out why she didn't break off with you sooner."

"It was me that called the wedding off," Henry said.

Mary Ann stared at him speechless for a moment. "So that's the kind of guy you are?" she said with bitterness in her voice. "Now I'm positive that the same thing would have happened to me. You'd have jilted me sooner or later. Yes, I was a big fool to get involved with you. And to think I passed my chances with Norbert Shank. He wasn't the best looking guy in the world—and his father was an alcoholic—and to think I was kind of ashamed to get tied up with him on that account. Now, I came to my senses. Norbert is a damn, good, clean living guy, and believe me, if he could have had your opportunities, my what he would have done with them. You've passed them all up—while he had to climb out of the barnyard on his way up the ladder without anyone to help him. But he made it all right. I've' written to Norbert and informed him that I was coming to Washington to work, and he still wants a girl who's been fool enough to mess around with someone else all these months. He wrote back and said that he'd be waiting for me in Washington, and he'd forgive me for what I had done."

Henry lowered his head in shame and disgust and did not utter another word. He turned and walked quietly from the porch and got into his brother's car and sped away.

Mary Ann having departed for Washington, D.C. to work for the FBI, and to smooth out her relations with Norbert Shank, Henry felt that this was another episode that came to an end. He felt that there would never be another person who could make him so uncomfortable again, but he was wrong. The next person to treat him harshly was Jim Heeler, the boy whom Henry and Richard Rand had always classified as being gay while in school. Meeting him one afternoon in downtown Sinclair, where Henry was wandering somewhat aimlessly, Jim Heeler brought his hot rod to a stop and yelled.

"Hey Shane, just the guy I've been waiting to see. I wanted to talk to you about your girl. Everybody down at the Rainbow Grill seems to be worried about her. They don't think she has been looking too well these days." He felt sure that Jim Heeler was actually trying to needle him and was fully aware of the existing problem.

"Oh," Jim Heeler said acting very interested. "Well of course that shouldn't bother a former football hero like you. After all, you can get any girl you want in this town. Perhaps the girls don't care about the big football hero now that he is out of school." He started to laugh. "Poor Edith had to find out the hard way while you were running around having a ball of a time. Of course you'll be able to find other girls, but I don't think you'll find them too easy to persuade in Sinclair. Edith was such a lovely girl—smart and good looking at that. Well, I must pass the good news along to Andy Curtis the next time I see him over at the Eureka Store, that is if he hasn't already heard the news. You know he has been rather high in his praise of Edith Miller, but he didn't interfere thinking you always had the inside track."

Henry tried to swallow the lump in his throat. Here was a guy talking to him, sissy as they can come, reminding him that Edith was not, after all, in the least dependent upon him for affection. There were others who were interested in Edith. This thought hurt his pride.

Jim Heeler started his hot rod. "Hope you like the army, Shane," he went on with an abrupt change of subject. "You know a big football hero like you might meet up with a WAC, you never know."

"I don't exactly like the idea of going into the army," Henry said. "Why should I?"

"Why, you're exactly the sort of guy the army needs," Jim Heeler said sarcastically. "You're full of fight, full of spirit, and you're well adapted to run through the enemy lines. I should think you'd have enlisted long before you were drafted."

"Are you going to be spared, Heeler?" Henry said hurriedly. "They need all the men they can get. Oh, that's right, I almost forgot, you're really not a man, but a cocksucker."

"Watch what the hell you're saying, Shane. For you information the army is not to get me. I've a bad heart, and besides my father knows all the members of the local draft board."

"That's tough shit to take! Are you sure you have a bad heart?"

"The family doctor said I have a bad heart. Anyway I'm fortunate enough not to have to go. Well, goodbye Shane."

Henry began to feel sorry, for he thought that many of the people were against him and in sympathy with Edith Miller. If the men still talked about Edith, then the girls spoke differently, and none of them, as Jim Heeler had stated would have anything to do with him. Girls don't care to risk being jilted, they were apt to remind him if he so much as approached them to go out on a date. If Edith didn't suit him, then why would he need another girl? As far as the young men in Sinclair, he thought they were going out of their way to be nasty to him and pleasant to Edith. She was the topic of discussion at every male gathering to which he had either the leisure or inclination to attend, and when he heard and discovered this, he began to realize that perhaps he should have married her after all.

She would not call him on the phone or speak to him. He felt himself ostracized in Sinclair, and neither Jaystown nor Haysville, though he tried them both, seemed to appeal to him.

Driven by loneliness and frustration, he decided to go to Edith and apologize. This seemed to him to be the easiest thing to do, but the more he thought about it, the more difficult it seemed to resort to this approach. He had been disloyal to Edith, running around with Mary Ann Rockingham, he admitted. Perhaps, he thought, her life might be more pleasant without him. He started on his way to Edith's house on many occasions, only to turn back feeling foolish, and that it might be better not to undertake such a venture.

At last, having acquired the necessary courage, he managed to make it to Edith's house one bright Friday afternoon. He saw her sitting comfortably on the glider occupied in reading, looking contented and attractive in a sky, blue dress. "Hello," he said as he walked up on to the porch. Edith did not appear to hear him. "Hello," he said again as a flash of redness appeared on his face.

"Hello," Edith said quietly without looking up. It was the first time she had spoken to him since their bitter quarrel several weeks before. "How have you been?"

Henry coughed, and fumbled with his hands. He was surprised that Edith asked about his well being. He immediately began to search for new questions. "I thought I'd come over and apologize," he uttered desperately.

Edith did not respond, but merely raised her head and stared at him. He could feel his face growing redder, and then he reached into his pocket for a handkerchief and mopped the perspiration from his forehead. "Warm day, isn't it?" he said.

"Yes. It's likely to be warmer over the weekend." Something in her voice made him look at her in puzzlement, as he felt the perspiration running down the inner side of his arms. There was no possible doubt about it now—he was making a fool of himself. Edith was amused and began to laugh. She had been amused ever since he came up on the porch.

Henry, overcome with embarrassment, walked slowly from the porch thinking. She missed him so little and was getting along well without him, and she had all the right to sit there and laugh. Suddenly he was overcome with anger. "I'll show her," he said. Brushing away his feelings of resentment and hurt pride, he rushed back on to the porch. What could he really say to her? His only hope was to beg her for forgiveness. It would not be easy or a pleasant thing to do, and he hated anything that was not easy and pleasant. He had to clear up the matter with Edith, and if he didn't now, there never would be another opportunity. "Edith," he burst out. "I'm sorry I deceived you; I'm ashamed of what I had done to hurt you. Please forgive me. I'd do anything for you, if you'll forgive me."

"Forgive you!" Edith shouted.

"Yes, forgive me," he said touchingly.

"Is that all you expect me to do, forgive you after what you had done to me?" She rose and came towards him, staring at him with her big, dark eyes that made it difficult for him to meet.

"Please," he pleaded again. "I'm sorry, I never would have done it if it wasn't for my getting drafted into the army. I wanted to marry you, but I couldn't under the circumstances."

"Are you using that as an excuse for deceiving me?"

"It was the only way. I couldn't marry you with the war going on the way it is. I often thought of the possibilities of not returning. Then how would you have felt being a young widow?"

"That's still no excuse for you to run around with that good for nothing Mary Ann Rockingham. It was disgraceful for you to have done what you did, but it was even more disgraceful considering that we were engaged to be married."

"I suppose you're right," he said sheepishly. "I'll never let it happen again, Edith. I'm sorry, honestly I am. Please forgive me."

"How can I forgive you? I'm not going to forgive you."

"Don't you believe me that I'm sorry," he said

"Yes, I believe you, because I know you Henry Shane. You're just miserable now because you don't have anyone else to run to. If I were to forgive you, you'd turn around and pull the same dirty trick on me again. You'd forget all about me if you were in another position of having a good time."

"Honest, I wouldn't—I swear to God I wouldn't!"

"We're finished," she said frankly. "I'm not going to give you another chance, even though it's going to break my heart for not giving in to you."

"Well, at least we can still be friends, can't we?" He said in a dejected tone.

"Yes, we can still be friends. I must go in now. Please leave." She turned away, and gently brushed away the tears that were trickling down her cheeks.

How could he have possibly thought she would forgive him. If only she would have, he thought. But she didn't. She had always been so sympathetic and very understanding in the past, but now he couldn't get to her at all. He realized he was a big fool to have deceived her. Now he deserved this fate. That was the conclusion he reached as he departed from her house.

As expected Henry Shane was drafted into the army later in the summer. On the day of his departure, he had hoped that Edith would call him and bid him a farewell, but she didn't. His hours were few in Sinclair, and he let them pass away willingly. Once he did not know what to do with his time after breaking up with Edith or where to wander, but now there were more important things he had to think of. A war was on, and he was called upon to serve his country. At last he had to bid farewell to Sinclair, his friends, his brother, mother and father to accept the role of a soldier.

There had been hardships in this type of environment, but the easiness and the hospitality of the people that comprised this town made up for the simple life they had to lead in carving a living from the depths of the black deposits. He went to his favorite spot overlooking the valley just above Saint Anthony's Cemetery and sat there thinking of the days that had skid past him. No longer feeling like a youth, but a man destined for an unknown future, There was no early morning fog over the valley, nor any early morning coolness, instead of these, the sky, the coal tipples, all along the fringes of the adjacent hills overlooking the valley.

In the distance he could see the water tower, appearing small from his vantage point, below were the houses of Sinclair with their drab, colorless exteriors. As he looked at the hill beyond, he caught a glimpse of a distant figure that appeared to be a woman carrying a sack, bending and picking particles of coal. Now and then she would stop and look around, and then she slowly disappeared behind an enormous mound of black earth.

With the sound of the whistle echoing loudly and clearly across the valley, this indicated the beginning of another work shift. He stood and observed the swaying, little coal cars carrying miners into the depths of the earth. He then proceeded slowly down the hill to the main road where he saw an old, hunched-back miner returning from the night shift at the mine. He was waddling along with his lunch bucket, and the miner's lamp jiggled from side to side on his metal cap. He recognized the miner to be Mudja, an old timer, who had emigrated to Sinclair from Poland many years ago. He stopped. "You go army, Henry," Mudja said.

"Yes, I leave today," Henry responded.

"Take care," Mudja said. "God bless you." As he departed, he turned around and waved his hand, and Henry returned the gesture.

When Henry arrived at Fort Bixler for basic training, he immediately knew that army life was a far cry from the confines of Sinclair.

He adequately prepared to face the enemy—at least in a fighting spirit.

Men at Fort Bixler had entered the army from all walks of life. Some enlisted, but the majority of them were drafted against their wishes. They all realized the importance of being well prepared, and they all worked towards the eventual battle, knowing that it would come. When their training was completed, it was a different problem. They felt they had accomplished what they had set out to do. Aggressive, weather beaten, and confident, they believed they were ready to be sent to the war front. And they were impatient at the thought of waiting. They were filled with anxiety, and now regretted the thought of informing their parents and sweethearts that they were to be sent to the port of embarkation for deployment to a war zone. Everything that they had done was pointed in that direction. They were now classified as potential soldiers, green and inexperienced, but still they were soldiers. They had learned their job, and were led to believe that their unit was the best that ever passed through the portals of the base.

Henry Shane's knowledge of military life and combat had come from movies he had seen or books he had read. "War movies always impressed me," he often would say, but later realized that the movies could not possibly reveal all the truths of military life. War movies that he had seen were entertaining and glamorous. Soldiers trained by dashing through fields, climbed barricades, swing on ropes across obstacles or streams, and poked at lifeless dummies with bayonets. Machine guns never fired anything but tracers. Soldiers always marched with spotless uniforms in precision and in rhythm to John P. Sousa's, STARS AND STRIPES FOREVER. All of these things took place, as he remembered, to a background of spirited music to arouse the emotions, but there was more to military life that could never be revealed in a movie. Although he knew that the movie producers made an important contribution to the war effort, the general public, he often thought, believed that all a soldier had to do to train for battle was to hurdle streams and go through obstacle courses, but they had their right to believe so. War movies depicted the average American going off to war. At the military bases, the barracks always appeared to be comfortable and spotless. Soldiers in freshly pressed uniforms sat around and studied the military handbook, and discussed with one another how the sweetheart was doing back home, and the importance of knowing more than the next guy to receive a promotion. The sergeants always explained the importance of keeping the body clean and keeping it well groomed. During inspections an officer in full dress uniform and wearing white gloves, strode proudly from bunk to bunk, followed by a group of men of a lesser rank carrying notebooks to write down all the gigs. Those who made simple, ordinary human mistakes of not acting like a soldier were assigned to KP, or other meager, annoying details.

Henry remembered the climax of the movies, showing soldiers in some desperate situation in a war zone where saddened faces continued to talk as much as they had done while back in the states. The movie ends with a dramatic outburst of spirited music, leaving women to wipe away all tears, and the men to blow their nose. With the feeling of compassion in their hearts, they walked up the aisle and out on to the street, only to forget the true hardships encountered by soldiers at the front.

When Henry Shane was sent to the Pacific Theater of Operation, he learned from actual combat experience that war was a combination of what he had seen in the movie, and a living hell that could never be fully described.

Eight

Edith Miller was sitting on the front porch glider moving it gently back and forth, listening. She could hear the sound of a bird in the nearby tree, while far away another type of sound, a whistle from Mine 35 designating the end of a workday. The whistle sounded disheartening to her ears. In the distance she saw Sinclair High School and the football stadium, which brought back memories of Henry Shane. Oh, the stadium she thought, the stadium that roared for several autumn seasons when Henry would lead Sinclair's football team to victory.

Oh, how proud I was then, she thought, to be Henry's girl. The girl of a football star. There will be other football stars now. Henry's name will fade from my memory with the passing of time.

The growth of summer was at its peak. The bird, the whistle, and now the rumble of coal cars far away on a distant track, very far away so that it did not interrupt the drowsy, late afternoon tranquility. She thought of all the summers past, but now sitting there they all became entangled into one. She thought, if the bird would sing forever, the coal cars would stay in the remote distance, the smell of the flowers would remain, then nothing would be a dream. As she thought these things, the bird flew away, the whistle ceased, the sound of the rumbling coal cars drew nearer, and she once again thought of the deceitful Henry Shane.

Suddenly she awoke from her trance. She heard a car coming down the road below, and she knew it was Andy Curtis. He always came by her house at about the same time everyday from his job at the mine. Andy lived but two houses away from her, but never made an attempt

The Wailing Wind

to date her. On this beautiful, late summer afternoon he honked the horn and waved at her as he pulled up along the curb.

Edith stood up with a sigh of relief and pushed back her long, black hair. "Hi," she yelled to him, leaning over the banister as he stepped from his car.

He looked up, "Hi, it's really nice to have a life of leisure," he said jokingly. "Why don't you come down here and give me a hand with these groceries?"

"Don't tell me that you do the shopping in your household?" she said laughing.

"No, I usually don't," he remarked. "That's my mom's job, but she wasn't feeling too well this morning, and asked me to stop at the Eureka Store on my way back from work. I got off a little early today, so I don't mind."

"I guess your mom appreciates having someone around the house who is kind and considerate."

"I meant to ask you, Edith, What ever happened between you and that young fellow you were running around with? What's his name?"

"You mean Henry Shane. He was drafted into the army. It's all over now, and has been almost the entire summer. I don't know where he is stationed, and I could care less."

'I don't know whether I should ask you this, but, but," he said hesitantly. "Why don't you and I go out together this evening? Maybe we can go to a restaurant and have supper together, and afterwards take in a movie. There's a wonderful movie over at Jaystown. How does that sound?"

"That's a splendid idea," Edith said. "Okay, I'll go with you."

"I'll go in and take a bath, and in the mean time you can pretty yourself up a little," Andy said in an elated tone. Later that evening they went to the Heritage Restaurant in Jaystown, and then took in a movie at the Mountain Theater. It was late when they left the theater. The moon was full, and the air pleasant and comfortable. They drove to the Melody Club, a nightclub located on route 56 between Jaystown and Sinclair. They parked the car and proceeded to the entrance of the establishment. They stopped.

"No minors permitted," Edith said sadly as she looked at the sign.

"Don't worry about that?" Andy said laughing. "Around here all the bars have those kind of signs. It's just a matter of formality to make one believe they're abiding by the liquor laws. The guys that own these kind of places are interested in making a few dollars, so they'll serve anyone that wants to drink."

"Are you sure?" Edith said reluctantly.

"Come on. Let's go in. I'm certain they'll serve you."

A few weeks ago, she would not have accepted the offer. Now she was free of Henry and could do as she pleased. She sat there looking at Andy. He was a mature man, seven years older than she was. He knew his way around. He looked like a picture of health, but was not physically fit to enter the army, and remained in Sinclair to keep the home fires burning. He had risen from the status of a lowly miner to that of a mine foreman in a relatively short period of time.

Edith looked around the bar. It was just like any other drinking establishment, with crazy decorations and walnut stained, wooden booths and dim lights. The patrons seemed to be friendly and many of them roared with laughter as they danced to the polka music. After a few drinks, Edith became frightened at the thoughts that were darting through her numb brain. It made her think of Henry Shane and Mary Ann Rockingham shacking up together, and all the other places they had frequented without her knowledge.

"Let's get out of here, Andy? Please!"

"Lord, you're a jumpy girl," Andy said.

"I know I am. I'm sorry, Andy."

They got into the car and drove off. Edith began to cry. Andy was upset. "What the hell is the matter with you? Did I do or say something to offend you? Please tell me what's wrong?"

"Don't remind me? Please don't? I'm just moody, I guess."

"Moody from what?" Andy said.

"I don't know," she cried. "Oh, Andy I do feel so upset, and I don't feel sure of myself."

"You're still in love with Henry Shane, aren't you? You miss him now that he is gone."

"No, Andy, please don't remind me? It's all over with him."

They were along a dirt road now and he turned into a narrow passage, concealing the car from the road. "Pull yourself together, Edith," Andy said. "Forget him, it's not worth it." He put his arm around her and she leaned her head upon his shoulder and cried harder. Andy didn't say anything, he just sat there running his fingers through her hair. Her desire and longing for Henry Shane crept up in her for a moment that she thought that the man sitting beside her was Henry. Then in a sudden rage, she flung her arms around him crying.

"Oh, Andy, please, please!"

"Please, what?" he said hoarsely.

"I don't know," she said faintly. She lifted her face to his in the summer moonlight. Her lips began to quiver and her breathing became heavier. "Kiss me, Andy," she pleaded.

He bent swiftly over her. They kissed gently, then passionately. She pressed her well-developed breasts against him. She searched his body. His hands worked expertly to remove her dress and lingerie, and then her brassiere. Within a short period of time she was completely naked on the front seat of the car. The moonlight revealed the beautiful contour of her body. A body that she had not permitted anyone to see in the light not even Henry Shane. She pressed her body against him as she continued to search his body. He returned the pressure with force. The drinks they had made them bold and daring. They joined their burning bodies together. Then it was still, so still she could hear Andy's heavy breathing, and the beating of his heart. She slowly proceeded to put on her clothes. Shortly, he started the car, released the brake, and drove slowly away, her head resting upon his shoulder

The name and memory of Henry Shane gradually faded from Edith's mind. She grew fond of Andy Curtis, and in turn he did everything possible to please her and to make her happy. He had taken her to many elaborate and plush eating and drinking establishments, dance halls and to athletic events. But most of all, they enjoyed going to a movie and strolling through the community park on pleasant, warm nights. After the movie, they could often be seen walking sedately along the sidewalks, heading directly to the park.

One night, Edith automatically drew him to a halt in front of a store. "Baby clothes are certainly cute," she said, staring. "They're nicer than the way they use to make them. Today they make all kinds of fancy things for babies." She drew back from the window and looked up at him. "Do you like babies, Andy? I mean cute babies."

"I've always liked babies," he said. "Why are you so interested in babies all of a sudden?"

She grinned and said, "Now Andy, don't pretend to be so dumb?"

"You mean you're pregnant." he mumbled.

"No, Andy, I'm not pregnant." The streetlights were dimmer as they turned into the park. At this time of the night the town was quiet, and the inhabitants rested comfortably in the realms of their household.

"Don't you honestly know what I was trying to say, Andy?"

"Oh, sure, now I remember. You like babies."

"Silly, can't you take a hint," she said casually. Then she stopped talking. They continued to walk slowly, arm in arm, always toward their favorite spot in the darkness ahead.

"Andy," she whispered. "You've never mentioned that you would like to marry me."

"Are you kidding me, Edith? Do you really want to marry a guy like me?"

"Why not." she responded.

"I didn't realize you were that serious about me, Edith," he said happily. "Are you sure?"

"Yes, I'm sure," she said. "The sooner the better."

"Gee, I'm delighted that you want to marry me. To think I didn't have the guts to ask you myself. How about that, you proposing to me? I'm honored." He took her into his arms and hugged her. Suddenly they were startled. From the darkness nearby, came a crying sound.

"It's somebody crying," Andy said quickly. They looked at each other, turned and walked in the direction of the sound. Huddled against a tree was a young girl. Her hair hung wildly upon her head and the upper part of her dress was torn into shreds. She was weeping, her hands covering her face. They looked at each other, but she did not notice them. Andy cleared his throat. "What happened?" he asked.

The girl started to talk. She wept. She peered at them fearfully. "Please help me!" she begged. "Would you please help me?"

"Of course we will help you," Edith said. "Tell us what happened?"

"I just went down to the Rainbow Grill, and I met this fellow down there. I never saw him before. He seemed so nice, gentlemanly like. He asked to take me home. Oh, God, I didn't know. Oh, what he tried to do to me. I begged him not to. I pleaded, and then he hit me. He twisted my arm, and forced me. Then, I didn't know what happened. He ran off and left me like this."

Andy took her arm gently. In the darkness she trembled. Then Edith took the other arm and they led her toward the lighted street.

"Where do you live?" Edith asked.

"I live on Walnut Street," she said. "125 Walnut Street. Oh, Lord, what are my mother and father going to say?"

She was a small, pretty girl, well developed for her age and would have easily passed for seventeen or eighteen. "Now don't you worry? We'll have you home in a hurry," Edith said.

The girl weeping again. "I went out and intended to stay a short while. I told my mother, I promised her I wouldn't stay long. Oh, God, I promised. All I wanted was a little fun. Why did I go with him? Why?"

As they neared the house, the girl pleaded. "I don't want to go in. I don't want them to see me like this!"

Andy knocked on the door. The door opened. A tall man peered at them, and said, "What can I do for you?" The tall man suddenly shrank upon seeing the bloody face of his daughter. He promptly called over his shoulder: "Mary, Mary, come quickly!"

"Oh, my poor daughter, oh child! What has happened to you?" she said alarmingly. They stepped forward and seized the girl's arms. "Mary, call a doctor!"

"You'd better call the police too," Andy said.

"I'm sorry daddy, I'm sorry," the girl cried out.

"You'll learn not to hang around on street corners. I've warned you time and time again," the father said.

"I just went down to the Rainbow Grill," she wept.

"You know what's going to happen to you now, you're not going to go out at night anymore. We've had enough of you running around. This is the last time."

"Please, daddy, not now. Don't discuss it now?"

He hurried up the stairs with her to the bedroom, and the mother followed them, weeping with each step.

"We better be going," Andy said. "She's okay now."

"Yes," Edith said. "Wait! What's going to happen to her now?"

"You heard what her father said," Andy grumbled. "He told her to keep away from those joints downtown. When a girl goes down there, she's asking for trouble, especially if she gives a guy the come on look. That's what happened. I know, the Rainbow Grill is suppose to be a hangout for young people, but it makes no difference."

"And you never know what may have happened to her in that park," Edith said trembling. "She may have even been killed by that sex lunatic." she stared at Andy with terror in her eyes. "And not knowing if she was killed or laying hurt somewhere. The entire town will be in an uproar when the news breaks. The parents will want to know the whereabouts of their children. A girl can't even go out and have a little fun anymore."

"A guy has to be a loony to go that far against a girl's wishes,"

Andy said. "Probably a lot of girls around that would have obliged without a struggle."

"She'll be all right now," Edith said. They stood outside of the door. They looked at each other. They walked into the darkness again and the air was now cool against their face.

"You know, Andy, I'm glad that you're going to marry me. Then we don't have to worry about sneaking off into a dark, secluded area to make love. We can do that in our very own home."

As Edith Miller had suggested to Andy Curtis, she wanted to get married, and the sooner the better. After making brief plans, they drove to Colby, Maryland. With them were Nancy Smith, a former classmate of Edith's, and John Sterling who worked with Andy at Mine 35. Andy was thrilled with the idea of getting married as quickly as possible, and eliminating the formality and long waiting period that was required in Sinclair. This matrimonial plan was like a game to Andy, and he enjoyed the change of atmosphere and the role he was assuming. Of Edith and her nearness he was conscious, the bride, awaiting the rites that would legalize their desire of matrimony.

When they arrived in Colby, they went directly to the marriage license bureau. But outside the entrance to the building, Edith hesitated.

"Are you all right, Edith?" Andy said.

"Yes," she said. A smile came upon her face and she sighed.

Andy's face brightened and his eyelashes quivered, and he had a sudden feeling that he knew her and everything about her thoughts. He accepted her for what she was.

"I love you, Andy," she whispered.

"Come on! Let's go in!" He responded. He took her hand and they entered the building. They walked down the hall with Nancy and John following closely behind. They came to a desk where a clerk was seated.

"Looks like you're ready to take the big step," the clerk said earnestly.

"It's now or never," Andy replied. Nancy and John giggled.

"You're going to have to fill out this form," the clerk said.

Andy and Edith went about the formality of filling out the form. When the form was completed, they answered a few questions directed to them by the clerk. Then they paid the fee for the marriage license.

"You can have your choice of a minister or a justice of the peace in this town," the clerk said. "We certainly have enough of them. A lot of young couples come here from other states to get married. Many of the officials make a darn good living for conducting marriage ceremonies. Like I said, you've got plenty to choose from."

They decided that they would prefer to have a minister marry them—a Lutheran minister. They asked the clerk where they could locate a Lutheran minister.

"Well," the clerk said. "We have two Lutheran ministers in this town. There's Reverend King up on High Street, and Reverend Riley just one block from here."

"Which one do you want to go to, Edith?" Andy asked.

"It really doesn't matter. Let's go to see Reverend Riley. He is only one block away and we can walk from here."

Then they rushed out into the street towards Reverend Riley's church. When they arrived at the church, Andy looked at Edith. She knew the time had come.

"Come on Andy. Let's get it over with."

"You don't care about the way you're getting married, Edith."

"Not a bit," she replied.

They located the minister. The ceremony was brief and informal. They were surprised that it did not take long before the minister said: "I now pronounce you man and wife." The minister closed his book. He smiled and said, "God bless you both."

Andy and Edith felt uneasy, and they realized now they were man and wife. They hesitated, and there was nothing more to say, and suddenly John Sterling said, "Kiss the bride, Andy."

And Andy expertly leaned to Edith and kissed her. Upon the completion of the marriage ceremony, they drove back to Sinclair with Nancy Smith and John Sterling. After bidding them farewell, they proceeded on their honeymoon to New York State.

So here they began their life in wedlock. No rice was thrown, no car horns honked, and no trumpets sounded to climax the ceremony. In their persons there was no change. They felt no closer to each other than they had previously. Now they only had the legal assurance of legitimate relationship. Now they could be accepted by society as man and wife.

They spent their first night in a motel. Edith still thinking of the marriage recalling the briefness of the ceremony and the final words of the minister, and now facing the unknown future of living with Andy Curtis. Now she was married and was alone with Andy. But they had been alone before under different circumstances. Now they were man and wife in a motel many miles from Sinclair.

"You're kind of quiet," Andy said, while she went and sat down near the dresser, thinking about the same type of wedding she had planned with Henry Shane, but it did not work out as she had hoped. Suddenly she said:

"It seems so funny. Do you feel married, Andy?"

"I guess so," He began to wonder why she had presented him with that type of question. She was his woman now, and he began to anticipate what really was on her mind.

"How did you think you would feel?" Andy said.

She looked at him and said, "Do you honestly and truly feel like a married man? After all I'm not a virgin as you well know."

Andy laughed. "Sure, I know you're not a virgin, but I still feel you're my wife. I don't care about your past. I'm only interested in the present and the future."

She began to straighten the room, opening suitcases, putting clothes on hangers, and rearranging her personal belongings. He watched her to try to determine what she really had on her mind and simply asked, What's troubling you, Edith?"

"I'm thinking about our marriage and how it's going to be. About having children. I'm trying to feel like a loyal and dedicated wife. I hope I can make you happy, Andy."

"Then you really weren't sure about me, Edith?"

"No, it's not that, Andy?" She said. "I was sure the first night we were together on that dirt road near Sinclair. I knew, at least I was thinking about it."

"Oh, come on now, Edith! I don't believe that."

"Yes, Andy the very first night we were together. Anyway we 're married now. Why are we talking about it? Everything turned out as we planned it."

"I'm happy," Andy said. He rose, excited finally by the awareness that he was alone with Edith behind closed doors. "I'm getting sleepy."

"Yes, I am too." She stopped arranging the clothes and went to the window to close the drapes.

Andy got into his pajamas. Her face smiling, she picked up her negligee and walked to the bathroom and closed the door behind her. There he lay on the bed waiting for her glorious re-entry. After a long time she came out. She looked quite different than previous times that Andy had seen her. Her body was enticing, and an aroma of perfume filled the room. She crawled slowly into the bed. They looked at one another with hunger in their eyes. She reached over and put out the light.

"Well," she said. "We're married." She turned and threw her arms over him and put her mouth near his ear. "What are you waiting for, honey?"

"Why in the hell did I put on my pajamas?" Andy responded. He quickly pushed her aside and removed his pajamas. He assisted her in the removal of her negligee. Instantly he felt the warmth of her body and the firm breasts protruding against his chest, and he was overcome with passionate joy. She lay passive, then began to breathe faster, waiting and now panting. His hands found the crucial spots, his mouth the nipples of her breast. He caressed her, she hesitated, but then was aware she was married, no longer resisting, and moved up and down in rhythm with Andy. She cried out, and then she was still.

She lay there nestled against him, exploring his body with her hand. "Did you like it?" she asked suddenly. "I mean did you really enjoy it like the other times."

"Oh, Lord, it was wonderful. It was better than the other times."

"What's it really like for a man?"

"The same as for a woman, I guess. It felt like I was walking on a cloud, and a thrilling sensation crept over my entire body."

"I got the same feeling that you did, but I really can't explain it. It just felt so wonderful."

"Did I hurt you?" Andy asked.

"No, Andy you didn't hurt me, and you didn't hurt me the other times either?"

Andy rolled the covers into a big ball and threw them on to the floor. He reached over and put on the light. "Since we are married now, I want to get a better view of your body," Andy said.

She cuddled closer to him and gazed into his widened eyes, she breathed faster as she glanced at his naked body, feeling him look at her nakedness, and she closed her eyes.

"It's beautiful, it's beautiful," he said with a thrilling emotion in his voice. Her mouth was open, and he bent over and kissed her.

"Now! Again, again," she pleaded. She cried out, "oh, oh."

He lay there thinking. She was his now. This is what it will be like for a long time. Had he really satisfied her. Would he be able to please her forever and ever. He moved his head to look at her. She was asleep.

Within a year after their marriage, the residence of Andy Curtis had become one of great popularity. Like the mines, it was discussed in the conversations of many local people, for many were entertained there. All the people who visited the Curtis residence were impressed by the charm and beauty of Edith Curtis, one of the few women in Sinclair who had a knack of being a good hostess. No one truly disliked Edith.

The Weaver's were the first to come to her house, and the O'Hara's, the Smith's, the Anderson's and many others followed them from

Sinclair. Moreover, the Curtis household became more than any other in Sinclair a place where people met, talked and danced together, and where young miners met girls, and visitors from Jaystown saw Coal Region hospitality at its best.

So now Andy Curtis had become a Coal Region gentleman and the head of a Coal Region household. The long social climb that had started the day he became a mine foreman had reached its peak when he was appointed a mine superintendent. Now he had all the manners appropriate to his position at the mine. Deep within, he knew he did not belong to the class of the laboring miners. His promotion came about as a result of hard work. In particular he lacked the primary prerequisites of a supervisor authority. The feeling of power over others Andy lacked completely. He had acquired authority in spite of himself, the prestige of money, and the power of an executive over his understudies, but he never learned to like domination of workers. His approach to order always had the appearance of a request rather than a command. When a problem occurred with one of the miners, he often sought the advice of his superiors, and when a miner proved difficult, Andy would release him with considerable regret. With utmost respect he had observed the other mine foremen under his jurisdiction make men work to the best of their ability. Andy, however, could not imitate his subordinates. He got his way, when it was necessary, but always by coaxing. He did not have the command to make anyone do anything and no one knew this as well as his wife. Edith had entered his life by mere fate, but now she had come to stay in his household as his wife. Her time was her own and she came and went as she pleased. She was very energetic and full of radical ideas, and took it upon herself to renovate the Curtis house. So Andy found himself within a short period of time the head of a house dominated by his wife, whereas in the past he relied mainly on the services of his mother.

The elderly Mrs. Curtis had insisted that Andy remain in the house after his marriage to Edith. Now, it no longer looked like the same house. Edith had the kitchen and living room enlarged and had the house completely refinished from top to bottom. Like her deceased mother, she loved large pictures on the wall that made the rooms look more colorful and attractive.

Here in the Curtis house she could be found serving coffee and tea to the local women friends, and also beer to Andy's acquaintances, for she had learned that miners did not care much for the sophisticated things in life.

Edith's hospitality attracted many people. Often a group of young miners would drive over in the evenings, knowing they would be welcomed. As a result many mothers would bring their pretty daughters over to flirt with the young men. There were always a few men that were musically talented, and would contribute their time in forming a band. Often the music would lure other bystanders, and they could be seen dancing and whirling while others looked on in bewilderment.

Edith loved dancing and she was well versed in the latest trends. She was able to express all her feelings and graces in the manner in which she danced, and incorporated her own fervor into her partner. She could polka with perfect rhythm with many of the talented men, and when the party reached a high level of liveliness she could go into a jitterbug with a male partner that would have made any woman envious. Best of all, she was well versed in the know-how of making a dull party come to life.

Andy often watched her with jealous eyes. She seemed to have more spirit in her than almost any other woman, and this troubled him. He was soon aware of the many possible rivals. Edith attracted many young men to her house without trying, and she lured them to her side in the same manner, their eyes glistening with passionate desire.

Everyone who came to her parties could see that Robert Heim was falling in love with her. He was a businessman, twenty-eight years old, who had graduated from Yale University. He was a handsome man, tall and muscular, with a wave of black hair, dark complexion, brown eyes and he possessed a charming personality.

On a dance floor he was stiff as a board. Having learned to dance at Yale, he danced correctly, keeping his partner away from him, embracing her gently only when it was necessary. Later, Edith evidently felt it a part of her duty as a hostess to loosen him up. She moved in upon him with graceful tactics and clinched him in her arms, and at the end of the dance he wore an embarrassed grin, while Edith stood looking at him with passionate eyes. "I will make a good dancer out of you yet," she often would say.

After that incident, Andy observed that Robert Heim followed her all the time with his eyes, and he tried to dance with her as often as possible. Later, it seemed that he only came to the Curtis house to look at Edith and to be in her company.

Andy couldn't understand whether Edith felt a genuine interest in Robert Heim or whether she feared he might be an annoying presence. Her attentive gestures toward all male visitors always were of grave concern to him. She seemed to be attracted to all men, with her casual mannerisms.

Likewise, many women looked at Robert Heim with keen interest, and when Edith noticed this, she would eventually worm her way toward him, talk with him, shake his hand when he was about to leave.

Afterwards she questioned Andy about him and wanted to know what type of work he did and where he lived. Andy would tell her all he knew about him and his interest in business ventures, and often suggested to Edith that she should have him to the house for Sunday dinner. Edith firmly refused to cater to Andy's suggestion.

Evidently, Andy thought, Robert Heim was out of the picture with Edith, at least for the present time. Fearing he might be offended, Andy drove to Jaystown to visit him and was surprised to receive a warm welcome. Robert Heim poured whiskey and talked about the mining industry, steel mills and railroads. Robert was full of ideas about going into business for himself after the war. "All I need is a little more cash and I'll venture going into the construction business myself," he said. "I'll move to the Philadelphia area. After the war, the veterans will be coming back looking for work, and they are going to locate in an area where they have the best opportunity for employment. Yeah, the house construction business would be the ideal thing. Families will need houses, and there's good money in that type of construction. Why don't we form a partnership, Andy?"

Andy hesitated. "Well, it would be a good business risk. But it would take a lot of money to get started. I don't think I'll have enough cash to get started, Robert. By damn, such a project would require considerable thought and inquiry."

It occurred to Andy that it might be a good proposition to back Robert in Philadelphia, but he said nothing further about his possible involvement. So he merely listened to Robert with care making positive gesture and comments, and then changed the conversation to something else before leaving. Robert shook his hand and smiled. He had enjoyed talking to someone else about his tentative project.

"Good luck," Andy said. "Anytime you get bored with drinking alone and Jaystown women, come over to Sinclair and pay us a visit."

"I'll do that," Robert replied. "Your wife is a wonderful person. She's so popular. I thought I'd never get to dance with her the last time I was over in Sinclair, and I did want to say goodbye to her."

"I hope you're not going to leave us too soon," Andy said.

"No, not really. I'm going to Philadelphia the day after tomorrow and check out a few details on my proposed project."

"It appears that you are serious about going into the house construction business," Andy nodded.

"This is just a business trip. Nothing official yet. If I think it'll work out, I'll just come back to Jaystown and round up my personal belongings and pull up stakes for good."

"I'm sorry to hear that," Andy said.

"I'm sorry to go," Robert told him bluntly. "This Coal Region gets into your blood—you can't beat the friendly people and their hospitality. I've stayed around here long enough. The odds are favorable for me to succeed in the house construction business."

"Good luck, and take care of yourself," Andy responded.

Nine

Meanwhile, Henry Shane was discharged from the army in September of 1946. He was merely going home for a visit, he thought as sound as any man, but he knew he would be weary and restless in Sinclair. On the train bringing him home, he looked about with a new attitude and a new out look. When the train slowed he was waiting in the vestibule. He alighted from the train. He was in Sinclair. The pavement under his feet, the familiar station, the churches, the barrooms, the houses and the sulfuric odors, he acknowledged them with his senses, his desire for them unaffected by the contact, made keener by their promise of home. He looked about grinning. Behind him the train moved off silently. "Sinclair!" he said fiercely. "I'm in Sinclair!" Lifting his duffel bag, he walked friskily toward the center of town and on all sides of him familiar things fell into view, the dusty street, the town hall and the well remembered bandstand. It was midnight when he reached the center of town. There was no one there to greet him—no crowds—no bands—no friends—not even his own brother. This is the way he wanted to come home and without any fan fare. Several weeks earlier, he had sent his brother a telegram assuring him that he was well and would be home shortly, but never designated a date of arrival.

The entire town was asleep. There were no signs of life except for a few shabby, stray dogs roaming the streets in quest of food. He sat down on a stone bench in front of the war memorial and wiped the perspiration from his forehead with a handkerchief. He sat there in silence, thinking of the Sinclair that he had left behind to go into the army. Many dismal thoughts wandered through his mind as he stared at the dimly lighted street, and the shadows of various objects in the environment before him.

He mumbled, "What the hell kind of future will I have here?" Like all Coal Region communities, Sinclair was built in proximity to the coal mine. A railroad trestle marked the western approaches to the town. All the houses were constructed of the same type of material and were similar in design. The only distinguishing factors were that the houses were painted of various colors, now fading, drab and deteriorating with the passing of time.

He shook his head from side to side as if he could not tolerate the scenes he saw lying before him. The silence of the night was interrupted when he heard a dog barking in the distance. He stood, stretched himself, and reached for his duffel bag that he picked up and threw over his right shoulder, and walked slowly down the street in the direction of his household.

When Henry Shane returned, he found that Sinclair was a town, even then, where it was very difficult to acquire decent employment unless one had some political connections.

Several weeks had passed since his return from the war but he still had not acquired a job. He became desperate and seriously considered working in the coal mine, and on several occasions the thought occurred to him of approaching Andy Curtis, the superintendent of Mine 35. Why in the hell should Andy go out of his way to give me a job? Andy knows damn well that I was involved with Edith for several years before she decided to marry him. If anything, he probably anticipated that I would be killed in the war. Maybe there is a small chance that he isn't the type of man who will hold a grudge.

To put an end to this suspense, he went reluctantly to Andy's house. The equation of his value had dwindled sadly since his return from the war, but he was in a desperate need of a job that paid a half-decent salary. To his disappointment, he found out from a neighbor that Andy and Edith had gone to Pellersville. He had a sense of injury and dejection.

I must try work at something and cease to worry and lie awake at night, he thought.

He had nothing to do but visit the local taverns, write letters or walk the streets and wait hopefully for positive responses to his inquiries for employment. Weeks had gone by, but no word of acceptance had reached him; not even the coal mine or the steel mill in Jaystown. He merely received replies, "Thank you for applying, but we have no positions available at the present time. We will keep your application on file for future reference." Nothing but thank you typed on a piece of paper-cold, formal, prompt, ready-made, and more than likely mailed to all unsuccessful applicants. And he was in about the same fix-rejected with thank you—politely, firmly, thoroughly rejected. For a time he felt like an outcast. He began to see there was no clamorous demand for him in the great society, as his brother Lee on occasions would call it.

Nevertheless, he didn't give up hope. He went to the J. P. Smith Steel Company in Jaystown to find that Mr. Smith had gone to Philadelphia, and Mr. O'Hara, his associate was too busy to see him. Now, he concluded that he would be willing to take a job in one of the lesser paying occupations just out of desperation. Day after day he continued to go from one establishment to another, but was rejected everywhere with, "I'm sorry, we have no jobs available at this time."

He returned to his home and constantly appraised his life. First he checked his meager bank account, of which there was about two hundred dollars left. As to his talents, there were none left, except that of a soldier. Like trying to seek admission to a championship athletic event, if you were late in arriving—the gates were closed. He did buy some decent clothes upon being discharged from the army, anticipating he would need them in the event he would get a white collar job; but no more use for them than a piece of shit in an outhouse.

He still continued to answer advertisements and apply at business offices for something to give him a living, but with no success. Now, he began to feel the selfishness of men. He often whispered, "God, damn the warm and tender hearts of a war veteran when it begins to harden and grow cold. Beware of the time you loving mothers, that have sons that were called upon to make a sacrifice for their country."

Still Henry continued to have confidence, but very little cheerfulness. He even went to try his luck with the companies and business establishments in Pellersville, and there one of them kept him in suspense for a week. He waited in Pellersville hoping he might hear some word of employment. He could not accept the idea to report failure or to send for money from his brother. He would sooner go to work as a dishwasher.

One day, after a climax of ill luck, and reduction in cash, he decided to hitchhike back to Sinclair. Meanwhile his friends at the Ritz Tavern were enough to keep him in good spirits. One night he was introduced to a William O'Leary, an Irishman of a great gift of dignity and a nickname inseparably connected with his handicap. He was a crew foreman for the Pennsylvania Railroad, and was known as Stump O'Leary, to honor him because of an arm that was severed near the elbow, the result of a freak accident that occurred while working on the railroad. He drank excessively at times, but never to the loss of his dignity or self-respect. In his drinking glass, the self-respecting manner of the man grew and expanded.

"I understand you are looking for a job, my boy," Stump said forcefully.

"Yes," Henry responded. "I will soon be out of money and I'm at my wit's end, but I haven't given up hope. It's damn tough to find a job in this region."

"What luck?" Stump said sadly.

"It's bad luck for me. Only a few dollars in my pocket and nothing to fall back on."

Stump gazed into his drinking glass. "If I were you, I'd take any type of job that's honest. Upon my word, I'd rather drive spikes on the railroad than remain idle."

"So would I," Henry responded immediately.

"Would you, really," Stump said with animation as he looked at Henry from head to foot.

"I told you, that I would undertake anything that's honest."

"That's right, you did," Stump agreed. "It seems to me like you're not accustomed to hard work."

"I can do the work," Henry said in desperation.

He looked at Henry sternly and said, "I'll tell you what to do. Tomorrow morning you report to me at seven o'clock. We are replacing many of the old railroad ties between Sinclair and Jaystown. We can use some extra help. If you want the job—be there at the western outskirts of town near the trestle."

"I'll be there," Henry said. "And by the way, Stump, thanks a lot. I appreciate it."

"Forget about it, boy. I'm more than happy to help out a war veteran." He swallowed the remaining contents of his glass—bid everyone a goodnight and left the tavern.

The following day Henry Shane reported to the railroad job site. Upon seeing Henry, Stump O'Leary approached him and said, "Come along."

They walked a short distance until they came upon a gang of burly men uprooting deteriorating railroad ties. "Joe Downey!" Stump shouted.

A hearty voice answered, "What the hell do you want, Stump?" Joe Downey came out of the crowd of men, using his steel bar as a staff.

"A good day to you!" Stump said.

"Same to you and many more of them," Joe Downey replied.

"How about doing me a favor?"

"And what is that?" Joe Downey said.

"A place for this war veteran on your crew. Will you do it?"

"Indeed I will," Joe Downey confirmed, and he did.

Henry went to work that cold, blustery December morning wearing a short, heavy workingman's coat and a pull over knit cap save a bright pair of gloves that aroused the ridicule of his fellow workers. With this reception and the righteous determination of earning seventy-five cents an hour, he began the inelegant task of removing rails and ties—no easy occupation especially on a blustery day. He helped to shovel dirt and gravel and dig with a pick and bar under adverse conditions.

His arms and back ached, his face was wind-burned crimson when he quit work at three o'clock, and he went home with a feeling of having been run over by a steamroller. He had a strong sense of soul and body, the latter dominated by a mighty appetite.

That night, as he eased his aching body into bed, Henry realized how badly out of condition he was. It was a long time since he had done such hard work.

He left his home the following morning, sore and stiff as a board, but filled with self-determination. He was assigned to the same work crew again, working harder than the previous day.

He went home that second night with some personal satisfaction. It was good to work like this, to do a man's work against all odds and to at least be able to earn a livelihood. Some of the ache had left him, his muscles loosened and smooth moving. Yes, he thought, it was good to work again after the frustrating weeks in attempting to seek employment. It made him forget his longing for Edith Curtis, it eased his mind of the constant worry about survival.

After a few weeks, the work went better. He helped to lay new railroad ties and hammered the rails to the ties with spikes. He took his turn to huddle near the fire to warm his body, and to drink hot coffee.

One day, in the middle of the afternoon, He straightened up a moment to ease his back and to look about. There at the edge of the gang stood the renowned John P. Smith and his associate Vincent O'Hara, both dressed in heavy, hooded parkas. The latter beckoned him as he caught his eye. He went aside to greet them. John P. Smith extended his hand and said," So you're Henry Shane. You're the fellow that had been writing all those letters seeking employment with our company over in Jaystown. You don't give up, do you? Were you really sincere when you stated that you would rather work than beg or borrow?"

"That's right," Henry answered. "And you are not ashamed of any kind of work," Vincent O'Hara intervened.

"Ashamed! Why? I'm not quite sure of what you mean. It had never occurred to me that one had any cause to be ashamed of working. As long as it is honest work."

John P. Smith chuckled. "I guess you'll do for the job I have in mind for you. If you're interested, come to my office in Jaystown around ten o'clock tomorrow morning. By the way, don't worry about leaving this job on the railroad. I am one of the major stockholders, and I can use my influence to get your job back. Be in my office tomorrow morning and I'll give you all the details. I can assure you that you'll be making much more money than you would working on the railroad."

If Henry had been a knight in shining armor he could not have been treated with more distinguished courtesy by those hard handed, fellow railroad workers the rest of the day. He bid them farewell at the end of the workday, and went home wondering why John P. Smith had singled him out for a special work assignment.

To put an end to this suspense, he went the following morning to the office of John P. Smith in Jaystown. A secretary, who immediately directed him to John P. Smith, who was sitting behind a large mahogany desk, greeted him

"Sit down! Sit down!" John P. Smith shouted. "I have a job for you, son. I want to give you an opportunity to make some money. You have good qualities, my boy, and everyone is entitled to a break now and then. Yes, I have a job for you, and you're just the right man for the job."

"What's the catch?" Henry asked.

"There isn't any catch. I'll be very honest with you, Henry. I don't have any ulterior motives. Therefore, there isn't any need for you to be suspicious of me."

Henry stared into John P. Smith's eyes and waited quietly for him to go on.

"Didn't I ask you to come to my office? Did I sound like a man who was going to give you the run around? I'd ask you again, because you're the kind of man I need in my company. This job I have in mind for you will require a lot of guts. It appears to me that you are a gutsy person and had a lot of experience in crucial situations while serving in the army. Jobs are hard to come by in these parts, and I figured you would jump at the chance of making a lot of money. This is business, son. Please get the notion out of your head that I'm trying to con you into taking a shady job."

"All right," Henry said. "Now what about this job?"

"It's in Coalport," John P. Smith said. "You know that I have acquired a coal mine there."

"Yes, I know. I read about it in the newspaper."

"So you do know. All right. Now when I acquired the McLaughlin and Jones Coal Company, I found it to be in a pathetic economic state. Those previous owners had overextended themselves and were on the verge of bankruptcy. Why, the wages they were paying those miners were way out of line, considering the low output of coal from the mine. Productivity is the name of the game, my boy."

"So," Henry said. "You decided to cut the wages and to furlough miners to compensate. What did you do about improving the working conditions in the mine?"

"Nothing," John P. Smith said. "There was nothing I could do. I did inherit a damn terrible mess. That stupid idea that McLaughlin and Jones had of catering to the miners just didn't pan out. The very day I took over the mine, I announced that the wages would be cut down to a reasonable figure until we were able to reorganize and eventually reap a profit from my investment in the mine. They didn't give me a chance to explain my position. The rotten bastards went on strike.

A coal miner, Henry thought, could starve to death on your reasonable wages; but what business is that of mine? He stuttered, "You—you want to hire me to break the strike. You are asking me to be a strikebreaker."

"That's right, my boy," John P. smith replied immediately. "I told you that I would give you an opportunity to make a lot of money. I'll pay you four hundred dollars a week, and give you a substantial bonus of two thousand dollars if you succeed in breaking the strike."

"What happens if I fail to break the strike?" Henry asked.

"You still will get your money. I'll assure you of that and even put it in writing," John P. Smith replied. "I'll permit you to have a reasonable expense account. You can hire anyone you need, spend as much money that is reasonable, but break that damn strike!"

Breaking the strike, Henry thought, must be John P. Smith's top priority. "I'll have to think about it," he said. "When do I have to let you know?"

"As soon as possible," John P. Smith answered. "Breaking the strike is very important to me. I can't afford to wait. I'd appreciate it if you can make the decision right now."

"All right, Mr. smith. Let me think about it for a moment. Did I hear you say that I can hire anyone I need to help break the strike?"

"Yes, of course I said that," John P. Smith answered quickly. "By the way, I already took it upon myself to hire your friend, Richard Rand a few days ago. You and Richard can get your heads together and decide how you're going to handle this situation."

Henry stared at John P. Smith, his jaw dropping. "You mean to say that you hired Richard Rand! He has a job with the Crystal Coal Company in Sinclair. I didn't think that Richard would get himself involved in this mess."

John P. Smith smiled and said, "So, you thought he wouldn't come to work for me. Why? Because he thought I was a son of a bitch. He is a very clever man. You should know that money could buy most people. Well, I approached him politely, and it didn't take much of an effort to persuade him to take the job. There's something about working as a petty employee of a coal company that is a blow to one's ego. Richard Rand wants to improve his status in life, like any sensible man. By the way, he is the one that told me about you. That's the main reason why my associate, Vincent O'Hara, and I decided to contact you. We were

The Wailing Wind

impressed with your determination in attempting to seek employment in our steel mill. Now, this job I'm offering you will pay three times the amount of money you would have earned working in the mill or on the railroad. Anyway, Richard Rand said to tell you that he'd cooperate with you to the fullest extent if you take the job. Now, go ahead and think about it. Take five or ten minutes. I think that is sufficient time."

John P. smith sat there chewing on the end of his cigar, gazing first at Henry's puzzled face and then out the window.

Think! Henry laughed inside of his mind. What the hell kind of thinking do I really need to do? I have thought. Nobody else in my predicament would refuse the job. I need the money I have to look out for myself and nobody else will. Perhaps I might be lucky enough to break the strike, which would be a feather in my cap. Still there is that possibility that one of those angry coal miners might blow my head off; and then I wouldn't have to worry about a job anymore. Anyway, if it works out I may be on easy street and John P. Smith will more than likely offer me a better position within his organization. Why don't I stop wasting my time, he thought?

"I'll take the job," Henry said suddenly. "When do I start?"

"Now," John P. smith said. "I'll have my secretary prepare the contract which you can sign, and I'll have her call the train station over in Sinclair for your tickets. By the way, Richard Rand will meet you at the station."

"You were certain I'd take the job, weren't you?"

"Yes," John P. Smith answered. "You were in a desperate need of a good paying job. You had to start somewhere, and I knew you would jump at the chance. Money talks so to speak."

When Henry Shane arrived at the station in Sinclair, cold drizzle was falling. The clouds were gray, and the wind that blew across the open platform was bitter cold. He greeted Richard Rand who had arrived earlier to pick up their tickets. They boarded the train together and eventually found themselves sprawled in their seats. Henry appeared to be relaxed and comfortable, but his face was frowning.

"I don't particularly like working as a strike breaker," he said.

"You should have thought about that before you committed yourself," Richard responded. "It's a job, isn't it? What are you bitching about? Count your blessings that John P. Smith was kind enough to hire you."

"I took this job because I need the money, but now I'm not sure whether I did the right thing."

"Yeah, I know," Richard said quietly. "Some jobs are just too damn miserable. What the hell are we supposed to do? We are from the working class and don't have a pot to piss in. Have you forgotten how it was most of our lives? Do you think I like to come home every night with my whole body aching and not enough money to make ends meet. That type of feeling can make a man pretty damn mean and nasty."

"I just can't picture myself beating the hell out of another man who is struggling for survival and defending what he thinks is right," Henry said sadly. "I don't have the brass balls to do something like that. I don't have the meanness in me, and that is what this job requires—just plain old meanness."

"I suppose you're right, Henry. Nobody has the right to live high and mighty when the house he owns, the food he eats, the automobile he drives, and the clothes he wears on his back were obtained by conniving and taking advantage of another lowly human being. Nobody—not John P. Smith, not Vincent O'Hara, not me—not even you."

Henry looked at him and said, "I'm going to do my best to avoid any beatings or bloodshed. John P. Smith gave me an expense account and I'm going to take advantage of it. I'm going to spread some of his money around where I think it will do the most good. I'll approach the leader of the strike and offer him a substantial sum of money and convince him to call off the strike. I'm not anxious to kick anybody in the ass or break someone's arm or leg. It's not necessary. Like I said, I'll distribute the money among some influential individuals where it will encourage them to convince others to support our cause."

"You must think that everybody has his price, don't you?" Richard said.

"I'm inclined to believe they do," Henry replied as he looked out of the window at the rain that was changing into a mixture of sleet and snow.

"I'll be damned, I think you're right. Only, sometimes it isn't just the money."

Henry burped. The loud sound attracted the attention of the other men and women sitting nearby, and they merely glared at him.

The train rumbled westward among the hills through areas of depressing bleakness, sleet and snow whipped under a gray and gloomy sky. Here and there tumble down and deteriorated clapboard houses clung to the hillside, dark and depressing against the patches of snow, and the smoke coming forth from the chimneys lay back over the houses and cast a shadow on them.

Several miles from Coalport itself, the engineer reduced the speed of the locomotive prior to approaching a sharp and dangerous curve near a ravine. The train seemed to glide around the curve and moved slowly towards Coalport. Shortly, the train stopped near an old crumbling building that was designated as Coalport's passenger and freight terminal. They alighted from the train, looking about the deplorable environment.

Coalport was a dismal and gloomy town. Even the snow appeared to have a dirty, gray cast, and the main street was an unrelieved sea of slush. The houses were not well kept, but aside from the facts that under the film of smoke and grime the remains of a thin coat of paint could be seen. The houses were like the company houses that were commonplace near the mines in Sinclair.

There was no one at the terminal to greet them, so they picked up their suitcases and walked up the street ankle deep in the icy slush. There was nobody on the street. From the sky there still poured a mixture of rain, sleet and snow. On this day, however, a foggy, sulphurous haze with the stench of rotten eggs permeated the air. On the hillside they saw the mine tipple's huge, gigantic structure where the coal from the mine is dumped, sorted, cleaned and loaded into trucks and railroad cars. They walked to the bottom of the hill and turned toward the mine. Potholes and ruts that made walking difficult ravaged the road leading to the mine.

Outside the mine, they saw a group of miners, dark silhouettes against the dirty whiteness, their breaths steaming from their nostrils in streamers that rose above their heads like clouds. Henry and Richard did not pay any attention to them. They looked about until they found what they sought; the mine superintendent's house, an ugly clapboard structure nestled between piles of slag with the eerie desolate periphery of dead trees around it. They walked through the slush up to the porch. Henry knocked on the door with his fist. A thin, mustached man with a worried expression greeted them.

"I'm Henry Shane, and this is my friend Richard Rand. You must be Michael Finley."

"That's right," Michael Finley replied. "We have been expecting you. I'm damn glad to see you. Come in and warm yourselves near the stove."

Henry walked towards the stove, but Richard gazed down sheepishly at his wet and dirty shoes. Michael Finley noticed the hesitation. "Hell oh mighty, don't worry about your shoes? We're quite used to sloppy conditions around here."

He led them through the living room and paused near the entrance to the kitchen. "Rachael," he called, "the men from Sinclair are here!" Then turning he said, "This is my wife Rachael."

Mrs. Finley stepped away from the kitchen stove. She was an attractive, well-developed woman and appeared to be much younger than her husband.

"Oh my!" she said. "You're soaking wet! You better get into some dry clothes. Pick up your suitcases and I'll show you to your room." They followed her up the stairway and waited while she opened the door.

"This will be your room while you're here in Coalport. If you have to use the washroom, it's down there at the end of the hallway. When you have cleaned up and changed your clothes, please come right down for supper." Mrs. Finley smiled and left the room.

The bedroom was large and comfortably furnished with twin beds, a dresser and several chairs. There was a louvered, heating ventilator in the middle of the room, but the room was so cold that they shivered when they removed their dirty clothing and put on their robes and proceeded to the washroom. Changed into dry clothing, they went down the stairway and rejoined Michael Finley sitting at the kitchen table. "Sit down and eat your supper, gentlemen," Michael Finley said politely.

Henry looked at Michael Finley wonderingly. How in the hell had this quiet, meek mannered man ever become a superintendent of a coal mine? He had anticipated meeting a rough, tobacco chewing man, muscular and aggressive, but Michael Finley was different.

Michael Finley recognized the puzzled expression on Henry's face. "I was hired by Mr. McLaughlin, gentlemen. John P. Smith kept me on the payroll after he bought the Coal Company, though he doesn't really know me very well. I doubt that he will keep me very long once he gets organized."

"I don't know anything about that," Henry said.

"I know, but I immediately recognized the puzzled look on your face. I'm not cut out to be a mine superintendent. If you did get that impression, you're right. After McLaughlin and Jones sold out to John P. Smith, I considered getting out of the coal business and moving out of the state. Now, I'm certain with all the turmoil and strikes we have been having around here lately. I'm going to submit my resignation to John P. Smith at the end of the week. I'm sick and tired of all the bullshit day in and day out. There seems to be no end to it. Oh, I could do well enough if it weren't for all the crap. I could make the mine productive again if I was to get some cooperation from Mr. Smith, but that isn't likely to happen. I can see the handwriting on the wall, and so can those other poor bastards that have to mine the coal. So what is the end result—a strike. Now, gentlemen, I know why John P. Smith hired you and sent you to Coalport—you're strikebreakers."

"Yes, if that is what you want to call us," Henry replied. "By the way, Mr. Finley, you mentioned something about making the mine productive again. How would you?"

Michael Finley thought a moment, smiled and responded, "By paying the miners even more than McLaughlin and Jones paid them. Giving them an incentive to work. By increasing their pay portal to portal. Most of all, by improving the working conditions in the mine. You see, I'm in sympathy with the strikers even though I am a part of management. That is one of the reasons I am submitting my resignation. It's always the poor little guy that gets screwed."

"They're good people once you get to know them," Mrs. Finley intervened. "They'll give you the shirt off their back, and that coal mine is so dangerous. Why, in less than six months five miners were killed and fifteen others crippled for life, not to mention other injuries besides. Coal mine accidents take their daily toll around here, but many people forget about the other dangers inflicted upon the miners due to the coal dust. While working in the mine, the miners are covered from head to foot with coal dust. It gets in their hair, on their clothes and on their skin. The rims of their eyes are coated with it. It gets into their mouth and they swallow it. They breath so much of it into their lungs that until the day they die they never stop spitting up coal dust. Some of those poor miners cough so hard that it is a miracle that they have any lungs left. Eventually you notice those poor souls getting short of breath even when they walk across the street. Call it what you want silicosis or miner's asthma. In plain and simple words, they are miners' lung diseases that will cause terrible suffering and lead to death."

Michael Finley coughed as his wife completed her brief remarks and turned to Henry.

"May I ask you what your specific plans are to end the strike, Mr. Shane?"

"I'll try to get in touch with the leader of this strike and talk to him face to face. I'll try to convince him to call off the strike, and pay him a substantial sum of money if he cooperates."

Michael Finley smiled a slow, pleasant smile. "If you want to know who the leader is, it's Charles Bane, but trying to bribe him won't work."

"Why not? Doesn't he need money?" Henry asked immediately.

" I'm certain he needs money as much as anyone around here," Michael Finley said. "Not at the expense of the coal miners he represents."

"Well, that may be true, but there won't be any harm in trying, is there?"

"I suppose not," Michael Finley responded.

"Then where in the hell does Charles Bane live?" Henry asked.

"Down the road near the train station. You can't miss it. There is a picket fence around the yard. You'll like him, and find him to be an interesting man. He's a war veteran just like yourself, but somewhat older. I think he served with an airborne division in Europe. I'm sure you'll find something in common to talk about."

Henry wiped his mouth with a napkin, pushed his chair away from the table and stood up. "Let's go, Richard," he said.

"Ok," Richard answered. "Let me finish my supper first."

"It's damn wet and sloppy outside," Michael Finley said. "I have an extra pair of boots that either one of you can use."

"Thanks," Henry replied. "It really won't be necessary."

Once Henry Shane and Richard Rand left the house, they realized that it had grown much colder. By walking along the edge of the road, they were able to find solid areas where the slush had frozen and they arrived at Charles Bane's house with their shoes almost dry. They walked on to the porch and knocked on the door. Charles Bane opened the door and invited them to enter

Charles Bane was a tall, powerfully built man, with a broad chest and muscular arms, and he looked like a weightlifter. "What can I do for you?" he asked quickly.

"Mr. Bane," Henry began, but he was interrupted by the sound of someone wailing in another room. It was an eerie sound, penetrating and frightening. It went on for several minutes before it subsided into a low, steady sobbing.

"That's my father you hear," Charles Bane explained. "He's dying. Suffering from a coal miner's lung disease and unable to eat or sleep. It seems that one problem is never without the other."

"Then it should not be difficult to explain my position of a strikebreaker," Henry said. "Use your influence to end the coal strike. Get your men to go back to work. You can't afford to be without work. Your father needs all the support he can get from you to buy food and medicine."

"Yes, I know," Charles Bane replied as he lowered his head. "Even when we work, it seems as if we have nothing to show for our efforts. Sometimes it is necessary to make a sacrifice for awhile and fight for what we think is right. I know what my father went through in that damn rotten coal mine. And I remember the daily suffering my mother encountered before she passed away. She used to worry a lot. She often thought what her reaction would be if they brought my father home a corpse. Why, she never knew that when he went to work in the mine if he would come back that evening. It was this sort of worrying that was really hard for her. Now, you're asking me to force the miners back to work. My father, you say, needs food and medicine. He is so sick now, because when I did work I still could not afford to pay for adequate medical services. He will die regardless of whether I work or if I do not. Under the present circumstances I think it is better for all of us to fight for better wages and better working conditions in the mine."

Henry frowned. My own father must have suffered like this, he thought bitterly. Richard Rand is right. Some types of work are just too damn miserable.

"You do want to help your father, Mr. Bane?" Henry asked.

Charles Bane nodded his head. "Of course, I do. How can I?"

"It's simple. Just call off the coal strike. I can give you enough money so that you can send your father to a good hospital where he can get the best medical attention possible." Henry replied.

Charles Bane studied Henry's remarks curiously. "You're trying to bribe me. You're suggesting that I take your money and approach the other miners and say to them; go back into the mine and work your asses off as you did before. Risk your asses and have nothing to show for it. These miners are concerned with the problem of getting hurt. You see, when a miner gets hurt, this preys on the other men's minds. You know damn well that you really have to be careful in work around a mine either on the bottom or at topside. I know that most of the miners were concerned about the welfare of their children, and what would happen to their family if they got killed or injured. I'm not trying to spread a lot of bullshit either. A miner really worries about his work. It's a dreadful thought that is always with him. You see, there are so many damn ways of getting hurt. One of the most dangerous ways of getting hurt is when the roof collapses, and this occurs most often in the summertime. In the summertime, the mine takes in moisture and all the workings are wet. When the weather changes in the autumn, everything gets dry and dusty. Most of the explosions in the mine usually take place in the autumn or winter because the amount of moisture has subsided. Yes sir, there are so many damn ways you can get injured in the mine, from collapsing timbers, from crumbling walls, and from the machinery. I know of many miners who have been killed or injured in the mine. I can remember a fellow miner that had to have one arm and leg amputated and then complications set in his other leg and the doctors had to amputate that one too, and all he could say was, "Oh my poor family and my poor children." I helped to load many men who were injured or killed in the mine on to the meat wagon. The Coal Company really didn't give a shit about them either, and they don't give a damn about us now. It takes a lot of nerve on your part to ask us to go back to work all day in that dangerous mine and come out into the cold hungry and deprived. All we want is enough money to provide a decent life for our families, and the Coal Company to be concerned for our safety and welfare. We don't want our children to grow up with brittle bones or with swollen bellies and legs just like the starving children from some of those African countries. Is it this you are asking of me?"

Henry Shane remained speechless for a moment and then he began to speak softly. "The only thing I'm asking you to do is to have some consideration for the welfare of your own father. I'm not interested in all that other bullshit."

"My father," Charles Bane said. "What about all those other miners that are on the verge of death? I know my own father. He could not tolerate a life bought at such a price. The shame would break his heart. No, Mr. Shane, what you ask of me is a thing I can't do. I'm not about to sell my soul to the Coal Company."

"Then there's no use in my trying to change your mind," Henry snapped back. "Let's get the hell out of here, Richard."

"Don't rush me?" Richard said sharply. Then he reached into his back pocket for his wallet. He fondled the wallet momentarily and came out with some bills. "This money can be used to help your father. Please take it. I swear to God that there are no strings attached. I agree with what you are doing here in Coalport, and I hope you and your followers don't give in to John P. Smith."

Outside in the cold, blustery night, the anger and the shame inside Henry Shane were bitter as the weather itself. Because his own participation in the plot to break the strike was something he could not tolerate, he turned angrily toward Richard.

"That was a damn stupid thing for you to sympathize with Charles Bane! What if John P. Smith finds out?"

"I don't give a fuck!" Richard said forcefully. "Staring at you right now makes me want to vomit."

"Then vomit all over the fucking place if you want to." Henry said, and walked away, leaving Richard dumbfounded.

He did not even look back at Richard. He walked on, his gaze straight forward, his eyes quite, speculative, almost peaceful, sparkling a little from some humorous thought which he shared with God. He came upon a barroom, and pushed open the door. The noise inside subsided the moment he entered, and instantly heard derogatory remarks directed towards him, combined with profanity, until the nods, nudges, gestures had run from patron to patron; and the silence was there before him.

The bartender was pouring beer from a bottle into a mug for a client. He went on pouring, not seeing the beer brim over the edge and gather around the bottom of the mug in a yellowish pool, thickening, spreading until it ran over the side of the bar and dripped on to the floor.

Then Henry Shane began to speak. "It's a damn shame to waste good beer, mister. I hope my presence in this establishment isn't making you nervous. Would you please pour me a shot of whiskey?" He gulped the whiskey, and immediately his facial expressions revealed signs of displeasure.

"I don't want any trouble in here," the bartender said. "I sort of suspected who you were the moment you entered the bar. The miners know why you came to Coalport. I don't even know your name, but I know damn well that you're one of those strikebreakers. If you're not careful, you're going to get your ass blown off."

"There isn't going to be any trouble if I can help it," Henry said softly. "Pour me another shot, and stop your worrying,"

He picked up the shot glass, looking at the whiskey as if it were the most precious thing in the world, his eyes sober, calm, and peaceful. Then he lifted the glass to his lips, and gulped the contents quickly. By the time he set the glass back on the bar, he noticed that the majority of the patrons were leaving the barroom. The bartender left his position from behind the bar and came and stood next to him.

"There's one thing I noticed about you, mister," the bartender said. "You have the balls to come in here knowing damn well that most of the clients are coal miners. Yes, sir, it takes a lot of guts, and you certainly have them. I do admire you for that fact. By the way, what is your name?"

"Henry—Henry Shane from Sinclair," he answered. "And yours."

"Scott Martin," the bartender replied. "Here, let me pour you another drink. It's on the house."

"Thank you. I don't mind if I do." He stood there drinking and talking easily, slowly with the bartender for a long time. The bartender, a former miner, rambled on about the coal mines where the miners were sentenced to a miserable life at hard labor and a grueling, painful existence.

"They were treated with contempt, and if they ever went on strike, they and their families were left to suffer," Scott Martin said. "That meant all of us! Can you see why it is so important for the miners to take a firm stand against the Coal Company? If they don't, the Coal Company will continue to shit all over them again," he exclaimed, pounding his fist on the bar. Scott Martin continued. "The miners would come into this barroom and release their frustrations in the most unusual ways. This barroom, like most barrooms in the Coal Region, was sometimes the scene of grand-scale brawls. It was like war in here. When everything was operating smoothly over at the mine, the miners would come in here every weekend and raise a lot of hell."

Scott Martin recounted enthusiastically the night a drunken man stabbed his best friend to death, and another incident involving broken whiskey bottles and bloody gashes. He left the impression that the barroom now was much calmer than a few years ago.

"Mind you," Scott Martin said. "There were some other crazy things that happened in here other than violence. I can remember the night an attractive woman was standing over in that corner holding the cocks of two of the miners, while a third man was trying to fuck her. Then there was this divorced woman from Clarkstown who would come in here every Saturday night. She loved to suck cock. She would take any miner who wanted a blow job into the back room and charge five dollars for her services. Some miners tried to fuck her, but she always said that she didn't like to fuck, but she certainly didn't mind sucking cocks. The old timers say that there used to be a lot of women like that around here."

"Yeah," Henry said. "We have the same old shit happening in Sinclair."

He began to feel restless and weary. He persuaded the bartender to sell him a fifth of whiskey to take back to his room. He wasn't getting anywhere talking to the bartender. He had more pressing problems confronting him and the bartender knew it. He left the barroom and walked aimlessly down the frozen roadway toward Michael Finley's house.

Later that night, he opened the bottle of whiskey and got drunk. When Richard Rand came into the room, he found Henry sprawled out in a chair, his eyes glazed and his lips sagging.

The next morning Henry took the train to Jaystown to confer with John P. Smith and to recruit scab workers for the mine. When he returned to Coalport, he brought with him some of the filthiest, toughest, and the most vulgar specimens of humanity that Richard Rand had ever seen in a lifetime. He also recruited a number of men to serve as mine guards, every one of them with a rifle, revolver or a riot club.

He accompanied his diversified crew up to the ridge near the portal of the mine where the striking miners had assembled. "We are going in there to dig coal," Henry said. "Those of you who want to join us may do so. If you don't, then I suggest that you get the hell out of here. We don't want any trouble. We just want to go into the mine peacefully. So, please disperse and go home until this problem can be resolved."

The striking miners moved closer to the portal and huddled together under a threatening sky. The wind whipped down in gusts, driving the snow that had fallen earlier against them. One man left the group and ran away towards town. Then, as Henry's scab-workers and guards moved forward, other men could be seen scaling the hillside. From an advantage point he could see them coming, looking like a dark, advancing military column against the surface of the snow.

He ordered his crew to move forward toward the striking miners who stood in the driving snow gusts before the entrance to the mine. The wind seemed to cry. It sounded to him like a lost child wailing for its mother.

They were moving cautiously toward the striking miners when suddenly someone threw a chunk of ice. It struck a mine guard on the face, felling him. Immediately the air was filled with flying debris and the sound of swinging riot clubs against one another reverberated across the hillside.

"Don't fire your weapons!" Henry shouted to the mine guards. "I don't want any bloodshed." Nevertheless, his pleas fell upon deaf ears. He heard the sound of revolver fire, and the loud, sharp cracking of rifles. Then there were several men squirming with pain on the snow-covered ground, and near them pools of blood spreading and steaming in the cold air.

Henry Shane and Richard Rand ran frantically toward the guards who had fired their weapons, but before they could reach them the issue was decided. The striking miners made one desperate surge forward. A youthful miner, swinging a shovel, reached Henry Shane and attempted to hit him across the side of the head, but Henry ducked quickly to avoid the blow.

The guards continued to fire their weapons into the air, and shortly the terrified, striking miners of Coalport ran off, stumbling and falling in the snow on the hillside. Henry, raving like a maniac, ran after the miner who attempted to hit him across the side of the head with a shovel. Richard pursued them, gaining steadily, so that he was close by when the miner entered a dilapidated, clapboard house, with Henry in hot pursuit of the miner.

Inside of the house it was dark and dismal, but Henry put out his hands and caught the miner. His hands encircled the miner's throat, but a woman's pleading voice cried out, "Please, don't hurt him?"

Henry turned the miner loose, and at that moment Richard entered the room. They heard the scrape of a match, and shortly a kerosene lamp spread its smoky, golden glow about the room.

Suddenly Henry felt a slow sickness spreading through out his body, as he saw an old man sitting in a wheelchair and apparently an invalid from sort of mine accident. Henry took a step backward, glancing warily at the miner who still panted from exhaustion, then again his eyes shifted to the old man in the wheelchair.

It was then that Henry turned and drew his right fist back and smashed it with all his force against the wall. Then he hurriedly left the house with Richard hard upon his heels. Outside in the cold, blustery wind, they heard the faint sound of sirens as Coalport gathered up her wounded miners. Henry and Richard walked through the snow toward Michael Finley's house, their heads bowed, their footsteps dragging.

"I'm quitting this fucking job," Henry said. "I've seen enough of this bullshit. We take better care of our fucking pets in this country than we do of our own people. Can you imagine all the miners that can't breathe because their lungs are rotten from coal dust, and all the miners that lost either their arms or legs and the Coal Company not giving one ounce of shit? I listened to what Charles Bane was trying to say about poor wages and unsafe working conditions. The miners were always hungry, always too tired, always driven and even Charles Bane can't do anything to improve the working conditions in the mines because John P. Smith isn't about to cater to them. That rotten, goddamned son of a bitch, I hope he burns in hell! I'm quitting this fucking job! Do you hear me? Quitting, and John P. Smith can shove his money up his ass."

"I hear you, Henry. You're going to quit," Richard said almost in tears now. "What are you going to do now?"

Henry looked at Richard. He was trying to think of something to say, words to express a disgust that was endless. Some jobs, he thought slowly, bitterly are just too damn rotten. And once more he started to think about the insecurity of living in Sinclair. How could he answer Richard Rand's question? So, he simply said, "Oh, I guess I can always re-enlist in the army."

The following morning, Lee Shane joined his brother at breakfast, but though he was puzzled at Henry's sadness and the quiet hurt in his face, he chattered away at a great rate. One thing he said caused Henry to lift his head and stare at him eagerly.

"Don't worry?" Lee said to his brother. "You'll find another job."

Henry put his coffee cup down on the table and looked at him. "I want you to get this thing straight, Lee. I wasn't fired. I quit. I quit a good paying job. Now, I don't have a pot to piss in."

Lee sat across the table studying his brother with his grave, dark eyes wondering what to say next. Shortly he said, "Now Henry, don't worry yourself? I know why you quit that job over in Coalport. I say God bless your tender heart that you did quit."

"You know?" Henry said wonderingly. "I never said a word about it."

"You didn't have to mention it," Lee replied. "It's in the newspaper."

Lee picked up the newspaper and pointed at the headlines that stated, Coal Miners Riot in Coalport. "Here read about it yourself, and afterwards you can tell me how it really was over in Coalport. Maybe, you now realize how some men like John P. Smith will cheat, steal and even resort to bloodshed for the mere sake of acquiring wealth and power, and they lie to cover up the real truth about their lives."

Henry read the account of the story swiftly, then looked up, his eyes fastened upon his brother's face. "Some of those miners were roughed up badly," Henry said quietly. "The blood from their wounds dripped on the snow, steaming in the cold. It wasn't just a struggle. It was violence, pure and simple violence where miners were beaten who tried to defend their simple rights the only way they knew how. I was in on it—and I was so ashamed I decided to quit. As long as I live, I will never forget what I had witnessed in Coalport. The trouble with me is that I won't stay sorry long enough. I'll get involved in something else, and before you know it, I'll do some more damage. Well, that's how it is? Now, I must go out and find another job. Maybe, I would be better off getting the hell out of the Coal Region and re-enlist in the army."

"There's good in you," Lee said. "Don't be down on yourself? I always said as far back as I can remember that you had a lot of compassion. Only you don't seem to give yourself much of a chance. Perhaps this terrible episode that occurred over in Coalport will help change your attitude about life in general."

Henry's brief experience as a strikebreaker in Coalport did not change his attitude. He became depressed, and the constant struggle in attempting to make an appropriate decision as to whether to remain in Sinclair or re-enlist in the army preyed on his mind. Being unemployed and restless, the idleness enabled him to frequent many of the drinking establishments in Sinclair.

One cold and blustery night in mid February he emerged from his room he occupied in his brother's house and walked down the staircase. He was fortunate enough not to encounter his brother or his sister-in-law as he was descending the stairs. They occupied the floor beneath him, and their living room with its usually open door was entered from the bottom of the staircase. Whenever he went out, he was obliged to pass within their view, which often produced a barrage of personal questions embarrassing him and causing him to grit his teeth.

It was not that he deliberately tried to avoid his brother, but that for sometime he had been overwhelmed by stress and anxiety akin to burnout. He had withdrawn from society and isolated himself since his return from Coalport that he was ready to shun not merely his brother, but everyone. His job as a strikebreaker for John P. Smith had once weighed heavily upon him, but of late, he had lost his sensitiveness on that issue.

He had given up most of his daily extracurricular activities. In his own heart, he knew he was not a typical introvert, nevertheless his mind and body were telling him to slow down. Still to be detained by his brother or sister-in-law at the bottom of the stairs, to have to listen to all their inquisitive questions, hear their complaints, and have to make excuses and apologies in return—no, he preferred to descend the staircase without interruptions. The persistent sense of disgust that had begun to overwhelm him this night had now become so intense that he longed to find some escape from the mental anguish. He walked quietly to the closet, and put on his coat.

He opened the door and stepped on to the edge of the snow-covered porch. He stopped. He raised his hands to the top of his shoulder and lifted the collar of his coat. Then he proceeded to pull the knit cap over his ears, took a deep breath and slowly descended the steps, and proceeded towards the Star Tavern.

Ten

It had not been easy for Henry and his brother in Sinclair. As far as it goes, it wasn't easy for anyone who resided in the Coal Region who had to struggle for survival. First his mother died while he was fighting against the Japanese in the Pacific. Exactly two years later, his father passed away, thus putting an end to the contention of doctors that his father would linger on for weeks with the dreaded disease of cancer. All these things just constituted a normal series of events in one's life when he thought about them objectively. With the family estate yet to be settled, he felt that the road before him was still closed to once again render service to his country.

"It's a shame that we have to try to settle the family estate shortly after father's death," Lee said. "As you suggested, Henry, we better discuss it now. Get it straightened out—it's better that way. You aren't a kid anymore, and you have a good head on your shoulders. The war has changed you. You have to get more serious about life. You've got to settle down—make up your mind as to what you want to do. Perhaps it was the war. What you had done in the Pacific was fine. It brought honor and respect to our family and to our town."

"Thanks," Henry said sarcastically. "What I did in the Pacific was a duty to my country. I would do it again if necessary. Get off my back, Lee."

His brother looked at him and quickly said, "Are you sick in the head? I didn't mean it the way you interpreted it. I was just trying to help you find yourself."

"Yes, I'm sick," Henry shouted. "Sick of this town and sick of thinking of Edith Curtis, and regretting not marrying her when I had the opportunity to do so. What the hell kind of future do I have?" He turned to his older brother, and his voice was now calm.

"Don't worry about it, Lee? I don't care about the property. It's worth more to you than it is to me. Anyway, its value isn't what it was when the mines were in full operation. Mom and dad tried to improve it, but we'll never get the money out of it that they had put into it. Besides, I don't care about the place anymore. The worse thing about it, time will deteriorate the house if someone doesn't look after it."

Seeing the expression on Lee's face, he realized he should not have said what he did.

"What the hell kind of attitude is that?" Lee responded. "I was always under the impression that you were a caring and understanding person."

"I can't help it. I'm sick of this place. Take my share if you wish. Pay me what you think my rightful share should be. Hell, Lee, I'll give you my share! Take it as a gift, just give me enough money to get out of town."

"Thinking of re-enlisting in the army? So, that's what the hell is bothering you?"

Henry smiled. "Perhaps it is. Anyway, anything is better than living in this stagnant town. Maybe I shouldn't have come back after the war."

Lee looked at his younger brother. "You're not kidding, Henry? You're very serious about re-enlisting in the army."

"Yes, I am. If I stay here I won't have a pot to piss in. Do you remember the prosperous mines we had around Sinclair when we were kids? So what do we have now? Most of the younger fellows are leaving this town looking for greener pastures. This town is not for me. You are married, and I am not. You have something to keep you here. You have a family and a job, but I have other plans and objectives. If I were married, I'd assume the same attitude, live and work for my family. In the army I can find what I'm looking for. Other fellows have, you know."

"More haven't," Lee said. "Still there is that added risk of being involved in another war and not returning. I know you're capable of taking care of yourself. You proved that you were able to do that. I wish the hell you wouldn't re-enlist. I'll miss you, Henry."

Henry felt the strain of emotion in his brother's voice. Why, he means it, he thought. I'll be damned if he doesn't have a heart after all. Lee shook his head repeatedly.

"No" Henry said. "I've got to re-enlist, Lee. Don't ask me again why, because I don't exactly know. I've just got to re-enlist that's all."

Lee pushed back his black wavy hair and stared at him. "Are you sure you're not running away from something? Maybe Edith Curtis for instance."

Henry looked away from him. Then he turned and looked into his brother's eyes." Yes," He said frankly. Perhaps I am."

"That was a hell of a thing," he mumbled. "Serving your country in the war, and the moment you leave she turns around and marries someone else. I know, I was against the marriage at the time, but she could have waited."

Henry put his hands into his pocket and lowered his head. "She wasn't to blame," He said. "It wasn't all of her fault, anyway. We had some bitter words about my going in to the army the first time. She wanted to marry me before I left and I was against it," He added softly. "It would have been a hell of a thing."

"It wasn't fair for her to take action like that," Lee said.

"Perhaps, we both got all worked up for no reason at all. Anyway, it was mainly my fault because I two-timed her. I started to take Mary Ann Rockingham out on the side. It ended with Edith saying she definitely wouldn't wait for me to return to marry her. I said, "I don't give a damn if you don't wait for me. I didn't think she would have taken me so seriously. I thought she really loved me, and would forgive me for what I had done." Lee looked at the expression on his brother's face. He frowned. Cleared his throat and said, "Maybe she has changed her mind about you."

Henry didn't answer him. There was a long period of silence and then Lee began to speak. "Look, Henry. There has been some awful rumors about you and Edith."

"What the hell kind of rumors?" He asked with surprise in his voice. "What kind of rumors?"

"Now, don't get all worked up, Henry. I only asked you because I was concerned. After all, I don't like the reputation of our family ruined because of some ridiculous rumor. I know you better than that, Henry."

"You mean to say some of those bastards are saying that I am seeing Edith on the sly."

"Yes, I can see why some of those people are saying it," Lee replied. "Edith isn't getting along with Andy. She makes no bones about it either."

"I'm crazy about her—and perhaps that shows too," Henry remarked. "I can truthfully say that all those sons of bitches are wrong, they're wrong." He looked at Lee and grinned. "Really, I don't know if I can put it into words. Perhaps what I mean to say is that what went on before with Edith and me was a true love, but its finished. I can look back on it—those wonderful days that we spent together. I would prefer those happy days remain in my mind as they were. Now anything we may do, anything at all would kind of mar those wonderful moments. She married Andy, and this I must learn to accept, regardless of how I feel about her."

"I'm glad that all those damn rumors aren't true. You must still be careful. That Andy Curtis is a revengeful man. He is the type of man that isn't going to let anyone step on his toes, let alone someone fooling around with his wife."

"I wouldn't want to get mixed up with him," Henry said. "I have no reason to fight him. I've got to save my fighting spirit for the army. Any man, who wants to fight with me from now on, I'm going to ignore him, just as a matter of principle."

"People might call you a coward," Lee replied.

"What the hell do I care? Fighting is useless and won't solve anything, Lee."

"Perhaps we'd better be getting back into the house," Lee suggested.

"Not me, I'm going to drive over to the Curtis house and say goodbye to Edith, and inform Andy that there is no truth to all the rumors about my involvement with Edith."

"You're what!" Lee said. "Andy will be home at this hour of the day."

"I want him to be. I'm going in broad daylight. Since, as you said, those damn people are talking, this would be the best approach. Isn't it?"

Lee stood there startled. "All right. Be careful, and don't get involved, Henry?"

It was a pleasant, warm evening. Andy Curtis sat on the front porch with his wife, Edith. He was reading the newspaper and resting after the evening meal. Occasionally he would look up and stare at his wife in a confused manner. There were certain rumors he had heard at the mine about his wife that bothered him. Many thoughts began to fall in place within his mind. What if those rumors were true? What if she and Henry Shane have been seeing each other? One thing bothered him. When? He had been at home with his wife every night and in her company away from home. It was impossible, but the rumors continued to spread. Perhaps Henry was responsible for spreading the rumors to get even with Edith, Andy thought. I should mention it to him. Perhaps— during the day. I'm a mine superintendent. I have to supervise the miners over at Mine 35, and all that damn Henry Shane would have to do is come over here and play up to my wife while I'm at work. Maybe, this is the reason why my wife is so frigid towards me at night."

Andy Curtis was infuriated. In response to his thinking, he heard the screeching wheels of an automobile coming around the corner. "Some nut," he said to Edith, "is sure in a hell of a hurry."

Edith didn't utter a word. She was often like that now, moody or falling into a stupor. The automobile came down the street and came to a sudden halt in front of the their house.

"It's that damn Henry Shane," Andy moaned. "That's damn fine of him to come by."

"Well, if it isn't Henry," Edith said with a thrill in her voice. "Nobody else would be crazy enough to drive like that."

Andy stared at her. "He also comes here while I'm working at the mine. Tell me, Edith, does he?"

"No," she said. "This is the first time he has ever been here, Andy."

"Don't lie to me?" Andy shouted. "Then why in the hell all the rumors."

"I'm not lying. I'm not going to lie to you or anyone else. I'm not a fool to lie to you, but I could care less about what you think. Do you think that if Henry had been seeing me, and if he wanted me to go away with him, I'd be here now, Andy?"

"You whore, Edith!" He said, but Henry was there now standing on the porch. Andy stood up. His face was red with rage. "Henry Shane," He said. "It appears to me that you and I have a bone to pick. I have been hearing a lot of rumors about you whoring around with my wife."

"I know," Henry said quietly. "That's the reason I am here, Andy. I heard a lot about it myself from my brother. Rumors are always like that. The persons that are suppose to be involved are the last ones to hear about them."

"What the hell do you have to say for yourself?"

Henry looked at him. "I came over to get this thing straightened out for any embarrassment I may have caused you and Edith. It never did occur to me, Andy, that I'd have to tell you it's not true about Edith and me. I see I do. That surprises me. All right, then, since you appear to have your doubts, I'll tell you once and for all. It isn't true, Andy, not a damn word of it."

"How do I know that? What about the days I am over at the mine? What real proof do I have?"

Henry's lips tightened. "My honest to goodness word. The word of a gentleman."

"He doesn't know what a gentleman is," Edith said sarcastically. "He hasn't the slightest idea of what the word gentleman means."

"That wasn't a very nice thing to say, Edith. It appears that you two are not getting along together."

"A husband deserves a little more respect than that."

"Don't make me laugh, Henry? Respect, oh my God."

Henry looked from one of them to the other. "It looks like I came at the wrong time. Most of all, I came to say goodbye to you, Edith. I'm going back into the army. For many reasons. I'll honestly admit that you're one of them. All those days, while I was in the Pacific, I thought about you, feeling sorry for the way I two-timed you. So Andy, you won't have to hear all those damn people talk about my whoring around with your wife. Perhaps it is a good thing I am re-enlisting."

Edith stood there with a lump in her throat. I won't cry, she thought. I won't! "Yes," she managed to say, "I believe it's the best thing, Henry."

"Goodbye, Andy," He said and put forth his hand.

Andy stood there in astonishment, looking down at his out stretched hand. Then he grasped it.

Edith wondered if he had taken Henry's hand because he didn't give a damn anymore, or because it was just a matter of formality. One or the other, she knew he really didn't want to.

"So long, Edith," He replied.

With tears in her eyes, she watched him get into his car and drive away. She walked to the gate and leaned against it, still watching the car as it moved out of sight. Inwardly she had a feeling of disappointment. She expected Henry to kiss her. Now she knew it might be all over. What could she do to win his affection? She turned and walked slowly up the steps to the porch. Without saying a word to her husband, she entered the house and slammed the door.

Andy merely looked at the closed door with a feeling of anxiety. He knew that there was something going on between his wife and Henry Shane. Why didn't she speak to him after Henry's departure? Why didn't she return to her chair on the porch? Perhaps she feared what he was going to say. An urge came upon him to slap her face, bring her to her senses. Their marriage had been somewhat successful until Henry returned from the war, he thought. Then suddenly Edith began to change. She became irritable and frigid, and maybe, he once thought, all the whispering about town was not just gossip. Edith had borne him no child. If she had, her attentions would remain at home instead of running or sitting about without anything to do. Andy had tried to get her pregnant, but to no avail.

It was dark when Andy re-entered the house. His mother greeted him in the parlor. "I thought you might want some coffee before retiring, Andy?" she said. "I have a pot of coffee on the stove now."

"No, thank you," Andy replied. "Where is Edith?"

"She told me she was going to bed," his mother responded. This was not surprising to Andy, for he knew Edith was hiding something from him. He went to the bathroom, took a shower, and then went directly to the refrigerator in the kitchen for a can of beer. He sat at the kitchen table, his mother sitting directly across from him, her arms resting on the table. When Henry was a bachelor, and when his mother was the only one in the house with him, she often sat there, as she did now, and they had engaged in interesting discussions. They were never futile discussions. His mother never sat there in that manner unless she had something to say that was important. All the rumors had come to her ears. Andy had the impression that all the women folk who resided in Sinclair communicated with each other, and perhaps his mother knew a great deal more about Edith's relationship with Henry Shane than what he did.

Prior to his marriage to Edith, his mother often warned him, sometimes critically, about Edith's restless behavior. Like many elderly people in Sinclair, she lived by the traditions, morals and values of the foreign stock. At the beginning, she mentioned to Andy, casually, that it would be a mistake to marry a restless girl like Edith. Eventually, she learned to accept the fact that Andy loved Edith.

Most of their discussions had ceased when Andy got married. The elderly Mrs. Curtis seldom sat at the kitchen table, and never discussed issues in the presence of Edith. As head of the household, Edith had replaced her, and she knew it. Nevertheless, Edith had often begged and pleaded with Andy to buy another house, a house she could call her own, and a house located in another section of town, but Andy had refused to move. He found it difficult to offend his mother by permitting her to live alone in a big house. Edith showed no resentment or ill feelings toward Andy after his refusal to move. She displayed no emotional out bursts. She accepted this as Andy's will.

Andy hesitated, Then he looked at his mother expectantly. He knew she was going to tell him something soon, something she thought he ought to know.

"Do you think Edith has been well?" She asked suddenly. Andy knew it was customary for her to inquire about Edith's well being.

"Yes, I believe she is well," Andy replied. "Why do you ask?" There was a deep silence in the room. His mother spoke again. When she did, it was with words of warning that had annoyed him so often before.

"I think you better keep a close eye on Edith." She said.

"Why do you ask?" Andy demanded.

"Your wife might become unfaithful to you. I saw the way she looked at Henry Shane when he was here this evening." Again she withdrew into silence. Neither her eyes or her lips revealed her inner feelings, yet Andy felt uneasy and knew she was about to say more.

Then she spoke softly. "There's no telling what Edith may do. She runs about the town freely while you are at work. Why do you permit her to do that? What can you expect from a pretty and young wife?"

Andy placed the can of beer on the table and suddenly realized he could not finish it. He understood perfectly well what his mother was trying to say. She could only mean one thing. Edith is seeing another man, and more than likely it is Henry Shane. He realized it was difficult for his mother to inform him of this heart breaking news. He knew she had spoken these words because of the general feelings of suspicion and gossip that was spreading throughout Sinclair. He believed it unwise to question his mother any further. It had already been an embarrassing situation for her.

Could this man possibly be Henry Shane, or is it some other man? He thought. Henry was here this evening and assured him that he was not seeing Edith. If it is not Henry, then who might this other man be? He looked at his mother who was still sitting at the table. She would not have remained seated unless she had other things on her mind.

"Imagine," she said. "Your wife running around with another man right under your nose." She stood, as she began to depart from the kitchen, she suddenly turned and said, "Be brave, my son. Don't do anything that you might regret?" Then she walked slowly up the steps to her bedroom.

His mother's words could mean that Edith had been seeing Henry Shane in secret after his return from the war, or at least someone had carried the tale and did an effective job of convincing others. At first it appeared to be a ridiculous rumor. Why would Edith be seeing a man who had hurt her terribly? Andy had always assumed that Henry Shane had removed himself from her life several years ago.

Now he began to worry, trying to remember when Edith may have been in the company of Henry. Suddenly he remembered them dancing together several months ago at the Polish Club, shortly after his return from the war, and their lengthy conversation at the bar, and how he had taken her hand into his. Perhaps they had agreed to see each other, he thought. Then the rumors started, for in Sinclair no one could escape an illicit encounter or a secret romance, and it was well known that Henry Shane had once been in love with Edith. It was possible then, he thought, that Henry might still have a power over Edith. No, there would be nothing impossible about it if they came together again.

What he needed now was something to relieve his mind and to calm his nerves. He went to the cupboard and reached for a bottle of whiskey and a glass. He carried them into the parlor, and poured a double shot. Then he sat down on the couch, and put the bottle on the floor, drank the whiskey quickly, feeling the alcohol burning in his stomach, feeling a welcoming relief throughout his body that seemed to make him think more clearly.

In times of distress he had often resorted to drinking. He could drink and drink until he would find himself in an unrealistic world. So now he was telling himself that what had happened in his relationship with Edith was only what could have happened to any man in a similar position. He had been aware of Henry Shane as a possible rival ever since he returned to Sinclair. What would another man do if he suspected his wife of infidelity? In this case he might warn Henry Shane or even kill him, but although a man must fight to defend his honor, such action would be insane. Perhaps, he thought, it would be wise to ignore the matter and continue to live as he had done in the past, or merely tell Edith to get the hell out of the house. After all, adultery was grounds for a divorce, and many other men had found themselves confronted with the problem of an unfaithful wife.

Andy poured another double shot of whiskey and took a deep breath. He was not yet inebriated, but it seemed to him that now his mind was free, that his mood was carrying him away from this heartbreaking pain. If now he was going to live up to his stature as a worthy man, it was necessary for him to commit himself to some definite course of action. He knew he might have failed in his relationship with Edith. She loved me in the beginning, he thought. Or did she? Edith was an extraordinary woman, passionate and always wanting to satisfy her beastly desire. Recently, she had been very frigid. Thinking of Henry Shane, and how long Edith had gone steady with him in the past, he began to feel the bitterness of betrayal on the part of his wife. A strain of violence flowed through his veins, and he tightened his fists. Anger and hatred invaded his mind, this sudden feeling that he had not known since the time of the "Great Coal Strike." Briefly it crowded his mind, obstructing his thinking. It didn't last long for Andy was too much of a realist to be dominated by emotions of anger and hatred.

He came to his senses, It was not Henry Shane he had to be concerned about at this crucial moment, but Edith. What could be done? How could he approach her? What will her reaction be? What he had to face now was the possibility that Edith no longer needed him. He remembered how she had entered his life several years ago, as a broken hearted girl, standing on the porch and responding to his friendly, neighborly gestures. She had needed a man to provide her with security, someone to comfort her in a time of despair. With her cleverness, and the thought of seeking revenge on Henry Shane for his refusal to marry her, she seized him as the ideal bait to fulfill her ambition. He remembered the night she had placed her head upon his shoulder, weeping, and suddenly permitting him to kiss her with ease. Then feeling her passionate urge coming upon her, begging him to carry out the act of flaming desire. Then later, he thought, how she had persuaded him to go to Colby, Maryland to elope.

Maybe, Henry Shane will leave Sinclair and re-enlist in the army, he thought. He said he would, but maybe he said that to get himself off the hook. Now Andy, feeling tired and weary didn't want to remember anymore. He arose from the couch and proceeded up the stairs to the bedroom. He had forgotten that Edith was in bed. As he opened the door, she was startled, and quickly sat up. Then she slowly got out of bed, and he merely stared at her. It was a painful stare that revealed many things. No wonder, Andy thought, that other men would be interested in Edith. She is beautiful. Her face was flushed, and her long, black hair dangled freely over her shoulder, and her lips were the color of cherry wine. She had on the usual transparent negligee that she always liked to wear, revealing the outline of her body.

She looked at him, and they stood for a long, silent period of time, staring at each other without uttering a word. Her face had changed from a flush of red to a pale white, and then her eyelashes began to quiver, and he could see tears flowing freely down her cheeks.

"I didn't want to!" She screamed. "I didn't know you would find out! It wasn't with Henry Shane. Honest to God, Andy, it wasn't!"

"Then Henry was telling me the truth. He wasn't seeing you, and to think I almost got the urge to kill him. If it wasn't Henry Shane, then who in the hell was it?"

"I can't tell you, Andy! I can't! I can't!" She wept.

"How in the hell did the rumors start involving you with Henry Shane?" He asked bitterly. "I should have known better, and to think I almost permitted my emotions to get the best of me. All this time I was suspicious of him, practically condemned him because of your peculiar behavior and the malicious rumors. Mother knew about you running around with this guy, didn't she? Tell me, Edith! Tell me the truth!"

"Yes, yes, yes!" She screamed. "I told her all about it after she became suspicious. I begged and pleaded with her not to tell you. Oh, Andy, what have I done?"

Andy became enraged, and fiercely grasped Edith's throat. "Tell me who the son of a bitch is that you're whoring around with!"

"You're hurting me, Andy, please, please don't?" Then with his right hand, he slapped her across the face.

"I feel sorry for you," he said chokingly. Earlier he had gone into the bedroom to comfort her, and perhaps forgive her, but now it was an unbearable moment, and he could never put himself up to it.

Weeping, Edith covered her face with her hands, and then ran and threw herself on to the bed. Then she heard the bedroom door close.

Andy stood outside of the bedroom. H e could hear her crying. He could not bear to re-enter. He wondered whether he would ever again sleep in the same bedroom with her. He walked slowly down the steps and into the parlor. He picked up the whiskey bottle and glass and poured another double shot of whiskey. He then stretched out on the couch. Now he wanted to rest.

During the next few days that followed, Andy worked diligently at Mine 35. After his return from the mine, he would sit at the supper table, just as usual, except that nothing now was the same as it had been. His mother sat motionlessly, with sealed lips, whenever he questioned her about Edith's secret lover. Andy knew that she would never divulge the identity of the mystery man, for she feared that her son would commit murder. In his relationship with Edith, he had

The Wailing Wind

contemplated divorce, but disregarded the idea in favor of making her life miserable. He often thought that a divorce would be an easy way out for her, and this is what she had been hoping for, so that she could be free to re-marry at her discretion.

It seemed with the passing of time, a deeper barrier came between them, and that it pushed them further and further apart. Once they had enjoyed each other's companionship, but now they had turned in different directions. They often saw compassion in each other's eyes, and one felt sorry for the other, and that was all they knew. What had become between them seemed like an act of fate that they could not prevent.

Several weeks later, the entire community was shocked when they heard of the death of Andy's mother. Rumors once again continued to spread like fire throughout Sinclair. It was rumored that she had died from a broken heart, died from the constant pressures imposed upon her by the infidelity of her daughter-in-law, but Andy did not place the blame of his mother's death upon Edith. He knew that she had been ill for sometime, suffering from high blood pressure.

Now Andy went back to a life of solitude, such as he had lived in the years prior to his marriage to Edith. Sometimes before retiring for the night, he would go out into the coolness of the air and walk about the peaceful and quiet streets of the sleeping town. The sky with its bright stars, and the moon hanging low over the broad Allegheny Mountains gave him a feeling of tranquillity that soothed his pain and confused mind.

Occasionally he sat on the front porch, and now and then he had a visitor, usually an acquaintance on his way back home from a local bar. These visitors he always welcomed, for there was no one in his household, since his mother's death, he could tell his troubles to, but Andy still remained the hospitable man he had always been.

One night, John sterling was a welcomed visitor, for he had not visited his house for some time. John Sterling was well respected in the realms of Sinclair, where respect was an important aspect of one's life. He had proven himself to be a good citizen and a hard worker. He was a happy go lucky type of man who enjoyed drinking beer, therefore he was well known by all the bartenders and male citizenry that frequented the taprooms in Sinclair. He had been one of Andy's best friends, but since Andy's marriage to Edith their close friendship had somewhat declined. They no longer sat at a bar during their leisure time, talking and sharing their pitchers of beer. In fact they were never together except at the brief wedding ceremony in Colby, Maryland where John stood as Andy's best man, and once during a local mine union picnic. Andy on many occasions attempted to invite him to the house for dinner, but he flatly refused because he didn't particular care for Edith.

Like all "coal crackers," he had a sense of pride. John Sterling would not have stopped to see Andy unless he had something very important on his mind, and Andy knew that. John Sterling knew all about Andy's problems with Edith, as did almost everyone in Sinclair, and he evidently stopped to see Andy to extend his sympathy, or to pass on to him some worth while information. When John came up on to the porch, Andy immediately stood and greeted him with a firm handshake.

"It's been a hell of a long time since I've seen you," Andy said in an elated tone.

"You know how it is, Andy. After you got married I didn't want to impose upon you, so I started to associate with a different crowd. Since I'm not married I can afford to do that."

"Really good to see you, boy, really good to see you. How about a beer, John?"

"Okay, Andy, I'll have a cold one with you." Andy went into the house, and shortly returned with several bottles of beer.

John Sterling was the type of man who knew when to keep his mouth shut and how to be diplomatic when he did speak. Only once did he mention Edith by name, a woman he never liked, but always acknowledged her beauty, chiefly because he knew the type of woman she was, and now sitting there listening to Andy discuss his problems, he was overcome with compassion.

Andy knew that John Sterling didn't just stop by to have a beer. "Why did you stop and see me, John?" Andy asked suddenly.

John changed his sitting position, reached into his pocket for his cigarettes, lit one, and took a deep drag, exhaled, coughed and began to talk. "I don't know whether I should tell you what I really have on my mind, but if its going to be of any help or comfort to you, I'm willing to stick my neck out. You know, Andy, you and me had been good friends, so what I'm going to say has nothing to do with our former relationship. Most of all, don't get angry at me for telling you."

"Tell me what!" Andy said excitingly.

"You know, all those damn rumors about your wife whoring around with that soldier boy, Henry Shane—that was just a lot of bullshit."

"Hell, I know that," Andy quickly responded. "Edith broke down and told me it wasn't Henry Shane she was having an affair with, but she never did tell me who it really was. To this day I don't have the slightest idea as to why, and how she was able to run around with another man right under my nose. My mother knew, I'm almost sure, but she never revealed the man's identity for fear I might do something drastic, and to think, she went to her grave with sealed lips. I'll admit, I thought sure as hell it was Henry Shane she was running around with, and so did everyone else."

"I can understand a mother's reasoning, but I think she should have told you," John said.

"Yeah, maybe she should have," Andy said in a whisper. "If she would have told me, then I know I would have killed the son of a bitch."

"It was a shame how some of those damn people tried to get Henry Shane involved, but you can't blame them, it's your damn wife that is to blame. She must have told other people how she always felt about Henry Shane—and to boot—she married you while she was still basically in love with him. As long as he remained away from Sinclair, she forgot about him momentarily, and as soon as he came back from the war, that old love spark ignited in her heart. You might as well face reality, Andy. Even though Edith may have been running around on you, it's Henry Shane that she really loves, not you or anybody else. People in this town aren't so dumb. They notice things like that. Oh, sure, Edith may have told you she loved you, and appeared to be affectionate during your early days of courtship and marriage, and catered to your wishes—but women in general are funny creatures just like the weather. I'm willing to bet that Henry Shane still has a crush on your wife."

"Yeah, I know it," Andy said sadly. "Why in the hell was I fool enough to get involved with Edith? Now life—her life—is going to be miserable. I made up my mind some time ago not to file for a divorce, and if she wants a divorce, she's going to have to fight like hell to get one."

"Suppose you have the right to feel as you do about your wife," John said. "If she was my wife, I'd have kicked her the hell out of the house long ago. Anyway, since you already know it wasn't Henry Shane who was whoring around with your wife on the sly, I'm going to tell you the name of the man who is involved with Edith."

Andy, startled by the words that came forth from John Sterling's mouth, quickly stood up in shock and uttered: "You're what!"

"I told you not to get all shook up. Sit down and let me finish what I have to say to you."

"Tell me! Tell me! Who was it?"

"Look, Andy, sit down, try to be calm and I'll tell you." Andy sat down on the chair and tried to be calm as John Sterling had suggested.

"Remember Robert Heim, your friend who said that he was going away to Philadelphia last summer to enter the house construction business, well he is the son of a bitch who is running around with Edith. Everybody thought he left the area, and this is why you never suspected him. Imagine, leaving and then coming back just to see Edith, your wife."

"How did you find out, John?" Andy said with tears trickling down his cheeks.

"Does anyone else know?"

"I don't believe so, Andy. I never mentioned it to anyone else, but you know how things are in a small town. Anyway, I felt that you should know so that you can get the pain out of your system. It was just a matter of coincidence that I found out."

"Please, John, go right ahead and tell me all about it."

"One day, when I had to take the truck over to Pellersville for machine parts, I was driving down this one way street and happened by chance to see this attractive woman standing near the entrance to the Hotel Warner. I thought I was seeing things, and I said to myself, that couldn't possibly be Edith Curtis. What in the hell would she be doing way over here in Pellersville, and you know Pellersville is quite a distance from Sinclair. So I decided to drive around the block to make sure my eyes were not deceiving me. To my surprise, it was Edith, and to make it more shocking, she greeted Robert Heim, and they walked arm in arm into the hotel. Now I don't know what happened after they went into the hotel together, but I have a pretty damn good idea. When I first saw them enter the hotel together, I decided to hang around and wait awhile, so I parked the truck a short distance from the hotel where I had a good view of the entrance. Hell oh mighty, I ended up waiting about two hours before they came out, and Robert Heim kissed Edith before she got into her car. Then he turned and went back into the hotel."

"Then my wife was stepping out on me while I was at work—and to think with Robert Heim. Now that you brought his name into the picture, I'm beginning to fit the pieces together. Last summer he showed a great interest in Edith, and I overlooked it because I didn't want to appear if I was a jealous husband. No wonder he told me that Edith was a wonderful woman."

"I'm sorry that I was compelled to tell you these things about your wife, Andy, but hearing all about the untrue tales regarding Henry Shane whoring around with your wife sort of got me down, so I thought it best that you know it was Robert Heim. Now I'm not defending Henry Shane either, because I know damn well how Edith feels about him, and I personally feel if he had a chance to do what Robert Heim did, he would do the same damn thing."

Andy made no comment and both of them were silent for a long time. Then Andy remarked at last. "I guess Robert Heim couldn't stay away from Edith. My wife always had a bad habit of playing up to other men."

Eleven

Andy had not seen Robert Heim since his return to the area, and he began to wonder whether he had truly carried out his plan to enter the house construction business. A few nights later he got the answer to that question. While sitting on the front porch, a blue Cadillac stopped in front of the house. A man got out of the car, and proceeded up the walk to the porch. It was a man he recognized immediately to be Robert Heim. Andy was not at all surprised to see Robert standing on the porch nervous and embarrassed. He suspected that Robert would come sooner or later, perhaps to plead with him to give Edith a divorce. So Andy merely pretended that he had no knowledge of Robert's relationship with Edith, and tried to refrain from going into an explosive out burst of aggressive hostility. He merely greeted him in the same manner as he had done in the past. "How are you doing?" Andy said. "Come and sit down?" Nervously Robert sat down, stretched out his legs, and immediately reached for his cigarettes. After lighting a cigarette and taking a few puffs, he seemed to be more relaxed. Andy noticed that his face was now more haggard than the previous times he had seen him. Perhaps, Andy thought, Robert was going through hell in his business ventures or displeased and ashamed with the affair he carried out with Edith.

Robert's expressions were chilling, and his present look did not reveal the pleasant signs of good humor and charm that Andy had so often seen before. Robert had been one of his friends, but since John Sterling had informed him of Robert's immoral conduct, the idea of friendship was supplanted with that of hatred. A feeling that Robert was worse than Judas, a feeling that crept into Andy's veins that almost carried him to a point of resorting to murder. Now Andy watched him with a feeling of pain and also of suspense. What, he wondered, would Robert say to him now? He knew Robert was bound to say something about Edith. He was a man for whom action was an important necessity.

"Andy, I don't really know how to begin, so I'll make a long story short. I feel like a heel because I have hurt you, but I do love your wife, and I can't help it."

Andy remained calm and uttered, "There were many men that loved Edith, but they loved her in a different way."

"That may be true," Robert responded, "but I love her so much that I want to marry her regardless of the consequences, and she told me that she had stopped loving you for some time now. I knew that you and Edith haven't been getting along together, and she wants a divorce."

"Wants a divorce!" Andy said sharply after remaining cool and calm since Robert Heim's arrival. "No damn wonder she wants a divorce, you're the sneaky son of a bitch that put her up to it in the first place. Pretending you were going to leave the area for good, then turning around and coming back. Not to Jaystown or Sinclair mind you, but to Pellersville. You had it all figured out, didn't you? You had it all planned last summer, made arrangements to see Edith at the Hotel Warner while I was at work. How often did you see her, Heim? Once, ten times or perhaps it was more often."

"All right," Robert said. "I did see her often, but it wasn't my idea. It was Edith who made the suggestion. She thought of the Hotel Warner over in Pellersville, and to meet me there every Wednesday. She wanted to be with me, and often mentioned the possibilities of asking you for a divorce. I can't help it if she has stopped loving you. That's your damn problem, not mine. If you would have treated her like a man is suppose to treat a woman, then this may not have happened."

"Why? Why, did it have to be you, Robert? My friend, a person I always had faith and confidence in—betraying me."

"Love is a strange thing," Robert said.

The Wailing Wind

"You're a fool, Robert if you think Edith loves you. She may no longer love me, but she really doesn't love you either."

"What the hell do you mean?"

"It's Henry Shane she loves," Andy replied.

With a puzzled look on his face, Robert said, "Who in the hell is Henry Shane?"

"That's your problem now. You find out for yourself who Henry Shane is. Why don't you ask Edith? I'm sure she knows more about him than I do."

Robert Heim lowered his head and nodded. "You knew that for some time."

"Yeah, I did, but he never tried to lure my wife away from me after he returned from the war. He wasn't a sneaky bastard like you were, and to think everybody was accusing him of whoring around with my wife, and all this time it was you, Heim. Let's face it, you're a rotten son of a bitch. Further more, as far as a divorce is concerned, there's not going to be one if I can help it. So you might as well forget it, pal. I'm not going to file for a divorce to please you or anyone else. So, you might as well get the hell out of here before I kill you."

"You're still not going to stop me from seeing Edith. I love her and I think she loves me regardless of what you said about Henry Shane."

Now Andy, overcome with rage, quickly turned to Robert and gripped his shirt, lifted him from the chair, and threw a smashing blow with his fist directly into his face. He fell on the porch, with blood running profusely from his nose. Stunned, he got to his feet slowly, and Andy gripped him with both hands and shook him violently. Now remembering vividly the words of his mother, "don't do anything drastic that you might regret, Andy," he released Robert and shouted. "Get the hell out of here, and I don't want to see your face again!" Robert Heim walked slowly from the porch, mumbled a few curse words, and headed for his car, got in, and sped quickly away from the scene.

Andy stood on the porch for a few minutes, puzzled, disturbed and still breathing heavily from the skirmish he had with Robert Heim. There was something ruthless about Heim, he thought. Staking a claim to my wife, pitting him against the possibilities of being murdered. Andy wondered what plan or hope Robert could have in acquiring Edith. He suspected that Robert was making a foolish and desperate gesture because he merely was in a desperate mood, that he had been moved by a passionate desire to put his charm to the test, to bring his inward feelings to a climax. There might be something insane and dangerous in that because Robert Heim had created a situation that definitely could lead to murder. What would happen, Andy continued to wonder, if Robert was fooling around with another man's wife instead of with Edith. Andy knew how patient and humble he was as a man. Did Heim know all of this? Had he taken this factor into consideration, thinking that he would give up Edith without a fight after he found out about her infidelity? Did Robert really believe that he would sit still and not defy him? These were not the most desirable qualities for dealing with a problem of this nature. It seemed to him that Robert had not anticipated the possible odds against him—in any case he did not figure that there was another contender in Edith's life—Henry Shane.

Standing there thinking of the deceitful Robert Heim, who obviously had underestimated him, he knew that Robert was a doomed man. Now Andy began to envisage, driving over to the Hotel Warner in Pellersville, armed with a rifle. He could envisage the pleading gestures of his wife. " Don't shoot, don't shoot, Andy?" Then there was a burst of fire. Even better, he imagined the cracking sounds of a double shot in the stillness of the hotel room where Edith and Robert Heim released their inner feelings of passion. Robert, the man who betrayed him—the man who had been his friend, and had become his enemy, and the one who had caused him great pain and suffering, now eliminated.

Andy shook his head, then looked up into the sky laden with bright stars. He was trying to see the entire picture clearly in his mind. He knew it was wrong to think of violence and murder, but he believed it was a situation that contained the making of a serious outcome. It appeared to him that Robert Heim had deliberately caused the problem, tried to lure Edith away from him. Why? Andy's pride was involved. He had come to feel that he had failed as a man, as a husband. So what could he do? Should he give up Edith and move away from Sinclair, completely out of her life. No, he couldn't do that. The very thought of giving into Edith and Robert would be intolerable. He would have to reconsider and inquire and consult with some of his friends.

Just how great and immediate were the possibilities of murder. Perhaps at that very moment, he had overstressed this easy approach of eliminating Robert from the picture. He had heard of several similar cases where the men were informed to stay away from somebody else's wife, and that these so called lovers had found it wise to heed the warning or face the possibilities of being completely eliminated from life.

Lee Shane looked worried when he came home from work. He of course had heard about Robert Heim's affair with Edith Curtis. Everybody in town was talking about it.

"Andy will kill him," He said directly to his brother, Henry. "If he doesn't stop seeing Edith, some of Andy's friends might even kill him."

"He should have told Robert Heim to stay the hell away," Henry said.

" Maybe, Andy did give him a warning in his own little way," Lee said. "Robert just didn't take heed to the warning."

Henry shook his head looking deeply distressed. "The worst part of it is that people here in Sinclair know how I feel about Edith."

"Yeah, that's what I have been trying to tell you for some time, and I wanted you to stay away from her. Now, don't you go and get involved in their problems?"

Henry didn't try to answer. After Lee left him, he sat thinking for a long time. Lee is right. This is Andy's problem. Why should I get involved? When a man faces a problem he has to analyze all of his values and beliefs. He has to look at the facts and then do what he thinks is right. To Henry, violence had always been somewhat of an evil, he feared it, and he had declined on many occasions to engage in open conflict with other men. So now, he thought, in all probability was violence in the making. If murder was committed, and he had done nothing to prevent it, was not he then against his own principles. He knew he could intervene and be of some assistance, for Edith more than likely would listen to what he had to say. He could inform her to stay away from Robert Heim, and then tell Robert that she no longer was interested in him.

For days Henry felt that something had to happen, something that would bring this situation to a climax. Perhaps this incident could answer all the questions that had been troubling him since his return from the war. How involved are Edith and Robert? If this man loved her, and she loved him, then they had a right to be together, then Andy should file for a divorce. This situation could also put his feelings for Edith to a test. It definitely would put Edith to a test.

Henry was now considering how to proceed. He knew he had to consult his best friend, Richard Rand, the person to whom he turned to for advice on many other occasions.

This time Richard came to him. He came late one evening, and for the first time in all the years that he had known him, Richard was emotionally disturbed. "Did you hear about Edith Curtis and Robert Heim?"

"Yes, I heard about it," Henry replied.

"That could mean a hell of a lot of trouble." Richard exclaimed. "Andy is liable to kill Robert Heim. I almost feel obligated to get in touch with Robert and warn him. I don't want to interfere, and it may not do any good if I do. Why in the hell did he get involved with her?"

"He won't listen to you anyway, Richard. I can almost assure you of that."

Richard stood looking at Henry for a moment, evidently bewildered. "You don't appear to be all shook up," Richard suddenly remarked.

"Yeah, maybe I should be shook up. Still this could mean trouble for me since Andy suspects me of loving Edith. I'm not in favor of seeing someone killed not even Andy Curtis. Perhaps we can to something to prevent violence."

"Maybe you're right, but what?" Richard demanded.

"If we should talk to Edith, maybe she will give up her foolish venture, and then we'll go and try to explain the situation to Andy."

"You know damn well that Andy and Edith can't possibly be happy together after what has happened," Richard said. "You also know that Robert is in love with Edith, and he's not the type of man that's going to give up on the idea very easily."

"I've heard that story before," Henry said.

"What are you doing, feeling sorry for yourself? Maybe you're thinking of cutting in yourself some how or the other." Richard said bluntly.

Henry looked at Richard with anger in his eyes.

"Well, am I right or wrong!" Richard exclaimed. "After all I heard all the gossip about you and Edith before, and honestly, Henry, I felt you were a fool to get involved with Edith. Since the word is out that Robert Heim is the guilty one, why get involved again. Look, I know you still have a crush on Edith, but you're different than Robert. He is nothing but an agitator, and I wish to hell he never would have come back to this area."

"Me too," Henry said with a smile. "But Robert Heim is an educated man, and has plenty of money, and he does know how to give all the women a big line of shit—so Edith was fool enough to fall for all the bullshit."

"Do you figure on forgetting about Edith?" Richard asked.

"I want you to contact Edith first and then Robert," Henry suggested.

"You want me to find out how Edith feels about you first," Richard said. "Is that it?"

"Yeah, that's it. I've thought about it ever since I heard about Edith running around with Robert. I can't possibly believe that she loves him. If she is truly in love with him, then I'll know where I stand."

Richard sat quietly for a long moment, and it was a moment of suspense for Henry. He knew he could not go directly to Edith with the question concerning his status; therefore he had to rely on his friend to do so. He was greatly relieved when Richard opened his mouth and began to speak. "Okay, I'll do it for you, Henry."

"I knew you wouldn't refuse. I know you can tell, if anyone can, whether she really loves Robert Heim or how I stand with her."

"All right, I'll see Edith as soon as possible," Richard promised. "I'm sure she'll tell me how she feels about Robert. As for him, he's going to be a dead goose if Andy gets a hold of him again. I'll talk to Robert too."

"Now don't forget, try and get in touch with them as soon as possible," Henry said firmly.

"As soon as I get some information on their status, I'll call you on the phone. If I'm going to be of any help in this case there's no time to lose."

After Richard departed, Henry sat for a long time thinking of his former relationship with Edith prior to his initial departure from Sinclair. He felt sure that if he had married her, she would have remained faithful to him. Then unexpectedly, his mind turned away from the thoughts of Edith, and he once again thought of his re-enlistment into the army. He knew once again there would be the annoying pain of departure, and then perhaps never returning to Sinclair. If he had remained, he would have dreaded what lay before him, a life of economical struggle for survival.

Late in the afternoon of the following day, Henry received a telephone call from Richard, informing him that Edith Curtis would talk to him about her relationship with Robert Heim, and that he was to meet her at the Roxy Club in Jaystown at eight o'clock that night.

Upon receiving the message, Henry sat down feeling somewhat relieved. Now everything was arranged, he thought. It remained only

The Wailing Wind

for him to see Edith and tell her how he still felt about her. That was all, but he knew it was not going to be easy to face her. Pain and confusion would still prevail, and possibly a scene filled with tears in that last moment, in what probably may be the last time he would ever see her again—unless Andy would give her a divorce. How could he tell her that he still loved her? Yet, knowing that she may have fallen in love with Robert Heim, there was a good possibility that she may rebuke him completely in favor of Robert Heim. It appeared to him now that Edith was the only woman in Sinclair he feared, because she could hurt him by merely stating that she did not love him like many people thought she did. He knew he had to see Edith, knew he never would have another opportunity to confer with her privately.

That evening he shaved, took a shower, and dressed in his best suit. He glared at himself in the mirror, and remembered another time, a few years ago when he dressed for a special occasion, the first time he went to Edith's house at the edge of Sinclair, the night he discovered his potential as a man instead of an inferior youth. As he looked into the mirror, he also recognized the figure before him to be mature, and his face still showing the signs of weariness from participation in the war. It was a more serious face now.

Henry departed for the Roxy club in Jaystown, and upon arriving met Edith in the parking lot. They entered the club, and Edith immediately said that Richard Rand had asked her to be there at eight o'clock to discuss some important issues.

Edith seemed a little puzzled, as she sat there, but she asked no questions. She only wondered how much Henry knew about her relationship with Robert Heim. She looked worried and somewhat more disturbed than he had seen her before, and then she spoke softly in her charming way.

"Why did you want to see me?" She asked as a smile appeared on her face.

"My orders finally came through recently informing me to report to Fort George, and I may not see you again for a long time."

"Is that all?" Edith said in a whisper.

"No. I also wanted to tell you how I always felt about you, Edith. You know damn well I still love you."

"That's too bad," she said as she looked at him sadly. At that moment the waiter arrived at their table.

"Do you care to order something to eat, or do you prefer to have something to drink first?"

"Both," Henry replied. "What do you wish to order, Edith?"

"The same as you," She responded.

After eating they sat there looking at each other, reminiscent of the days they had gone steady, drinking to a point where they were almost inebriated. Henry did most of the talking, aware that he had to be diplomatic in keeping the conversation from stirring into an emotional outburst. He felt it was better not to mention Robert Heim at this particular moment. It would not do to let anything interrupt the conversation between them, to let any discussion break the pleasant surface of their evening together. He had to create the proper atmosphere and then bring the matter before her prior to their departure. So he told her how he thought about her while he was in the Pacific, and about the reasons for re-enlisting in the army. He implied that not being able to have her was what had made it necessary for him to leave Sinclair. Edith was pleased to hear that he regretted not marrying her when he had the chance. Talking somehow gave him a feeling of relief. He found himself full of romantic words, almost saying them to a point where he had the urge of sweeping Edith into his arms. He knew he had penetrated her feelings. That in itself was an accomplishment in his favor. He could tell by her eyes that she was trying to communicate with him her inner thoughts, and also that everything he said interested her greatly, that she was pleased to be in his company. In particular she seemed to be stirred about the things he said regarding their companionship in the past.

She placed her hand beneath her chin and gazed at the ceiling as if she was in a trance. "I wonder how it would have been if I would have married you, Henry."

He felt like a man trying to evade an important question. He

The Wailing Wind

cleared his throat and said,

"I couldn't tell you." He hurried on to the most important question of the night. "Do you love Robert Heim?" He asked bluntly. "I've heard all kind of stories that you do love him, and that you have been seeing him secretly for sometime."

She looked at him as though she had anticipated this question. "Not really," she said. "Not in the same way that I loved you. Oh, Robert has been very nice to me, but he still acts like a college boy that never grew up—but he has been better to me than what Andy has been."

"I feel sorry for Andy," Henry said. "I don't think it was very nice of you to deceive him the way you did."

"What are you talking about?" she replied hastily. "You pulled the same dirty trick on me. You have no damn room to talk."

"Yes, I did, but remember, I wasn't married to you, and I was still free to make a decision. In your case you entered into a marriage contract with Andy, and you violated it."

"So," she said as she lowered her head to look at her watch.

"Is that all you're going to say about it?" He asked smartly.

She did not answer his question but merely said, "I think we better go, Henry."

Now he realized that his encounter with Edith Curtis was about to end, and he quickly attempted to search for new words. "When I leave you, Edith, I want you to believe me that I will always be thinking of you, no matter what you did, or who you were running around with. Please be careful. There is a lot of talk around Sinclair about Andy killing Robert Heim and even you, if he finds out that you are seeing him again. For your sake, I sure as hell wish that you would leave Sinclair before something drastic happens—like murder."

They stood and walked towards the door, opened it and shortly they were standing side by side in the dark parking lot. They stood for a moment facing each other, searching for appropriate words to say and neither of them able to speak. Then he took her by both arms and kissed her lightly on the cheek, and he knew at once that he made a serious mistake because she trembled, and she knew he felt the tremor. He released her and opened the door of her car, hoping she would not say anything, but as he closed the door, she quickly rolled down the window.

"I have loved you ever since the first time I met you," she said. "I will always love you, no matter what I may have done." She began to cry, and he tried to help by comforting her. "I have loved," she went on crying, "but I know I will never be able to have you, never, never!"

He knew this to be true. She had lost him before, and she has lost him now.

"I am happy and honored to hear that you still love me," he said flatly. "At least I am able to depart from Sinclair knowing that you do."

She started her car, and smiled at him, and then proceeded toward the main highway for Sinclair. He stood watching her car as it sped away, and then it was lost in the darkness.

After leaving the Roxy Club late that night, he drove directly to Richard Rand's house in Sinclair. Everything in the house was dark, and he knew that his friend had retired for the night. He walked on to the porch and knocked on the door. A light went on in the house, and he heard footsteps on the stairs, and shortly the door opened.

"Come in," Richard said as he rubbed his eyes.

"Did you get to see Robert Heim?" Henry asked quickly.

"Yeah I did, but that guy is really a smart ass. He told me that he loves Edith, and that Edith loves him. He also told me he wasn't going to stop seeing her either."

"That's strange. Edith didn't leave me with that impression," Henry said sharply. "What else did he say when you told him he better get his ass out of this area?"

"He just laughed and said that he wasn't going to leave—but then I told him that Andy was going to kill him—then he appeared to be somewhat concerned," Richard chuckled. "You know, I was right. Edith and Robert do have something in common with each other, bound together for some reasons I quite can't explain. I'm certain that they both will suffer once he stops seeing her."

"Did you bid him a farewell?" Henry asked.

"What the hell else could I do? He went along with my proposal that it would be better for him to stay away from Andy, at least I think he did."

"Did he say anything about Edith?" Henry asked. "Yeah, he wanted to run away with her. Take her to Philadelphia. He said he really loved her. I was surprised to hear that Edith was willing to go along with his plan."

"Then Edith was giving me a line of bullshit tonight at the Roxy Club. Why would she lie to me? I can't imagine Edith telling me one thing and then doing another. She told me that she loved me."

"Yeah," Richard remarked. "She may love you, but she may think that she'll never be able to get you anyway—so she found her ticket out of Sinclair. You often said there was nothing here in this town anymore and that the future looked dismal. Maybe she feels the same way as you do. What the hell kind of life would she have if she was to remain with Andy in that big house."

"Yes, you might have a good point, Richard."

"This is tough for you to take, Henry, but why should you be concerned. You're leaving Sinclair to go back into the army. Edith always remained out of your reach since her marriage to Andy. Now you're going to have to forget all about her. She'll have to work out her own problems and so will Andy."

"You have said enough. I don't want to hear anymore about Edith."

"Now you're talking sense," Richard agreed. "Let's not talk about your leaving Sinclair. You know how much I'll miss you. After all, who will I talk with now. We have been the best of friends, and we could say anything to each other without getting overly disturbed."

"Yes, we have been. I hope our friendship will be an everlasting one—no matter where I go or what may happen."

"You know, I'm envious of you for the decision you have made to leave Sinclair," Richard said. "I wish I had the courage to do what you're doing. Believe me, going back into the army is not a bad idea at that. Sure, you may have lost something you loved, but now you can go out into the world in search of new adventures."

Henry smiled. "This going away is not really a lot of fun. But it's not a new experience for me. When I was drafted during the war, it sort of hit me hard thinking of leaving Sinclair, and perhaps not ever returning. I painfully gave up Edith and departed, thinking it was the wise thing for me not to marry her at the time. But it wasn't."

"Perhaps what you are saying is true," Richard said. "Still you're not the same person who left here several years ago. It's different now, the war is over, but what lies before you I can not foresee."

"Neither can I. When I left for the army the first time, I only wanted to leave it, to come back to Sinclair, back to what I loved. Now I'm anxious to return to the army."

"When are you leaving, Henry?"

"Day after tomorrow. Well, I'd better be going, so that you can get back to bed."

"Don't worry about that? Here, sit down and we'll have a couple of cold beers. I'm not sleepy now, so you might as well stay for awhile."

So they sat and drank beer, just as they had often done in the past. When Henry rose and extended his hand, he saw tears in Richard's eyes.

"Don't forget to come back to Sinclair once in awhile," Richard said quietly. "It's not going to be the same around here without you."

"That I promise you," Henry told him.

"Don't wait too damn long–good luck Henry?"

Most of the next day, Henry spent working diligently among his personal belongings, amazed at how much he had accumulated in a relatively short period of time. Most of it he wanted to get rid of. He burned unimportant papers and books in the furnace, and gave most of his clothes to his brother. Only a few things he packed so he could travel lightly. This trip was not going to be filled with fear and anxiety

The Wailing Wind

as it had been several years ago when he was drafted. Now there was no war, and this time it was of his own choosing to depart from the realms of Sinclair. He knew that he was doing the only thing possible to escape the tension and frustrations of daily living in an environment where he had no conceivable future if he would have remained.

On the morning prior to his departure, he approached his brother. "Lee, would you be kind enough to drive me to the train station?"

"Of course," Lee said slowly. "I'll even drive you to the airport over in Jaystown if you want me to."

"No, thank you. I don't like the idea of waving goodbye from an airplane. I'd prefer to take the train—somehow it's different—just like leaving Sinclair for a few days. Besides I like the view from the train better."

"Maybe it'll be sometime before we see you again, Henry," Lee said touchingly.

"It's not as bad as all of that. I'll have leave coming, so when I'm able to, I'll be back to see you and your family. I'm going to try for an assignment in Japan, and if it does come through, I'll still get to see you before I go overseas."

They were silent looking at each other, then Henry spoke. "Oh by the way, since I still have some time before I depart, how about driving me out to the cemetery so I can pay my last respect to mom and dad."

"Sure," Lee said. "I think it's a fine thing for you to have remembered. Let's go."

Upon arriving at the cemetery, Lee parked his car and waited. Henry walked through Saint Anthony's Cemetery, going up the old familiar path that winded around the tombstones, to the place where his parents were laid to rest. They had buried his father there along side of his mother, in a clearing around which a few cedars stood. He stood beside the grave of his mother first with his hands folded, and then there was a deep sadness within his heart, tears flowed gently down his cheeks. Without understanding why, and in spite of his emotion and weariness, he felt that one of his great moments had come. The thought of his mother resting in peace, and the thought of her dwelling in the House of the Lord suddenly seemed to overcome him as no thing had overcome him before. He turned his head, half expecting to see some heavenly vision before him—but there was nothing to see and nothing to be heard, only something wonderful he had felt within his soul. He bowed his head and prayed. Slowly he raised his head and looked directly at the tombstone, stained from mud that had splattered upon it from falling rains, and inscribed were the words: "In loving memory of our mother, Katherine Shane, born March 24, 1895, died January 27, 1945."

Then he took a few steps towards his father's grave, seeing before him a clean headstone, for it had been more recently placed at the head of the grave. He knelt beside it. He tried to pray, but could not think of an appropriate prayer. So he knelt there a long time in silence. When he rose, a deep quiet entered in to him. Then he uttered, "God have mercy on your souls, mother and father. The only thing I can do now is pray for your eternal salvation." He blessed himself, and proceeded down the winding path to the dirt road where the car was parked. Lee got out of the car and stood beside him. They looked down at the quiet and peaceful valley. None of the joys that once flooded Henry's mind enveloped him now. The view of his birthplace did not comfort him, the broad Allegheny Mountains gave him no strength. Henry Shane was a different man at this moment, and his weariness was enhanced by a sense of non-accomplishment that hurt him almost as much as his hopelessness. He thought of Edith Curtis—doing nothing constructive—nothing that counted with her life. Andy Curtis, though he had lost Edith, had so much love and joy before he lost her to a disturber, now had to unwillingly forfeit everything that Edith had meant to him. At this very moment the ghost of her love also annoyed him painfully. Henry was not only overcome with painful, reminiscing thoughts, but with failure.

His trance was interrupted by his brother's words. "I better drive you to the station, Henry. The train is due to arrive soon."

"All right, Lee. Let's go."

When they arrived at the station, they had ample time to engage in brotherly conversation. "I guess this is goodbye, Lee," Henry said and put out his hand. But Lee instead of clasping his hand embraced his brother. He held him like that for a few seconds. Then he released him and as he stepped back he saw Edith Curtis coming on to the platform. Surprisingly he asked, "Isn't that Edith Curtis over there—she sure is looking this way? I didn't know she was taking this train, but she can't be, she doesn't have any luggage." Henry turned and saw Edith standing in the midst of the small crowd. She had a package in her hand, and he could see her hands moving nervously over it. Then the rumble of the train could be heard coming towards the station and Henry quickly said to his brother, "Please get my things on to the train. I'll be there shortly."

Then he was gone, walking towards Edith Curtis. There were people standing on the train platform that they both knew. It was always like that in Sinclair when the train came in. Henry passed them by without uttering a word of acknowledgement, without recognizing them or knowing who they were there. Now he stood before Edith and was silent.

She spoke. "I had to come and bid you a farewell. The last time you left Sinclair to go into the army, I didn't. I regretted it all this time. I know, all the people are going to talk about me again, but I don't care. They know I was involved with you some time ago, and also with Robert Heim in some way or the other, so it makes no difference to me. Let them see, let them know the truth."

The package she was holding in her hand fell, and she quickly reached down and picked it up. "Here," she said. "I want you to have this."

"What is it?" Henry asked.

"It's a picture of me. I want you to have it so that you can always remember me, and the good and pleasant moments we had together before my marriage to Andy."

The people on the train platform nudged each other, the whispers suddenly dying among them, all of them turning, staring in disbelief at what Edith Curtis was about to do, at a thing that a married woman should not have been doing.

"Edith," he said.

"Henry," she whispered. "Oh, Henry, I'm not a very strong woman, and I'm not a good woman. Don't think for a minute that I am, but I do love you with all my heart and soul, regardless of what anyone might say. You must tell me before you leave, that you're happy that I do. Oh Henry."

"I should have married you a long time ago, Edith. It would have been the right thing for me to do. Now, I can't help it. You've got to tell me the truth. Is it me you love, or is it Robert Heim?"

She looked into his eyes and said, "I told you the other night, it's you I really love and always will." She came up on tiptoe, put her arms around him, and her mouth on his was wild with passion. She held on to him trembling all over. He tightened his hold on her, and then their lips parted.

"If I only could be your wife—then I could be leaving with you."

"Yes, it should have been that way," Henry said softly. "Whenever I think of Sinclair, I'll think of you Edith, and the beautiful Allegheny Mountains—covered with trees and laden with the wild, roaming game, its beauty and tranquillity. I'll think of the past days when we strolled along the banks of the Stonycreek River, and most of all, I'll think of the bandstand in the middle of town where I first saw you. These are the things I want to remember for the rest of my life—do you understand?"

"Yes, darling, I understand."

"Henry," Lee suddenly yelled. "You better get on the train, it's about to leave."

"All right!" he called back. Putting his arms around Edith, bending, he found her lips again. Then he dropped his arms. "So long, Edith," he said.

She did not answer him. She merely brought her hands up to his face, and gently ran her fingers over his cheeks as though to memorize his facial features. Then she turned and walked slowly away with her head lowered, wiping away the tears from her eyes.

Twelve

Henry Shane left Sinclair to begin his second tour of duty in the army, and was assigned to a military unit at Fort George, Georgia. The area, in which his unit set up headquarters was an old army training sight commonly referred to in military circles as Tent City, located approximately nine miles from Hallensburg in Sakahoochee County.

The tents were laid out in neat rows beside the pine trees. They occupied fields that were not exactly classified as farmland, not quite wilderness, but that casual mixture of the two that seemed to be the greatest charm of the southern landscape.

Behind the rows of the officer's tents and the barren fields, a small valley deep in grass provided pasture for the cattle living out their short life on the hillside. Beyond this point, the scenic terrain continued in the same serenity, an unlimited number of pine trees, hills and streams.

It had been raining for several days when he arrived. The puddles of water that had refused to soak into the ground had trickled underneath the sides of the tents and gathered in new puddles around the cots. Morning had succeeded morning with gloomy skies. Sometimes in the late afternoon the sun came out for a brief moment, like a blessing, and made the large pine trees glitter. Then the sun set and immediately the stars were concealed. Night followed night without stars and created a dismal scene.

A small contingency of officers and enlisted men preceded the regiment to Fort George to lay out the camp area. Lieutenant John Harris had been one of the leaders. So as soon as the regiment had arrived, he was sought and questioned.

"What the hell do you do around here for entertainment?" was the first question asked by a young enlisted man.

"There my friend," said Lieutenant Harris who enjoyed the role of a spokesman. "You have a pertinent question."

"It's simple, lieutenant," volunteered another enlisted man. "You go to the movies at the base theater. The following day they show a new movie, so you go again. That's all there is to it."

"What's in Hallensburg besides theaters and restaurants?" Another asked.

Lieutenant Harris counted off on his fingers. "A whorehouse, beer and whiskey every night." He laughed and continued to speak. "There are many stores, service stations and churches of many denominations. After that you have the wide open country."

"How far is Kern City?" some one wanted to know.

"About thirty minutes—buses every two hours." someone replied.

"That's for me," many said in unison.

"One three day pass a month," continued Sergeant James Miller. "Then you have Federal City that is a nice little community. At Lake Edward you can rent a boat and go rowing or fishing on the lake. If you don't like any of those things, you can stay on the base and play with your dick or go raving mad."

Everybody chuckled. One of the men asked, "Is there a dancehall?"

"Now you ask," said another man.

"Five miles from here," said Lieutenant Harris. "The Nest. Two floors, a bar and a dance floor. A dance is held there every Friday and Saturday night, and that touches on the heart of the problem. The women, who keep you from going off your rocker."

Everybody laughed again. "What about them?" somebody asked. "You can get a three day pass," said Sergeant Miller. "You can go to Hallensburg. There are an assorted number of females of different resistances who live there. My recommendation is for you to stay the hell away from them. If you want girls, The Nest will oblige or you can walk the streets and take your pick, that is if you don't mind waking up some morning with a rotten prick in your hand."

On an ordinary morning there at Fort George they were awakened by the sound of the bugle—a hair raising sound that brought everybody out of a deep sleep. The sergeant had roll call, and then they marched around the drill area for awhile.

Breakfast usually was comprised of scrambled eggs, a strip of flabby bacon, cereal, coffee and toast. For variety the cooks omitted the scrambled eggs and had SOS. On Sundays there were pancakes or French toast, and on rare occasions fried sausage.

Everybody was on military duty by 0730. By 0800, the open fields and unobstructed grounds in the area were in use by the platoons for calisthenics. At 0900, the well-conditioned officers took their men for forty-five minute runs along a secondary road leading to Hallensburg. Rest periods of ten minutes divided the hours. If the timeless clouds burst, everyone crowded into one of the dark barracks for a lecture on map reading or the military tactics of the squad, while the rain beat steadfastly upon the galvanized covered roof.

On many occasions the men engaged in war activities while the regular officers with considerable experience observed the strategic action attentively.

The latrines in the training area were all outdoors, and the shower facilities were antiquated. There never was enough hot water, and often the showers were permeated with a damp and musty aroma. When toilet articles were needed and other essentials, a half ass PX was set up for business in a Quonset hut.

To escape the monotony, most of the men went to a nearby town at night. The southern girls were friendly and no one worried much about an intimate relationship. From time to time a prostitute from Hallensburg was caught in one of the tents or in an isolated area behind the encampment, but those incidents failed to disrupt the boredom that existed at the site. While at Fort George, Henry Shane tried desperately to forget about Edith Curtis. He knew he was unable to have Edith as his wife. Now he felt he had to make up for lost time. He no longer was concerned about moral principles and began to drink heavily and went on weekend sprees. All these evils came upon him in a relatively short period of time following his re-enlistment into the army. The type of establishment, the type of girl, the type of environment all played roles in the shaping of his destiny.

While at Fort George, he was introduced to a few buxom, sexy southern girls, anyone of them would have made a good wife. There was one girl in particular that he was found of. She was a simple and pleasant girl with blue eyes and dimples on her cheeks. Her mouth was wide and she always smiled at him. She had long silky, blond hair that fell over her shoulders. She had a figure that was attractive to most men. Most of all, Henry knew that she liked him, and Faye Cooper made it known that she did. Henry also knew that Faye was the right girl for him at the moment. He dated her frequently, but never attempted to lure her into an illicit affair.

One night he drove her home from the dance at the Nest, a nightspot that was a short distance from Fort George. He ached to ask for her love, but he couldn't put himself up to it. Although he had affairs with other women while at Fort George, he refused to seduce her because of his great respect for her, but most of all, his constant remembrance of Edith Curtis.

One night, while he was in the company of Faye Cooper, he noticed the tears flowing gently in a slow, thin stream from her eyes.

"Faye," he said. "You're crying. What's the matter, honey?"

"You," she said. "You're not affectionate with me, like you are with the other girls. I know you'll leave me, and I won't ever see you again. I know you really don't love me, but it hurts me that you don't." Then she turned and kissed him. She did not have many opportunities to kiss him, but she kissed him with sincerity.

Henry looked at her. "Faye," he whispered. "I do love you."

"Don't say anything?" She said and kissed him again with passion. She sat there in the car gazing at the moon, and then quickly put her head upon his shoulder. The tears were still coming forth from her eyes. "There's some other girl in your life," she said. "Isn't there?"

"Yes," he said frankly. "It's a rotten love, Faye. She is married and is living in Pennsylvania."

"Why don't you go back to her? Go back and get cleared up with her. Get her out of your mind for good. Then come back to Fort George. I'll be waiting for you. Tell her it's all over, and that you're not interested in a woman who already has been married."

Edith's face appeared in his mind. He knew that it would be difficult for him to inform Edith he no longer cared for her. It was unfair to mislead Faye. It was far from the truth.

" Marry me now," he said suddenly. "Faye, I love you enough that we can get married without mentioning it to Edith. I need you as much as you need me."

"No," she shouted." I'm not going to marry you now and regret it. I'm not going to share you with another woman. When you're angry with me, you'll always be thinking of her. When she is completely out of your life, come back and then I'll marry you."

"All right," Henry said. He knew that Faye was serious.

One early morning, out side the base post office at Fort George, Henry stood holding two letters, debating which one he should open first, Lee's or Edith's. He had no eagerness, but only a far off feeling of despair, mingled with a confused reluctance to alleviate himself of anymore disturbance of his already broken heart. Edith lived at a distance. It would be days, if ever, before he would see her again. He prayed that her letter would not arouse his emotions and cry out to him, reawakening the pain of lust. He pondered. Finally he opened the letter from his brother first.

"You certainly started something in Sinclair. Perhaps I better warn you long before you decide to come back here on leave. That was a damn foolish thing for you to have kissed Edith Curtis while standing on the train platform prior to your departure for the army. Everybody is talking about it. Most of the people feel certain you were fooling around with Andy's wife."

Henry continued to read. "Now that Andy is separated from Edith, the people in Sinclair think you were responsible for interfering with their marriage that caused Edith to violate her marriage vows. Andy has left Sinclair and is staying with the Clark's over in Twin Forks. It was a hell of a thing to happen. Now it seems that you are caught between Edith and Robert Heim. You told me that you wouldn't interfere with their marriage, and I believed you. Still that didn't give you the right to kiss her in front of all those people while standing on the train platform."

"Goddamn it," Henry said bitterly. "How in the hell things can be distorted to suit one's own narrow minded thinking? Sure as hell beats me."

He turned again to the letter. The rest of the contents were not important, inquiries as to how he liked the army, questions about meager details, life in the army, information about Lee's wife and children, complaints about how difficult it was to make ends meet in Sinclair.

He folded the letter and put it back into the envelope. Slowly he opened the other letter. An aroma of perfume coming forth from its contents, persisting through all those days since he kissed Edith while standing on the train platform back in Sinclair.

"My beloved," he read. "If it seems to you that I, a wife of another man, call you beloved, I'm sorry. I can't help it. You are my beloved, and the only man I have ever truly loved, or will love. I am writing this letter with a great passion for you. When you come home on leave, I hope to see you again, and continue where we left off at the station." Henry smiled and was delighted to read about her interest in him. Shortly, he became disturbed when he read further.

"As you probably were informed, Andy has left me and is living over at Twin Forks. As you knew, our marriage had been a failure after the first year. Your departure from Sinclair and enlistment into the army has given Andy a sense of relief. I know your brother has informed you of the scandal I caused by my unwisely behavior the day you left. Andy was wild with rage, but I calmed him. I convinced him that while it was true I loved you, there never was anything between us after my marriage to him. I even lied to him that it was your fault, not mine that the rumors were spread throughout town. Yes, I am a passionate woman, but being without you has made me so. I was a fool not to have married you in the first place, but for other than what has happened between you and me, I firmly believe we would have been good for each other. I understand why you haven't written to me. As you know, there is no longer the danger that your letters might fall into the wrong hands. Please write to me. Tell me about yourself. What you are thinking. Tell me that you love me. I long for you Henry. Oh, Henry, please come and see me when you come back to Sinclair."

Henry's hands trembling, folded the letter and put it into his pocket. The passion within him was very deep and quiet. He knew suddenly that he would have to go to Sinclair. He no longer was concerned about the rumors. His only thought now was of Edith. He wasted little time in putting in a request for a leave to return to Sinclair.

Thirteen

It was a bright morning in early July and the sun's ray, peering into the bedroom, fell on Ruth Shane's face. Her husband deliberated that she was growing lovelier and lovelier with each passing month. Just now, however, her face showed signs of slight discontent. He had noticed this expression in the past only when she spoke of the dullness of Sinclair. It had left her all together since the first glorious years if their marriage, but was now returning more and more frequently and far more plainly defined than Lee liked it to be.

"What's troubling you, Ruth?"

"Oh, not much, except that I'm wishing that I'll soon have the baby," Ruth replied.

Lee smiled, stood and walked over to the bed where Ruth was sitting. "Don't worry, Ruth, everything will be all right? It's not like having your first child. After all, this is your third pregnancy, and you should be rather use to the strain by now."

"It's easy for a man to say those things. He doesn't have to go through all the agony," Ruth remarked.

"What is really bothering you, Ruth?"

"Well, Lee, I'm concerned about whether we are going to have financial difficulties trying to rear three children."

"Don't worry about things like that now? We managed to get along with the other two children, and I'm damn sure we'll be able to manage with three."

"Maybe you're right. So I'll have to cut back to make ends meet—that is if I can. I really don't spend much money on myself compared to the other married women. We don't go out and socialize like we ought to, or even go to the theater."

"I know, Ruth. It doesn't seem fair to you, but we do have two wonderful children and another one on the way. I didn't realize how fortunate we really are, and we've had a good marriage, and have been somewhat comfortable and happy at that. It's a lot more than I ever expected, especially living and working in a place like Sinclair. We have a little money saved in the bank. I guess we will have to save it for a rainy day."

Something about Lee's tone seemed to annoy Ruth, so she decided that it was best for her to change the subject immediately.

"We had a letter from your brother Henry yesterday afternoon. I meant to tell you at supper last evening, but with all the commotion it slipped my mind. It seems as though Henry is bored waiting for his assignment to be approved to be relocated to an overseas installation. Anyway, he is getting a leave and is coming back to Sinclair to spend a few days with us."

Lee hesitated. "He certainly changed his opinion in a hurry about Sinclair. It seems that he told me that he didn't care if he ever came back to this town. On the other hand, it seems as if I'm obligated to be a good host. After all, he did turn over his share of the property to us."

"Of course," Ruth remarked. "If Henry is coming to Sinclair, we must be nice to him, after all he is your brother."

"When did he say he was coming?" Lee asked.

"He said he'd probably be here sometime within the next two weeks according to what he wrote in his letter."

Henry arrived in Sinclair a week later and Lee with his usual fair-mindedness admitted that his brother's disposition had changed considerably. He appeared to be reserved, but somewhat disturbed. It was evident that he had something on his mind. "What seems to be troubling you," Lee asked.

"Oh nothing really. I'm just exhausted. Why do you ask?"

"It appears to me that you have changed considerably since you left Sinclair to go into the army."

Henry smiled and merely said, "Not really, Lee."

Henry and Lee Shane engaged in a lengthy conversation. Lee spoke of the expectancy of their third child and the economic conditions in Sinclair while Henry elaborated on his exploits in the army. In the meantime, Ruth was trying to be a good hostess and prepared and served a delicious supper for all of them.

During the course of the supper, Lee asked, "Do you have anything special planned for tonight, Henry? If not, why don't we go to the movies? It will give us an opportunity to go out together, and besides Ruth would like that since she doesn't get out much anymore. We'll get Ruth's sister to watch the children."

"Yes, of course, I'd enjoy going to the movies," Henry replied. "First of all, if you don't mind, I'd like to go and visit Edith. I haven't seen her since the day at the railroad station when I was departing to go into the army. How is Edith doing anyway?"

Lee looked at Ruth. There was a deep silence. Then Ruth at last began to speak. "Edith has been getting along fine. Why she's been having some wonderful times from what we heard. She is still seeing Robert Heim, and we understand that he moved back in with his parents over at Jaystown."

"Moved back to Jaystown!" Henry exclaimed.

"Yeah," Lee said. "He was staying at the Hotel Warner over in Pellersville for awhile, but now he's back in Jaystown"

"I thought he was going away to Philadelphia," Henry replied.

"Yeah, that's what we thought, but I guess he has some business ventures going for him in Jaystown," Lee said.

"Yes, Edith has been doing all right for herself," Ruth intervened. "The Heim's have one of the finest houses in Jaystown, and they know many prominent people residing in this area. They always engage in many social activities and do a lot of entertaining in their house. Why we're only lowly mining folks compared to Edith. The Heim's have taken her on several trips to different parts of the country since you left, Henry. Miami, New York, and just recently she returned from Denver, Colorado. She sure has been around these past few months. I'll tell you that. She has been doing all right for herself. I don't believe she'll shun Robert Heim now that Andy has left her. Edith is a pretty woman, but she's also clever and knows what she wants out of life. Can you imagine she's driving a new Cadillac now? Edith must have a damn good bank account, but folks around here are saying that the Heim's have helped pay for it."

"She has plenty of time to rest and enjoy herself since her separation from Andy," Lee added. "You know, after Andy found out that Edith was running around with Robert Heim, he never considered getting a divorce, but merely tried to make Edith's life miserable. The first week after Andy's departure, she didn't even come out of her house—then the Heim's drove over in their big car and drove her off to Florida, I'd say that Robert Heim is looking out for her welfare."

"Looking out for her welfare!" Ruth exclaimed. "He's with her all the time now—she even stays over at the Heim's most of the time. She might as well marry him. It's strange though, but Andy still refused to grant Edith a divorce. I don't understand why he is willing to put up with all of Edith's bullshit."

"I'm glad she is happy now," Henry commented. "Still, I want to see her anyway. I can't stop thinking about her."

"Well, let's go to the movies tonight, and you can go and visit Edith tomorrow," Lee said.

Immediately after supper, they drove to Jaystown, and were fortunate to find a parking place near the theater. They purchased their tickets and were led by an usher to their seats. Before the lights went out, Lee gave Henry a sudden nudge with his elbow.

"Look," He whispered, "in the reserve section, the sixth row."

Henry turned his head in the direction indicated. He saw an elderly man and woman, and two younger men and two younger women. They were all well dressed. At the first glance, that was all Henry recognized. Then it suddenly dawned on him that the two elderly people were Mr. and Mrs. Heim, one of the younger men Robert Heim, one of the other women was his sister and the other Edith Curtis, whom he had not seen in several months.

The theater seemed to be swaying, then everything blurred. Henry shut his eyes. When he opened them, the row in the reserved section was filled. A few other people had joined the Heim's. One couple sat to the left of them and two more near Edith adding to the congestion. Shirley Heim was entirely absorbed in the man with the glasses, but Edith seemed more interested in Robert Heim. He kept leaning towards her and whispering in her ear, as she appeared to listen attentively.

"That dark haired fellow with glasses is Shirley Heim's companion, Gerald Smith, the son of John P. Smith the owner of the J. P. Smith Steel Company," Ruth said. "They didn't intend to be married until sometime in August, but since he's going to Europe on a special assignment they've put the wedding ahead. Edith is going to be the maid of honor in the wedding. Looks like Edith is interested in Robert Heim. She isn't the only woman who is crazy about him, though I guess she has the best chance of marrying him. I suppose they'll all go over to the Wedgwood to wine and dance after the movie."

"I thought Mr. and Mrs. Heim were extremely sophisticated to come to this theater, but they certainly don't mind stepping down," Henry said.

"Why don't you go and speak to Edith after the movies?" Lee asked.

"Barge into her, just like that! I'm not courageous enough to do something like that," Henry replied.

"Well, don't get upset!" Lee exclaimed. "I just thought you wanted to see her."

"I wouldn't know what to say to her anyway," Henry remarked.

Lee attempted to change the subject, but Henry was already disturbed and remained in such a bad mood for the remainder of the night.

The following day, immediately after lunch, Henry borrowed his brother's car and set out for Jaystown. He was determined to visit Edith at the Heim Estate. Eventually he arrived in Jaystown to find himself parking in front of a flower shop. He hesitated a moment, then entered the shop and approached a clerk.

"I want to buy some flowers. I want something for a lovely lady."

"Certainly, sir," the clerk responded. "The red roses cost two dollars a piece. Or these carnations that just came in are very attractive. They cost fifteen dollars for the smaller arrangement and twenty dollars for the larger arrangement."

Comparative wealth in Sinclair meant poverty in Jaystown Henry had discovered. He reached into his pocket for his wallet. "Not any like those, I'm afraid," Henry replied.

The clerk appeared to lose interest.

"I don't see any type of an arrangement that I particularly care for," Henry said.

"I can make you a special floral arrangement with an assortment of flowers," replied the clerk.

"Yes, that's what I want." When Henry paid for the arrangement, he asked the clerk for a pen and card, writing on it: "For Edith with all of my love." Then he turned and left the shop.

His destination was an enormous stone house on the north side of Jaystown. Its outer structure appeared to indicate exclusiveness. Henry, becoming a little nervous, as he walked onto the flagstone porch, rang the doorbell that sounded like church chimes. Shortly a tall man appeared, and immediately Henry came to the conclusion that he was the house servant.

"Is Edith Curtis here?"

"No, Mrs. Curtis is not here," the servant replied. "As a matter of fact there is no one at home."

"When do you expect them to return?" Henry asked.

"There is no saying when they will return, maybe it will be four or five o'clock," the servant replied.

"Do you mind if I wait to see Mrs. Curtis? I'm a friend, Henry Shane from Sinclair, and as you can see by my uniform I'm in the army and would like very much to see her before I return to my base." At that moment he regretted coming to the Heim household, but he had to speak to Edith and this was the only possible approach.

"All right, do come in," the servant said. "Will you please wait in the study. The minute she comes in I'll tell her you're here." The study was an enormous room with a picture window that provided one with a scenic view of Jaystown and surrounding mountains. Henry had never imagined a room such as this before. In the confines of his own home in Sinclair, where he once lived, there was no luxury and no space, no aristocratic atmosphere nor signs of wealth. When he looked around, he saw elaborate oil paintings on the wall, books and periodicals, and furniture that was typical of the early American period.

"It wasn't likely that Edith would turn up her nose on all these things," Henry whispered. "This was the kind of house that any woman would dream of living in and Edith had the best chance of acquiring all these wonderful things."

The grandfather clock in the corner of the room chimed and struck five o'clock. Henry, after pacing the floor for a considerable period of time decided to sit down. As he did, the servant appeared and said, "Looks like the Heim's won't be home for awhile. Do you care for a drink, Mr. Shane?"

"Yes, I'll have brandy on the rocks," Henry responded.

"As you wish, sir," replied the servant.

As he sat there sipping on his brandy, the rumble of thunder could be heard in the distance, and with each passing minute the thunderstorm was getting closer and closer. The early evening sun faded and was overshadowed by dark clouds that raced rapidly across the sky. Then the rain fell. It was after five thirty when he heard Edith's voice in the outer room. "Sure having a big storm," she said to the servant. There was a short pause.

"By the way Mrs. Curtis, there's a young gentleman here to see you. He says his name is Henry Shane. He is waiting for you in the study."

"Oh," she said. "Henry Shane. Thank you, Jonathan."

"Shall I get you a drink, Mrs. Curtis."

"Yes, do Jonathan, a martini will do. Please bring it into the study, and tell Robert I'll be with him shortly."

Henry heard her approaching the study, and this is what he had been waiting for. As she entered, he could see that now Edith, even more vividly than the night before that she was happy and relaxed and all of her frustrations and tensions had disappeared. Her face was the color of a pink rose, her dark eyes sparkled, her entire personality different.

"Henry, why did you come?" Edith asked. "Anyway, I'm glad that you are here. I've been staying with the Heim's, and they have been wonderful to me."

"That's nice," Henry said as he lowered his head.

"Isn't this a beautiful house, Henry? To think the Heim's have a servant to wait on them, and to take care of the house when they are gone. Isn't Robert fortunate in having all of these beautiful things?"

"Yes, I guess so," Henry said. "Luckier than most people."

Edith sat down, pulled off her white gloves, and took off her hat that was slightly wet. As he looked at her, her eyes further revealed signs of contentedness.

"Is every thing all right with you, Henry. How is the army? Are you going to stay very long in Sinclair?"

"Only a few days," He replied as he looked at her with sadness in his eyes.

"I'm sorry," she said. "If I only would have known exactly when you were coming. Didn't you get my letter?"

"Yes, of course I got your letter. That's why I took a leave—I just assumed that you would be in your own house back in Sinclair. When I arrived at my brother's house, they told me all about the escapades—

going to Miami, New York, Denver, and having a wonderful time with Robert Heim—now this—coming and going as you please. Why are you staying with the Heims? Why in the hell don't you just turn around and marry Robert?"

"It's not like you're thinking," she said bluntly. "The Heim's have been wonderful to me since my separation from Andy. They comforted me, and made life somewhat pleasant for me, not like the miserable days I spent with Andy."

"All those days with Andy couldn't have been so damn miserable, you married him, so you must have liked him some. Did you ever analyze the entire situation? Perhaps it was your fault that your marriage didn't work out. I hate to say this to you Edith, but everyone knows you were whoring around with Robert Heim. All those things you told me the night we were together at the Roxy Club, and at the train station, you just said them to make me feel good. To make me feel that I, Henry Shane was your only true love. You gave me a big line of bullshit. Like a fool, I believed you. I guess since you are separated from Andy, you've changed your mind about me."

"Perhaps you are right in saying some of these things," Edith responded. "What I said to you the day you left Sinclair, I said to you from the bottom of my heart. I've always loved you, and will to my dying day, but I have my own life to look out for. If you're honest, you'll admit that there is no place for me in your future."

"Oh, Henry. Why are you talking like this? You're only going to be here for a few days, and I should try and make them pleasant for you. By the way, Robert is having a dinner party tomorrow and I'm sure I can arrange it for you to attend. I'll find a female companion for you, a beautiful girl."

"It's awfully nice of you," Henry said. "I would prefer not to be asked to dinner. I just came over here for a special reason, and it seems like you're giving me the old screws."

"No!" Edith exclaimed. "It's not that at all, Henry. Please believe me!"

The servant brought in the martini. Edith took a sip. "This is just fine, Jonathan," she said.

"Thank you, madam," he replied as he turned to depart.

The room was overcome with a complete silence, then suddenly Henry broke the silence and shouted, "I'm going back to Fort George! I've had a rotten son of a bitch of a time since I came back to Sinclair, and was really pissed off in not finding you there. This having to come over to Jaystown just to speak to you is for the shits."

"Did you expect to find me at home, sitting in a rocking chair weeping and mourning because Andy wouldn't give me divorce?"

"No, I didn't," Henry replied. "It's a shame it had to turn out this way. I guess Andy knew he could never win you over, and therefore became all messed up with himself and life in general."

"Why how did you guess?" she said sarcastically. "I tried to make him understand how I felt, but he wouldn't take the hint. I made up my Goddamn mind to leave him several months after we were married, but I hated to walk out on the bastard. Yes, It must have been hard on Andy, but I'm glad it's all over now. It was Andy who decided to leave his own house."

"I suppose you'll be glad to see me go too," Henry said in a whisper.

"Oh, no, I'm not glad you're going. I hoped that you would have a longer leave." Edith put down her glass on the desk, and came and sat down beside him on the couch.

"Henry," she said, her voice trembling. "I haven't any right to ask you, but tell me the truth? Do you really love me, or are you just interested in my body?"

"Yes, Edith, I do love you and I know I'm a damn fool to do so. Yet, I know you're going to marry that fucking Robert Heim."

"No, I'm not going to marry Robert Heim," she replied. "I'm going to go back to Sinclair. I've spent as much time with the Heim's as I ought to, and merely for company and pleasure. I'm willing to prove to you that I still love you. I don't know whether I can, but I'll try."

"Then you would marry me instead of Robert Heim. You would give up all these luxuries and security just for the sake of a soldier boy."

For a minute she did not answer. She sat looking into his eyes, and Henry saw that some of her lovely color had suddenly faded. "I thought," he said, gaining new courage with each word, "that if you are willing, we can have a few happy hours together before I depart. We could go to some quiet little place in the mountains—neither of us has ever done that. When I go back to Fort George I can look for an apartment, and look forward to your coming; even though Andy won't give you a divorce."

Suddenly he turned and buried his face in the fold of her breast. "Edith," he said. "I've been so damn miserable and lonely without you all these years. I've wanted to be with you. I've wanted you to be my wife and bear my children. I've wanted to make up to you, and never realized it until I left Sinclair for the first time several years ago. Sinclair to me always meant you, Edith. Oh, Edith, I want you so."

"I know," she said slowly. "I've known that, of course since you returned from the war. That's one reason why I became miserable living with Andy. I couldn't bear the thought of having him make love to me, knowing that you were available. But you never made a move, you never went out of your way to see me—not until you decided to re-enlist in the army."

"I couldn't, Edith," he said sheepishly. "That's why I decided to re-enlist, always thinking I could never have you anyway. I swear, I love you."

She lifted his head from her breast. "You think love is just something to ease your tension—screwing everyday," she said. "Wanting, always wanting. Then suddenly throwing it away when you get bored with the same woman. Then after a prolonged period of time coming back in search of adventure. Son of a bitch, Henry, I'm not that damn stupid. If I married you this is the way it would be for you—and for me. The first little whore you would meet in your worldly travels with the army, you'd play up to her."

"Edith, please don't talk like that."

"Well, wouldn't you?" she remarked. "At least this is the way I have you pegged. Remember, Henry, you pulled the same rotten trick on me a few years ago, and I don't think you've changed that much in a short period of time."

"I thought I had a chance with you again," Henry said. "Perhaps, I don't. Do I?"

Edith frowned. "I don't even know whether I can put it into words very well. Love isn't something you talk about. It's something you feel in your heart. I can only tell you what love means to me as a woman. I can't for you. Perhaps you don't feel the same way as I do, though they say women can feel love more than men." She turned her head away from him and gazed at the ceiling. "You know, Henry, I'd like to live in a house similar to this one. It's much better than the one I'm living in back in Sinclair. Jaystown is a good town, but I can't say that I'm exactly crazy about it. I know the Heim's have plenty of money, and I could always have a servant and a nice car to drive the rest of my life, and have anything else I want. When a man you really don't love offers them to you, then it's a different story. Some women would jump at this opportunity, but me—no. Maybe I am a fool, nevertheless Andy left me some money in the bank to get along with comfortably. I can't help admitting it, but it's been a very difficult situation. Robert is an intelligent man, handsome and wealthy, but I found him to be a playboy. I tried to lure him deliberately, and forced my love upon him—so that I could have all these beautiful things you see before you. I thought it would work out, but now I can't go through with it."

Edith looked at Henry once again, her lips searching for more words. He was still sitting patiently beside her. She began to speak and her voice was very soft. "A woman must judge a man by his character, his principles, not by whether he is rich or poor. A woman should have a man that she wants to marry—to go to bed with every night and to be cuddled in his arms. A man who is a hard worker and good provider, one who'll share his problems, joy and sorrow."

Henry rose from the couch and walked towards the window. He

turned and came back. "You really don't love Robert Heim," he said. "So you're not going to remain in this house with him permanently. You don't want a man because he is rich. You mean to tell me you're willing to give up all these materialistic things for someone else that can't give you wealth and security."

"Yes," Edith said.

"Then, do you think it likely that you would be content with a person like me, Edith?" Henry said quickly.

"No," she said. "I don't think it would work out in marriage. We're too much alike, Henry. We're always seeking new thrills, new adventures. Several years ago, it would have worked out."

Henry lowered his head, "Of course I know it's impossible. It was idiotic of me to think that you would go away with me now after what I had pulled on you a few years ago, especially when you really cared for me then. I did ask for your forgiveness—and I know damn well I didn't deserve it, and didn't expect to get it."

"I wouldn't say that, Henry," she replied. "After all I didn't say I wouldn't forgive you. Stop feeling sorry for yourself."

"I guess you're right," he said softly.

"Let's forget about the past, about Andy, Robert Heim and look to the future," she said gaily. "I don't belong in this type of society anyway, so I'm going back to my own house in Sinclair." She rose from the couch and walked towards the door. "I'm going to say goodbye to the Heim's, and thank them dearly for everything they had done for me."

"What about Robert Heim?" Henry asked. "How are you going to explain to him?"

"Now don't you worry about Robert? I'll handle him."

"Now, how do I stand with you, Edith?" he asked bluntly.

She smiled and came towards him. She put her arms around him, came up on tiptoe and kissed him lightly on the lips. "I'll be at my house in Sinclair. Please come by and see me. Now run along, so I can clear myself with the Heim's."

"All right, I'll think about it, but I can't guarantee you I'll be

The Wailing Wind

there," Henry said.

"Oh, please do come, Henry!" She pleaded.

Edith was somewhat relieved over the separation from her husband, Andy Curtis. At last she was free to do as she pleased. Now she remembered her passionate desire for Henry, and all those rumors that were spread about them. Only if they were true. What could she hope for now that her husband is gone? Why did she suddenly sever her relationship with Robert Heim?

"I should simply move away from here," she whispered. "That would be the best thing for me to do." Then she realized that she had told Henry to come over to visit her.

There was a full moon. She could hear the sound of a train in the far off distance. She stood by her bedroom window, clad only in a transparent negligee, hearing the echo of the train whistle once again. After a short period of time, she went to bed. She lay there for sometime staring at the ceiling and unable to sleep.

Suddenly there was a knock on the outer door, and at first she thought she imagined it. The knock came again. "Come in!" she called. "It isn't locked." She didn't lock the door in her house that night. Why didn't she? Perhaps she was hoping. "Oh, God," she whispered to herself. "I only hope that it is Henry." Before she could utter another sound, the bedroom door opened.

"I saw the light in your window," Henry said. "I thought you were sick. I didn't know whether I would have the courage to come over to see you after you extended an invitation."

"No, I'm not sick. I just can't sleep, but I'm glad you came."

"Can I get you something," Henry said. "Maybe I should leave and try to get a bottle of brandy."

Then he left, before she had ample time to say anything of importance. She lay there wondering where he was going to get a bottle of brandy at that time of the night. She knew that all of the taverns were closed. Perhaps there was a bottle of brandy at Lee's house, she thought. She hoped that he would soon return.

He was gone for a short period of time, but in the meantime she began to grow sleepy after all. She put out the light. She didn't need it in the first place, for the moonlight lit the room. She lay there, wondering how wonderful it would be to have Henry in her arms. She closed her eyes, dozed and dreamed.

She was startled when she heard the door open very softly. She quickly turned and put on the light. She saw Henry standing there looking at her, holding a bottle of brandy.

Henry smiled and said, "You look very becoming in that transparent negligee." He turned and placed the bottle of brandy on the nightstand.

"Really," she remarked. She tilted her head and sighed.

Watching her smooth down her negligee, Henry said, "Not all woman are as beautiful as you are, Edith."

She pushed her long, black hair back with her slim hand, and then leaned back and took a deep breath. She smiled, turned her body, and treated him to a glance of her breasts. She didn't want him to go away and urged him to come over and sit on the bed.

Henry sat down on the bed facing her. Then he was invading the privacy of her bosom. "I'm wondering if you've just put on the negligee to induce me into an affair, and how you would react to my fondling you."

She looked at him with bewildered eyes. "Gracious!" she remarked. "Is that all you're thinking about?"

"One more thing, Edith," Henry said. "Do you always wear a transparent negligee when you go to bed?"

"All right, Henry. Quit the kidding. I put on a negligee because it is more comfortable. Any objections?"

"Of course not. I'm pleased in fact. You didn't respond to my main question? How would you react to my fondling you?"

Her lips revealed a challenging twist. As he looked at her face, she met his eyes with more passionate intentions than he had ever seen in them before. She had thrown her desires directly at him. She awaited his response, and was hoping for a place in his heart with no mistaken thoughts regarding the future. She was not discounting her values as she turned and said, "Care for a drink, Henry."

She rose from the bed. Watching him looking at her in swift appraisal, she walked from the bedroom. Shortly she returned with several glasses and a bucket of ice.

"Do you want a large or small glass of brandy?"

"A small glass of brandy will be just fine," he replied.

She talked about her married life with Andy as she prepared the drinks, and Henry listened attentively. All the time studying her, admiring her beauty and gracefulness. She was far more polished than Faye Cooper, he thought.

"To our future," he said while touching glasses.

She smiled and said, "May the time we spend together be happy."

Henry placed his hand on her cheek as her mouth carved into a smile. "Now if I were such a woman—I'd want to mess around."

"You don't want to get involved with me, Edith. You just want to mess around."

Her soft voice varied in tone just as her lips changed into lovely shapes. Both intrigued him, and sent his mind wandering recklessly ahead to the next move. Now, he thought would be the proper time to sweep Edith into his arms, but Edith was ahead of him in her thoughts.

"Let's go and sit on the bed," she said. "The bed is much softer than the couch."

He took off his shoes and dropped them on the floor. She stretched out on the bed, passionately waiting. He smiled at her. Then without any wasted motion, took off his clothes and draped them over the back of a chair near the bed. "Move over, "he said.

"What difference does it make," she whispered. "What if people do find out about our affair?" She lay there thinking about their affairs before her marriage to Andy. Then very quietly she moved to the far side of the bed, and stretched out her arms to him. I wonder what he'll be like after all these years, she thought. Oh, God, it has been so long!

Her eyes were wide, curious and expectant. Henry waited no longer and reached out and pulled her to him fiercely. She did not resist. She pressed her firm, yielding breasts eagerly against him. The room was filled with an aroma of sweet smelling perfume, and intoxicating as the softness of her breasts in his hands. The darkness of her eyes seemed to fade as he searched for her lips, and then she was like burning fire. He knew that she was responding with a passionate craving. She gasped for a breath of air, then clung to him in desperation. In the dim light of the room she was fascinating, her body lifting and falling, a moaning coming forth from deep in her throat

It was now morning and the rays of the sun had awakened her. Henry turned to her and began fondling her breast. Then he stopped.

"What's wrong, Henry?" she whispered. "Wasn't I good enough?"

"Nothing," he said. "I suddenly feel guilty about what I have done. Especially since you are still legally married to Andy."

She stared at him, and her throat tightened. She frowned, moved her lips, forming words to say. What could she say? Then she quickly said, "I didn't love my husband anyway."

He put his arms around her gently. Slowly he got out of bed. "It would be wonderful, If I could marry you, but this way you'll always be able to go to bed with whom ever you desire. I'm sure you'll always be here waiting when I want you."

"You—you're not leaving?" she asked quickly.

"Yes," Henry replied his voice endlessly deep. "Yes, I'm going back to Fort George tomorrow, and I'd like to spend some time with my brother and his family before I leave." Then without glancing at her again, he reached for his military uniform that was draped carelessly over the back of a chair. Edith watched him as he dressed. "There must be something I can say at a time like this, but what is it? Don't leave me my love, or you rotten son of a bitch. I have to live out my life knowing I love a man who doesn't really love me."

He was finished dressing now and stood there before her. "Well. Edith, I'm sorry but I do love you in my own little way."

She got out of bed then and faced him. "I love you Henry," she said softly. "I have always known I was wrong to love you. I have even hated myself for it, and at times even hated you for making me want you so. I can't help it. I'll go on loving you and wanting you all my life, but the hatred and bitterness will go on too, until it overwhelms us both."

"I hope to hell you're finished," Henry said, his voice filled with contempt.

"Yes," she replied, and walked down the stairs with him to the front door. "I suppose," she whispered, as his hand enveloped the doorknob, "suppose I'm not here when you decide to return to Sinclair again."

"I'll take that chance," Henry said. Then he was gone.

Edith stood there in astonishment, staring at the closed door. For the first time, she regretted having an affair with Henry Shane.

The next day, when Lee Shane returned to his home from his job at the mine, he immediately approached his brother. "Henry," he said. "I heard from some of the fellows over at the mine that Edith was rushed to the hospital last night."

"Oh, my God!" Henry exclaimed. "What happened? I was just with her yesterday, and told her I was going back to Fort George today."

"That answers your question, Henry," Lee said sarcastically.

"What hospital is she in?" Henry asked.

"The Good Samaritan Hospital over in Jaystown," Lee replied.

"Why the Good Samaritan? Why didn't they take her over to the Sinclair Hospital?

"How in the hell do I know?" Lee remarked.

"She's not dead, is she?"

"No, she is not dead. Not yet," Lee said. "Do you want to wait until after supper before we go to the hospital to see her?"

"No. For Christ's sake, Lee, let's go now!"

Hearing the commotion, Ruth Shane entered the living room and demanded to know what had happened. Henry proceeded to explain while Lee changed his clothes.

Shortly they went down to the car that Lee had parked in front of the house. Henry gave the address of the hospital and they drove off. Henry sat tight-lipped and motionless, looking neither to the right nor to the left. Lee touched Henry's arm.

"Tell me the truth, what happened yesterday?" Lee demanded. "I have to know."

Henry looked at his brother with anger in his eyes. "Hell, Lee, you know more about what happened than I do. Those fellows over at the mine gave you the scoop."

"Yes, I know, but that's not what I am referring to. I want to know what really happened between you and Edith when you were together yesterday."

"Nothing," Henry said softly.

"Something had to happen," Lee interjected. "Some of the fellows over at the mine mentioned that she took a walk in that terrible rain storm we had late yesterday afternoon. One of her close neighbors happened to remember the habit she'd gotten into of going up to Saint Anthony's Cemetery to visit her mother's grave site—remember she died shortly after you were drafted into the army during World War II—so they were able to find her. Too late, though. She overdosed. The fellows were saying that the doctors at the Good Samaritan Hospital don't give her much of a chance. You can chalk her on the list of women who got in your way, Henry."

"That's a hell of thing to say!" Henry shouted. "You know damn well that's not true!"

"Do, I?" Lee said. "You know that Edith loved you with a great passion. Maybe it would have been better for you to have married her."

When they arrived at the hospital, the unit clerk directed them to the door of Edith's room, but there one of the nurses motioned to them to wait. They proceeded to the waiting room.

Looking at Henry, Lee saw the sweat appearing on his brother's forehead, saw the slight, almost unnoticeable tremor run through his body, heard the constant strumming of his fingers against the arm of the chair. Suddenly Lee felt a strange surge of pity for his brother.

The door opened and the doctor came out. Seeing the doctor clad in a scrub suit, Henry stood up immediately. His face was pale and the trembling in his limbs increased so violently that Lee put out a steadying hand. The doctor stared at Henry curiously, noting the distorted effort of his speech, out of control now, to shape the question.

"No," the doctor said suddenly. "She is not dead. She will recover. She took a turn for the better a short time ago."

Henry's knees buckled suddenly, so that he might have fallen if his brother had not pushed a chair forward. As it was, he sat there a long time wiping the perspiration from his forehead with a handkerchief.

"You can go in to see her now," the doctor said. Then nodding to Lee and the nurse, he left the waiting room. Henry got to his feet and walked into Edith's room. She lay there upon her bed so small and pale that she was half lost among the sheets and pillow. When she saw him, she let out a cry, and Henry went down on his knees beside her and buried his face in the fold of her breast.

"Don't cry, Henry?" she whispered. "Please, don't cry?"

Then as he raised his head she kissed him covering his face with light, feathery kisses, filled with such agony of tenderness that the pain inside her heart was like fire.

"I shouldn't kiss you," she said. "You aren't mine anymore. It was so good of you to come—so good and wonderful. You know I tried to commit suicide. It wasn't very brave of me. Only, I didn't know how I could bear living without you. I still don't. I'll try, my darling, for your sake. I wouldn't want to give you any cause for regret."

"I should have married you," Henry said suddenly. "I was a fool. I love you Edith, and nobody else on earth is going to take your place."

Her right hand, pale and cold, came up and rested on his cheek. "No, Henry," she said softly. "Our marriage would not have worked out. Go back to Fort George—and I shall always pray for your happiness."

"What about your happiness, Edith?" Henry asked.

"Oh, I shall find it in a different way, a different place perhaps. Living the best way I know how. It won't be the same happiness I would have known with you, Henry; but it will be very real, nevertheless, very quiet and rewarding."

She took a deep breath and continued, "You know, I can always go back to Robert Heim. As for you, Henry, you'll find somebody else. Some nice young girl who will make a good wife."

Henry's hands trembled fiercely. "After having known you, Edith?" He said. "Never."

The nurse entered the room and tapped Henry on the shoulder and said, "It's time to leave, sir."

"I'll write to you, Edith, when I get back to Fort George," Henry said, but Edith shook her head.

"No," she said weakly. "Don't? Please don't write? Go back to Fort George and forget about me."

Henry Shane coming out of the hospital suddenly wondered why Edith severed their relationship. Still he had his own life to think of. He knew that Faye Cooper waited in Hallensburg. So thinking, he sat in the car beside his brother and directed him to drive him back to Sinclair to pick up his duffel bag, and then to the train station.

After many hours he was back in Hallensburg again after a train ride that had seemed endless. He was walking up the now familiar street once more in the darkness and rain. At last he was standing on the porch, hesitating before knocking on the door. He heard the doorknob turn, and it was done, He was standing inside the room facing Faye Cooper.

She stood there under the light, paler than he had ever seen her before—and apparently more beautiful. "Henry," she cried out. "You came back to me! I can't believe it!"

Fourteen

It was Henry's intention to go back to Fort George that same night, but Faye persuaded him to remain in Hallensburg. Her apartment was very cool and comfortable which the quarters at Fort George were not. The presence of Henry Shane triggered an emotional response in Faye Cooper. "Besides," she said modestly, "a man and woman, who is in love always discuss marriage, don't they?"

Henry frowned as he nodded his head in agreement. The truth of the matter was that Henry was emotionally disturbed. All his life he had taken his pleasures when the opportunity presented itself, to his advantage and without thought. It was also true, as he told Faye was that he had never known a woman of moral excellence and strict rearing and training. Faye Cooper was all these things. She was undefiled, Henry discovered, in body but certainly not in thought. It was this observation that shocked him. He had all of his life the dissipated man's dream of marrying a model of excellence. He had expected sensitivity, bashfulness and prudence. He had even looked forward to these things as an added adventure that would lend keen enjoyment to the whole process, and instead he had found great enthusiasm.

He at first was bewildered and confused. Faye was very playful and full of eager desire that was almost inexhaustible. "A family!" Faye chuckled when he mentioned the possibility of such an outcome. "We will have a family later. Right now I want to keep my figure and enjoy myself. Besides I want to keep you sexually occupied so that you won't have the time or energy to satisfy another woman. I am a jealous woman, Henry." She said.

She stood up then and came toward him, the night-light revealing the features and expressions of her face. "Henry," she whispered, "don't think about the negative aspects of our relationship anymore tonight. Later, we will discuss it. Tonight is my night—no ours. Please don't disrupt our indifferences over this or for any other reason."

"No!" Henry said, the word nearly suppressed in his throat. He was furious with anger. He was a man of many desires, of extraordinary sexual appetite, but tonight he had no desire for a woman. Tonight it would be hypocritical to make love in light of what had happened to Edith.

"Henry," Faye whispered. "Please, Henry."

"Some other time," Henry said. "Not now. I have no interest in fondling you at the moment." It was an expedient reason, and not what he meant at all. It was a pretext, an escape from reality, and even it denied him.

Faye reached for his blouse that was hanging on a hook in the closet and handed it to him. "We'll go and find a justice of the peace. Do you still want to get married, Henry? Tell me, do you?"

"Yes," he replied. In a strange way he did. He was attracted to her as he had been attracted to many other women, gladly, inconsiderately with a tendency to emotional excitement. Not like his affection for Edith. This was a different situation. He loved Edith with all his heart and soul.

"There isn't a justice of the peace available at this time of the night that will marry us," he told Faye flatly.

"Then we will go to another community," Faye said. "There is one over in Kern City that is available at any hour of the night. It's only about a half-hours drive from here. Please, Henry, let's go to Kern City."

He allowed her to take his hand and lead him to the car that was parked along the street. He helped her into the car and then took the wheel himself. The car moved through the dark night, and the car's engine muffled into soundlessness.

They found a justice of the peace in Kern City, dressed in pajamas and slippers who heard their marital vows while his wife stood by and served as a witness. A twenty dollar bill dimmed the justice of the peace's facial expression at the contrast between the neatness and attractiveness of Faye's attire and Henry's military uniform.

At the completion of the marriage ceremony, Henry asked the justice of the peace the where about of lodging for the night. "Mrs. Holihan has a boarding house and she does take newly weds. Just go one block down the street to the big Victorian house on the corner. Go on to the porch and knock on the door."

Mrs. Holihan was a tall, slender woman of such subtle doubtfulness that she had to be convinced of the marriage ceremony and required Henry to show her a copy of the marriage certificate that was signed by the justice of the peace.

As late as it was, she offered to prepare some snacks for them. The snacks were appealing, but Henry could not eat very well. He sat pondering over the snacks that Mrs. Holihan placed before him. Faye saw the sickly expression on his face, but said nothing.

Shortly they climbed the stairs to their room. Inside, an electric fan was turned on to produce cool currents of air, and to assist in the ventilation of the room. A queen size bed dominated the room, but Henry merely stood there looking at Faye without uttering a word.

Faye, who was standing in front of the mirror, looked over her shoulder. "Help me with the zipper," she said. Henry's fingers upon the zipper were awkward and uneasy. She opened her brown, leather suitcase and pulled out a pale blue negligee. "Don't look now, Henry?" she said.

When he looked again she was sitting on the bed, her hair spread out over her shoulder like a protective cover. Still Henry stood there as if in a stupor making no effort to undress.

"Come here," she whispered.

He went over to her and when he was close she put up her arms and began to caress him and dabbing his lips with her soft fingers.

Suddenly, in a jerky motion he brought up his hands and broke her firm hold.

"I can't!" he said in a harsh and rough voice. "Tonight I just can't! I'm not in the mood!" Then he turned and walked to the door. He opened it, and without hesitation he slammed it, and quickly went down the steps into the dark, silent night.

Faye sat there on the bed, propped up against the pillows, and stared at the door that Henry had just closed behind him. My wedding night she thought, my wedding night! How many times have I longed for this night! Then suddenly, softly she began to chuckle. She chuckled very quietly, but her body was trembling. It went on and she could not stop. It was not until she lifted her hand to her face and found it to be very moist. She realized that the sounds she was making were no longer chuckles. No—not chuckles. She was weeping.

Early the next morning, Henry sat up in bed and gazed at the sleeping figure of his wife. It was long before daylight but a dresser light was still on. Looking at Faye outstretched in the semi-darkness, sleeping peacefully, Henry mumbled to himself.

"I must be crazy. I ought to be one of the happiest men in the world, and I'm not. I have one of the prettiest women that one can find, and I'm sitting here thinking about negative things. I have an opportunity to be satisfied and a content man, and I'm actually disappointed. I have a woman here that I may not be able to satisfy. Yet, I'm acting like a hungry dog searching for food in the desolate streets. I don't understand what the hell is bothering me. He brought his firmly developed hands up and placed them on his face, with his elbows resting on his knees.

"I wonder," he uttered softly, "how things would have been if I would have married Edith." The instance he expressed his feelings, he regretted it. It was out now, the very thing that had been worrying him since the night of his marriage to Faye—that extraordinary wedding night that had not been a wedding night at all. He began to have hallucinations of Edith. He shouted her name, and it seemed that she was present in the room with him. He could see her pretty face and well-developed body. She was standing there talking to him in a mild and refined manner, but he could not hear the words. She was talking to him about something—something that he badly needed to know, but his ears failed him on this occasion. Then he realized that there was something wrong, for he could no longer see the image of Edith's face. He was suddenly aware that he was trembling, his entire body perspiring.

He sprang from the bed and paced the floor. Though he could not see Edith, she was everywhere about him, his outstretched hands missing contact with her figure. He realized with disappointment that was difficult to explain that she would always be present between him and Faye, and that never again in his lifetime would he be completely happy. There was nothing unusual about that. He was aware of that before. What confused him, what he couldn't explain, were the agonizing thoughts of Edith that tormented him. Something was amiss.

"I'm out of my fucking mind," he groaned. "I'm a goof. I better lie down and try to get some sleep." After being affected with insomnia, and a lapse of time, he finally fell asleep. Even his sleep was troubled, filled with ridiculous dreams he forgot about the moment they were completed.

He was aroused finally by Faye's loud voice and her hands shaking him repeatedly. He sat up, blinking, and staring into Faye's face momentarily, and then began rubbing his eyes with his fingers.

"If I ever again," she said forcefully, "You call me Edith while you are asleep, I'll kill you, Henry Shane!" Then she got out of bed and walked sedately to the bathroom, leaving Henry alone in the room in a state of perplexity.

Fifteen

Robert Heim had reluctantly stayed away from Edith with a feeling of rejection for several weeks after Henry Shane returned to Fort George. Edith, overcome with loneliness, decided finally to send Robert a letter.

"People in Sinclair aren't concerned about us," she wrote. "They've got other more pressing things on their minds—things a hell of a lot more important than worrying about you and me, Robert. I'm very lonely and depressed, and I'm anxious to see you. Since my separation from Andy, he still has not consented to a divorce. He has been gone now for several months—and it has been a hell of a lot longer than that since I ceased to really care for him. I do expect him to return any day now to pick up his personal belongings. Please come to visit me as soon as possible. It would do me good to sit and talk with you and even to look at you, Robert, if you will excuse the boldness. So, please come. I kind of think that wherever Andy is, he probably doesn't give a damn about us anymore one way or the other."

Robert Heim came to Edith's house the very day he received her letter, parking his car along Pine Street, walking up the steps on to the porch to meet Edith with feelings of suspense and compassion and exaltation depicted in his eyes. He stood there, like that, looking at her trying to get it out of his system, trying to put it into words; the suspense, the compassion, and the exaltation, but he could not. The absence of a continuous relationship with Edith caused him to become tense and frustrated.

"Edith," he whispered. "Edith."

She had stepped forward, her hands outstretched in welcome, and drawn him very simply and naturally and peacefully into her arms.

There wasn't anymore time for self-pity, because his face was above hers, kissing her passionately, shutting out what was left of any painful thoughts in his mind. When he released her, she stood there staring at him.

"That really was some welcome kiss," Robert said. "That was a pretty damn passionate kiss by a woman that is still suppose to be married."

"Damn you!" Edith said. "What the hell do you expect me to do? I haven't seen you for several months."

"I'll kiss you more and make love to you when I get around to it," Robert said. "Right now you're looking at a starved and famished man. I'm so damn hungry that I could eat the asshole out of a cow. Don't tell me that Coal Region people don't have any hospitality about them?"

The food she had prepared for her own supper was still in the oven. She hadn't eaten it, not only because she hadn't the time to eat the roast chicken and vegetables—if only she had begun to eat as soon as it was cooked—but because she hadn't really felt like eating it at all. She had attributed it to loneliness, but it was more. It was true that her house was situated some distance from the center of town, near the outskirts of Sinclair, on the beginning of coal lands that stretched westward toward the Allegheny Mountains and the setting sun. So, the days ran together with the passing of time, fading into weeks, into months even, seldom socializing with other people, and at rare intervals, her relatives. There were times when she found herself talking to herself aloud, merely she thought, to hear the sound of a human voice. What was more frustrating was the absence of a man in the night to comfort her.

"All right," she said suddenly to Robert Heim. "I'll prepare your supper."

She set the table and removed the food from the oven. She could sense Robert's eyes upon her, and then suddenly, a feeling she had often had, a need, a hunger, caused her to become motionless, paralyzing her slim, shapely body before his eyes. It was then, at that moment that her body began to tremble. She knew that without turning that Robert had gotten up from the chair and come over to her. Then he embraced her trembling body.

"It's a hell of a thing to be lonely, isn't it, Edith?" he said, and his voice was soft and gentle.

"Yes," she said. "It's terrible." Robert returned to the table and she sat there watching him eat. There was no hunger in her, at least not any such simple hunger. The way he ate, gulping down his food, was enough to warm the cockles of any woman. Andy Curtis, she remembered, merely picked at his food, too worn out and tired to eat, really—the pressures of his job at the mine had so overcome him that his mouth had forgotten how to smile.

Robert finished his supper, and wiped his mouth with a napkin. Then he reached into his shirt pocket for his cigarettes. She got him a match, and he lit a cigarette, sighing with satisfaction, leaning back in the chair, smiling. This is the good life, he thought. Having a woman wait on you hand and foot.

He didn't say anything. He just sat there, staring at her, until looking through the window, he saw that it was getting dark after sunset, and the big maple tree near the gate, was a faint image now, shadow after shadow, and far off in the sky, a single, brilliant star.

He got up from his chair then, very slowly. He was not a man to hurry about anything. Seeing him get up and coming toward her, Edith got up too.

"Come here, Edith," he said gently.

She stood there, staring at him for a moment. Then without any protest or hesitation whatsoever, moved slowly, quietly into his waiting arms. Shortly they climbed the stairs to the bedroom and closed the door behind them.

They were asleep now. At last the sun had risen in the east. The sunlight, peering through the window, enabled Edith to see Robert lying there with his lean, muscular body. One arm was flung backward under his head, the hair of his arm pit showing, the mat of hair covering his chest, stomach and genital region, the contour of his tanned body, and she sitting up looking at him and touching him shamelessly, admiring his body with her eyes.

"I enjoy sex, and I know I will be damned to the fires of hell because I am an adulteress," she whispered. "I can't help it. Lord, it was wonderful and this is what a man is like, a real man." She whispered his name over and over again. She remembered how it had been with every detail, leading to her orgasm. She didn't even compare him with her husband, Andy, and not even remembering the moments with Henry Shane. Those moments were out of her mind, gone and forgotten. Her body was still tingling with the slow endless pleasure that now the ecstasy was agony, so that she had bitten her lip, to keep from crying out, until the remembering was too much for her to bear. She bent her head and kissed his sleeping mouth with her own, cruelly, savagely, and awakened him.

They remained naked in the full glare of the morning sunlight and talked. There was plenty of time for talking now. "Yes," Edith said. "I expect Andy to be returning to this house any day now. He said that he would never give me a divorce, but we never discussed any arrangements for a legal separation. I had heard that he is living in Twin Forks."

"Why did you marry him?" Robert asked immediately.

"He was a good and gentle man, and I was very lonely at the time. Most of all, I was jilted by Henry Shane who was suppose to marry me in the first place, but Henry was drafted into the army and I was left all alone. After Henry left Sinclair, Andy started to stop by quite frequently to look after me. At the time, I thought it was mighty kind and considerate of him. So one thing led to another and we decided to go to Maryland to get married."

"That rotten bastard," Robert remarked.

"No, you're wrong about him, Robert. He never mistreated me or even said an improper word. Even when we were courting, it was me who suggested that we get married. It's kind of rough living alone in the Coal Region. Anyway, it doesn't matter what went wrong with our marriage now. The important question is, what kind of plans are we going to make, Robert."

"Plans! What the hell are you talking about? We are not going to plan anything, Edith."

"My God, Robert, Andy is bound to come back soon. Let's leave Sinclair. We can move into your parent's house over in Jaystown. I'm sure they will not object if you tell them we are planning to get married. I used to spend a lot of time over there anyway after Andy left me."

Robert grinned and said, "We're not going anywhere, not to Jaystown nor to Pellersville until this problem with Andy is resolved once and for all. Besides I like living in Sinclair for the time being. It is quiet here, and it is a change from the hustle and bustle of Jaystown. "Don't you worry about Andy? I'll deal with him when the time comes."

Ironically it was Robert Heim who did the worrying. He had seduced Andy's wife, but equally Edith had seduced him. Robert smiled, thinking of enticing Edith, but was concerned about Andy returning with a gang of miners. I won't have a chance against them, he thought. I remember how Paul Hoban back in Jaystown caught a salesman screwing his wife, Christy. He got so pissed off that he put a double load of buckshot through the salesman's belly. He held the shotgun so close that when he pulled the trigger it tore a hole in him the size of a canon ball. Then after that, beat the living shit out of Christy Hoban that she nearly died. The startling thing about it was that Paul Hoban never spent a moment in jail. The same thing can happen to me in this situation, he thought.

As expected, Andy Curtis did eventually return to his house in Sinclair. The first thing that surprised Andy when he unlocked the door and entered the house was the dining room table cluttered with dishes and the cigarette butts in an ashtray. Several beer bottles were toppled on their side, and the liquid that came forth from the bottles spread out on the tablecloth. Many things designated that a dinner guest was present, things that an average person may not have recognized, but that struck Andy Curtis like a bolt out of the blue. He walked quickly out of the house, with raging fire in his eyes. He saw

Edith and Robert Heim walking down the narrow path from the nearby hillside with their arms clasped around one another.

Andy stood there waiting for them. Robert Heim studied him, not even bothering to look at Edith's stricken face, deciding at once what it was that must be done, until, coming closer, he dropped his arm from Edith's waist, and pushed her aside, saying quietly, no emotion at all in his voice. "Get the hell away from here, Edith. Get your ass in the house."

She ran quickly towards the house, leaving the two men facing each other. They didn't say anything. Andy's hand reached into his pocket and came out with a revolver. Robert Heim stared at him without fear and said, "What are you trying to prove, Andy? I know damn well that you are not a murderer."

"I know I'm not," Andy relied. "I don't intend to use this weapon unless I have to. You're nothing but a rotten bastard, Heim. You've pressed your luck far enough."

"What the hell are you talking about, Andy?" Robert Heim shouted. "That I've lured your wife away from you. It isn't my fault that she has stopped loving you, and I've pleaded with you to give her a divorce. I'm here now, and by damn I'm staying too, and for your information, Edith is staying too. It appears to me about the only smart thing for you to do is get your ass into your car and drive away from here quietly—just like the way you came."

"I'm telling you for the last time, Heim, you're the one who better get lost in a hurry," Andy said quickly.

"What if I don't?" Robert said.

Andy studied him. Then he remarked, "I guess I'm going to have to put a little lead into your body. Hell, Robert I don't really want to do that. I think you have irritated me long enough. You have seduced my wife and she legally belongs to me. If I have to kill you to keep Edith, I'll kill you. I'll kill you without any regrets, but I'll do it. I don't give a damn what happens to me afterwards."

Andy stood there trembling with rage in his eyes, so that Edith, seeing him from the porch, could read his thoughts, feel almost if by touch the temptation that plagued him. "Oh my God!" she cried out. "Robert is going to force Andy to pull the trigger."

She rushed from the porch frantically, and hurled herself between them. "No, Andy!" she shouted. "There isn't going to be any cold-blooded murder over me! Put that damn revolver away! Do you hear me, put it away!"

Slowly Andy let the revolver drop and then he placed it into the pocket of his jacket. Edith turned to Andy and whispered, "Please, Andy listen to me. I don't have any excuses. I'm an immoral woman and you're too good for me. You always were, and I shouldn't have married you in the first place. So go away, Andy, and let us be."

His eyes held hers. She wanted to turn away from them but she couldn't. She had to stand there and watch his expression of humiliation—the death of a man's pride, his reputation, his respect, his dignity and self esteem. She had to watch it, being unable to turn away her eyes from his total sorrow.

"All right, Edith," he said, his voice so soft and low that she felt, rather than heard the sound. "If it makes you feel better, I'll go."

He walked towards his car so feebly that Robert Heim had to assist him. Then he got into his car and drove off, his head bent far over the steering wheel. Robert Heim seeing it threw back his head and laughed aloud.

Edith was annoyed at the sound of Robert's laughter. She rushed towards him, and attempted to punch him on his chest with her fists. He stepped aside, with the grace of an athlete, and his hand came up, palm open striking her across the face, sending her down to the ground weeping at his feet.

"Get up," he said mildly. "You should have stayed in the house. Then this would not have happened."

Edith struggled slowly to her feet. "You rotten son of a bitch," she shouted. "You lousy rotten bastard." Robert took a step towards her. "Get the hell away from me!" she screamed. "You wild son of a bitch, a good for nothing dirty, wild son of a bitch."

Grinning, Robert locked his arms around her so tightly that she had difficulty in breathing. "Yes, you're right—I am a son of a bitch, but Edith, you're not an infallible woman. You did your share of constant bitching as I remember like, please Robert, take me away from Sinclair," he mimicked, "take me far away from Andy where he won't be able to find us. It appears I heard those familiar words quite frequently."

"Oh, damn you!" Edith said. "I hate you!"

"No you don't," Robert replied. "You need me, and you're never going to get rid of me—because you can't." Then his hand came up and gripped her chin, holding it firmly. He lowered his head and tenderly kissed her moist lips. Robert Heim picked her up, and carried her across the threshold into the house.

"Robert," Edith said, "It's strange. I thought I was going to die of shame at first. The problems with Andy and Henry Shane were insurmountable. Do you know what, Robert? I'm not ashamed anymore. I don't have the time to be concerned about them anymore. I'm just too damn happy being with you."

"I'm glad," Robert said. "I'm not that bad of a fellow, once you get to know me."

"You," Edith whispered, "are the best, absolutely the best lover in the whole wide world."

"How do you know that, Edith?" Robert asked. "How many men did you have sex with to prove that?"

"If I were to tell you, you'd be mighty angry."

"Sure as hell would," Robert grinned. "It would mess up my work schedule. I'd have to take time off to wipe them all out—everyone of them."

Edith looked at him and her dark eyes were wide. "Would you really do that, Robert? Would you kill a man who was trying to make out with me?"

"Just for looking, let alone trying to screw you," Robert said. He sighed wearily and changed the subject. "Christ, I'll be glad when I can get my business ventures rolling, and then I can move on to bigger and better things."

"I'm certain that will be soon, and I think it's going to be sooner than you think, Robert."

It wasn't. The days blurred into weeks, lost in an abyss and the pain of waiting. It appeared to Edith that Robert Heim was more concerned about his sex life rather than his business ventures that he was neglecting. Still, Robert couldn't leave her. Not with what there was between them now. He had lost count long ago of the women he had intercourse with, but he knew with certainty that there had been no woman like Edith. He'd never give her up. He'd rather die first. That would be much easier for him to do, but being around Edith for long periods of time were very distracting. They came together many times at night, in the morning, and in the middle of the afternoon. They had sexual intercourse so often that they stopped keeping tract.

There were nights now when they fell into bed exhausted, and fell asleep as soon as their heads touched the pillows. Robert had a hard time waking Edith in the mornings. Often she was near tears when she dragged herself out of bed and began to dress. How long, he asked himself, is it going to be like this? How long before she learns to despise me? He was concerned about her on many mornings lying there on the bed in the dimly lighted bedroom, mumbling in her sleep.

It was many mornings later, it seemed to him, when he heard her call him. When he straightened up he saw the rays of sunlight through the window and Edith standing there. Something was wrong with Edith. Her face was as white as snow, and her lips were trembling. He saw her double over suddenly, and the sounds that came forth from her mouth were those of spasms of nausea.

Quickly Robert jumped from the bed and hurried towards her. "What's wrong with you, Edith?" he asked nervously.

Edith did not respond to the question and staggered across the room to lie upon the bed. The pain had subsided, but she began to cry. "I knew," she sobbed. "Oh, Robert I knew I would get pregnant sooner or later. To think, I am still legally married to Andy. I tried to convince myself that it couldn't happen. Andy and I tried desperately to have a child. I always thought it was my fault that we didn't, but now

I know that Andy must have been sterile. Oh, Robert, what am I going to do now?"

"Damn it Edith, that's not a difficult question to answer. I guess you'll have to have the little bastard and take care of it like any normal mother would."

She looked at him. She didn't say anything. He watched her moving about, gathering her clothes and putting them on.

"Where are you going?" he asked.

Edith turned and her face was flushed. "To see Andy," she said.

"For Christ's sake, Edith," he grumbled. Then he stopped. It was futile to discuss anything with Edith at the present time, but curiously he asked, "where in the hell is Andy staying since he left his house?"

"He's staying with the Clark's over in Twin Forks. William Clark and Andy were mine associates at one time," Edith said.

She came over and put her hand on Robert's arm. "This baby is going to be ours," she said softly. "I told you often that I'm not ashamed of getting involved with you. I'm really not, Robert, and I'm very happy. What else can I say, but we were meant for each other, and that is good enough for me. What I had done before was wrong—a big mistake, Robert. I should have waited knowing that some day you'd come along. I didn't wait—I had to go ahead and marry Andy for spite—to get even with Henry Shane."

"Edith," Robert muttered.

"Please, Robert, I'm doing the talking. I've gone to bed with you, God knows how often. There isn't anyone that is going to cast shame on this child I have been praying to have for a long time. It's your child as well as mine, and that makes it even better. Just to think, it's going to be our child."

"Are you going to tell Andy that you're pregnant? What else are you going to ask him?"

Edith lowered her head for a moment. When she raised it, her voice was calm. "I'm going to beg him for a divorce again. My child must have a name. I don't give a damn what other people are going to say. They don't understand, Robert. I don't want my child to always be called a bastard."

"You really are kind of worked up, Edith," Robert said. "Don't you think it's in my place to approach Andy again?"

"No, Robert, he didn't listen to you before. What makes you think he's going to listen to you now?"

"I guess you're right," he said softly.

She stood there a long time, looking at him, and finally she said, "I'm leaving now."

"If that's what you want to do, it's fine with me," Robert said wearily.

She kissed him lightly on the cheek, left the house and walked slowly towards the car that was parked along the street.

It was a long way to the Clark house in Twin Forks where Andy was staying since his departure from Sinclair. It was a very hot day and the road lay before her in a faint gleam of heat, the lines of everything were hazy, blurred by the heat waves rising from the sun-baked macadam.

As she drove into the mountains, the air appeared to be cooler. She drove on slowly, applying the brakes occasionally as she rounded the treacherous curves on the road descending towards Twin Forks. She scarcely felt any discomfort, felt only the silent tumult going on inside her mind.

I've got no choice, she thought. I've got to face him and beg him for a divorce. I've got to tell him that I'm going to have a child, the child he wanted and couldn't have. I've got to tell him I got pregnant from my involvement with Robert Heim. Then the worst part about it, I've got to stand there and watch the expression on his face when I tell him that he no longer is important to me nor is Robert Heim. It's the child that concerns me now.

She went on, driving the weary miles unaware of their going until she came to the outskirts of Twin Forks and saw William Clark's house. Thank god, she thought. Andy is here. His car is parked along the street. What is the Clark's going to say when they see me? They're likely to tell me to get the hell out of here, and I can't blame them if they do. I'm not fit to keep company with decent people anymore.

Edith got out of her car and proceeded towards the house. As she climbed the steps on to the porch, she noticed that the door was ajar. There were no signs of the Clark's being at home, but as she entered the house, she saw Andy sitting alone at a table.

She took a deep breath, and held it. She came up behind him very quietly, and when she was close, she saw a bottle of whiskey and a revolver on the table. The breath she was holding came out in a rasping sound.

"Christ, Andy," she cried out. "What the hell are you trying to prove?"

He turned and she saw his glazed eyes. "How are you, Edith?" he asked quietly.

Quickly she responded, "I have deceived you. Although I don't love you I think you're a good man, but you can't take away your own life."

"I've thought about it," he said. "I don't have anything to live for now. All my plans, all my hopes and dreams are broken."

"Why should they be, Andy. Why?"

He looked at her. "You ask me why, Edith? You of all people." She stood there speechless for a moment only when he looked at her face did he see tears flowing freely from her eyes.

"Please sit down, Edith. I'll make you some coffee."

"No, thank you, Andy. I don't have anytime to drink coffee. I came here mainly to talk to you. I've got to ask you something. I hate worse than anything to have to, but I just got to ask you again, Andy."

"Then why in the hell don't you ask me?" Andy said.

"Please give me a divorce," Edith said softly. "Please, Andy, please."

"So you can marry Robert Heim. Is that it?"

"Yes," she whispered quickly.

He had to lean forward to hear the words. "It appears to me that you took your good old time coming around to see me about a divorce, considering the way you have been living in sin."

"I guess you're right, Andy. I begged you several times to give me a divorce, but you wouldn't. As time went on I felt guilty. I was ashamed to face you again."

"Was ashamed?" Andy said.

"Honest to God, Andy, I still am. Now I must have a divorce. It is the best thing for us to do. I am pleading for a divorce, because it isn't for my sake any longer, not even for Robert Heim."

"Hell oh mighty, I can't do that," Andy said. "I don't have the courage to condemn you in public and file for a divorce, then hearing all those vicious rumors about you committing adultery."

"I am an adulteress," Edith wept. "I did commit adultery and that is sufficient grounds for you to file for a divorce."

"What's life going to be like for you, Edith, if I grant you the request for a divorce."

"Terrible," Edith said. "Please, Andy, please give me a divorce."

"You're pregnant, aren't you? That's the reason why you came to see me."

Edith lowered her head in shame and whispered, "yes."

Andy didn't say anything. He turned and stared directly at the revolver lying on the table for a long time. When he looked at her again, he was relatively calm. "All right, Edith, I am going to give you a divorce. Just wait here a few minutes." He walked into an adjacent room. When he returned, he had a large, tan envelope in his hand. "Here," he said. "Take this envelope and give it to Attorney John Wilkins over at the Law Building in Sinclair. Don't ask me any questions? Just do as I say. By the time he opens that envelope, your request for a divorce will be granted."

"Andy," she cried out, "I always thought it took a hell of a long time to get a divorce?"

"You said that you want to be free to marry Robert Heim. Now stop your bitching and do as I told you to do, before I change my mind."

She stood there staring at him, until, finally, the revolver lying on the table caught her attention again. She began to tremble and stuttered as she began to speak again. "What's—what's that revolver doing on the table? What in the hell are you going to do with it, Andy?"

He smiled at her. "What I'm going to do with that revolver is none of your damn business, Edith." He walked her to the door. He hesitated momentarily, and then kissed her lightly on the cheek. "Goodbye, Edith. Don't forget to give that envelope to Attorney John Wilkins it's important that you do?"

"Yes, Andy, I'll give the envelope to Attorney John Wilkins."

"I pray to God that you're going to be happy with Robert Heim. Now, you take care of the baby when it arrives. Do you hear me?"

"Yes, Andy, I hear you," she replied as she got into her car and drove away in the direction of Sinclair.

Robert Heim was waiting at the house in Sinclair when she got back from Twin Forks. He was nervous and anxious. "Well, what the hell did Andy say?" he asked forcefully.

"Andy is willing to give me a divorce," Edith said tiredly. "He promised to initiate the proceedings as soon as possible."

"I told you," Robert grinned. "There's nothing to worry about. Come on now, get cleaned up and I'll take you out to a restaurant so that we can have dinner together."

"I'm not hungry. I'm not the least bit hungry."

"You're going to have to eat," Robert told her sharply. ""You're carrying a child now and it's going to require all the nutriments you can possibly give it."

"Yes, I know. I don't feel like going out to a restaurant. I'll just prepare a little food and we can eat in the dining room."

That night she lay there in her bed unable to sleep. She turned it all over in her mind. It didn't make sense what Andy Curtis had said to her, she thought. They didn't change the law, nobody could get a divorce in a couple of days unless they went to Mexico. There was no logic to it at all. Andy couldn't give me a divorce. It wasn't that easy or that quick, but he said that I'd be free to marry Robert Heim. Then she suddenly remembered the revolver lying on the table and she quickly sat upright in bed.

"Oh, my God," she cried out. "Andy is out of his mind! He has been driven to insanity by what I have done to him—by me who he was good to and loved and worshipped—that's it—of course that's it! He's going to kill himself. Oh, my God, Andy is going to commit suicide."

The moon's sparkling light radiated through the oak trees and brightened the night. From a nearby tree, an owl hooted. Then it was silent, so silent she could hear Robert's breathing and the beating of her own heart. She couldn't tolerate it. She couldn't bear the silence. She was overcome with fear, suddenly. Something is going to happen, she told herself, and I'll have no control over it. The owl hooted again, creating an eerie and weird feeling. Edith sat there with her body trembling. Then far off, a dog howled, the sound quavering in the still night.

The following day Attorney John Wilkins arrived unexpectedly at Edith's house in Sinclair. Robert Heim took one hand off of the lawn mower, and wiped the perspiration from his forehead with his handkerchief. Edith, who was sitting on a swing on the front porch, recognized the man sitting in the car to be Attorney John Wilkins. She walked from the porch and moved closer to Robert Heim.

"How do you do, Mr. Wilkins?" Robert said.

Attorney Wilkins didn't answer him. He just sat there in his car staring at the two of them with an expression on his face that Edith and Robert couldn't define. Then he threw a partially consumed cigarette on to the pavement.

"What the hell is on your mind?" Robert asked.

"You know damn well what's on my mind, Mr. Heim," Attorney Wilkins said sarcastically. "You're the one who is responsible for what happened to Andy Curtis."

"For Christ's sake," Robert said. "I don't know what the hell you're talking about. The only damn thing I know is that Edith went to Twin Forks to ask Andy for a divorce. That's the extent of my knowledge of her visitation to Twin Forks."

Attorney Wilkins studied him for a few minutes. "By damn, you mean to stand there, and tell me you don't know what the hell I'm talking about."

"I swear to God, I don't," Robert said.

"All right. Maybe you don't know what happened to Andy Curtis. Anyway, I'm certain you know that Edith went to her husband and asked him to give her a divorce so she could eventually marry you. Would you believe it? He granted her request for a divorce the quick and easy way."

"What do you mean the quick and easy way," Robert Heim intervened.

"It was a terrible tragedy," Attorney Wilkins said slowly and clearly. "He put the end of a revolver into his mouth and pulled the trigger. That's what he meant when he said he was going to permit Edith to marry you. It's really sad indeed to see a man do a way with himself in the prime of his life."

"Oh, my God, oh my god!" Edith cried out hysterically. "Oh, Jesus Christ, no!" She doubled over, her entire body trembling, the tears flowing profusely from her eyes, her hands clutching her stomach, pressing hard to relief the pain. "I suspected it! I suspected it when I saw the revolver on the table. I didn't think much about it until last night. Oh, my God."

"Edith, that's enough of this bullshit," Robert Heim said cruelly. "Let's go into the house. You're not in any condition to carry on like a deranged woman."

He took her by the arm and led her away from the front yard. A few yards away, he looked back. "Don't you leave, Mr. Wilkins?" he said. "I've got some important business to discuss with you. It doesn't have anything to do with Andy Curtis."

Edith staggered beside him like a drunken person, moving slowly and awkwardly. "Goddamn it, Edith," he said. "Don't carry on like a child throwing a tantrum? It isn't your fault that Andy put a revolver into his mouth and pulled the trigger. It's not your fault at all, so face reality."

She didn't answer him, but permitted him to lead her into the house. She lay down on the couch and turned her face away from him. It was futile trying to talk to her and Robert knew it. So he left the house and stood in the yard looking at Attorney Wilkins sitting in his car. Shortly, Attorney Wilkins got out of the car and stood there looking at Robert Heim. Then he walked towards him.

"It's not in my place to pass judgement on anyone," he said softly. "It's none of my damn business as to what happened between Edith and Andy, I guess, but I'm certain it's God's. I am an attorney, and I know damn well that it was immoral the way you were involved with Edith. You, Robert Heim, seduced another man's wife and impregnated her. You have not only taken his wife, but your actions caused him to commit suicide. The worst part about it is that the law won't be able to apprehend you. I'm assuming that this incident should make you feel mighty happy and proud."

Robert Heim lowered his head and didn't answer him. Gradually he raised his head and looked at Attorney Wilkins, and the expression on his face didn't change.

"I don't know if Edith told you, Robert," Attorney Wilkins said. "Andy instructed her to deliver a tan envelope to me. Do you know what was in the envelope?"

"No, I don't. I don't have the slightest idea. Edith never mentioned the envelope she received from Andy."

"Well, I'm going to tell you—it was his last will and testament," Attorney Wilkins said bluntly. "He really loved Edith. He left everything that he owned to her in spite of her immorality. That's what you call love, my boy. The will is legal and valid. There aren't any surviving relatives, and if there were, they might have contested the will. Since his mother's death, Andy was alone in the world. So all of Andy's possessions go to Edith and her heirs. I guess when you get around to marrying Edith that makes you a part owner of her possessions. If there is anything I can do for you, please feel free to call on me."

"As a matter of fact there is something you can do for me, Mr. Wilkins. I'm going to need a good lawyer to handle my legal affairs."

Attorney Wilkins looked at him from head to foot. "I wish I could refuse you," he said softly. "It is my policy to render assistance to those that are in need of help. Now, what is it that I can do for you specifically?"

"Well, Mr. Wilkins, you know I'm involved in several business ventures and most of my money is tied up. Since you are on the Board of Directors over at the Citizen's National Bank, I'm going to ask you to help me get a substantial loan from them."

"What do you have in mind?" Attorney Wilkins asked quickly.

"I'm interested in acquiring some land near the Stonycreek River. If I can get the land, I'm going to construct a coal storage depot and a large loading dock so that I can ship the coal by freight or barge to Pellersville and points west."

"It seems like a damn good idea," Attorney Wilkins said.

"Yeah, but there is only one major problem."

"What is that?" Attorney Wilkins asked.

"Vito Rizzo!" Robert said emphatically. "He's the stubborn old bastard that owns the land. To boot, he's involved in some half-ass coal mining operation that doesn't amount to an ounce of shit. Anyway, my first major concern is with the bank. If I can't get a loan from the bank, then it would be ridiculous and a waste of time trying to convince Vito Rizzo to sell the land. I know damn well that the land is of no use to him. If he finds out why I want to buy the land, the rotten son of a bitch won't sell it to me just for spite."

Attorney Wilkins began to smile. "I don't think you're going to have trouble with the bank. Since the Citizen's National Bank's policy doesn't say anything about doing business with a man because he is a big prick and a rotten son of a bitch, I'm certain the bank will grant you a loan. After all, they're in business to make money too. You need the money, the land is valuable and your business venture is bound to be profitable. As you know, and I know, you're going to have a hell of a time getting Vito Rizzo to sell the land to you. Anyway, I must readily admit that you're one of the best Goddamned businessmen I've ever known."

"Thank you," Robert said.

"You come to my office tomorrow morning and then I'll accompany you over to the bank. I'm certain there will be no problem whatsoever with the bank. Better yet, make sure you come in early when there aren't too many people on the street. It seems that the people in town are damned upset over the death of Andy Curtis. It might not be safe for you to come in at all. Anyway, I'll see you tomorrow, Heim, if you feel up to it."

"Wait, before you leave, Mr. Wilkins. When are they going to bury Andy Curtis?"

"Day after tomorrow," Attorney Wilkins said. "There will be no viewing—coffin will be closed so nobody can see his face. They'll have private services and invite only his closest friends—then they'll take him up to Saint Anthony's Cemetery and bury him alongside of his mother and father." He paused, staring at Robert Heim. "On second thought, I think it would be wiser for you to wait for a few days after the funeral before coming downtown to see me. As I said before, the people in this town are pretty damn upset and some of them might rough you up a bit or even try to kill you. Anyhow, I'll see you in a couple days, Heim. I'm sure the loan can wait, considering the present circumstances."

Robert Heim didn't answer him, or even watch him go. Instead, he walked to the back of the house and leaned on a fence, gazing in the direction of the Stonycreek River. I'll build the coal loading dock there, he thought, and after that, a coal storage depot. I'll hire more workers, and get ready to make a big profit by the end of next year.

Something eluded him. He stood tall and erect near the fence and ran his fingers through his hair. He should have been happy, but he wasn't. He was, he realized suddenly, downright miserable. Goddamn that Andy Curtis! He thought. Why in the hell did he have to commit suicide? Why didn't he part from Edith graciously? Now, all the people in town are upset and will be out after my ass. Andy is dead, but all the rumors relating to his death will haunt me. I forced him to leave his own house, took his wife, but there still is something amiss. I still don't understand why he suddenly committed suicide knowing that Edith was always unfaithful. I have everything but I still feel that my ass has been whipped. Why in the hell do I feel like this?

It wasn't a thought he could support very long. A slow, painful anger overcame him. He wanted to strike out and to hit his fist against anything in sight. Son of a bitch, I can't compete against a dead man, he thought. I've got to get all this bullshit out of my mind and sure as hell as I'm standing here I'm going to end up in a mental institution.

Then a thought came to his mind with a strange feeling that was like a triumph. "Those rotten bastards downtown are pissed off at me, and that damn Attorney Wilkins had the balls to come up here to warn me to stay undercover for a few days. Hell, I didn't tell Andy to commit suicide. Why should I crawl in a hole and end up as a recluse because of the actions of another man? I'll show those people, I'll show them that I have a lot of guts and I'm not one bit afraid of them. They're going to accept me whether they like it or not."

He turned and walked slowly toward the house. When he entered it, he was somewhat relieved. Edith was resting on the couch with her face to the backrest. She didn't turn over as he came into the room. She lay very still until she heard him open the door to the gun cabinet, and after that, the sound the revolver made when he spun the chamber with his thumb. Then she sat up quickly and stared at him, wild-eyed. "Robert," she cried out. "What are you going to do with that revolver?"

"Don't you worry about the revolver, Edith? I'm not going to go anywhere in this town without any protection, and I have no intentions of using this revolver unless I have to. Furthermore, I'm not going to live in isolation the rest of my life because of what Andy had done. So,

I'm going to take a little walk, right down Rosemore Avenue where everyone can see me. I'm going to do it now, and get it over with. It seems that there is a group of people downtown that don't care too much about me and the things they think I had done to break up your marriage. It's time they find out who Robert Heim is once and for all."

"Robert," Edith said tearfully. "For God's sake, Robert."

"I'll be back shortly. Don't you worry? Nothing is going to happen to me."

She arose from the couch, facing him. "I'm not concerned about you!" she said forcefully. "It's your child I'm concerned about, Robert. Go and get all crippled or possibly killed! Leave me helpless and alone to rear your child. Go on, if that is what you want!"

He thrust the revolver into a holster and strapped it tightly to his chest, concealing it with his shirt. As he put out his arms to embrace her, she whirled away, crying.

"Why don't you listen to me, Robert? Even Attorney Wilkins warned you about going downtown to face those people that are all upset. Please, Robert, don't make matters worse!"

He straightened up, his face revealing expressions of annoyance. "All right, Edith. I'm leaving now. We'll carry on this conversation when I get back."

Then he departed from the room and closed the door very quietly behind him.

When he walked from Pine Street on to Rosemore Avenue, a silence moved before him. The warm breeze that stirred in his face seemed to increase in velocity, and the usually unnoticed sounds increased—a car with screeching brakes, a dog's bark, a child wailing, the shrill sound of the whistle far out beyond the town's limits sounding clearly, piercing against the stillness. Most of the men he encountered ignored him, apparently they were thinking about other more pressing affairs far removed from him. He dared not to engage in conversation with any of them. He walked on, his arms swinging at his side, and his shoes striking the pavement sounded loud in the silent street. He walked forward slowly to the center of Sinclair.

Once he reached the center of town, consisting of a few stores, barrooms, a post office; and a recently constructed office building, he could think of no way out of his problems. He went into the first barroom that he came upon, but the men there ignored him with elaborate casualness. He thought of ordering a round of drinks for everyone present, but he decided against it almost at once. If any man refused his offer, he'd be obliged to fight. He was certain he was still physically able to challenge any man there. Win or lose, he thought, fighting wasn't going to help solve his problems. He stood there leaning against the bar with the revolver pressing against his chest, and with no thoughts of fear that had haunted him earlier in the week.

He had two quick shots of whiskey and walked out frowning. He wasn't getting anywhere and he knew it. He walked aimlessly down the sidewalk, stepping into the dusty street occasionally to avoid bumping into anyone, because of Edith's warning that he must keep away from trouble stuck like glue in his mind. He stopped before entering the Law Building, hesitated momentarily before entering Attorney Wilkin's office.

That was the end of it, the hostile mob that was never formed, the talk of being physically abused or murdered, of being driven out of town on a rail. He stood there in the Law Building, talking easily, slowly with Attorney Wilkins for a long time. Upon the completion of his business conversation, he left the building and walked once more to the house on Pine Street where Edith waited anxiously for his return.

The next morning Robert Heim looked at Edith with his dark and dreary eyes. She was very big with child now, sitting there calmly across the table from him. Robert cursed savagely.

"Son of a bitch, Edith. I've permitted my imagination to get the best of me just worrying about what those people were going to do to me. I guess I deliberately tried to push those Coal Region people a little too far. Lord, but they're proud. Still, I've got to get that land near the river. I've got to figure a way as to how to approach Vito Rizzo. That's another big worry for me. I don't have a coal storage depot, and I don't know what the hell to do with the coal that's coming from the stripping. Once I solve that problem and hire some more reliable workers to maintain the coal storage depot, I'll be independent of these people. Until then, it's tough sledding. I've got to do something to change the minds' of these people." He finished eating his breakfast, pushed his chair away from the table and stood up.

Edith looked at him questioningly. "Going somewhere, Robert," she said.

"Yes," he replied. "I think I'll drive over to Vito Rizzo's place and kind of check out the land I'm interested in acquiring. Maybe if I were to talk to him a little—act friendly like—he might come across."

"Robert, it won't do any good. I know the Rizzo's. They're awfully stubborn people, and I don't think you're going to change their mind about selling the land to you."

"Well," Robert said. "There's no harm in trying. Nothing ventured, nothing gained."

"All right, Robert. Please don't let them get you all upset. If you lose your temper and get into a fight, it will be about the worse thing you could do."

"Sure as hell would," Robert sighed. "All right, Edith, I'll be careful. I know damn well those Italians stick together like flypaper, so I don't have any intentions of arousing Vito Rizzo's blood brothers." He bent down and kissed Edith quickly. Then he walked out of the house.

Sixteen

There was nothing that upset Robert Heim more than attempting to purchase land owned by Vito Rizzo, that in reality was actually needed for his business venture. This land was located near the Stonycreek River where he could build a coal storage depot, and thus transport with ease his coal to Pellersville. The only available land to suit him for the construction of a coal storage depot was land located at a higher elevation, useless for growing crops but escaped flooding water from the Stonycreek River. Yet, Vito Rizzo was a very stubborn man and refused to part with the land, although all the money offered to him was of greater value than the land itself.

There was something else on Robert Heim's mind: the tendency to dislike Vito Rizzo with a passion. Vito irritated him, denied him, and conquered him by the mere reality of his presence on the face of the earth. It was not an intricate issue, it merely indicated that Vito Rizzo was what Robert Heim wanted to be, could not, in reality ever be sensitive, and a kind and sweet-tempered man. It was somewhat disputable which of the two things Robert Heim wanted the most to fulfil; to purchase Vito Rizzo's land or to degrade his pride.

"The damn, aloof Italian bastard!" Robert whispered as he drove toward Vito Rizzo's house that was very attractive in comparison to those occupied by the coal miners who lived in company row. "I'll be dammed, if I'll let him shun me."

Robert Heim saw as he drove closer, that Vito Rizzo was sitting on a swing on the front porch. He was talking to several of his neighbors. His wife Jean was in the kitchen, Robert assumed, preparing food for supper and the thought of her slender figure and black hair excited him immensely. I'm going to make out with that woman some day, he thought. He drove his automobile in front of the house, opened the door, and stepped onto the pavement. Upon seeing him, Vito Rizzo stood up with an easy and refined motion. He was a short, stout man with black hair, a round, puffy face out of which his dark eyes continued to blink indefinitely.

"Robert Heim," he said, "It's a pleasure to see you."

At that moment, Robert was uneasy, and the blood began to throb in his body with more than the usual force. "Yes," he uttered, "I'm here to see you and I believe you know why, Vito. I want to buy some of your land near the Stonycreek River. Why don't you face reality? The land isn't really of any great value to you, and it would be worth a hell of a lot to me if I use it for the storage of coal."

"Sell it," Vito Rizzo said. "Just because it isn't farm land."

Robert Heim chuckled, "Anyone can see that the land isn't farm land." Robert looked directly into Vito's eyes. "All right, I'll have to tell you the truth—even if it encourages you to raise the price of the land. It is a suitable place because it is near the river. The land itself doesn't interest me much, except in so far as I could possibly do some farming if I was to clear and fertilize the land. The area I'm seeking has deep water right out in front of you—barge water. I'll build myself a dock, transport the coal to Pellersville, and to other points to the west. I could save myself a hell of a lot of money in freight and storage costs. Now do you see why I want to buy the land."

Vito Rizzo attempted to change the subject immediately. "Do you care for a glass of wine, Robert?"

"You mean you aren't going to sell the land to me," Robert said loudly. "Believe me, Vito, the money I will give you for this land, you could purchase yourself a decent plot of ground somewhere else."

"How about another glass of wine, Robert?" Vito said softly.

"All right, I don't mind if I do have another glass of wine. You know Vito, I must admit that you are one of the toughest sons of bitches I ever had to negotiate with."

"That's hard to believe," Vito said calmly. "I'm just the son of an Italian immigrant trying to mind my own business. The land means more to us than just trying to earn a livelihood. My sentimental attachment to this land has nothing to do with its commercial value or lack of it. As you indicated, I could buy other land and use it accordingly. We like the scenery here. Do you notice how the sunlight reflects off of the water onto the tall oak trees bordering the river? Look at the bending river flowing between the avenue of trees. I find it rather gratifying to observe the scenery. Secondly, I have no desire whatsoever to become wealthy. This may sound peculiar to you."

"Peculiar!" Robert exclaimed. "Vito, you're really stubborn!"

"Maybe I am," Vito smiled. "Do you want another glass of wine?"

"Thanks, I don't mind if I do," Robert said quickly. "Look, Vito, if it is a question of the price I am offering you for the land, I'll kindly increase it."

"It's not the land itself," Vito said firmly. "We had some prosperity this year on the farm and at the mine. The good Lord has been kind to us, and as I said before, it is the scenic view that is important to us. It is priceless. You don't have enough money to buy the land from me."

"Well, I'll be a son of a bitch," Robert said angrily.

"I rather think you're one," Vito said. "Any man that has no perception of beautiful scenery, so driven by his intuition is most apt to be entrusted to everlasting punishment. Don't you ever stop thinking of getting wealthy, Heim? You should know by this time that there is more to life than just money."

Robert Heim stared at Vito with an expression of contempt. "Are you calling me greedy and selfish, Vito?"

"No, the statement was rather apologetic. I'm sorry you received the wrong impression because I consider it to be disrespectful to insult a guest in my house."

Slowly Robert Heim smiled.

"I thought you would understand," Vito said. "If you are so determined, upon having your own coal storage depot near the

Stonycreek River, then why don't you purchase a piece of land from one of those families on the other side of the river. Some of those people might not appreciate nature like we do. There are plenty of other locations along the river."

"Not like this location," Robert Heim said. "Your land is directly in front of me, and it appears that there are no obstructions on the river at this point. If you were a clever businessman, you would build a coal storage depot yourself if you had any worth while collateral. That's the most important factor, isn't it?"

"Look, Vito," Robert said earnestly. "I'll clear the land and build a coal storage depot for you. I'll loan you the money, and all I would want out of the transaction would be the right of way to cross your property and use the coal depot with you. I will not exert any pressure on you. Hell, you could reimburse me at your discretion."

"No, I'm not interested in your proposal," Vito said forcefully.

"I can't believe it! Would you mind telling me what is wrong with my offer?"

"Not at all," Vito said. "I just don't like having an obligation to any person. That's one thought. Another is that I would have little use of the coal depot, while your vehicles would continuously rumble over my property. I wouldn't approve of it. I prefer to live in an area that is calm and peaceful."

Robert frowned. "I guess there is nothing else to be said to convince you."

"No," Vito said. "I don't think there is much more to say. Anyway, don't deprive us of the pleasure of your visitations just because we can't agree on business terms. Come and see us someday and bring your mistress. Jean has been anxious to meet her. She has heard so much about her."

"I imagine she has," Robert said quickly. But, he thought, it would be a cold day in hell before I bring Edith over here to be criticized by a sophisticated Italian woman. Robert did not express his thoughts openly, but did manage to say, "thank you kindly, I'll tell Edith." Then he got into his car and drove away.

There the subject may have rested, but for two aspects: Robert Heim's stubbornness and Jean Rizzo. Robert Heim pondered over the state of affairs for several days, searching deeply into his own mind to try to determine what Vito Rizzo's real philosophy of life was, and how he might understand it.

Vito Rizzo had told him the truth that there were people in the world that were uninterested in money, to whom the fluffy clouds in the sky, the sun's defined rays pervading among the trees, the water of the river ripping against the embankment near Sinclair, were priceless. Robert was incapable of understanding the existence of such a mood of mind. He loved his own dense, succulent woodlands with an intense passion, but he would never admit to himself, did not in fact realize that the appearance had something to do with it. If it ever had been forced upon his conscientiousness that he, too, like every man living, was at least to a certain extent an admirer of scenery. If he did not understand this, he would have been overcome with confusion.

One of the things that bothered him most about his relationship with Edith was that basic as it was upon the craving of all desires—a strong desire for devoted attachment—he didn't understand it. "Damn if I know what I see in her," he told himself time after time. He thought Edith was deficient in some qualities that were prevalent in other women. She was not as passionate towards him as she should have been. The wild, raging passion he was able to arouse from time to time in other women, simply did not occur easily in Edith. She yielded to his embraces, but more, he was certain, merely as a means to hold him than from any excitable sensation of the act itself. She did not, of course, find it offensive. She accepted it as she accepted it all of her life, with mild endurance. He wore himself into exhaustion attempting to encourage Edith to have an orgasm, a state of emotional excitement he was accustomed to successively induce in other women he had known. When he could not succeed, he accused her of being frigid.

"I am not frigid," Edith protested. "I love you very much. I like sexual intercourse—very much."

"Why?" Robert Heim questioned cruelly. "You are difficult to arouse in recent weeks."

"Yes, I know," Edith whispered. "Yet, it was the most sensational feeling—like the fragrance of roses." This comment startled Robert Heim—like the tintinnabulation of bells.

"Damn!" he said loudly, but he still continued to live with her just the same. Her pleasing, facial features attracted him, and the softness of her voice enticed him, but he still sought the affection of other women.

Nevertheless, he thought Jean Rizzo was his kind of woman that excited him. Always lamenting, he thought with pleasure, the way a woman should be. What he meant was that the relationship between a man and woman was to him in its leading principle, a struggle, a clash, a disagreement of course that after several encounters and minor disagreements the man eventually succeeded. "The wilder they are, the better I like them," he would often say to others. He was of course, not nearly so obsessive of a man as he thought of himself as being. Even his sexual appetite was no simple desire, but carried with it other aspects of his existence, his greediness for gain, for he thought of a woman before anything else, like she was his property in much the same way he thought all of his workers were his property. He always had a need for authority, even in the fondling of women. He attempted to make a woman yield and forced her to surrender to his will, but in the case of Edith, he struggled to make her moan, to weaken, and to move violently.

Jean Rizzo was another issue. He thought of her often now, his mind functioning at an intense pace—that amounted to no more than an impulse—sensual skill. I'll direct compliments towards her, he thought. I'll have that coal storage depot. There isn't anything like a woman persuading her husband into something that he doesn't want to do. So the next time he visited the Rizzo homestead, he was cautious to choose a time when Vito would be away from the house, out in town, or supervising his workers at the mine.

Jean Rizzo greeted him with politeness. "Come in Robert," she said. "I'll use the telephone and try to locate Vito."

"No, don't," Robert said quickly. "I would prefer to talk to you, Jean, if I may."

"Well," Jean hesitated. "I can't imagine what you would want to talk to me about."

"I would like to talk to you about the same thing I talked to your husband about, Jean. I thought I could convince you to support my offer to Vito. When a woman is determined to persuade her husband—he doesn't have a chance."

"I see," Jean Rizzo said softly. "You want me to persuade Vito to sell the land near the river. My God, you are an obstinate man, Robert Heim. How many times do you have to be told we like the land?"

"You would like the land located somewhere else just as well, Jean." Robert said calmly. "You probably would like the land a little better from my way of thinking, because the money I'm willing to pay your husband, he could purchase more productive land. He could also afford to buy elaborate shirts, suits and ties. He could wear the kind of clothes that will make him look like a distinguished man. If you don't mind my saying so, Jean, you're an attractive woman, but you would look more attractive in modern clothes."

"As a matter of fact," Jean said coldly, "I do mind your saying so. I like praiseworthy remarks, every woman does. Those words coming from your mouth, are not praiseworthy, they are insults!"

"Well, I'll be damned!" Robert said in astonishment.

"I don't like your language," Jean said angrily. "I'm afraid I shall have to ask you to leave—now!"

Robert stood there pondering. "You're a mighty conceited woman, aren't you. I thought you would like a little flattery. There isn't anything else I can say—nothing at all."

Then he moved forward and forcefully seized her, holding her body with his left arm, raising his right hand to grab her chin, to stop the jerky movement of her head. She didn't say anything, she just went on resisting until he held her firmly, bending his head down to find her lips. It was then that she did the thing that was to him unthinkable. Jean Rizzo opened her mouth and spat directly into his face. He released her at once, and stepped back, searching for his handkerchief. He wiped his face and stood there staring at her, unaware of the fact that his body was trembling from the episode.

"I shall not tell Vito," Jean said quietly. "I think he would want to challenge you and he might be killed. I'll say this, Robert Heim, I hope you have learned a lesson. I know, all your experience has been with the cunning barroom whores, but now you have met a faithful woman. I will not dishonor my husband. The vows we had taken are everlasting. So go home now to the kind of woman you are used to, go home to the woman you are shacking up with, whose husband committed suicide."

She trembled, and became indistinct before his eyes. He was overcome with anger, and everything that Jean Rizzo said was mere nonsense to his ears. "Shut the fuck up," he roared. "Don't you bad mouth Edith with your slanderous remarks? Don't you dare?"

"The truth hurts, doesn't it?" Jean snickered. "Or are you just a phony? You have a right to defend Edith, but there will be a time when she will betray you the same way she betrayed her husband. Adultery gets to be repetitious."

Jean Rizzo's words disturbed Robert tremendously. He subconsciously raised his hand and slapped her face. The blow against her face sounded like the sharp noise of a revolver shot, and she fell down quickly before him, lying there like a wounded warrior. Then his anger diminished, and there were no other abusive thoughts in his brain. He attempted to assist her to her feet, but she refused.

"Don't touch me!" she said in a surly voice. Don't put your filthy hands on me!" She stood up wobbling from side to side. "Incredible!" she said. "Other people have told me that there were men like you." Then in an abrupt, revived wave of frenzy, she screamed at him.

"Get the hell out of here! If you ever come back again, I shall kill you and that means shooting you in the gut without warning. Get the hell out of here! Get out!"

Robert Heim was bewildered, lowered his head, walked to his car and drove away. He did not go directly to Edith's house. He was not in a mood to confront Edith. Instead he went to the Ritz Tavern in Sinclair where he frequently spent his leisure time, beaming in the hearty acceptance of the coal miners, buying them beer, periodic boasting of his exploits that was directed to them—the mighty man before the impoverished miners, the protectorate encircled by his followers. They were aware that they were being duped, but on the other hand, they thought Robert Heim was a fine and reputable man, but with little aspirations. "There is nothing outstanding about him," some inebriated miners would say.

Robert leaned against the bar and drank his whiskey with the other men, passing the bottle from one man to another and engaging in conversation with the well-versed clientele. Tonight he appeared to be exhausted, and after awhile the clientele noticed it. Still, they went about engaging in their routine pastime, the intensive activities for the usual gratification of the other clients.

Many clients amused themselves by deliberately irritating other clientele and causing brawls. Often the tavern became a violent environment crowded with rugged and boisterous men who quarreled and fought over insignificant matters. The conclusion inevitably produced broken arms or legs, bloody or smashed noses, swollen and damaged eyes, broken teeth, whirling bottles that caused severe gashes, and occasionally the appearance and use of switch blade knives created a hysterical scene.

Several lean, rough breaker men were engaged in an arm wrestling match at the end of the bar, while one of the fellows timed them with a pocket watch. Others were attempting to tolerate the weariness and humidity of the evening by having a whiskey drinking contest, to determine how much a person could drink at a gulp, without taking the bottle from the lips, the eventual loser required to pay for all the drinks consumed.

Tonight they were confining themselves to one of their quiet pastimes. At the rear, right corner of the tavern, a battered dartboard was hanging on the wall. The local dart club members were engaged in a contest with a rival dart club from a nearby community to determine the county championship.

A group of men were gathered in the middle of the tavern where they were competing with each other in a penny-tossing contest. The center point was a brass spittoon that served, as a container to catch the pennies that were aimed with precision behind white chalk marks drawn on the floor. At each round the distance between the spittoon and the marks were increased until the lowest scoring competitor was eliminated.

Robert Heim mingled with the clientele, always feeling comfortable among them. It gave him great pleasure to participate in their simple pastimes. If he felt it beneath his loftiness as an entrepreneur to gratify in them, he none the less urged them on. He inspired them, and offered to buy them beer and whiskey, first to those who were coal miners, and then to the other clientele avoiding signs of favoritism, and finally for the two bit whores from company row, just for the hell of it. They accepted him not as one of themselves, but as something more such as an associate and an able leader. They fell into the customary practice of respecting him, yielding to his skills and opinions, seeking advice and solutions from him to solve various problems.

His sullen mood that night was real. A woman had rejected him with disdain, and he was unaccustomed to being rejected. Vito Rizzo had abruptly stopped him from attaining his ambition, and there was nothing he could do about it. One of the clientele, Paul Williams noticed the sad expression on Robert's face.

Finally Paul Williams shifted his chewing tobacco from one side of his puffy check to the other side and nudged one of his associates. "Something is bothering Robert Heim," he said. "I have never seen him look so depressed before."

The others nodded signifying an agreement. "Go and ask him

what is bothering him, Nick," Paul Williams said. "Maybe we can help him solve his problems."

Nick Polski walked over to where Robert sat, pondering over his glass of whiskey. "What is bothering you, Robert?" He asked with that faultless, fool's seriousness that was a visible sign of his kind.

"Oh, Nick! Sit down and join me. Hey, Frank, another glass of the same kind for Nick, here."

"You look very depressed and exhausted, Robert," Nick said. "I don't think I have ever seen you look so bad before."

"I have a major problem, Nick," Robert said with a deep sigh.

"Tell me about it," Nick said quickly. "Maybe we can help you out."

Robert's natural reaction would have been to laugh. But he didn't. Instead, for no other reason than a benevolent need to get the entire event off of his chest, he told Nick the story, neglecting, however, to tell him the about the specific incident with Jean Rizzo.

"The worse part about it," Robert continued, "is that plot of ground is of no value to Vito. He isn't a farmer. If it weren't for the antique cars he has stored in his barn, he wouldn't have a pot to piss in. I wish someone would destroy that damn barn."

"Why?" Nick asked.

"Then he would have to sell the land, don't you see? Or else the Citizen's National Bank can acquire the land from him—damn Italian bastard."

"Yes, I see," Nick said. "Thanks for the whiskey, Robert. Thanks a lot."

So it was that Robert Heim was entirely unprepared for Vito Rizzo's decent upon him the next day. Vito came driving on to Edith's property, accompanied by several of his henchmen.

"There he is," Vito said quickly as soon as he saw Robert sitting on the porch. "Go and work him over!"

Several of his henchmen attacked Robert, holding him with their rough, callused hands. It was the second incident in the last several days that he was insulted. First, Jean Rizzo spat in his face, and now Vito had sent his henchmen upon him.

"What the hell is going on!" Robert shouted. "Vito, you're going to pay for this!"

Vito sat in his car, a grin igniting his face. "I suppose that you don't know," he said quietly, "that my barn was blown up sometime during the night. I suppose you don't give a damn that I have lost an investment and that I have no other recourse but to turn over my property deed to your very close friend, Mr. Harold Stone at the bank."

Robert stared at him, with a smirk expression showing on his face. "That son of a bitch, Nick Polski!" he said aloud, uttering his name subconsciously before he had time to suppress the sudden thought.

"Oh, so you did know about my barn being destroyed!" Vito smiled. "So Robert Heim, we are going to beat the living shit out of you. Perhaps, who knows, I might even be able to arouse in you some small sense of appreciation for the meaning of the words, respect and decency. "Tony, hold him tight!" Vito said forcefully.

Vito's direct command was a mistake. The henchmen, who were strong, apparently knew very little about the dirty tactics of fighting. Robert moved with an unexpected physical force, bringing his knee up swiftly against a man's testicles, and the man doubled up in pain and dropped to the ground moaning, grasping one of the most delicate parts of his body. Robert attempted to retrieve his revolver from the holster, but his bungling maneuver failed him.

Once again Vito Rizzo said forcefully, "I hate to do this." He reached for his revolver and shot Robert Heim in the chest. Vito sat in his car looking at the outstretched body lying on the ground. He sighed deeply. "Let's go," he said to his henchmen. "I think we better get the hell out of here before the police arrive."

Edith heard the firing of the revolver. She ran quickly from the house and saw Robert Heim lying helplessly on the front lawn. He stared aimlessly at Edith. She was shocked and had to stand there and accept the tragedy with heavy tears in her eyes. Then she became hysterical and began to scream, arousing the tranquillity of the neighborhood. "Robert, Robert! What have they done to you?"

Vincent Jones, a neighbor, hearing the commotion and seeing that Robert was felled by a bullet quickly telephoned the hospital for an ambulance to report to the scene of the tragedy. When the medical attendants arrived, they lifted Robert onto a stretcher and placed him in the ambulance. Edith stopped crying, but she stood there with facial expressions displaying the signs of terror. "Is he dead?" she uttered.

"No, madam," one of the attendants said politely, "but he is in serious condition."

"He is dying," Edith said, her voice tense against the excitability rising within her. "I told him to stay away from Vito Rizzo, but he wouldn't listen to me."

"Edith," Robert whispered, but his voice failed him.

"Robert!" Edith shouted. "For God's sake, Robert! Robert!"

The attendants assisted Edith into the ambulance to accompany the wounded Robert Heim to the hospital. When the ambulance arrived at the Sinclair Hospital, the attendants immediately transported Robert to the emergency room where a medical staff was awaiting his arrival.

"Bring him in here," a nurse said.

They laid him on a litter, and began to remove his clothes. "Take off his shoes," another nurse commanded. Then she turned to one of the practical nurses that was standing nearby, "Please bring me a pair of bandage scissors. Thelma, get the intravenous started. Hurry!"

Edith stood there watching as the nurse cut the bloodstained clothing away from his body. The wound was located on the left side of his chest, and it still bled profusely.

Immediately, a doctor dressed in scrubs arrived on the scene. Edith looked at the doctor seeking answers from him regarding Robert's condition.

"There are many suppositions in this case," the doctor stated. "We will try to do our very best, and that is all I can say at the present time."

"That is all I can hope and pray for now," Edith replied. She returned to the waiting room to await the outcome of Robert's tragedy. While there she was approached by Vincent Jones who immediately said, "Aren't you interested in who shot Robert?"

"Yes, I am, but I already know who shot Robert. It was VitoRizzo." "It wasn't entirely Robert's fault," Vincent Jones responded. "It was Vito Rizzo and the dispute was over some land near the Stonycreek River, and the destruction of a barn on Vito's farm." Vincent could see some of the relief on Edith's face. "I said that Vito was entirely wrong. Robert never sent anyone to destroy his barn. That's not the way he operates. He has more class than that to resort to those kinds of tactics. I'll be back later to see how Robert is doing."

Edith didn't even hear him depart. She was too upset. There was nothing she could do but wait for the outcome. She sat nervously in the chair twiddling her thumbs. She could hear the raspy voices coming forth from a nearby room, the continuous, chronic coughing of the elderly patients, the rapid rustling of garments in the corridor, and the noise appeared louder and louder as time elapsed.

On the outside windowpane, a leaf meandered slowly from a maple tree and clung to the glass. It was now so still that her ears were overwhelmed by the excessive sounds of silence: the ticking of the clock, the patter of heels against the floor as nurses walked across it, the uniform sound of her own breathing, the throb of her own heart.

"Dear God," she prayed, "he is a sinful man. He has violated all of the religious rules bestowed to humans, but he is the only man I have now. He is my child's father. Please God, grant me my wish. Save him! I need him to support my child and me. God, please don't take him away from me! God, please grant me my wish!" Then she lowered her head and cried.

The doctor examined Robert's chest with a stethoscope listening for activity of the heart and lungs. Shortly, he leaned gently over Robert's body and put up his right hand and with his fingers he delicately drew down the lids over his glassy eyes.

Steve Mallory, the police chief, was in his office sitting on a chair with his feet propped on the desk, reading the latest edition of THE JAYSTOWN TRIBUNE. He looked up when he saw Vito Rizzo enter the office.

"What a big surprise," he said. "My men have been looking for you for the greater part of the day."

Vito reached into his jacket for the revolver and placed it on the desk. "I come to give myself up," he said quietly. "I shot Robert Heim. I understand they took him by ambulance to the Sinclair Hospital. I am sorry I had to shoot him, but he was harassing and tormenting my wife. I became infuriated and lost control of my reasoning power. Well, Steve, I think you should give me the opportunity to contact my lawyer, and then put me behind bars. I'll take my chances with the law."

Part III

A Soldier's Life in the Far East

1948-1953

Seventeen

Henry Shane arrived in Yokohama, Japan, located on the Island of Honshu. After undergoing the brief military clearance at the port, he was sent directly by train to Camp Fuji near the city of Tokyo. Camp Fuji was a visible indication of the power and glory of the United States Army, reminding the Japanese people that they had been conquered by a great nation. Colorful barracks were sprawled on many acres near the western fringes of this thickly populated oriental city. Soldiers could be seen drilling on the dusty parade ground, while others were engaged in meager details.

In the barracks at night, soldiers gambled. A card game or crap game was almost always going on among the men. In their scant leisure time they made their way into Tokyo to drink or to be in the company of Japanese girls. In Tokyo, soldiers had a good time and were never discouraged by the language barrier that existed. Camp Fuji was a boom to the economy of Tokyo and surrounding villages. It gave the people a sense of security they had lacked under the Japanese militarists, for the American soldiers spent their monthly pay in local business establishments and barrooms.

At Camp Fuji, Henry Shane had a good and mutually useful friendship with Sergeant Joe Poletti who informed him of the conditions in Japan under the occupation. To Henry's delight, he was well versed on the aspects of the nightlife on the Ginza.

"Before you decide what you want to do in Tokyo, Henry, you will need several things," Joe Poletti said. "You'll need plenty of money, plenty of will power, and sure as hell you'd better know where you're going."

"How are the bars up in Shimbashi," Henry asked. "I heard a lot about them from several of the other men."

"It's better to stay away from the joints up there," Joe Poletti said. "If a fellow isn't a drinker before he goes there, the chances are that he will be if he stays there long enough. I know, because I used to go over to Shimbashi, that is until I wised up. Those bastards will give you anything to drink just to get your money."

"I'll just have to be careful," Henry said. "It's going to be tough for me to stay away from the booze when every other business establishment is a bar, and I know damn well I'm not just going to sit in the barracks at night and twiddle my thumbs."

"If you can stand the pace, you're a good man, Henry. You'd better be prepared for a damn hangover in the mornings from drinking that rot gut they sell."

"What do most of the guys do to pass their time away? Where do they usually hang out?" Henry asked frankly.

"Just like back in the states. A typical evening usually starts off innocently, you know," Poletti said as he smiled. "You go out with a couple of your buddies or you meet a few other GI's at a bar, and after a few drinks, someone suggests you make a quick run of the Ginza. Lord, that does it." Joe Poletti coughed, and then continued to talk. "Ginza bars are damn well standardized, not like the bars up in northern Japan. The bartenders are shrewd operators, and they know their business and can make any kind of drink you want. The places are usually loaded with paid hostesses loitering in the semi darkness."

"Well, that's no different than back in the states," Henry remarked.

Yes, that may be true, but this country has too many women, that are what makes the difference. The GI can have a ball here because everything is wide open. One thing that is damn convenient about the girls in Japan is the fact that they are pretty well classified."

"What do you mean that they are classified?" Henry asked.

"It's hard to explain—anyway, you'll know what I mean when I get done talking," Poletti said. "There are those girls in the upper class—to be looked at and admired, but you can't get your paws on them. Then the rich girls, and awfully expensive ones too, who might be lured with a tactful approach. Then the run of the mill type that take a little bargaining, but well worth the effort, and finally the anxious to please girls who will go into high gear at the sight of your money."

"I see what you mean, Poletti. I'd better damn well know what I'm doing. I imagine being over here for awhile can make a person go wild. Those anxious to please girls are probably the ones that are infected with a venereal disease," Henry said disgustingly.

"Yeah," Poletti said. "You can't tell that to some of the stupid jerks we have in our outfit. They'll still go out and mess around them, and before you know the medics have their hands full. Some of those Japanese girls are rather clever though, and they take care of themselves."

"What about the girls that work in the bars?" Henry asked.

Joe Poletti hesitated and then began to talk again. "Those kind of girls usually average about a thousand yen per hour. So be careful as to how many girls you invite to your table. You know the GI's are well known for their free spending. The fewer girls mean lesser mouths to feed. Oh, before I forget, Henry, one nice thing about it all, many places remain open long beyond the police curfew on the pretense they are restaurants. These are the places that the Ginza girls come to after their own places have closed. Many of these girls on a night off are found in these places, surrounded by GI's with plenty of money to throw away." Joe Poletti paused a moment and then continued to talk. "Many of those places cater to the security forces who wander off their base and go slumming in the Japanese night life." Joe Poletti reached into his pocket for his cigarettes. "Care for a smoke."

"No, thanks."

"Don't misunderstand me?" Poletti said. "You can have a hell of a good time over here, but be careful." He took a drag on his cigarette. "By the way, are you married, Henry?"

Henry's face reddened. "Yes, I am. I married a girl I met while stationed at Fort George. I really don't know why I did. I thought I loved her, but now that I'm in Japan, I'm not sure. Once I get settled, she's going to come over. Don't let my being married stop you from talking. Go right ahead where you left off. I'm interested in knowing more about this country."

"Now, where in the hell was I?" Poletti said.

"You were talking about the girls that hung around the bars."

"Anyway," Poletti continued, "the girls take turns in sitting around looking pretty and otherwise useless, that is until a special GI friend drops in. Most of the girls speak a few words of English of the standard barroom vocabulary that usually sounds like hell, and consists of single phrases. If you are the lovable type, they probably will take a little smooching, but it all depends on the size of the tip. The girls live on the tips and whatever they can make afterwards. Their main objective is to get your money. Just about the time you get bored, the girl on your lap decides to go to the benjo. Then you get up, stagger to the bar, pay your bill if you're able to, and wander down the street to the next bar."

"What happens if you can't make out with the girls sitting at the bar?" Henry asked in a serious manner.

Joe Poletti began to laugh. "If you can't make out, you might as well give up the idea of luring a bargirl. I'm sure you'll make out, that is if you have some money to throw around, If you can't make out, then you'll have to get a friend to fix you up. Try a blind date perhaps. Then you know what happens?"

"I don't have the slightest idea," Henry responded.

Joe Poletti chuckled and said, "You usually get stuck with a girl for the entire weekend." At first, Poletti roared with laughter. "You might end up with a girl that is enough to ruin your romantic ideas. She could turn out to be as blind as a bat, and wears glasses for the effect only. You know, just like the girls' back in the states. Some of them were pretty damn good at covering it up. If you get stuck with a girl like that, then it's time to make a quick get away, make up some kind of excuse about a last minute detail. If you're loaded, it probably won't make any difference what girl you're with. Things always shape up after a few drinks, and you'll decide the weekend might turn out good after all."

"I heard a lot about those kind of weekends," Henry said laughingly.

"Yeah, they're all right, Henry, no kidding. Many of the guys look forward to the weekend. No wonder, the quiet Japanese inn, the mamasan and the sake puts you in a good mood. Then the hot water test. Mamasan shuffles in and informs you that the bath is ready. You look at the girls around you and yell out, What the hell is going on? If the girls blush and put on an act, you are in with them. If they go to the bath first, they're probably old professionals, and if they say, well, what are you waiting for, then you've had it brother."

"I think I'm going to like it over here in Japan," Henry said. "Everything you've told me certainly sounds interesting. I'll go out and find out for myself what it really is like."

"As I said, Henry, you've got to be careful where you go in Tokyo. A place to stay away from after dark is Shimbashi. Sneaky little men come upon you and whisper something about a nice clean place around the corner. You know what that means. I've told you all the things I've experienced during my stay in Japan."

"Thanks," Henry said. "I certainly appreciate it."

Upon arriving in Japan, Henry Shane realized that there was a new generation of Japanese womanhood. Although he never had been in Japan before, he had heard many accounts of the nightlife, not only from Joe Poletti, but also from other servicemen who served there with the occupational forces. Yes, he thought deeply, I am a veteran of a war, and never had the opportunity to enjoy or experience such a lavish and leisure life. Now my opportunity has come. The Japanese girls have come a long way from the early, post war period of candy bar presents and the Lucky Strike cigarettes. These beautiful girls know the taste of freedom and prosperity and won't be satisfied with just beer. They know the best places to eat and won't settle for anything less.

After being in Japan for several weeks, Henry knew it was so easy to sin. It was so convenient. Anyway, he knew what it was to sin. He started first by calling a Geisha House. He explained that he had a desire to have supper and relaxation.

Mamasan asked him, "What will you drink? What will you have to eat? What do you wish to satisfy your needs, fat, tall, or skinny? Do you wish to stay all night? Make up your mind," she says bluntly.

"Oh, a little sukiyaki, sake, and perhaps a hot bath, a massage and then to bed," Henry replied.

He arrives at the house, and partially drunk. The small girls are lined up in a row alongside of the mamasan. As he stalked along the corridor, he heard the sound of pattering feet. He realized that these girls were only the maids, and the other girls would come later. Then they gave him a kimono and he changed in to it, before settling down to the main events of the evening.

"If you are nervous about taking your clothes off in front of the girls, you can turn the other way," the mamasan said. "Its much less trouble than to chase them out."

Then he saw the girls enter with the sake and food in an unending procession. Eventually he saw other girls come into the room from the area of the sliding doors. They entered noisily, bowed and waited restfully while he examined them.

He was overwhelmed with joy. "It's just like the guys said would happen," Henry whispered. He asked the girls what their names were, and he could only remember that they sounded like Chiyoko, Ritsuko, and Seiko. He knew if he were willing to pay more, his choice would be better. After a careful study of the girls, he selected one that he thought would be an expert in bedroom tactics, thus Ritsuko was his choice.

He did not say much to Ritsuko, but spent considerable time evaluating her facial features. He drank sake and Ritsuko drank with him. Finally Henry had enough of the sake and was bored with the simple conversation that they both really didn't understand. That was the signal. Ritsuko clapped her hands and the other girls entered the room to clear away the remains. Without any hesitation, he asked Ritsuko to scrub his back. She catered to his wish.

He staggered down the corridor, feeling the effects of the alcohol he had consumed prior to his arrival, and now the sake. He came to the bath. He put his foot into the tub and found that the water was scalding hot and he yelled, "How in the hell am I going to be able to get into that!" Quickly another girl entered uttering words of apology, "Gomennasai, gomennasai," and without a blush sent him scurrying for cover. She knew what his problem was, and immediately turned on the cold water. There he sat relaxing until he was aware that more hot water was pouring into the tub constantly.

"Some son of a bitch left the hot water on," he yelled. "Come and turn the damn water off before I'm scalded alive!" Suddenly Ritsuko appeared.

"You no use soap in water, GI," she said with a smile. "You come here, Ritsuko soap back." After he was soaped and rinsed, Ritsuko skillfully obtained a towel, and made him more comfortable. Henry, by this time felt in a playful mood and tried to return the compliment, but he knew that this wasn't the right place for such a foolish gesture. Back to the tub he went, and shortly there after found himself back in a kimono and escorted to his room. How pleasant the atmosphere, he thought. Clothes were neatly folded and others hanging in the corner, lanterns were dimly lighted, and an aroma of oriental perfume was detected throughout the room. Then Ritsuko glided into the room and found herself in his warm embrace.

The next morning he woke up with a terrible hangover, and had no recollection of how he ever got into bed with Ritsuko. The adventure ended with a sad bottle of beer as the glare of the dawn's early light and the hustle and bustle of the city brought him once again to his senses. The early dawn shattered his illusion of the night on the Ginza. It seemed that many hammers pounded on his head, and he solemnly moaned, "Never again."

The next night, he was on the prowl again in search of a new adventure, lured by the shrill screeches of the beckoning Ginza.

So it came to pass that Henry spent most of his free time in Tokyo, fascinated by the grasping environment, for it offered him a means that he could readily release all of his tension and frustrations. He still had another month of carefree living, and then his wife Faye would be there with him. The thought of Faye coming to Japan frightened him, for it meant settling down to a life of general routine. Why, he often thought, did I marry Faye? I really didn't love her. He knew that his attitude would remain entirely unchanged. It was Edith Curtis he loved. He remembered suddenly the letter his brother Lee had written to him while he was still at Fort George. "Would it shock you if I were to inform you that Edith Curtis has turned out to be a whore." Upon receiving the news from his brother, he remembered how infuriated he became and sent a bitter letter of denunciation to Edith. How foolish I was to have done such a thing, he often thought. The same label should have been attached to my name. I am no better, and I had the nerve to condemn her for the same actions I am guilty of. Why did I walk out on Edith? Now he often realized that if he didn't walk out on her back in Sinclair, he would have taken her once again in his arms and married her. He also knew that he would have been a damn fool to do so, but on many other occasions he regarded himself as a fool. Now he had no intentions of ever going back to Sinclair. The further he stayed away from Edith, the better. He realized he was fooling no one but himself, because deeply rooted in his mind were the tender memories of Edith prior to her marriage to Andy Curtis. What it was, the thing that kept his hopes alive all these years, no other than the thought of Edith. Now, his mind with bitter thoughts in search of the why of things had led him into this state of dismay. Edith, whom he had dedicated his young life to, his high school sweetheart, turned a whore, lying possibly at that moment in bed with another man back in Sinclair.

A lonely soldier can create for himself many problems in the darkness of his mind. Finally Henry Shane fled into the familiar refuge of drunkenness again, and driven by his beastly needs, his desires, his shattered moral principles submerged under the influence of alcohol. He once again found himself staggering down the street reading off the names of the bars: The Bar Cherry, The Juraku, and The Bamboo

Bar. There seemed no end to them, nor to the brawling mill of the loud, voiced, drunken men crowding their entrances. Prostitutes standing along the street sizing things up with their mouths open in a grin, and the gold teeth drawing his attention.

"Hey, GI, where you go? Want to come my house."

He finally managed to make it to the Orient Room where he renewed his sorry state. The bar tender was very short, black haired, and noticeably slant of eye and easy of grin. Slanted as his eyes were above his cheekbones, watchful and wolf thoughtful, they trapped him.

"What you have to drink, GI?"

"Bottle of Nippon Beer," Henry stammered.

With the beer bottle in his hand, Henry glanced around the barroom. Some men were lying on the floor, men seated lay forward with their heads on beer soaked tables. Some men were moaning; they thought they were singing. Others were engaged in drunken argument. An occasional bottle fell to the floor with a crash that sent shattered pieces of glass in all directions.

There were many Josans present—a kiss here, a stroke there, and an uttered, "I like you GI." They went from table to table clasping the various men in their arms.

Apparently, Henry thought, some men had been lying on the floor for a considerable period of time, and some had been kicked out, some had been lying in the doorway and had sobered a little owing to air. One look at the pitiful sight in the barroom still prompted him to make inquiries about a reputable house of prostitution.

"Where is the whorehouse?" Henry asked the bartender.

"You go Shimbashi, GI," the bartender said with a smile. "Plenty houses there."

Neglecting the warning by Joe Poletti to stay away from Shimbashi, he staggered from the bar out on to the street and flagged a taxi. Upon entering the taxi he informed the driver that he wished to be taken to Shimbashi. "Why you go Shimbashi?" the driver asked him with a wide grin on his face. "Better you go back base. No good to go to Shimbashi when GI have too much drink."

"I'm not drunk," Henry said. "I may be feeling good, but I'm not drunk. I just want to find a nice house with pretty girls."

"All right, GI, I take you to number one house."

Shortly the taxi arrived in Shimbashi, and came to a sudden stop in front of an elaborate building. Henry got out of the taxi, reached into his pocket for his wallet and paid the driver.

"You go knock on door, GI, tell mamasan Yoshi sent you." He grinned, put his taxi into gear, and drove off into the night.

Henry walked slowly to the door, knocked, and before long an elderly woman dressed in a colorful kimono stood before him.

"What you want, Yank?" the mamasan said in a rough voice.

"Yoshi told me that this is a number one house," Henry replied.

"All right, you come in house. Cost you five thousand yen."

"Five thousand yen," Henry said in astonishment. "What the hell is this, a gyp joint?"

"You no like, you go. I no tell you to come. Mamasan have number one girls. Cost much money."

Henry looked around and saw he was in a reputable house of prostitution. The taxi driver wasn't kidding when he told me he would drive me to a clean establishment, he thought as he looked at the girls. The sight of the pretty young girls and the thought of going to bed with one prompted him to say, "All right mamasan, I'll give you five thousand yen."

"You can pick girl you like," the mamasan said. "Then I take you to room, and you have nice time. Many GI come here, all like. Come back many, many times. Hope you like too."

He had gone to bed with one, a slender, well developed young girl, selected by him to be as different as possible from Edith, Faye or any other girl he had relations with before. He was ineffective, for the alcohol was taking its toll. The youthful and eager girl became inpatient with his inability to respond. The urge was not strong enough, not strong enough to meet his needs, his lust. He quickly got out of bed, put on his clothes, and fled from the establishment to the sound of the whores' mocking laughter. He never returned to Shimbashi again. Instead, he lingered at the Bar Cherry where he drank beer to weary himself into sleep. Instead the long hours of stillness, gazing upon the strangeness of this oriental city, upon the darkness and hapless shape of his despair.

Eighteen

At the Bar Cherry, Henry repeatedly found himself seated opposite an attractive girl, often too far away for ready conversation, but always in a position where he could study her with ease. He found out from those who frequented the bar that her name was Keiko. By his keen observation and interest in her, he became intimately familiar with Keiko. He studied her appearance and mannerisms, with all of her charm, with her fluttering eyelashes, with her quick, restless movements, and her slight knowledge of English. The more he looked at her the more he was impressed that she was different and not at all like the other Japanese girls he had met or seen. Many of the GI's, he thought liked their girls to be somewhat bold and daring. Keiko was none of these things. Her voice had a soft quality rather than the rough note that was characteristic of most of the Japanese girls that frequented the bars. Her laugh was pleasant and meaningful in contrast to the put on chuckling gestures of the others. Her body was strikingly appealing, and she always showed good taste and originality in her dress. Japanese women in Tokyo at this time were then undergoing a period of transformation. The styles from the states were finding their way into the market, and all the girls who could afford it wore the kind of dresses that were common in San Francisco, New York or Chicago. Now Henry was visualizing how striking Keiko would look in clothing that could reveal the true contour of her body. This thought, too, was evidently prevalent in the minds of the other GI's, for they all looked at her with similar intensity. Nevertheless, in her usual restless manner, she would toss her pretty, well developed legs about so that she seemed to want the men to look at them with hungry eyes.

Henry found himself to be increasingly fascinated by her. To his way of thinking, she was more attractive than the other girls with soft eyes who were the center of GI attention in all the other bars. He hoped, although he wasn't sure of it, that Keiko planned her visits to the Bar Cherry to coincide with his. She became aware of his presence, and now some type of relation was bound to occur between them. Henry was also of the opinion that she had adorned her body and revealed herself primarily for him, and the thought of a relationship with her encouraged him immensely.

For several nights he saw no evidence that Keiko was thinking in the same manner he was. He received his first jolt, when he and Joe Poletti, after duties at the base had come to the Bar Cherry for a few drinks. The two of them were engaged in a friendly discussion when Henry suddenly got the urge to approach Keiko boldly.

"Why in the hell didn't I have the courage to get acquainted with Keiko?" he said frankly. "I like that girl."

"Maybe you're worried about your wife," Poletti said jokingly.

"My wife!" Henry responded. "I don't give a damn what she thinks. She isn't here yet so why should I worry about her. In the first place, I told you I never really loved her." He stopped talking and continued to stare at Keiko.

Shortly Poletti broke the silence, "You sure as hell are attracted to that girl. Why don't you call her over before some other guy makes out with her?"

"Not a bad idea," Henry said. He took a sip of beer, set his bottle on the table, and motioned to Keiko to come over to their table. Keiko hesitated, smiled and walked sedately towards him.

"Sit down, Keiko," Henry said.

"How you know my name

"Some of the GI's told me who you were."

"Oh, by the way, this is my friend, Joe Poletti."

"All GI's name Joe," she said as a smile came upon her face.

"No kidding, Keiko, his real name is Joe Poletti."

"That's right, my name is Joe Poletti."

"What's your name?" Keiko asked while looking directly into Henry's eyes.

"My name is Henry Shane."

"I see you many times," Keiko remarked. "All the time you look at Keiko, but you no come sit with Keiko."

"I guess I didn't have the courage," Henry said.

"All other GI's no afraid of Keiko, but I no like all GI. Some drink too much. Some nice."

"What's a nice girl like you doing in a place like this anyway?" Henry asked boldly.

Keiko looked at him with bewildered eyes, then a frown came upon her face. "Look GI," she said bluntly. "You nice guy." Then she paused looking at him with her sad eyes. "Most Japanese girls tell GI sob story why they get job in barroom. Tell how GI make them go to bed. Then Josan get pregnant and have babysan, and then GI go back states."

She hesitated, gazing past them, her tear-laden eyes filled with a memory. "Funny, I like GI once. He comes from Iowa back in states. Him has nice face, blue eyes, and light hair. I young girl, but I tell GI to come my house. Then we go to bed. But him nice boy, and then he go back states. Keiko never hear from him again." She wiped the tears away from her eyes. "See what Keiko try to say. You nice too, but best Keiko no fool around you. Now Keiko leave table."

"No, I don't want you to leave, Keiko," Henry said sadly. "Do we, Joe?"

"Just sit there, Keiko," Joe Poletti said. "We understand."

Keiko did not speak, but gave Henry a long steady look that seemed to be filled with a meaning. Then she smiled very slightly, lowered her eyes and fussed with her hair. Henry knew that Keiko liked him, for he saw it in her eyes. He felt at once flattered but also annoyed. He knew that she could never be anything more than an escape for his frustrations, and another lengthy affair would be, he thought, practically impossible for his wife Faye was due to arrive in Japan in the near future.

Henry had by this time learned a great deal about the morals of the Japanese girls, if only because the barracks at the base was so full of gossip about them. All the GI's who lived there was promptly informed on the girl situation upon their arrival in Japan. So almost every soldier had a long list of establishments to visit, and a long list of girls' names that were available.

So it was only to be understood that Keiko would practice upon the traditional aspects of her class. Henry had originally felt uneasy about her, but now he was the aggressor, the new man at the fringes of her life, perhaps the only man at that moment that understood her. She wanted him to feel her charm and power as a woman, to respond to it as best he could, and this he was determined to do. If having an affair with Keiko meant losing his wife, then, he could care less. In fact he was more concerned of displeasing Keiko than the possibilities of open hostility with his wife. Although Faye may have been prettier, he obviously felt that Keiko had a more charming personality. So he became infatuated with Keiko, trying hard to leave the impression that he was delighted and pleased that she had extended him a challenge, hoping she would understand.

For several nights now, although he saw Keiko, there was not another exchange of words regarding a possible relationship with her, and he began to think he had attributed too much importance on their first meeting. He found himself dejected and disappointed. Naturally he didn't want trouble at the Bar Cherry—no man would be foolish enough to deliberately do so in an oriental barroom—yet there was a thought in him, a hope, that Keiko was going to bestow her affection upon him. There were nights now when Henry was more convinced that she had forgotten him or perhaps found another GI that was more appealing.

Because of military duties, Henry did not see her again for about a week, and then only briefly when he and Joe Poletti met at the Bar cherry for their usual round of drinks. He did find himself sitting uncomfortably opposite Keiko while Joe Poletti was engrossed in conversation with other GI's. She looked at him in a peculiar manner. This time there wasn't a trace of a smile upon her face. Instead, she frowned, heavily and purposefully, almost as if she hated him. Why, Henry thought. He felt distinctly hurt as though she had thrown a knife at him. Her look revealed as plainly as words that he had neglected her that he was a son of a bitch, that he had earned the dirty looks. Now what could he do? It was evident that something had gotten into Keiko. He rushed to her and seized her by the arm.

"What have I done to offend you, Keiko?" he said sharply.

"You no do anything. That's why Keiko sad. Some GI's say you married and wife come to Japan soon. I like you. I no care you married. Why you no like Keiko? If you like Keiko, you take Keiko home. All you do is look around and look at Keiko, then you just drink and drink."

"So that is what is bothering you," Henry uttered. "Why in the hell didn't you say so? How am I suppose to know what's going through your mind? All of this time I merely thought you didn't want me to bother you."

"Okay, you come my house Saturday after you finish work at base."

"Why Saturday? Why not tonight?"

"No can stay all night then. You work base and Keiko no want you to get in trouble. Better Saturday night, then you can stay all weekend."

"Where do you live, Keiko?" Henry said anxiously.

"Me live at number two, Shoten, Nishi Tachi. Just tell taxi driver, he know. You sure you come my house."

"Of course," Henry said, and before he could speak another word she turned and darted out of the Bar Cherry, while he stood there bewildered and amazed at the speed of her departure.

At home on Saturday, Keiko sat in her room sipping on tea, although it was much too hot for tea. She needed something to relax her nerves. Repeatedly she thought she heard a faint rap at her door and sat listening. Once she went and slid open the door, thinking Henry would be there, but he wasn't. "Maybe he forgot," she whispered to herself. It was now eleven o'clock, and Henry had not yet arrived. The night was becoming cool, and the silence caused Keiko to become more restless. Then she unmistakably this time heard a taping at the door that was often in Nishi Tachi the signal of a suitor. When she slid open the door, Henry Shane stood before her. He permitted her to look at him for a moment, then stepped through the doorway, dropped his traveling bag, laughed and said, "You thought I wouldn't come. Well, I got tied up today—went out looking for a house and had a hell of a time finding one. You know my wife is coming to Japan, and I sure as hell was worried about not finding a house. The billeting office over at the base told me they're all booked up and they'd have to put my name on a waiting list to be eligible for quarters there. What do you think I did?"

"No understand," Keiko responded.

"Well, I decided to come over to Nishi Tachi to look for a house, and to my surprise I found a damn nice place. So, I told the guy I would rent it. It really isn't far from here."

"I no care about house. I glad you come. Please sit down."

It sounded a little too formal, he thought. Perhaps he should have seized her in his arms the moment he stepped through the doorway, but such a bold gesture may have alarmed her. In fact, now that his glorious moment had come, he felt unsure of himself, if only because he knew so little about her. It dawned on him suddenly that so far as any understanding of each other was concerned, they were strangers. He had never before been alone with her, even for a moment. To him she had only been a number in a barroom and they had met each other merely through friendly gestures.

"Care for tea," Keiko said.

"Yes, thank you," Henry responded.

There he sat silently with a smile on his face. To Keiko it appeared to be a deceiving smile. He knew he wasn't making it easy for Keiko to understand him. His approach to a woman had always been to make friends first, by way of casual conversation, to create an atmosphere free of tension and laden with mutual understanding. But to Keiko, it was not her way, at least where Henry was concerned. To her, a man was like a package, full of surprises, to be challenged.

Henry understood this from his observations of Japanese woman. Among the average girls, where they shared a struggle for survival, there was more of a companionship, but to them sex was not a game, but a means by which they could earn a livelihood. To Henry Shane, illicit sexual behavior was a sin and its sinfulness was part of the resistance. She was not an overwhelming woman. To this, she knew, she was inadequate. She had neither the desire nor the technique.

"It was kind of you to come," she said. "I always want to talk to you, now Keiko have chance."

Henry rose immediately, shook his head, grunted faintly that indicated his opinion of a woman who would invite a man into the house for the weekend only as an opportunity to engage in a conversation.

"I didn't just come over here to talk," he said bluntly.

She was afraid of him and he knew it. Her facial expressions told him that much. He placed his hand upon her shoulder.

"Please," she said gently. "You must not do that." She stood with her head lowered, and her face revealed signs of anger, her mouth was tightly closed. Her look startled him and caused him to momentarily withdraw into his past so he was again the humble man who had so long looked up at women in their colorful dresses, sitting on a pedestal, a feeling they were forever beyond his reach.

They stood looking at each other in deep silence. Then she smiled a little which expressed to him a challenge, and it was not a mere gesture of formality. He never resorted to violence in luring a woman. This method he lacked, but he knew now he faced a crisis. He had to take some sort of action, and quickly before Keiko turned completely away from him. If he didn't, he would be disgraced, and possibly hated. Thinking of this, he gathered all of his strength and courage and moved toward her with passion in his eyes, pulled her fiercely into his arms in what he hoped wasn't a fatal approach, carried her quickly into the bedroom, and proceeded earnestly to remove her clothes. She kicked and squirmed, tried to get up, but he was not about to stop. He was determined to strip Keiko of her clothes regardless of the consequences.

"She screamed, "No! No!"

Exhausted from the struggling, she gave up her resistance suddenly when his hand explored her naked body. The struggle appeared as if they were seeking revenge for the tension that had built up since they first cast their eyes upon one another. She stretched out on the bed, and gasped for air. Later she sat up and kissed him with loving tenderness, encouraging him in a manner he had never before encountered. Keiko was born in a country, and of rare women for whom sex had been a profession for years, and they made an art of it. This was part of her tradition, but the method of approach was her very own. She indeed was a master in the art of love. Therefore, Henry was deeply enchanted by Keiko for she not only satisfied his desires, but with it, she had shed her entire personality that was shameless, and one that intrigued him. After spending the weekend with Keiko, it appeared also, when he was about to depart that she put on all her manners along with her dress.

"You come back, see me again," she said pleasantly.

"Yes, I'll be back," he said. "By the way, Keiko, I'm looking for a good house girl to serve in my household when my wife arrives. Do you know of anyone?"

"Good girl hard to find," she said. "Maybe wife no like to have house girl."

"Oh, I know she will, because she hates to do house work, and most of the other married GI's have a girl working in their house."

"Maybe Keiko take job. How much you pay?"

"You're kidding," Henry said surprisingly. He paused, "I don't know what the pay is going to be yet."

"Keiko tell truth. I think about it, let you know next time I see you." Henry slid open the door and peered out into the darkness of the night, listened for a long moment, then turned around and kissed Keiko, then he departed for the base.

Henry did come again, and many other times to Keiko's house. He enjoyed her company, but she was careful to keep her desires to a minimum. She had the impression that he came to her only when he was tense and frustrated. Yet when he was about to depart, he always appeared relaxed and well at ease, and free of guilt. Sin he accepted as a necessary part of his existence. For him, every act of passion was well worth the effort leaving him pure and tranquil.

Some of his actions she came to understand, as she might have understood any man by observing his behavior, but for days Henry remained a stranger and a mystery to her, a man who wanted her body and her love, but nothing more.

Then suddenly one day, Henry began to talk freely, and once he started to talk, words poured from his mouth in a steady flow. Keiko had surmised that he never talked much to anyone before, certainly not to a woman, and she led him on by careful questioning, feeling by his talk he would release some of his tension. Mostly, he talked about his youth in Sinclair, Pennsylvania and how he had gone steady with Edith Miller and wished that he never had walked out on her. He told Keiko about the hardships back in Sinclair, and why he re-enlisted in the army. As to his boyhood days, he talked easily and with pleasure, but he evidently found it rather difficult to tell her about his later years. He never mentioned why he had married Faye Cooper and did not divulge any of his inner secrets of passion.

"You are different, Keiko," he would always say casually. "You're not like the other Japanese girls. You treat a man as though he were your best friend." Keiko and Henry were humans of different kinds and born of different cultures, and they would never think or feel alike in regard to politics, but they had something in common, a burning love and a mutual understanding.

Therefore with a little persuasion on his part, and as she had promised, she informed him of her decision regarding employment in his household. Willingly she accepted his offer.

Several weeks later, on a bright Saturday afternoon, Henry's wife arrived at Tokyo International Airport. He was there to greet her with open arms. After embracing each other, and exchanging kisses, they set forth to their new residence in Nishi Tachi. At her first glance at the house, Faye was deeply excited and enchanted at the thought of living in the mysterious Orient.

Upon entering the house, an attractive Japanese girl, bowing greeted her and uttering, "Welcome to Japan, Mrs. Shane."

"Who is this girl?" Faye said surprisingly.

"Oh, this is Keiko, our house girl," Henry responded.

"House girl! I don't need a house girl. I can do the work myself."

"Most of the married GI's hired house girls to work in their household, besides it's good for the economy, and it makes for better public relations."

"Oh, I see" Faye said. "Are you sure that this is all there is to it?" She and Henry looked at each other in silence, then he turned and went into the kitchen where Keiko was busy preparing the evening meal.

"How your wife like house?" Keiko said in a whisper.

Henry looked away from her with an uncertain expression and said, "I don't know, she went into the bedroom."

"She no say anything, Henry," Keiko said with disappointment.

They expected Faye to enter the kitchen, and listened for her step, and not hearing it, Henry called her. "Faye, supper is ready." She did not answer, and after a few minutes he went to the bedroom and opened the door. The room was now partially dark, but in the shadows he saw her sitting near the window, and knew she had not taken off her traveling dress. She did not move, but Henry said politely, "Supper is ready. Aren't you coming?"

"I don't feel a bit hungry," she replied.

It was the trip, Henry thought, but he expected her to rise and walk into the kitchen and seat herself at the table. Instead, she remained seated, and he could not think of anything appropriate to say.

"I'm assuming you're awfully tired after the long flight across the Pacific." Turning her head at his remark she answered, "I'm more tired than you think."

Her words fell upon him with a strange shock of bewilderment. He had often heard people say they were tired, but not in the manner in which Faye said it and for a minute compassion prevailed. He thought, Faye did look tired and lonely sitting there.

"Are you sure there is nothing else bothering you, Faye?"

She frowned. "If you wanted to hire a house girl you should have waited and told me before you did."

"Why should I have waited? I thought Keiko would be as good as a house girl you could find over here."

Faye had been what Henry had always thought, sophisticated, and she was the first to admit that she enjoyed being waited on—but now he was fully aware of the repercussion that would arise while Keiko was present in their household. The first scene of open anger between he and his wife was evident the moment she cast her eyes upon Keiko. The problem was there and had to be dealt with.

"You'll have to get rid of her," Faye said.

"I can't do that," Henry replied.

"You better send me back to the states and be done with it. I guess there have been other women who came over here one day and left the next."

Her words burned into him, but he controlled his emotions. "I won't let you do that. That settles it."

There was a moments pause in their conversation and suddenly Faye said in a soft voice. "All right, I'll give it a try. I'll do the best I can for you, but I can't guarantee you it's going to work out."

The change in her tone reassured him. "Of course you and Keiko will get along fine together. There's a lot of things Keiko can do for you."

For several weeks thereafter, Faye and Keiko did appear to get along together. It was Faye who suggested that Keiko should have an occasional night off, and certain privileges should be granted to her. Keiko was a typical Japanese girl, and Faye thought it best not to permit her to feel a sharp contrast between the life she had left and the general routine of work in their household.

Keiko was living under their roof now as a servant to Mrs. Shane, and she only had the opportunity to see Henry in the mornings and at supper when he returned from the base, and occasionally over the weekends. The moments in his company were not comparable to those when she was free to linger in his arms, and the times she had spent with him at the Bar Cherry prior to his wife's arrival in Japan. Now Keiko on her nights off, frequently found herself going back to her former hangout in Tokyo to mingle with former friends.

It was during her absence, that Henry felt most intensely the desire to be alone with Keiko once again. For many weeks after his wife's arrival, the emotion had remained in him as a silent pain, coupled with sadness, and the thought of losing Keiko forever worried him. He did not even know whether any other GI was in the same predicament as he was in, or whether he was the sole victim of this disturbing inner feeling of passion.

Against his wife's wishes, Henry once again found himself in the habit of taking a taxi into Tokyo, and bringing Keiko home on nights when some form of entertainment drew her to the Bar Cherry. The thought of not being alone in the house with Keiko made him unhappy. Faye sensing this became very annoyed, and his unhappiness aroused her anger on many occasions. Thus she became very difficult to live with. Faye had not been jealous since the first day she set eyes on Keiko, but lately she had complained about the way Keiko did her housework, and thought of other meager and insignificant things to condemn her efficiency. There had been other signs of displeasure in Faye.

One morning, as he dressed in the semi-darkness, the light flickering in the panes of the window, he heard Faye speak from the bed. "If you want to have a house girl, you're going to get another one. Keiko isn't working out according to my expectations."

He had thought she had been asleep, and the sound of her grumpy voice had startled him, though of late she had been very explosive in her manner of speech. He turned and looked at her where she lay stretched out on the bed, her face revealing the emotion of anger.

"Who would I get to take her place?" Henry said in an angry tone. "We went over the same damn thing the first day you got here."

"If you can't get a decent girl, then we'll do without a house girl," she remarked.

"Then we'll do without," Henry replied.

Henry turned away again and walked over to the wash basin. "Why in the hell should we let Keiko go? She has been doing her share of work, and doing a damn good job at that. It's not that we're paying her a fortune to work in our house, so what the hell are you complaining about now."

"Complaining! I have all the right to complain. You're suppose to be my husband and I don't like the idea of her being around here. And further more, I don't like the way she has been looking at you. I'm not blind, you know—and to boot—I don't like the way you have been looking at her either. In the first place, I have a damn sneaking suspicion that there was something going on between you and Keiko even before I came to Japan, and that's why you brought her here."

Henry glaring at his face in the mirror threw his head back to wipe the soap away from his chin. His hands were shaky, but the remark that his wife made was an excuse for him to make an immediate outburst of defensive gestures. "What the hell are you talking about?" He shouted at the top of his voice. "I could make the same damn remarks about you. What did you do back in the states while I was in Japan—run around with other men?"

Henry paced back and forth across the bedroom floor nodding his head from side to side. "Here I thought you would appreciate my getting a house girl so that you wouldn't be tied down. If that's what is bugging you, then you go out and get a different girl, if not, the hell with it."

"Well, I'd like to talk to you about it," Faye said sarcastically.

"Okay, but I don't have the time now. I'm going to be late getting to the base as it is." Henry jerked his arms into his shirt, put on his tie, combed his hair, and as he went toward the door Faye said, "Aren't you going to kiss me?"

"Hell no!" he replied as he slid open the main door and stepped into the cool air of the morning.

Faye's attitude frightened Henry more than the insinuations about Keiko. It was a fact that since Faye came to Japan, he had ignored her, and most of all he failed to bestow loving affection upon her. Faye was just as guilty as he was, he thought, for she would fall asleep at his side at night without indicating that she desired affection. Henry knew he had stupidly assumed that she would not notice how he felt about Keiko. Several times in the past he had been aware of Faye deliberately letting things happen without making any remarks, or pretending she did not notice what was taking place, and now all of a sudden revealing that she had known all the time what was transpiring. Until recently, there had been no reason in his thoughts for such apprehension. Now Faye herself was beginning to gradually fade into a little world of her own.

Henry realized that to date that his life was truly lived in thought of Edith Curtis back in Sinclair. Faye had always been aware of this, but now she could no longer conceive of it being other wise. With Keiko in his presence, his trend of thought began to change in her favor.

As the days passed, Faye became very moody and restless. There were times now when she would withdraw into a deep silence and would not speak unless it was absolutely necessary. She completely ignored Henry when he would return from the base. Henry sensing her unusual behavior, became irritated, and once again sought a way of escape from all the tension that existed within the walls of their dwelling. All during these trying days, neither Henry nor Faye had mentioned the possibilities of a separation or a divorce. Nevertheless, Henry knew that the turning point in his life was about to be reached.

Nineteen

As Henry Shane stood near the entrance to the Bar Cherry, he saw within the hazy, smoke filled establishment that the crowd was becoming thinner and less noisy. Occasionally the rays of the Japanese lanterns lit up the faces of the dark haired silkily clad girls.

The Japanese men, uninterested in the remaining girls, were the first to depart to the street, while many American soldiers remained to seek further adventures.

"Aren't you going home soon, Keiko," a voice yelled from the corner of the bar.

Henry's heart skipped a beat, for this was the girl he was waiting for, and feared that another smooth talking man might lure her. From where he stood he could not see who was trying to attract the attention of Keiko. Then he heard Keiko speak. "No, GI! I wait for friend to take me home."

Then a wave of shyness held Henry back, for Keiko was their house girl, and it was at this very bar that he had encouraged her to come and serve in their household. He had enjoyed Keiko's company in the days prior to his wife's arrival in Japan. Those days with Keiko had been memorable ones for Henry, for she had given him something of her own easiness and enjoyment of life. Now, he was thinking in the same fashion as in his school days back in Sinclair, when he tried to bestow his affections upon other girls.

Henry stood there staring into the hazy dimness, and Keiko left the bar alone, pausing near the outside entrance to the Bar Cherry. She was about the last girl to have left the bar, and she stood there wondering why Henry looked so bewildered. Then a slant eyed Japanese man approached, coming so close to her that it appeared he was going to seize her.

"Mamasan going to be mad," he said. "You no find GI to bring to house. Mamasan no like. Mamasan need money."

At that moment Henry came forth from the bar and saw that the Japanese man was giving her a rough time. "Get the hell out of here you pimp!" he yelled. "I'll break every damn bone in your body if you bother her again." Henry gripped the man's shirt and shook him violently.

"No, no, I no tell mamasan," the man cried out. Frightened, the Japanese man ran down the street and vanished into the darkness.

"What the hell was he talking about, Keiko? I no tell mamasan."

Keiko half in tears began to speak. "Before I meet you, I stay with mamasan She gives me food, place to sleep. Then one day mamasan say, "you must pay to stay house. I no can find job, so I go on street and find GI, and take mamasan's house for short time, and many times GI stay all night. Since I work your place, I no bother GI. You pay, I no need to walk street." She began to cry.

Henry put his arms around her to comfort her. "I understand. Don't worry? Some of the girls I knew back in the states weren't any better."

Keiko seemed pleased that Henry understood her actions, and twirled the end of her long hair about her fingers. Not for a minute would he have cast her off, though it seemed to him that his entire life was in her hands.

"Wait, I'll flag a taxi so that we can go home," Henry said.

She stood there, looking at him, smiling in a manner that indicated security. He noticed that she was at ease, no longer looking or turning her head from side to side, as she had done in the past as if to be looking for someone on the street. A moment later they heard the screeching wheels of the taxi. "Where you want to go?" The cab driver said.

"Nishi Tachi," Henry said.

"Hope you have nice time," the cab driver called back to them over his shoulder.

Henry laughed and gave Keiko a nudge with his elbow.

The taxi moved so rapidly through the streets and that only the shadowy silhouettes of figures could be seen. Moments later the taxi came to a halt. "Can go no further. You must walk rest of way," the cab driver said.

"How much?" Henry said.

"Three hundred sixty yen," the cab driver said politely.

"Thank you," he said and drove off into the night.

"You thought I wouldn't come for you, Keiko."

"I no think you would come. I know your wife no like me. Maybe she no want me to work in your house."

"Oh, she's probably asleep anyway. Don't worry?" He hesitated. "What if I didn't come for you?"

"Me no afraid," she giggled. "I walk."

They walked together in the gloom of the night, an unknown destiny glittering about them beneath the darkness.

"Why didn't you let that GI take you home, Keiko. The one who seemed to know you at the Bar Cherry."

"I no need other GI, now," she said.

Her mannerisms and his conversation ran together like molasses. He had the feeling of accomplishment and a sense of security as he searched for an appropriate phrase, and brought out the words, "Let's hustle along."

He put his arms around her waist and drew her body closer to him. It was darker now since they were approaching an area that was not lighted. It was so dark that he could barely see the outline of her body. He pressed his cheek against her face. He longed to stop there, and stay with her all night in the darkness of the night. They moved cautiously forward, step by step, fearing that they might fall in to a ditch along the way. They laughed and giggled and talked as they went along. "Would you like to go with us to Yoshida someday, Keiko?" Henry asked softly. "We can climb Mt. Fujiyama and have a wonderful experience. There are a lot of men in our outfit that go there on weekends. They always have a lot of fun."

"Your wife no like," Keiko said.

"Well, if she doesn't want to go, then you and I will go. Would you go?"

"You take me, Henry," Keiko said with sincerity. "I like to go, if your wife no stop me."

"All right, we'll go next weekend if the weather is nice. You won't be afraid to climb Mt. Fujiyama, will you?"

"Me no afraid" she said. She tossed her hair back, leaving the impression that she felt indifferent, and suddenly she released her hold on him and began to walk rapidly.

"To tell the truth, I no afraid to climb Mt. Fujiyama. I afraid of your wife," she said suddenly. "What American women say and think about Japanese girls, true?"

She stopped, and he felt in the darkness that her face was quickly lifted to his. "Soon your wife tell me to go. Wife pretty, but she no likes you. She no likes me. I think you no like her either. Why you marry her?"

"Is that the way all Japanese girls think about GI's and their wives and sweethearts?" Henry said. "You mean my wife isn't the right kind of woman for me?"

They halted, and they stood facing one another trying to search for facial expressions on one another's face, but it was too dark.

"I know I was street girl, but no more," Keiko said sadly. "Maybe I no smart like your wife, but I make good wife for man. Your wife no say much to you. She no says much to me. That's why I know she no like you, she no like me."

"I know," Henry said. "She doesn't hardly say anything, and sometimes I realize I made a big mistake marrying her. I did like a girl back in my hometown and she loved me, but I made a terrible mistake of two timing her and stepped out on her behind her back."

"You ask wife why she marry you, Henry? Maybe wife think I love you, so best I quit work in your house."

"I don't want you to quit, Keiko. You're the only girl I have ever had confidence in. You make me feel like a man. At least you're honest, and I admire you for that. Maybe Faye married me to get a free ticket to see the world, and when she is bored she'll just get up and walk out on me. I guess it's damn tough being married to a soldier. Soldiers do get awfully moody and restless, and it's important to have someone around that is affectionate and understanding."

Henry did not want Keiko to quit her job in his household. The fact that she mentioned it caused his stomach to curl into a winding knot. Again he searched for an expressive phrase, and again, putting his arms around her merely said, "Let's go."

They walked in silence through the narrow passageway until they saw the outline of a structure that was recognized as his house. He had rented the house prior to his wife's arrival in Japan. Up until that time he resided on the base, and attempted to seek quarters for he and his wife there, but the billeting office had informed him of a waiting list.

Here and there stood other structures in a congested row, mute and cold as a cemetery. The night was so still that they heard the dirt crunching under their feet. A dog whined in the distance, breaking the silence. Keiko cuddled closer to Henry and hastened her walk. At length they sighted the portal of the house, and as they approached it, he knew the journey of the night was over and brought back into his mind many insecure thoughts.

"Don't quit and leave us, Keiko?" he said sadly.

"Where I go, If I quit?" Keiko said. "I no want to go back to street."

The answer sent a stream of joy bubbling through his veins. He forgot about everything, and hugged her so tightly that he felt the warmth in his heart.

"You aren't going to leave us, are you Keiko?"

"No, I no leave now," she said. "I know you want me to stay."

"I'll never want you to leave," he whispered. "We'll always go on living together in a dream world, and someday we'll be able to understand each other better."

He let his thoughts possess him as they walked to the sliding door. He was never happy with his wife when he withdrew his mind to these dreams. Keiko following close beside him stumbled on some object and quickly clutched his arm to steady her. The sensation that went tingling up his spine was reminiscent of his younger days. For the first time since his wife's arrival in Japan, he pulled Keiko into his arms, and she did not resist. He kissed her passionately and warmly.

"Oh, it's been so long, Keiko," he said affectionately. "If only I could, but I can't."

Then he had a distant vision of his cold wife lying in bed beside him, lying there like a dead body, not responding to his caresses and affection. Then he tried to slide the door, but it would not move. He pounded on the door, but no response. He pounded again and then listened thinking he heard a sound in the house. Maybe, he thought, there was someone in there with her. He pounded again, and finally heard soft footsteps coming towards the door. Then the door slid open, and there stood his wife. Against the dimness of the room, she looked becoming as she clutched her robe tightly against her breast. On the other hand, her face showed signs of distortion, her puckered lips deepened the lines of her face, and her eyes expressed signs of anger and hatred. Henry still in a trance with his moments with Keiko, the sight was pathetic. He now knew that he had never known what his wife really looked like. She turned without uttering a word, and he and Keiko proceeded to take off their shoes before entering the main room.

"You weren't worried about us, Faye?" Henry said smartly, placing his shoes on a rack.

"No, I've learned to live and accept your nonsense," she said sarcastically. "Why in the hell should I worry about you? Remember, you are just as much to blame for our marriage not working out."

Keiko came forward, and said, "I so sorry Mrs. Shane. Anything I can do before I go sleep?"

"There's not a damn thing you can do for me, but to get the hell away from me," Faye said angrily. "I didn't need a house girl anyway. If it weren't for my husband feeling sorry for you, you wouldn't be here. I know why he was so interested in bringing you here as a house girl, and I know all about your relationship with him before I came to Japan. As far as I'm concerned, you can have the son of a bitch all to yourself."

She continued to stare at Henry, and the rays of the shaded lantern brought out the feeling of relief on her face. Suddenly she began to laugh. "It's all over, Henry," Faye said with a thrill in her voice. I'm going back to the states and file for a divorce. I should never have married you in the first place, because you never really loved me. I always knew that you loved Edith Curtis who lives in Sinclair, but you'll get a taste of your own medicine. You only married me as an outlet to relieve your sexual frustrations. Now you can enjoy yourself living with this slant eyed whore. She'll take care of you."

She was overcome with mocking laughter. "Oh, I know," she continued to laugh. "It'll last for awhile, then there will be someone else to take her place after you become bored to death with her."

Henry did not respond, and moved slowly towards his bedroom. As he did so, he noticed Keiko, and he caught a gleaming and satisfying look on her face. He entered the bedroom with his head lowered, and his wife did not follow him as she normally had done in the past.

Now in the bright morning, Henry resting comfortably on the bed began to think of his wife Faye. How she has changed since she came to Japan, he thought? He remembered how pretty she looked back in Hallensburg, and how she would cuddle up to him on cold, wintry nights shivering from the cold. I didn't love her. Why in the hell did I marry her? He had been reluctant in having her come to

Japan for fear she would not be able to adjust to oriental living, and encounter long periods of loneliness due to his irregular military duties. He took the view that his wife was going to make the best of it since this was a good opportunity for her to travel and see part of the world.

He had no doubt that Faye had spoken the truth in saying that she did not love him, nor did he love her. Perhaps, he thought, she had someone else. He got out of bed, put on his robe and entered the small kitchen. Keiko was pouring hot tea into cups. Faye was already seated at the table. Henry paused at the sight of her. Instead of her usual blue robe, and hair up in curlers, she had on her best traveling suit, and her hair was combed smoothly. On the floor beside her were several suitcases.

"Why, where are you going?" He said.

"I told you last night that I was going to leave you, and I meant it," she remarked.

"Do you have to leave so soon? When you said you were leaving I didn't know you wanted to leave this morning."

"Yes, I think it best I depart before something drastic happens. Now you can have Keiko all to yourself. She'll take care of you. When you come home from the base everyday she'll be waiting. At least she loves you more than what I did, if you want to call it love."

"How are you going to leave?" He asked. "How did you make arrangements so quickly?"

She laughed and said, "Don't you worry about this woman anymore? You lead your own life and I'll lead my mine. If it bothers you so much, I called the Tokyo International Airport long before you were awake and booked a flight to the states. Now, does that satisfy your curiosity?"

"I'm sorry it turned out this way, Faye," He said. "I guess it's for our own good that we get a divorce. I'm man enough to accept it graciously. After all there is a lot of truth in what you said last night about our relationship."

For a moment his sense of relief was so great that he failed to recognize all other feelings. There was no doubt in his mind that Faye had spoken the truth, but wondered why Faye was parting without any ill signs of emotion. He then became suddenly conscious that he was staring at Keiko who was standing there all this time without uttering a word. Then with some effort he turned back to his wife.

"I suppose you wouldn't mind if I go with you to the airport," he said. And as he spoke these words, he regretted the suggestion, and expected her to say, "Go to hell." But to his surprise, she didn't.

"If you want to, but it really isn't necessary," she said sarcastically. "On second thought, at least you'll be able to give me a hand with my suitcases."

"All right, I'll go with you to the airport," he said willingly. "I don't have to report to the base until 1400 hours today, and I'll have ample time to see you off."

Upon their arrival at Tokyo International Airport, they saw on the roof of the terminal building, a shrine, with a red Torii that the Japanese felt safeguarded the airport as well as the passengers who embarked on the planes from this building to the far corners of the world.

Henry tried to say something befitting the view, but there was only one thought on his mind, the fact that, for the very first time since Keiko came to them as a house girl, Faye was to be away at night—and for many nights and never to return. He wondered if Keiko was thinking of the same thing.

His stay with Faye at the airport was very brief. He kissed her on the cheek as a gesture of formality and said, "so long Faye. I wish you all the happiness in the years ahead."

"Goodbye, Henry," she said. "I hope you can find happiness too." That was all. She turned and boarded the plane without looking back.

All the way back to the base he continued to think of Keiko. He pictured what it would be like alone with her in the house. For the first time in months they would be alone in doors, and they would live like man and wife. The vividness of his thoughts and the satisfaction of knowing that Faye wouldn't be there made him elated. Henry had always been thrilled in the quest of a new experience or a daring adventure. In Sinclair, as a youth, he had the reputation of being a live wire after meeting Edith Miller, and he had gloried in being classified as a great athlete, and the cessation of such honors had decreased his desire to return to his native habitat.

With his marriage to Faye, he had settled down comparatively. The craving for a new experience and adventure deepened within month after month until he reached a breaking point. This point was reached upon his arrival in Japan, where the environment lured him into the excitement that appealed to his interests and emotions.

He left the base that night in a wave of glory and started on his weary ride back to Nishi Tachi. The air was damper than earlier in the day and a thick, heavy overcast threatened another torrential downpour. A quiet peace hung over the Japanese huts of Nishi Tachi, as though they felt the expectancy of the rain. His ears were alert for the voices of the prostitutes that normally crowded the narrow streets, but not a sound broke the deep silence of the night.

As he approached his house, he saw through the branches of the cherry tree near the portal, a light twinkling in the window. She's in there waiting for me, he thought, and remembered the sarcastic words of Faye when she classified Keiko as a slant eyed whore. He reached the sliding door, but it did not yield. Startled, he pounded on it violently, then he thought that Keiko was alone and it was her fear of being alone that prompted her to lock the door at nightfall.

"Hey Keiko," he yelled. "It's me, Henry Shane. Let me in!" He stood there momentarily, and in a few seconds he heard the lock turn and the door slid open. And then Keiko faced him clad in a colorful kimono. She stood there, a Japanese lantern in her hand, and against the dark background she looked more attractive than ever. She held the lantern at shoulder level and it drew out the features of her beautiful face, the glitter of her lips, edged her dark eyebrows and eyelashes with a glowing luster. This matter of dress and facial care was a tribute to him for his devoted attention and trust in her well being.

She stood aside bowing and smiling. "Kohn-Bahn-wa, kohn-Bahn-wa."

As Henry entered, she moved away from him, walking softly on the matted tatami. She hung the lantern on a hook beside the table, and he saw that the table was carefully prepared for an evening meal, with rice cakes, roasted duck, salad, and tea. He was overwhelmed with the reception he had received upon entering the house, and with a sense of well being. Never did his wife render or bestow upon him such a welcome, he thought.

"Did you see wife go?" Keiko asked. "Make plane in time?"

"Yes, she made it to the airport in plenty of time."

The mention of Faye threw a sudden chill between them, and they sat a moment looking at each other before Keiko said with a grin. "I happy wife go. Now you and me together all the time. I afraid of wife no more. I take care of you, make you happy."

They finished eating and while Keiko cleared the table, Henry went to the sitting room to read the latest edition of THE STARS AND STRIPES. Shortly Keiko entered and seated herself on the floor. The sight of her sitting there was as he had dreamed while at the base. He felt his pocket for his tobacco pouch, and suddenly Keiko rushed to him and seized the pipe and tobacco pouch from his hands.

"I fix pipe," she said. Expertly she filled the pipe with tobacco and inserted it into his mouth. Then she ignited the tobacco with a match.

"A-REEa-TO-o, Keiko, A-REEa-TO-o," Henry said.

His late afternoon and evening work at the base made him feel listless and lightheaded, and he had a confused thought of being in another world where all was pleasure and time could not change it. The only problem, he thought, was that Keiko seemed a little more reserved than usual, but he was too comfortable in his reclining chair. After a moment he said, "Come over here my babysan and sit on my lap."

Keiko rose obediently and seated herself on his lap. She cuddled up to him and ran her fingers through his hair. There was a deep quiet throughout the house only interrupted by the rumbling sound of the train on the Chou Line heading for Tokyo and the Japanese clock ticking on the mantel and an occasional bark of a distant dog. The scent of a Far Eastern Perfume, mingled with the odor of Henry's pipe smoke, began to throw a gray haze about the dim room. All tension had vanished between them. Faye was gone forever, and so they began to talk easily and more freely.

"Henry, you say you take me to Yoshida. You promise if wife no go, you take me. Now wife leaves you and goes back to states. You take me, dozo, dozo."

"No, I didn't forget, Keiko. I promised you and I'll take you with me. We might go on Saturday if the weather is good."

She laughed and spoke with excitement in her voice, "A-REEa-TO-o, AREEa-TO-o." She tilted her head forward and kissed him. He kept his eyes fixed on her and was amazed at the way her facial expressions changed with each phase of their conversation. It was a pleasure for him to be with a woman that enjoyed his company. Her eyelashes fluttered as she threw her arms around him and said, "Oh, Henry, I love you. I hope I can stay with you all my life."

"We would be happy together," Henry sighed. "You'll probably meet some nice Japanese boy and marry him."

"No! No!" She shouted. "I no marry Japanese boy. Why you say that? What is the matter with you?"

"I only said that to get you all worked up," Henry said jokingly.

She raised her eyes to his. "I don't know if you joke. Last night wife say it's over, she no joke. You thought she joke. I love you, Henry, that is no joke."

"I believe you. I guess I'm still nervous about all women. I'm not going to think about it anymore."

"No, I want you to think about me, Henry."

The sudden tone of her voice made his face brighten again, not with a steady rush, but gradually flowing from his heart. She sat silent with her fingers moving lightly over his ears, and it seemed to him that a warm tingling current flowed up his spine toward the area of the immediate sensation. Cautiously he placed his hand on her breast. A faint tremble in her body seemed to indicate that she was fully aware of his gesture, and it had indicated that she had a sense of desire for him.

She smiled at him and it was a sign of challenge and invitation, making him conscious she was demanding affection. When they kissed, it was a hot, wild kiss, indicating she was ready to be carried over the threshold. After a moment she rose from his lap and stood there looking at him in acknowledgement of his immediate need. Keiko was offering herself, and he knew that if he failed to respond at this moment, he would lose her forever. He took her by the hand and led her to the bedroom door. It wasn't necessary for him to say anything. Her mannerisms seemed to communicate far better than words.

She turned to him and said, "Henry, I must pray to Buddha first."

When she closed the door, he felt that she was withdrawn into the mysterious realms of Japanese superstitions. He went back to his chair and sat down. Confusion entered his mind. Keiko, he thought, a girl that had been a street girl, a girl that was involved with him in sexual relations prior to Faye's arrival in Japan, now praying to the Buddha.

Now he was aware of all the possible repercussions. His heart was beating rapidly. His mind contained visions of his wife Faye, Edith Curtis, Mary Ann Rockingham, and other women he had affairs with. It seemed to him that it was now virtually impossible to turn his back on Keiko, a girl that truly loved him. The fulfillment of the act, under the present circumstances, had to be carried out or he would lose Keiko. He knew Keiko had planned it this way—a plan that would be the true test to determine Henry's love, if a love existed within him, she would know.

As he entered the bedroom, Keiko lay on top of the bed naked. She lay still with her eyes closed and her breathing was calm. He took off his clothes and got into bed beside her, turned and kissed her lightly on the lips. He kissed the nipples of her breast. At first there was no reaction, but as he searched her body with his hand, her lips parted to receive him, and her hand moving lightly over his body found the delicate area that aroused him beyond delight. She turned and flung herself upon him. Then it seemed to him that he was now free of his wife and the entire past.

In all the years of his past, he never encountered a girl that pleased him as much as Keiko. Her love, affection, and understanding brought him the happiness he had been seeking.

Henry had managed to rent a car, and as he had promised Keiko, they would go and spend the weekend climbing the sacred mountain of Japan, Mt. Fujiyama. They had made arrangements with Sergeant Joe Poletti and Meiko to escort them on their adventure. Poletti and Meiko had previously conquered Mt. Fujiyama, but they accepted the invitation without hesitation. They were fully aware of the Japanese saying: "he who does not climb Mt. Fujiyama once is a fool, and he who climbs Mt. Fujiyama more than once is a fool."

Saturday morning, after a military inspection at the base, they set out on their adventure. The road led into the hills through hamlets and towns. The roads were narrow, winding, and congested with carts. Peasants shouted and waved at the noise of the car horn, sounding constantly to clear the way, and at times without success.

In the early part of the afternoon, the slopes of Mt. Fujiyama became visible. It is not a mountain peak in comparison to other mountain peaks, but it stands alone, sloping up from the plains, gradually at first and then sharply. As they drove toward Mt. Fujiyama, only the lower level could be seen, a cloud hid the rest of the mountain.

"We better stop at Yoshida," Poletti said. "We can get something to eat, and buy some wooden staffs for the climb."

"Good idea," Henry remarked.

When the car stopped, many aggressive boys surrounded it and shouted, "You need guide boy! You need guide boy! Me number one guide boy!"

Henry laughed and remarked, "Those guides back at the Gettysburg Battlefield should come over here and get a lesson from these kids and try their approach."

After eating, Poletti informed the group of the fire festival in the

Fuji-Yoshida area. "Well, if we would have waited until next weekend, we would have been able to witness this gala night festival. This is something worth while seeing. Every year around the end of August, the Japanese build numerous bonfires through out the city, and at the same time all the people living in the huts on the mountain burn bonfires. From a distance it looks as though the entire city is aflame. We came over last year and witnessed the spectacle, and I think I would have enjoyed it again. It seems that the Japanese hold this festival to express their gratitude to the God of the Mountain for their safety during the climbing season that runs from the beginning of July to the end of August."

"It certainly would have been nice to see," Henry said. "Next weekend would not have suited Keiko."

"I think we better be going," Poletti said.

Before continuing on their adventure, they selected a young guide boy. He appeared to be a pleasant boy and had some knowledge of English. He got into the car, to the jeering yells of the other guide boys, "He no good guide boy! He number two guide boy!"

The guide boy put his head out of the car, and put his thumb to his nose, as the car drove off again down the dusty road.

The road up to the first station of Umagaeshi was covered by a bus service, but Henry decided to drive his car up the first stretch. It was a grind for the car, but they were determined to go as far as they could with the car, and failed to recognize the beautiful scenery.

At Umagaeshi they met other Japanese and American servicemen in the company of girls, preparing for the long, strenuous climb. Many of the Japanese men bound their legs with cloth, but on their feet wore only sandals. Many viewed the climb as a religious pilgrimage to the Sengen Shrine at the top of Mt. Fujiyama. Some men wore long, white robes and socks, and carried bells that jingled with every step.

They parked their car, and with the guide boy had a light picnic lunch that Keiko had prepared before setting out. They decide to hire horses to carry them over the easy stages. The road was rough, but there was some relief from the shade of the trees. Each station on the way up was clearly marked. The horses were getting tired and dripped with perspiration, but they moved steadily upward and made better progress than those climbers on foot.

The group welcomed rest at each sub-station. The houses were wooden with matted floors, and they had wooden benches placed outside for the weary climber to rest upon and beer and soft drinks for sale.

The air became cooler as they climbed to the edge of the tree line, and now the horses could no longer be used. Out from the tree line, the upper levels lay bare. "Top very nice," the guide boy said. He was an authority on the subject of climbing Mt. Fujiyama, for he went up and down the slopes of this sacred mountain every weekend during the climbing season.

Now they were walking on black volcanic cinders, remnants of the ashes of the fires that burned on Mt Fujyama many years ago. The path was winding and the climb became more difficult. The cinders were loose and shifting, and the progress was slow.

Below, visible now from high above the tree line lay the plain and Lake Yamanaha, Kawaguchi, and Nishi. Beyond the plain rose other mountains. The Izu Peninsula and the sea could be seen in the far distance.

Higher and higher they climbed, and the sky became bright with sunset. The colors spread and gradually began to fade, and as the sky darkened, the stars began to show in the heavens above.

"We better light our torches," Poletti said.

They took out their torches, ignited them and continued to climb higher and higher. The stations on the barren slopes now were constructed of stone, and their lights glittered brilliantly high above. Down on the plain, the lights of Yoshida and other villages began to twinkle. Below came a steady stream of climbers, in a torchlight procession weaving and swaying up the path.

"Many people will choose to continue the climb all night," Poletti said. "Someone always wants to set some kind of record."

"I'm not interested in setting a record," Henry remarked.

"After dark, this climb becomes pretty damn tough," Poletti said.

"Me tired," Keiko said in a weary tone. I like to stop for night"

The stone huts offered bedding and a night lodging, so they all decided to stay. They took off their shoes at the door, and the bedding was spread on the tatami in company with other Japanese men and woman. They stretched fully clothed on their mattresses on the floor.

Early in the morning, they were moving again. As the sun rose, the mountainside was warmed, and faces lit with smiles, reflecting the gladness of daybreak. Cameras clicked, and the pilgrims took up their chants, and little religious groups waved their flags.

Now some mountaineers were already beginning the descent. They had ribbons proudly pinned on their caps and shirts, symbols of success.

As Henry and Keiko remained silent, just climbing, resting every so often, breathing hard with the end of the climb seeming not to end. At last , several hours later, they passed under the Gateway of the Shinto Shrine, achieved their ribbons and the last chops on their sticks. Mt. Fujiyama was conquered.

They were delighted at the end of their climb for the rest and available refreshments. Little food could be carried or eaten on the climb and drinking had to be in quantities at frequent intervals, but it was good for them to pause and rejuvenate high above the plain. Patches of snow still could be seen near the top and inside the crater of Mt. Fujiyama.

The enormous crater, blackened and burned as if the volcanic fire had diminished just recently, remained an awesome sight. The black volcanic cinders did not hold any water. Mt. Fujiyama has no clear, cold mountain water. Only the ashes of the mighty fires that once ravaged the mountain remain.

Walking around the crater was a difficult task for them after climbing to the top of Mt. Fujiyama, but the shrine had to be seen. After resting for a short period of time, they decided to descend the mountain.

Descending was rapid and thrilling for them. Each step was sunk above the ankle in soft loose ash. Their sticks, that they were carrying, served to balance them, but there were tumbles and laughter, and before they realized it, the top of the mountain was at a distance and appeared to be inaccessible

Down from the mountain they came, tired and weary. Back under the shade of the trees, to normal walking on winding woodland paths. They were now on horseback again, down to Umagaeshi and to their parked car. "How incredible?" Henry remarked. "To think, we were on that mountain, that remote flattened peak."

They left the guide boy and started for home, too weary, too dirty to linger for food. They drove in silence. As they neared Tokyo, they looked back. There was Mt. Fujiyama dark against the evening sky, majestic, grand, and indeed the sacred mountain of Japan.

Twenty

Henry spent many happy months with Keiko—months crowded with everlasting memories, with excitement and adventure, some pleasant, and some tragic. Here he only wished to preserve the best moments of his existence, and to shut off the days of the pathetic past with Faye Cooper, Edith Curtis and Mary Ann Rockingham. Life in Japan had its fears as well as its pleasures and delights. He, as well as the Japanese feared the typhoons, the earthquakes, the floods, and the fires that rushed through the tinderbox houses.

One weekend in late September, unaware of a potential typhoon developing off the coast of Japan, they went on a cruise on the Inland Sea. The ship ran into violent waves, and as it was attempting to re-enter the port to seek shelter, it hit a massive rock, and rolled over, pushed by the strong winds of a typhoon. A SOS had been flashed three hours after the ship left port, but all rescue efforts were hindered by mountainous waves. There were many Japanese, Americans, and other foreigners aboard. Panic stricken passengers made desperate attempts to leave the ship after its engine was choked with sea water that resulted from the anchor chain snapping and the ship rolling over on its port side and then listing to star board. All holds were flooded, and many passengers disappeared in the raging waters of the sea. There was a terrible sound as the ship rolled over.

Henry quickly broke a window in the hold, and pushed Keiko through. He followed both dropping into the raging sea. Moments after they jumped, the entire hold became inundated with water. He heard Keiko screaming nearby in the water, He drifted near and held onto her for sometime, and she became quiet. An empty raft came by, and they struggled desperately to reach it, and then clinging to it, holding fast until their feet touched what they thought was the shore. Keiko was overcome with panic and started to run in the darkness, stumbled and fell into a big hole. Her weight came down upon her leg with a terrific force. There was a snapping sound, then a cry of pain. Her leg was broken. She sat there in agony, grasping her leg with both hands to alleviate the pain. She had never experienced the pain of a broken bone, and now in a state of shock she became delirious. "Henry! My Henry! Where are you?"

Henry was some distance away, trying to recover from the tragedy of the disaster. A blinding torrential rain was falling, and a cold wind moaned over the dreary, gray coast. He shivered with each blast of wind, slipped on the wet sand, stumbled over dead bodies that were washed up on to the sand mound. He lost his sense of direction. The waves of the sea pounded ferociously against the coastline, each wave getting larger and larger. He cried out several times, but the roaring of the waves muffled his voice.

Finally he came near the hole, and he heard a faint moan, then Keiko's voice. "I'm here, Henry. I can't walk."

"Don't worry?" he said. "I'll get you out of here?"

Keiko tried to smile, but her face was distorted with pain. "My leg broken," she said. "You nice to me. You take care of me."

Henry knelt beside her, and supported her with his arm. He ran his hand along her leg and recognized that she had a compound fracture. "You'll be all right, Keiko," he said. "Just be brave. We made it this far, and we're going to make it home."

Then he began to tremble, realizing they were not completely on secure ground, but in the midst of an elevated area some distance from the shore. He had momentarily forgotten about the rising tidal waves and feared they would be completely cut off. With the wind getting stronger, the waves of the sea would soon be upon them.

"Henry," Keiko whispered. "You no carry me in strong wind. I hear water come near hole. You go, Keiko stay."

Henry did not answer. He immediately inserted his arms beneath her body and lifted her. The great love for Keiko would not permit him to desert her. He knew now that their lives were in great peril, for the rising water had encircled the higher area on which they were stranded. He knew he could make it on his own if it required some wading or swimming across the inundated area before him. He felt the cold water beating against his legs in the darkness as he began to move from the high area toward the mainland. The wind blew harder than earlier in the day, and the typhoon seemed to be at its highest peak. The tides swept higher and higher behind him and before long the high area would be completely submerged.

"We'll make it, we'll make it!" Henry shouted. The water had risen above his shoulder. He now began to swim desperately, pulling Keiko behind him. Moments later they reached the main shore, and he fell to his knees in deep exhaustion.

"Keiko, Keiko, we made it!" he shouted.

Keiko was in severe pain and could no longer respond to his verbal excitement. Minutes later they heard, far off, the muffled sounds of sirens, gradually growing louder and louder as they approached. He locked his arms around Keiko, and embraced her.

"They know about the tragedy," he whispered. "Thank you God, thank you."

Keiko was lifted on to a stretcher, placed in an ambulance, and rushed to a hospital.

The next day, more than seventy search teams were busy combing the sea to recover bodies of those believed killed. It was determined that hundreds of people were believed to be dead as a result of an extensive search since the sinking of the ship amid the savage assault of the typhoon.

The tragedy was considered to have been caused mainly by faulty weather forecasts, in which the strength of the typhoon was not accurately predicted. Originally, predictions said the storm would bring fifty-five mile per hour winds on the sea, not dangerous enough to hamper a ship the size of the *Toya Muko*. It was later believed that one hundred twenty crewmembers of the ship attended the passengers until the very end, as only one crewmember was picked up while the others were swallowed in the depths of the sea.

The days blurred into weeks. Their life went on enslaving them in the ceaseless days of routine. There were nights now when they fell into bed and were asleep as their heads touched the pillows. Henry had difficulty in getting Keiko awake in the mornings. Often she would cry when she got out of bed in the morning and say, "Why you no marry me? Maybe some day you no like me."

Henry worried about things she would say to him, but feared discussing them with her.

"Don't worry, Keiko?" he would say. "I love you and I'm going to marry you."

One night he heard her calling him. He could see her standing near the lantern. Something was wrong with her. She was trembling, her mouth was slack, and the usual color of her face had faded into a pale yellow. She was having spasms and suffering from nausea, but managed to say, "I think I have babysan." Henry expected this to happen, and was elated when Keiko broke the news to him.

"I no shame," she said. "I happy—very happy. Babysan mine and yours. What I do before no good? Now Keiko makes you happy and babysan happy. You best man I ever know. Best man in whole world."

"How do you know that?" He said jokingly. "How many men did you have before?"

"I no tell you," Keiko said. "Maybe you get mad."

"I sure as hell would now," Henry said laughing. "Nobody is going to put their hands on you anymore. If they do, I'll kill them."

Keiko looked at him with her dark eyes. "You no do that Henry. You no kill other man for me."

"Oh, yes I would," he remarked.

"I glad you love me, Henry."

Henry's divorce from Faye Cooper became official in May of 1950, but he was still reluctant in taking Keiko as his wife. Their intimate relationship was short-lived, for the war clouds were beginning to form over the Korean Peninsula.

Twenty-One

It was in late June of 1950 that Henry Shane had to bid farewell to his pregnant mistress, Keiko, on the pier at Yokohama.

"You take care of the baby when it arrives, Keiko," Henry said proudly. "Don't worry about me? I'll be back."

With tears in his eyes, he embraced Keiko and kissed her. Then he picked up his duffel bag and joined the rest of the troops waiting to board the ship. Keiko stood on the pier awaiting the departure of the ship, weeping and fearing that Henry would never return.

He stood on the deck of the troop ship and watched Keiko waving to him and moments later she and the shoreline gradually began to disappear. Aboard were several thousand men, who like himself, were destined for combat in a strange and mysterious land. There was at that time nothing but loneliness in his heart, and a feeling that he may never have the opportunity to see Keiko again.

"Lord, am I ever sick," a voice behind him said. His accent unmistakably Pennsylvanian. "I'm not used to being on the ocean. The same damn thing happened on my way to Japan. It's only a few days to Pusan, and that is too damn long for me."

Henry turned. The soldier was slightly taller than he was. His hair was black, and his face pleasant. It was a typical friendly face that Henry had often seen.

"Where are you from?" He asked.

"Pennsylvania," Henry replied.

"By the way, my name is Norm—Norman Wright. I'm glad to find another Pennsylvanian aboard."

"Why?" Henry asked.

"There aren't too many Pennsylvanians aboard," Norman said. "Most of the guys are from the western states. Nice fellows mostly. There's one son of a bitch from my neck of the woods back in the states that has been giving me a rough time since we came aboard. Seems that his name is Morelli, Sergeant Tony Morelli. By the way, what did you say your name is?"

"I didn't," Henry said.

"Why, that's mighty unfriendly of you, seeing that we are both coal crackers."

"I was just in deep thought," Henry said and put out his hand. "My name is Henry Shane."

"I'm pleased to meet you, Sergeant Shane. Are you the same fellow that was a football star back at Sinclair High School a few years ago?"

"Yes," Henry said. "That was a long time ago."

"I knew it! You had a sweet little girl. If I remember correctly her name was Edith. That's right, it was Edith, Edith Miller."

"Right," Henry said. "That is all over with. Let's not discuss her, please. I married another girl back in the states, but we got divorced. So, I shacked up with a Japanese girl. She's nicer than any American girl I ever went with, and I know she loves me and I love her."

"You sure as hell brightened up when I mentioned the name Edith Miller," Norman said.

Henry looked out across the deep, blue water. "I used to go with Edith Miller, but it is a long story. All I know is that she married a fellow by the name of Andy Curtis, and later on he left her because she was fooling around with another man by the name of Robert Heim. I did see her once when I was on leave to Sinclair. As a matter of fact she wrote to me and told me how much she loved me, even after I two-timed her following our engagement. You know, when I got back from the war in the Pacific, I realized that I made a big mistake not marrying her when I had the chance. I think she is the main reason why I re-enlisted. I wanted to get away from her. I couldn't stand the thought of her being married to this guy, Andy Curtis. She sensed how I really felt about her after returning to Sinclair. A lot of those damn people back there started to spread a lot of rumors about me fooling around with Edith Curtis. Perhaps, it was because she wasn't getting along with Andy. Anyway, as I said, Andy left her and moved in with the Clark's over in Twin Forks, and then Edith started to write to me. So like a big, desperate fool, I took a leave and went back to Sinclair to see her. After I satisfy my beastly desires, I walk out on her again. Edith was a nice girl, but I understand she turned out to be a dilly. Honestly, I think I am the one responsible for making a big mess out of her life. I shouldn't have walked out on her. Later I found out that Andy Curtis committed suicide. I guess he could not tolerate Edith's immoral conduct with Robert Heim."

"It's too bad it turned out that way," Norman said. "After all that's the way the ball bounces. Sure you're going to feel guilty about her lousy life, but it seems to me that she should be old enough to realize the difference between right and wrong. I had a cute little girl back in Twin forks, and she started to whore around, so I gave her up. I felt bad about it, but I soon got over it. No, sir, I'm not going to run around with a whore. It was better that way, and by the time I got over it, I looked around and found myself another girl. Sweet little girl, blondest hair you ever did see. Figure a man can always make a new start with another girl though. Here, do you want to see her picture?"

"I guess so," Henry said.

Norman reached into his pocket and pulled out his wallet. Delicately, he searched for the picture. Upon finding it, he handed it to Henry.

"Nice looking girl. I hope everything works out for you, Norman."

"Sorry there aren't many more coal crackers aboard," Norman said. "Maybe we'll run into some buddies over in Korea. That's a hell of a place to go to meet up with some of your friends. That's our next stop, you know."

"Where in the hell do you think they are shipping us to?" Henry said. "That's where the war is going on and that's exactly where we are going to be, right up on the front line."

"More than likely Communist China will help those sons of bitches too," Norman said.

Henry looked at Norman, and then he smiled, very slowly. "Look Norman, I don't believe in becoming a hero, but I do believe in the principle of the damn thing. In the second place, I don't have anything to lose when the time comes for me to do something for my country."

"Yeah, but those Koreans all look alike," Norman said. "Understand that you can't tell the difference between friend and foe. So we should stick together."

"I'll put it to you straight, Norman. This war isn't going to be easy. I got a feeling that in the next couple of months, being around together is going to make for some mighty ragged nerves. I know from experience. War is a touchy subject. It makes bastards out of some guys. Be better if we didn't even think about dying. Don't you think, Norman?"

"Personally I don't have any strong feelings about this war," Norman said. "I just find that taking care of some other peoples' problems thousands of miles away is a crock of shit. When you get right down to it, people back home could make a big case out of this war. Maybe it isn't right for us to fight for something that we don't know we're fighting for. All a Korean has to do is work, bring a lot of kids into the world, and figure a way of getting a couple of bowls of rice on his table everyday. We have to do more than that in the type of society in which we live. We need more than rice. We have to plan for ourselves and for others through out the world. So we end up taking care of these Koreans anyway, trying to educate them, making them work, giving them the food to make ends meet. Hell, there were times when I felt like deserting our own army."

Henry stared at him, then he drew back his head and laughed. "Damn if you're not right," he said. "Funny thing, we've been so worked up about coming over here to defend the South Koreans on moral obligations, that we have forgotten the realistic side. If those damn communists had any brains, they would talk just like you just did, instead of getting us all worked up over nonsense. I don't think the communists think that way. Do you, Norman?"

"No, I guess not," Norman said. "It's hard to say if fighting is practical or not, but it doesn't look like it." Norman paused momentarily and glanced at the other personnel aboard the ship. Suddenly he began to speak.

"Henry, that's him. The guy I was telling you about. The short guy with all those stripes that's Sergeant Morelli and the other guy with him is Bernie Weaver. Morelli is from my neck of the woods back in Pennsylvania. It seems that I heard him say that he was from around Haysville."

"Haysville," Henry said surprisingly. "Hell, that's only a couple of miles from Sinclair."

"He probably knows you or heard of you," Norman remarked. "What a coincidence?"

Henry glanced over his shoulder at the two men. Tony Morelli was a tough looking sergeant. He looked like a typical sergeant that you normally would see in the movies. The fatigues he wore appeared as if they were tailored to fit the contour of his muscular body. Bernie Weaver was of a lesser rank, and not as sharp looking. He appeared to be somewhat younger and he was the kind of soldier, Henry thought, you had to really know before you could like him. They both came toward Henry and Norman.

"Oh, Norman," Morelli said. "I see you've found yourself a buddy aboard this ship. By the way, how is that little girl of yours doing back in Twin Forks, or don't you go with her anymore?"

"Just fine, Morelli, just fine," Norman replied.

"Say, aren't you going to introduce me to your buddy?" Morelli asked.

"Henry, this is Sergeant Tony Morelli."

"Pleasure to meet you," Henry responded.

Morelli looked at Henry and studied his face thoroughly. "You look very familiar to me Sergeant Shane. Seems that I should know you from somewhere. Maybe I have you mixed up with someone else. By the way, where are you from?"

"Pennsylvania, Sinclair, Pennsylvania," Henry replied.

"Well, well, what a coincidence?" Morelli said. "I believe you're the son of a bitch that was running around with Edith Curtis, or do you remember her better as Edith Miller? Does that name ring a bell with you? You see, I'm from Haysville, and that's only a few miles from where she lives. I met her in a tavern back there in Sinclair. The Moonlight Tavern, you know, up on Hillside Avenue. I took her out a couple of times when I went home on leave. She told me all about the guy she loved, Henry Shane, and here I'm standing right next to him now. This really is a small world."

"How in the hell did you get her to talk about me?" Henry asked.

"After a few beers," Morelli responded. "She kept on talking and talking, and it reached a point where I got tired of hearing her. She was married to a guy by the name of Andy Curtis. She never loved him, so she said. I assume you know that he committed suicide."

"Yes, I know. It was a terrible thing to happen."

"She really had eyes for you Shane, at least that's what everyone thought? I don't think it was gentlemanly for you to walk out on her. She told me all about the days you spent with her while going to school, and then two timing her for the favors of some neighbor girls over in Haysville. Can't say that I blame you, because a lot of guys tried to get their hands on those Rockingham sisters, and to think you made out with them."

"Damn you Morelli," Henry said angrily. "I got a good mind to punch you right in the fucking mouth."

Norman laid a hand on Henry's shoulder. "That's what I've been trying to tell you. Morelli is the type of person that enjoys giving other people a rough time with all of his bullshit. Take it easy, Henry. Control yourself when you're dealing with Morelli."

"You Henry Shane, aren't worthy of having a woman like Edith Curtis. She told me how you walked out on her after giving herself to you shortly after her husband left her. I understand she got all messed up with a guy by the name of Robert Heim.

"It's all over with Edith," Henry said in a low tone. "It has been for a long time. I'm not interested in what she had done in the past, and I don't give a damn what she does in the future. I found myself the type of woman I wanted, and I intend to marry her. I have her to worry about now, not Edith Curtis."

"My Shane, you really have turned over a new leaf," Morelli said mockingly.

"Goddamn it, there're many things you don't know Morelli," Henry said angrily. "Maybe you'll learn them in a hurry, that is if you have anytime, which isn't likely if you continue to spout off like you have been doing. You're not always going to be in a position to go around and blow off, because someday you're going to run into a mean tempered guy who's going to beat the hell out of you."

"Are you threatening me Sergeant Shane?" Morelli said forcefully.

Henry shook his head. "No, I never go around looking for a fight. I don't threaten people, and I don't go around and pry into other people's personal affairs. Fighting is for ignorant and savage people.

"You're a very clever man, Shane," Morelli said sarcastically. "You'll live a hell of a long time with your attitude, that is if the North Koreans don't get you over there in Korea."

All of this time, Bernie Weaver was standing nearby and merely absorbed the conversation that transpired between Sergeant Shane and Sergeant Morelli. Suddenly he said. "This is very interesting. Why are you against fighting?"

"Fighting doesn't prove a damn thing," Henry replied. "I and your friend here have been exchanging words of a personal nature. Suppose we did fight, what would it prove?"

"I suppose you're right," Bernie Weaver said. "I'm inclined to believe that at times it is necessary for a man to fight. A man has to stick up for what he believes. If you feel that what is taking place before you merits fighting then fight. Fighting doesn't settle the issue. It merely will prove who is the strongest and that's about it."

"You're all wet," Morelli intervened. "It does pay to fight sometimes."

"What does that have to do with our discussion about Edith Curtis?" Henry asked.

"Plenty," Morelli replied. "If you were married to Edith Curtis, I'm sure that you would have fought to preserve your honor. Especially if another man was trying to win her affections or if she would have gone to bed with him in a hotel, or had an affair with a stranger in a back room of a bar, or ran away to another state with a man. If you were any type of man you would retaliate. You would fight to keep your prize possession."

"Perhaps you have a good point," Henry said. "It's hardly a point that would merit violence. If she loved me, she wouldn't carry on an illicit affair, and if she didn't love me, I would be man enough to dissolve our relationship before violence would intercede. Everyone knows that a strong and powerful man can hold what he has acquired, but that doesn't make it entirely ethical to my way of thinking."

"Ethical," Morelli said. "That's not the right word for a person like you to use. Perhaps you can be classified as a strong man in this case or other cases. You seem to be free with your love of women, but on the other hand, I firmly believe you would fight if someone interfered with your prize possession."

"You're accusing me of being free with my love, and what about you Morelli? You admitted that you took out Edith Curtis, a woman that knows the score, and a woman that had been married. If you had the opportunity, you would take advantage of any woman, let alone Edith Curtis. Who in the hell are you trying to bullshit? I knew Edith Curtis, and knew her very well with all of her weaknesses. You said that you met her in the Moonlight Tavern back in Sinclair. What did you do Morelli? Did you just sit there and twiddle your thumbs?"

"No," Morelli said as his face reddened.

"Did you ever go to bed with Edith Curtis?" Henry said quietly. "Were you ever in her house? Were you? What's the matter? Aren't you man enough to admit that you are as much of an ass hole as I was?"

Sergeant Morelli lowered his head as he was overcome with embarrassment. "Yes, I was in her house, but–."

"But what," Henry asked.

"I was there on the last night of my leave," Morelli said reluctantly. "Honest, I was with her a couple of nights, but on that last night with her, she had too many drinks and seemed depressed. She said she wanted to go home alone, and I called a taxi for her and then she left. In the mean time I went back into the tavern and had a few more drinks. I wasn't drunk, but just feeling good. So, while I was sitting there, I was overcome with an urge to see her again, and I went over to her house. The door was still unlocked and I entered the house and walked into the bedroom. Edith was sitting at her dresser with her head buried in her hands. She had on a thin negligee. I could see her bosoms trembling. I thought she looked very becoming and–. Then I began to speak to her. "Now you don't have any reason to cry."

She frantically lifted her head. "How in the hell did you get into my house?"

I laughed and said, "your appealing body is refreshing to the mind. You have a body that no man can resist."

"You son of a bitch!" she yelled.

"Son of a bitch. That's not a very nice word for a woman to say. I just thought I would come over to see you before I left town."

"Get the hell out of here!" she screamed. "Do you hear me, get the hell out? I'm not a whore like many think I am. All men are alike. You're no different than that good for nothing bastard, Henry Shane."

"Oh for Christ's sake, Edith." I walked toward her and fiercely pulled her half-naked body tightly against me. I hungrily carried her to the bed. I told her to put her arms around me and kiss me. She hesitated.

"Edith you know what I want, and I'm sure you want the same thing."

"All right," she said. "Then get the hell out of here."

"She reached over and unbuckled my belt and assisted me in the removal of my clothes. She quietly catered to my wishes. I kissed her ears and throat, found her mouth and tormented her into a rage of passion until she succumbed to my beastly desires. She was now past the caring stage. I could hear her moaning with passion. Then she realized she was about to have an orgasm."

"Damn wonderful woman," Morelli said. "I'll never forget her. Mind you, I'm not bragging, but I'd venture to say that I had what she wanted. Perhaps I don't have the right to criticize your actions, Henry. I don't exactly blame you for feeling the way you did about her. Edith has what it takes in a woman to make a man want her. I'm sorry, but that's the way it goes. Let's forget all about it. I knew she craved sex, but she did have a special place for you in her heart."

"Forget it!" Henry said. "How can I forget it?"

"Well, we have no choice now, Henry," Morelli responded. "We have other matters to worry about. We have a war to fight. To my way of thinking, this now appears to be the immediate problem. I'm really sorry, please accept my apology."

Then Morelli put forth his hand, and Henry willingly clasped it in a friendly gesture. There was a deep silence. Then Morelli broke it by saying, "I understand you were in the service during World War II. Did you see any action?"

"Yes, I served in the Pacific, and was in combat in the Philippines. I venture to say that I had done my duty for my country, and feel I have gained the right to criticize and exploit my love life as I see fit."

"I agree with you," Bernie Weaver interceded. "I think you're the first man I've met aboard this troop ship who makes a hell of a lot of sense. Maybe you and I can get together sometime for a little discussion on the subject of love. What do you say?"

"Be glad to," Henry replied.

"That's great," Bernie Weaver said. "Let's go Morelli—and try not to be so worked up over your affair with Edith Curtis."

Again there was a moment of silence. "I'll be a son of a bitch," Norman chuckled after they departed. "Lord, but you sure as hell brought that old Morelli down a peg or two. To think, Bernie Weaver sided with you. Who would have thought of it? The honorable Sergeant Morelli was trying to accuse you of immoral behavior and free love. How about that?"

"Strange," Henry said. "I wonder why he admitted to me that he had a relationship with Edith. Maybe he felt the same way about Edith as I did once. I guess we were both damn fools, but I still don't trust that sneaky son of a bitch."

"Come on," Norman said. "Let's take a stroll around the deck."

Twenty-Two

The early part of Thanksgiving Day of 1950 started out as any other normal holiday for Sergeant Henry Shane. There was a lull in fighting, and the military cooks were serving roast turkey with all the trimmings that is somewhat a traditional occurrence in the armed forces. This is the first decent meal that they had received, and others were constituted of the cold, tasteless C rations that men in his infantry company had regularly eaten since the Inchon invasion in South Korea several months earlier.

Almost everything about that day seemed to be incomprehensible. The cold, blustery winds sweeping down from the wastelands of Siberia dropped the temperature so far below zero that it caused the once hot food to freeze immediately. The men rubbed their hands vigorously and constantly stamped their feet on the ground in an attempt to improve their circulation and to avoid frostbite.

A few days later, Sergeant Shane and his comrades found themselves huddled in an icy trench near the small town of Unsan, fighting ferociously for their lives. Hordes of Chinese soldiers—forces that the American high command had underestimated, and assumed their presence in numbers were so small that it was irrelevant. The Chinese attacked with their aggressive forces against the American lines with ferocity, and the attack was the most violent since the beginning of the Korean War.

At first it seemed impossible for the American forces on both sides of the valley to be overrun by the Chinese. The Americans had inflicted a heavy toll on the surging Chinese forces that their frozen bodies had to be cast aside during the lull in the fighting to open up avenues of fire. Then other Chinese soldiers would attack upon hearing the shrill sound of the bugle. They moved swiftly, trampling over dead bodies that already were frozen toward the vulnerable spots in the American defenses. Despite the subzero temperatures, the barrels of the weapons were extremely hot from the constant firing, and there was no safe shelter anywhere because the Chinese had penetrated every American position along the front.

It was so cold that the soldiers' breathes frosted in the air. The constant small arms fire from the Chinese was heard directly ahead, but the flashes from the guns were not seen. Shortly afterwards the Chinese fire became intense, and soon as they became certain that the Americans were counter attacking, they called for mortar support.

Shells striking nearby hurled shrapnel, dirt, and snow in all directions. As the intensity of the mortar barrage increased, the men buried themselves in the snow-covered ground. The soldiers constantly blew on their stiffening fingers and waited in their newly dug foxholes. The mortar barrage continued for some time, and the soldiers were no longer conscious of the bitter cold and snow. So intense was the mortar barrage from the Chinese positions that within a few minutes every communication line connecting the field units was severed.

Then the mortar barrage slackened, and then there was complete silence. Moments later, the Chinese charged frantically towards the American positions, blowing bugles and whistles screaming and firing. Everywhere the Chinese soldiers stiffened and fell and died, and their blood spotted the snow.

The Chinese were in great strength, and the forces behind, pressing upon the forces ahead made a massacre inevitable. Bodies of the dead piled up near the lower levels of the hill, and the Chinese, who followed, climbing over those bodies, became dead bodies themselves a few steps beyond.

At about this time the Chinese developed a gap in the front lines of a ROK battalion, and the elements of two companies lost contact with each other. It was then when Lieutenant Joe Carter and Sergeant Henry Shane were ordered to go forward with a patrol to investigate and repair the communication breakdown.

So when they successfully re-established contact between the ROK units, they turned around and struggled back through the deep snow. They followed a different route from the one they had taken previously.

Lieutenant Joe Carter was a former schoolteacher from New York. He was well respected by the men who served under him, and was classified as a pleasant and considerate officer. All through the bitter struggles of combat in North Korea, he often would talk about his return to the states and to continue his teaching career. His dream was never fulfilled. As they walked back to their lines, they emerged into a small clearing. They staggered through the deep snow to the other side, still unaware of the possibility of being ambushed.

Where the wooded area began again, the brush and trees had grown so close together that there was darkness beneath. They thought they were in friendly territory, and it never occurred to them to be cautious. They pushed aside the snow-covered brush and branches of the trees and stepped forward into a better-concealed area.

The Chinese fired upon them. Lieutenant Carter was knocked to the ground with a bullet wound in the right leg. Behind him, the other men dropped quickly to the snow covered ground.

"Get the men the hell out of here, Sergeant Shane," Lieutenant Carter shouted. "That's an order! I can't make it. I can't walk."

"God, I can't leave you here!" Henry shouted.

"Go, before it's too late," Lieutenant Carter said.

As the rest of the patrol struggled back to their own position, they looked back and saw the shadowy figures of Chinese soldiers seize Lieutenant Carter and drag him into the open clearance. It did not occur to them just then, that the enemy too might have captured them.

When the Chinese dragged Lieutenant Carter into the open clearance, they let him lie in the snow without administering first aid. Lieutenant Carter was carrying a pair of binoculars strapped around his shoulder. As soon as one of the Chinese soldiers noticed it, he grabbed the binoculars and displayed it to the others. They talked excitedly, and the soldier who was holding the binoculars smiled several times. Then another Chinese soldier walked calmly over to Lieutenant Carter, raised his rifle, and shot him in the head.

Later in the day, an American contingency came across Lieutenant Carter's frozen body, completely stripped of his boots and winter garments. They buried him, that same day not far from the Yalu River in the midst of a rocky, snow covered clearance. Captain O'Hara, the Chaplain, said a few words, and read a passage from the bible, his voice choked with tears. Henry Shane, Norman Wright, and the other soldiers from Lieutenant Carter's company said a prayer.

Except for the chaplain, no one prayed aloud. Its kind of strange, Henry thought, as he knelt there. A man like me praying for a man I hardly knew. I'm sick of killing, frightened, and I don't know what to do. When you face the good Lord, ask him for me, what I can do? I'm too mixed up to pray directly. Besides, you were a good man, and you probably can word it better than I can. Ask him if there is any hope for me? Ask him if I still have a chance to repent?

Henry stood there and looked at the freshly dug grave, and then lifted his head toward the heavens. "All right Lord, the time has come in my life when I must repent for all the immoral acts I had committed. I've got to end my bad ways. I promise, Lord, that if I get out of this war alive, I'll lead a good, moral, and honorable life."

The fight continued. By late afternoon, Captain Johnson's men had moved about two hundred yards in the deep snow. The casualties had been so heavy that every man not actively engaged in fighting was forced to evacuate the wounded. The Chinese mortar fire once again began to pound at the ROK and American positions. The wounded men had to be carried or dragged across the snow under the continuing fluttering of projectiles. The medics went out again and again to bring in the wounded.

Captain Johnson was in the snow about one hundred yards in front of his post, when he received a message from Lieutenant Peter Donnelley who was with a machine gun unit to Captain Johnson's rear.

"Chinese are coming up the hill to our left," he radioed. "They're about a quarter of a mile away."

Captain Johnson radioed back, "the twenty fifth is out there." Then there was little static and the voice on the radio crackled. "I have a twenty fifth officer with me. He said his men aren't out there. They've pulled back."

This was the first indication to Captain Johnson that something had gone wrong. Flank protection was the responsibility of the UN command. If the twenty-fifth had pulled back, then the flank is open.

"All right," Captain Johnson radioed to Lieutenant Donnelley. "Get those machine guns out to the edge of the thicket and see what the problem is?"

Five minutes later, Captain Corey then commanding Company A, also reported Chinese coming in on the flank. Captain Corey was holding his Company in reserve. He made his way to where Captain Johnson was sitting.

"This looks like the beginning of a catastrophe," Captain Corey said. "Do you want me to do anything about it?"

"Take the Reserve Company to the exposed flank," Captain Johnson said.

By the time Captain Corey had done this, and Lieutenant Donnelley had also positioned his machine guns along the edge of the hill, the small figures on the lower levels had opened fire. This settled all doubts of the effectiveness of the Chinese.

Accompanying the Chinese were several light field artillery units. They moved into position and poured fire directly into the American fortifications. Several more North Korean units joined in and began in company with the Chinese infantrymen, a gradual envelopment of the American positions. Sarcastically, Captain Johnson notified his regiment that his unit was in danger of being completely annihilated. Before anything could be done, the entire flank was under heavy Chinese attack.

At the edge of the hill, every available man joined the infantrymen under Lieutenant Donnelley and Captain Corey. As the Chinese and North Koreans reinforced their own positions, the action became fierce. The Russian made artillery pieces had very little cover and were exposed to aerial attack, but even from their exposed positions, they were not affected by small ground fire. They were firing point blank into the hill. The American men who were wounded stayed where they were and went on fighting to the very end, and before long the snow covered ground was splattered with blood and human flesh.

The situation was becoming critical. Captain Johnson became infuriated and radioed regiment again. The voice at the other end said, "we can't give you reinforcements, we can't give you reinforcements. Do your best? Do your best?"

The casualties had become so heavy that many of the more recently wounded were exposed to the bitter cold, lying helplessly on the snow covered ground with no hope of receiving medical attention.

The Chinese and North Koreans seemed well supplied with Russian ammunition, and even by then, several hours after the barrage had started, the shells were still coming down on the American positions.

Suddenly the shelling ceased. Chinese soldiers were once again swarming the hill like an army of ants, screaming and blowing bugles as they moved in quest of a do or die victory. As the early darkness hovered over the hill, and the snow falling, Captain Johnson knew that his men at the outlying flank would either retreat or be over run by superior forces. The cause was hopeless, but the men chose to fight to the bitter end. The men at the flank were completely wiped out by the barbaric hordes from across the Yalu River.

In a military sense, this was a costly defeat. Out of this battle arose the fighting spirit and will to resist and retain the spread of communism. The fight was carried to the last man. Sergeant Tony Morelli often wondered what a hero was. He thought a hero was something you became after the war was over. The wearing of campaign ribbons upon entering the hometown, or showing the sweetheart the wounds received in battle, or merely sitting in a rocking chair when old and gray and telling the younger generation about Seoul, Taegu,

Inchon, Pyongyang, or battles for the rugged, snow covered mountains of North Korea.

He remained at his position. He stared at the figures moving, creeping towards him in the swirling snow. The sound of the bugle sweeping down his spine, the fanatic screaming of opium fed Chinese, seeking to overcome the outlying fortification.

"Die you bastards!" he screamed. "Now I'll get even!" Then he cut them down with his automatic rifle.

Morelli saw some of them trying to rise, but their legs doubled. A bayonet of a fanatical and dedicated soldier of the Chinese Peoples' Republic who tried to storm his position slashed his pants. Morelli looked down and saw the white of the bone in his leg, sticking raggedly, sickeningly through the flesh.

Morelli staggered and hauled himself up on to the bunker, too sick to move anymore, the reaction gripping him, and below him, the Chinese jeering louder than ever, "Yankee die, Yankee die." In pain, Morelli shook his head.

"No," he whispered. "No."

The walls of the bunker reverberated with the gunfire. "Come and get me you bastards!" Morelli screamed.

The intense Chinese gun fire smashed Morelli to the ground, and he lay there groaning and bending over, feeling his guts, low down, the red hot stab of pain. He tried to rise, but toppled over into the snow. He lay there completely hidden from the Chinese fire, feeling the hand of death strangling him. His fingers moved feeling for the wound. It was low, very low in the stomach. A man could live for awhile with a wound like that, he thought. He reached for his medical pouch, and then he placed several sterile pads on the wound to stop the bleeding. He could feel the blood running inside of him, and the weakness in his mind was almost greater than his will to live.

He started to crawl, leaving a smear of blood on the snow. He crawled for several yards before he collapsed. For some unknown reason, the Chinese turned and moved in another direction.

The Wailing Wind

Meanwhile, Sergeant Henry Shane was instructed by Captain Johnson to access the threat of the Chinese on their present position.

"When you're ready to go Sergeant Shane, let me know," Captain Johnson said. "I want to know as soon as possible what the situation is at the right flank of our position."

Sergeant Shane folded the situation map. "Right now, sir."

"Are you coming, Norman?"

The wind outside was still whining. The snow was coming down more heavily now. "I don't like this," Henry said, his voice muffled under his collar.

"It may let up," Norman added.

"I don't mind the small arms fire so much," Henry said. "But I hate this damn artillery." He stopped talking. Then Norman looked at him.

"I'd go back and wait awhile if I were you, Henry," Norman said. "Maybe the weather conditions might be better later on. There's no sense in taking risks if you don't have to."

"I have to," Henry said. "Besides it was like an order, wasn't it, Norman? So, let's go and get it over with."

He did what he always did at moments like this, he committed himself to God. He had not been very religious since his boyhood days, but since coming to Korea, he found some reassurances in the form of a short prayer that always gave him some faith and courage.

None of them said anything. Isolated by the exposure, they walked forward steadily through the swirl of the snow. When a projectile exploded on the side of the hill, they fell flat on their stomach. Then they got up and continued to walk cautiously forward, still silent. In the terrible, booming storm of the night, fighting seemed insane.

Norman cursed when he slipped. Now they walked as rapidly as they could. Henry had noticed almost without seeing it that the fires caused by the heavy Chinese artillery barrage earlier in the evening, had died down. They had almost reached the out lying bunker outpost when another projectile came in. The sickening shrill that it made was ended before they could move. It fell nearby and exploded.

Henry felt two things at once: a violent crash on his eardrums and a hot bursting upheaval that slammed him into the air. "Oh, god," he screamed. Before he could close his eyes, he was smashed blindly into the snow-covered ground. He was stunned momentarily. His ears were ringing. He quickly felt his arms and legs to detect for wounds. Struggling, he got to his feet.

"Hurry up!" He shouted. "Let's get the hell out of here!"

"Over hurry!" Norman shouted. "Come over here! It's Morelli!"

"How do you know its Morelli?" Henry yelled back.

"I heard someone groaning after I hit the ground, and crawled toward the sound," Norman replied. "At first I thought it was you, Henry."

Henry hurried towards Norman, and upon reaching his location, he quickly got down on his knees and pointed a pen flashlight at the face of the wounded man. "It is Sergeant Morelli, and he is still alive," Henry said.

"Here, take this message back to Captain Johnson. Tell him the Chinese have pulled back from the right flank. Why, I don't know." Norman Wright raced into the darkness toward the command post.

It was there that Henry Shane found himself with the antagonizing Sergeant Morelli, in a pitiful state, on the verge of death. He knelt beside Morelli, seeing that he was still alive, feeling the fever burning in his flesh. Then as gentle as a father with his little son, he lifted Morelli's stocky body onto his shoulder and started back across the fringes of the hill. So thick was the swirling snow that he could barely sense where he was going. He stumbled over a body. Then he heard the groaning moan of a dying man.

"Yankee help me! Yankee help me!"

Henry lowered Morelli to the ground and reached into his pocket for the pen flashlight. He looked down at the ice and snow covered body of a Chinese soldier. He stood there looking at him with compassion, then that thing in him he always had, but which the priest back home brought to the surface, to the level of righteousness rose in him. The story of the Good Samaritan that Father Lewis had told so beautifully in a Sunday sermon so many years ago, that vast peace of soul too big for anger or hatred or revenge.

Here lying before him was a brother, but whose way of thinking, and way of life were entirely different than his. "Wait," Henry said. He took some of his rations and hurled them down within reach of the Chinese soldier's outstretched hands.

"Try to eat them," Henry said. "Soon as I get my friend taken care of I'll come back for you."

Henry realized that he was having a difficult time communicating with the Chinese soldier because of the language barrier.

The soldier lay there, feeling for the rations, because at the bottom of things men live and die by their beliefs and principles, but what they are the Chinese soldier could not believe this thing. It was beyond his barbaric knowledge of human relations, it shattered against his impenetrable disbelief that there was any man living who walked in honor and graceful peace.

The Chinese soldier pulled out a pistol from his coat and pointed it.

"Come get me!" He shouted. "Leave me here to die, you Yankee, and you die with me."

"Don't be a fool?" Henry said calmly. "I'll be back. Kill me, and you don't have a chance."

Then Henry lifted Morelli once more to his shoulder, and moved away. The Chinese soldier watched him go. He let Henry get several yards away, before his rage, his terror overcame him, his disbelief in Yankees, judged only by the primitive standards he had. He pointed carefully, and pulled the trigger. The bullet went through Henry's right side out of reach of his vital organs, but throwing him head over heels, falling, rolling and Morelli rolling with him, limp as a bag of rags.

Henry lying there felt the wound where the bullet had gone in and came out. His side was a mass of torn flesh, the blood running out of the wound and on to his clothes. He quickly jerked out the sterile pads from his medical pouch and placed them on the wound, cut off a piece of his shirt with a bayonet, and made a wad that he pressed against the wound. He could feel the strength going out of him now—when of all times he needed the strength.

He lay on the snow, his blood dripping on the frozen white. In agony, he staggered to his feet, and got his arms under Morelli. He could feel the tearing inside of him, the pain in his side, and a cold sweat coming forth from his forehead. He came on up, pulled up, he was sure by god's helping hand, seeing as he did so, that the snow had died off. Knowing what that meant, the possibilities of another Chinese counter attack, he proceeded to move toward an unoccupied Korean hut he had spotted earlier that afternoon. He stumbled and fell, got up and fell time and time again. The last few yards, he crawled, dragging Morelli's body behind.

A deep darkness had now come over the land. Henry lay inside the cold and dismal structure, seeing the curtain of white blasting out his vision, remembering with bitter sorrow his immoral behavior, and the girl he had denounced back in Sinclair.

Now with his compassion, there were more immediate things to be done. He had to live and tend to Morelli's wounds. He had no idea how difficult this would be with a wound in his side. He accomplished them finally, dominated by the force of will and courage. He made Morelli as comfortable as possible under the crude circumstances, and lay down on the cold earth of the hut, too weary to even attend his own wound.

"Norman will come back," he whispered. "He will find us, because I can not—I can not die."

When Norman finally reached them, the two of them were half frozen. He worked energetically, calmly, and proceeded immediately to build a fire. He saw that Morelli's wounds were already dressed, but that Henry's bled profusely in a steady flow. Norman had some clean and sterile bandages. They would serve well. He needed water. He took off his helmet, raced out into the whining wilderness, scooping up snow with his helmet. Then he raced back into the hut and placed the helmet over the fire to melt the snow. It would take time to boil, he thought. Henry was in a bad way, but he knew that Morelli would not make it. He could not understand how he survived so long.

While in the hut Norman heard in the far off distant the faint sound of bugles coming down with the wind that sounded like sinners begging for God's mercy from the depths of hell. He listened, but it did not come again. He realized suddenly, like all the soldiers at the front lines, that the Chinese were preparing to make another assault.

The water was hot now. He soaked Henry's wound, pressing hard to clean the area, then Morellis, easing them both. He sprinkled sulfa powder over the wounds. He stood there watching them. Henry's eyes twitching with pain, tried to smile.

Suddenly Norman realized that he had to get them out of there. He only had the power to move one at a time. He stood there staring and what was in his heart a pain greater than both of their wounds.

"One man will have to stay behind," Norman said. "I'm only capable of carrying one man. When the snow slackens, we'll move out."

He bathed their faces with warm water and forced a few trickles of water from his canteen down their throats. Morelli's flesh was as hot as fire, burning with fever. He started to mumble suddenly, then he became delirious.

"Help will come! I know it will!" Morelli screamed.

Slowly Henry struggled to his knees and lifted his head toward the barren ceiling of the hut. He folded his hands and began to pray quietly, not realizing that he gradually prayed aloud. From his private darkness and immoral life, he repented for his sins. He saw before him a vision of Father Lewis, the Parish priest back in his hometown of Sinclair, Pennsylvania, blessing him before the altar of Christ. He remembered after many years the exotic and beautiful prayers of the church, taught to him by Sister Mary at Saint Anthony's Church.

Norman, with tears in his eyes prayed with him. "Oh mighty

God, give me the strength and wisdom to do the right thing, because the one I leave behind will surely die or be captured by the enemy. Why have you placed me in such a difficult position? Tell me God, why? Morelli is a good soldier and was gentle with you, God, in recent months. And I have respected him all these days we were together in Korea. I disliked him once, but the war has changed him into a moral Christian. He is a soldier, so gallant of a soldier with courage in him that is the glory of God and his country, because he dominates it now with respect and love for his maker. And him, I respect as a soldier, as a countryman should respect a soldier—with all of my heart, with my life, and my soul. Thou have put upon me the difficult task of choosing between them. Between this good and gentle soldier, for whom I have great fondness, and Henry Shane who is my best friend."

Norman could not bear it He could not support the sight of their faces, tear streaked before the firelight. He turned his head away from the fire, and looked straight into Morelli's eyes. That was unbearable too, so he closed his own, retreating easily into darkness.

He sat there feeling the weakness in his own body, growing greater than his compassion and confusion. He added wood to the fire to keep it through the night. He lay down beside it, and though he did not think he could, he wept like a child.

Sometime during the cold and blustery night, Morelli was aroused from his agony.

"I must find God! I must! He will save us—he will not let us die! I know he will save us!"

He started to crawl toward the exit of the hut, enraged by the burning heat of the fever, by his faith in God, by his own still human desire to live. Once outside of the hut, he crawled a mere yard, before the icy blast of polar-Siberian wind brought him to his senses momentarily. He realized he was outside of the hut, and half turned to crawl back again. Then he remembered why he was sent to Korea and with that a love and desires to serve his country.

He lifted his head to the call of the whining wind and prayed.

The Wailing Wind

"Oh, God," he whispered. "It is a mortal sin for me to take my own life. I merely beg you to put an end to my misery. If you will not grant me my desire to live, I pray that you end my life here in this wilderness." He crawled for several more yards through the deep and drifting snow. In the morning, Sergeant Norman Wright found him, a short distance from the hut. He knelt before the frozen body of Sergeant Tony Morelli. He wept, with the tears freezing on his face.

Later in the morning Henry Shane came to his senses. He was braced against the inside wall of the hut with a number of other soldiers, none of whom seemed particularly surprised when he looked at them. Evidently he had been unconscious for sometime and was not aware that the other soldiers had entered the hut to seek refuge from the weather.

It was rather dim and gloomy in the hut. There were no sounds of weapons firing outside, and nobody seemed to be doing anything. Henry didn't see anybody he knew with the exception of Norman Wright, and he was ashamed to ask why he was there. So after a few minutes, Norman Wright assisted him to his feet and he staggered in the direction of the door. No one stopped him. Emerging from the hut, he found himself at the edge of a bitter, cold wilderness. It was empty of human beings. Shortly, Norman Wright joined him and gave him support with his arm, clasping it around his mid section. They walked slowly and grudgingly through the barren wasteland for several hours until they came to a road. There still were no signs of human life. On the side of the road however, was the remains of a North Korean military vehicle that was strafed by the machine guns of an aircraft. The vehicle was still smoldering and the remains of two soldiers' could be seen sitting on the front seat. As they approached the vehicle, they recognized the charred bodies to have been officers. They gazed unemotionally at the charred bodies and moved on.

They had no idea where they were or where they were going, but in the distance they saw an abandoned American weapon's carrier, so they headed in that direction. The sky had become almost completely overcast by then. There was a cold blustery wind blowing and stirring the snow on the ground, and though they saw a hut to the left of the road junction near the weapon's carrier, there were no signs of human beings anywhere. It never occurred to them that they were in enemy territory, and wandering directly into the inevitable—captivity.

Joseph T. Renaldi

Part IV

Immorality to Reconciliation

Twenty-Three

The days, passing were kind of like dripping blood that was reducing the endurance in Edith Curtis. These were the days that spread slowly, out of the Stonycreek River's visible vapors, moving silently into darkness and converting into a misty appearance to the call of the wailing wind. There were also the days that came up in a vast cover of the sun and cast the luster of rays over the landscape and aroused the call of the wild.

There were the somnolent days with the frisky squirrels leaping from one tree top to another and a conglomeration of birds singing incessantly in the tree tops, with the sun taking the tension off of everything so that the difference between what was, and what was not, became indistinct. The days all had one thing in common, because they nonchalantly passed.

The days passed, and with their passing they drained the enthusiasm out of Edith, and she was not aware of the decline in her endurance because it was happening silently. She still had a desire for indulgence, love, copulation and gratification that she tried to do exactly the same things she had done before, but without her former ease. Every new relationship began to lose its fierce pleasure, and each sexual act left her a little more spent, and that love itself had lost its meaning. The men who previously would have excited her, now merely passing her by with no more than a casual remark. Now, she no longer desired the same things as she had in previous years. Now, with the passing of each day she was approaching the crossroad in her life.

"Do you like Wayne Trent?" Edith asked Melissa.

"Yes, I like him very much," Melissa said enthusiastically. "He is so much more fun than Jason Snead. Besides, I need a father. Don't you think so, mother?"

Edith stared at her illegitimate daughter who was born out of wedlock when she was the mistress of Robert Heim. Melissa, at the age of seven, was an intelligent girl, and relatively tall and slender. There was something that could not be defined regarding her beauty. There was something existing inwardly, Edith thought, something not precise. How can a seven-year-old girl be voluptuous? There was, Edith decided, at least an indication of the characteristics that might lead Melissa to the same destiny that she herself had experienced. She would have to be extremely protective of her daughter. She must protect her well.

Edith was confronted with another phase of Melissa's development. She was growing up. She was unusually active, she had become even more so in the past few months. She was beginning to ask questions about her father. How long could she withhold the truth from her, she thought. She had never lied to her daughter. Melissa knew, for example, that she was born out of wedlock. It was she who had questioned Edith about the whereabouts of her father. Edith had been bothered by this question, but she always managed to change the subject.

Wayne Trent was coming this night to take Edith to a theater, and then to a restaurant. Melissa would remain in the care of a conscientious sitter, Helen Stringer. I do care for Wayne Trent, Edith thought, indeed I do. The problem is, she said to herself, I am still attracted to Jason Snead. Nothing seems to make me feel any different, but she was not really certain. If she were to leave Sinclair—go far away—and settle down with a husband who would care for her and Melissa, she might forget about Jason Snead. Was it not, after all, her moral duty to Melissa, to her, and to the institution of matrimony, to forget Jason Snead? She rubbed her forehead with her fingers. The pain annoyed her. Yet she must think. She must make a decision—it is either Wayne Trent or Jason Snead. It really was uncomplicated. All she had to do was give Wayne a positive answer. Even the difference in their philosophy was not relevant. He had often said this to her.

It was so elementary on the surface, but all Jason Snead had to do was caress her and she was overwhelmed by the sensual pleasures. He could kiss her briefly, thoughtlessly, his mind going astray, and she yielded to his fervent and ardent touch. It was like that.

Oh Lord, she thought, I can not control myself when I'm with him.

She would sever the relationship, if she possessed the discipline. If only her deeply ingrained weakness did not forsake her, if all her carnal desires and yearnings, and the burning in her flesh and the compassion that softened her very heart, did not deceive her. If the insurgency of her very existence against what should be, in approval of what was did not mislead her.

She heard the doorbell ringing incessantly at the front door. "I'm coming, Wayne," she yelled. Finally tonight I'll be with you, she thought, as she opened the door and stood there in the shadow of the dim porch light, her face blushing and becoming so that seeing it, Wayne Trent stood there as if in a stupor.

"Edith," he uttered. "I'm so happy to see you."

"Come in," she said softly. "We won't go to a restaurant or theater tonight. I have something important to talk to you about."

He followed her silently into the living room, his mind filled with deep affection and faithfulness that she could not sense the feeling though she did not look directly into his eyes.

"Please sit down," she said. "Would you care for a drink. Maybe you would like to have a beer or a glass of wine?"

"Yes, I think I will have a glass of wine. God knows I need a drink. You were so attractive standing there in the doorway, Edith. There was something about your facial features that puzzled me. I really don't know what it was."

"I do know," Edith said. "I have made a decision regarding our relationship."

"Oh, Lord!" He cried out. "Please don't tell me that we are through."

"Don't get upset, Wayne?" She said emphatically. "That was not

The Wailing Wind

the answer I was going to give you."

He stood in the middle of the room now scratching his head. "Edith," he said, "you are going to accept me."

The expression of compassion on his face was very pleasing to see. It was an intense and genuine expression—graceful and with charm. What she was about to do was the epitome of all deceits. She was about to accept a matrimonial proposal from a suitor under false pretenses. She was about to permit him to wed a woman, whom he really did not know, whom he believed to be honest and sincere.

Edith lifted her head haughtily. Wayne seeing this motion was certain that never again would he see anyone so attractive.

"Yes," she finally said. "I was about to tell you that I would marry you, but now I can't. I would have to lie to you in order to give you a positive answer—and you are too good of a person to accept lies."

"I don't understand, Edith. Please explain it further. How could you lie to anyone? I can't accept it. I have never seen anyone so gracious and refined."

Edith leaned forward, her pride lessening as if it never existed. "Please, Wayne, please leave," she said. "I don't want to tell you again."

Wayne rose to his feet. "There isn't anything," he said boldly, "that would make a damn difference about how I feel about you."

"Are you positive, Wayne?" Edith asked.

"You're damn right I'm sure," Wayne responded quickly.

"All right," she said looking directly into his eyes. "I had been Robert Heim's mistress for many months and had a child out of wedlock. I am neither gracious nor refined. Why would you want someone like me for your wife?"

She stood there, seeing the expression on his face distorted from agony, the suffering depicted in his eyes so plain and sympathetic, that even to gaze at them was touching. She walked to the coat tree and with finesse and picked up his hat and handed it to him.

"Goodbye, Wayne," she said.

He did not respond. She accompanied him to the door, opened it for him, and watched him walk discontentedly through the doorway. Then, very quietly, she closed the door behind him.

The following morning, in the confines of his own room, Wayne Trent ran a hand over his face, feeling the rough whiskers beginning to grow. He was aware too that he had muscular soreness in his legs that annoyed him and made it a chore to walk. He had no idea whatsoever how far he had walked after leaving Edith's house the day before. He could not even remember the names of the streets through which he had roamed.

Perhaps, no one had the fortitude to tolerate anything like this. There is such a thing as compassion. He remembered when his Irish setter had been unintentionally shot in a hunting accident near Twin Forks, and he himself had taken the dog to a veterinary hospital where the dog was injected with a large amount of sodium penethol. The Irish setter had been squirming and yelping of pain, and the veterinarian had stilled it. Was there no one available to stop this procedure? Must he daily know this—this degrading of his devotion? He decided to walk through Sinclair to release his tension.

While walking through Sinclair, he looked up and saw the outline of the incomplete Taylor Bridge in the distance. The morning sun cast its rays upon the structure making it appear as if it were constructed of tooth picks. It took him at least one half hour to reach the bridge for he had been at the western end of Sinclair when he glimpsed the structure.

When he started out, he felt the warm, whirling breeze against his face. On the Stonycreek River, below, a few coal barges were moving down stream towards Pellersville. The sun beyond Sinclair cast a golden brilliance over everything. There was a feeling of freedom, of walking on thin air itself—nothing between him and the river below, except the bridge itself and peace and tranquillity. The uniqueness of the bridge appealed to him. He stood near the railing on the bridge and breathed in the clean, cool air. He could feel the agony leaving him and his dazed mind being rejuvenated.

She said she would marry me, he thought, but I would not accept her. How is it then that I am here seeking extinction in preference to losing her, and when losing her would be of my own discretion. I love her. What kind of love is it that has no clemency in it? In what way did she ruin her reputation? How actually is she defiled? Is it because she bedded with the wrong man? Is it because she was forced into an illicit relationship? Dear Lord, I have catered to women in whorehouses, he thought. Who am I to condemn her?

He became lightheaded as he stared down toward the rushing water below. I could rescue her from this situation, he thought. Am I going to relinquish her to that son of a bitch, Jason Snead? What is in store for Edith, except to live a degrading and lonely life? I have been thinking about compassion. Is this the way I display it? Isn't Edith—whatever her mistakes have been, whatever she is doing with her life now—is important to me? If I marry her, I can bring her comfort, happiness, and joy.

He turned and walked back to the Sinclair side of the river. After a lengthy walk, he reached his parked car, and sat on the front seat contemplating his relationship with Edith. Later he drove to Edith's house. He never realized that Edith might have had other commitments.

In this situation, at least fortune favored him. As he approached her house, he saw her descending the steps of her front porch. He stopped his car immediately. He opened the car door and yelled, "Edith, Edith!" He ran swiftly towards her.

Edith saw him coming. She stopped walking, and her eyes were melancholy and inquisitive. "Edith," he said.

"What's on your mind, Wayne?" She asked.

"I have been an ass! I am asking for your forgiveness."

"Forgiveness for what?" she responded sharply

"For my rude behavior. I tried to convince you that my affection for you was insignificant. I lied to you. You told me about your background, and as far as I am concerned it has no affect on my genuine feelings for you. It is over with that. I didn't realize it. Let's go on as if nothing ever happened."

She stood there, her eyes fiercely staring at his face.

"You made your share of mistakes," He said. "Nevertheless, who am I to condemn you? It isn't my duty to judge you and sentence you. All that I can do is ask for your love. I would appreciate a positive answer. Please, Edith."

"No," she replied quickly. "Does it really matter how you feel about me?"

"I guess not," he said emphatically. "It really doesn't matter how you feel, but it is important to me. Nothing matters except that I want to marry you, if you will accept me. Will you, Edith? I would be most thankful."

She did not say a word. She was flabbergasted and her face so pale as if she had seen a ghost. Her facial expressions remained unchanged except that now her heavy eyes were laden with tears. He stood there in silence, listening to the throbbing of his own heart.

The teardrops flowed over the edges of her eyelids spilling over her lashes and making steady, wet streaks on her face. Wayne remembered a picture of Our Lady of Sorrows he had seen in a catechism at Saint Anthony's Church. Edith's face reminded him of the figure in the picture, now enlightened with kindness and affection, the corners of her mouth quivering.

"You would be thankful," she said. "You would be thankful for rescuing me from my damnation, for taking me away from my indecent life and all the anguish that I have lived with all these years. No, Wayne, I must be the one who should be thankful." He extended his arms and she came to him happily.

"No more of that nonsense," he said in a hoarse voice. "If you weren't kind, just and affectionate, I would not ask you to be my wife. You have paid your dues to society for all your mistakes."

"Do you think so, Wayne?" She said.

"I honestly do, Edith. Kiss me quickly. I have errands to do. I have to go to the jewelry store and check on the prices of the wedding rings."

Edith kissed him tenderly, then she embraced him.

"Nothing will prevent us from getting married now! Nothing at all," he said.

"You are certain, aren't you?" Edith said. "Listen carefully, I have to tell you something that is very important, Wayne. I am a little uncomfortable, I think. I'm very thankful that you want to be marrying me—honestly thankful. It will be a great honor to be your wife. I want you to understand my feelings at the present time, but I truly want to love you, but hopefully I will, Wayne, with the passing of time." She smiled at him softly. "I think I'm going to take advantage of you now," Edith sighed. "I want you to drive me to Saint Anthony's Church. I want to talk to Father Lewis, the parish priest and get some advice from him. I want to ask him some questions regarding our marriage and my standing with the church. I'll telephone him first."

"That's a good idea," Wayne said.

The day was clear and there were fluffy, white clouds in the sky above Saint Anthony's Church. Even the heavy wooden doors had lost their prohibitive look. One of the doors stood ajar, and through the opening Edith could see the black, metallic stand with the flickering flames of the candles grouped together. There was a feeling of a pleasant accomplishment in her heart now. She walked hurriedly toward the door of the church, but before entering the church she changed her mind and walked up the sidewalk that led to the parish rectory. Watching her depart, Wayne Trent mumbled the words of a prayer that he had remembered from his childhood days.

Father Lewis saw Edith as she entered the rectory. She approached him immediately and clasped his warm hands, sobbing intermittently that her words were not definable.

"Relax, my dear," he said calmly. "I was expecting you to come to see me sooner. God, in his own little way always directs the sinners to the church. Please come, there is a place to discuss these sinful problems." Then grasping her left hand, he led her from a room in the rectory through a corridor into the church where a confessional box was located. Many sins, annoyances, and sorrows were confessed to the priest in the confessional box, thus seeking absolution.

Walking home through the crowded street, Edith's steps were striking the pavement noiselessly, though she was aware of the complex problems still confronting her. She must call Jason Snead and inform him of her future plans. This was a humble thing, not something to be carried out like a fling in the night. It was going to require an immoral approach. He would do everything within his power to stop her. Before she would have been frightened. She would have been uncertain of her own vigorousness. Now she was not afraid. Her attraction to Jason Snead was somewhat of a compelling force strongly surrounded by a glowing, yellow light. Let Jason do as he pleases, she thought. He could not change her mind.

She called him on the telephone and waited patiently for him to respond to her questions. She knew it would not take him long for him to arrive at her house. She was completely surprised. Shortly the doorbell was ringing incessantly. She walked through the living room and opened the front door. Jason stood there shaking violently.

"You whore!" He uttered loudly. "You lying rotten whore!"

"Watch your language," she responded quietly. "Please come into the house. This issue is our own private affair. There is no need to announce it to the entire neighborhood."

Inside the house, she turned suddenly to Helen, her sitter and instructed her to take Melissa for walk. What must be said to Jason now was not for a child to hear. Shortly afterwards Helen and Melissa left the house before Jason approached Edith.

"So, you have decided to marry Wayne Trent for all of his wealth and not for love. What the hell is the matter with you? Wasn't I good enough for you? You wouldn't accept any of my offers. Why, do you think it is any different to sponge from some other rotten son of a bitch? Tell me!"

"There is a considerable difference," Edith said. "You know what I'm talking about. Regardless of what you are going to say to disrupt my plans, I am going to be Wayne Trent's wife. Didn't you realize that I would capitalize on the opportunity to marry Wayne? Now I can lead a honorable life and come face to face with respectable people without disgrace."

"You said you loved me!" Jason replied. "Me and only me!"

"It is an evil love," Edith said. "Nevertheless, I have often wished that I didn't love you at all."

"You are going to stand there and try to convince me that marrying Wayne isn't wrong. Standing before a minister or a justice of the peace pretending to cherish the vows of matrimony, but in reality deceiving Wayne. I don't think you will uphold the vows of matrimony. There is an obstacle in your way, Edith. You are not going to marry Wayne Trent because I'm going to tell him the truth about all of your escapades of the past."

"You wouldn't!" Edith said astonishingly.

"Yes, I would," Jason replied quickly. "I'm going to let him know that you were my mistress and we had sexual intercourse on many occasions. When I get done talking about you, all the whores are going to look like upstanding pillars of the community. When he hears all of these stories about you, Edith, do you think he will have the courage to marry you?"

"I think he will," Edith said casually.

"Then you are a horse's ass to believe he will marry you," Jason Snead answered.

"There isn't a man on the face of the earth who would marry you after hearing all about your immoral affairs."

"Wayne Trent will marry me," Edith said emphatically. "Go and talk to him so that you can find out for yourself what I told him about my character and reputation. I have told him about my relationship with you. It is time you realize that all men are not selfish and domineering like you."

"You really told him about us!" Jason said astonishingly. "I can't believe it!"

"Yes, Jason," Edith said confidently. "If you don't believe me, go and talk to him."

"When you told him the truth, it didn't disturb him. Hell oh mighty, Edith, he must be a pussy."

"He is a different man than what you are, Jason," Edith said.

Jason studied her, his facial expressions displaying the signs of disapproval. Edith knew he was going to plead with her to change her mind.

"Look, Edith," he said modestly. "You can't marry Wayne. Why do you want to hurt my feelings? Don't you understand how much I need you—how much I love you?"

"You really don't give a damn about me, Jason Snead," Edith said smartly.

"I'll show you how much I love you!" He said in a sharp, angry tone, and he pulled her quickly into his arms. Edith protested his rude behavior and his attempts to overwhelm her with kisses. She violently moved her head from side to side to avoid his advances.

"I don't have the will nor the strength to fight you, Jason," she said. "If you try that again, so help me God, I'll inform the authorities that you molested me. Don't you believe me, Jason? Look into my eyes and you will believe what I am saying to you. I will tell you once again that I am serious about reporting you to the authorities. Let me go!"

She could feel his firm hold slowly releasing her. He stepped back and stared at her. His face depicted bewilderment and the signs of defeat, and for a short space of time she regretted her actions. Then she came to her senses.

"Goodbye, Jason," she said softly, as she put out her hand. Subconsciously he was clasping and shaking her hand. He stood there shaking her hand for a moment. Then suddenly, he released his firm grip. "You haven't seen the last of me," he said forcefully and walked through the doorway and out on to the street.

Edith was never intimidated by the threatening remarks made by Jason Snead. Several days after his departure, Wayne Trent and Edith

Curtis were united in marriage and continued to reside in Sinclair. It appeared that their marriage was sound.

One day, Edith stared at the face of her husband, Wayne Trent. Then she looked out the front window at the gloomy environment of Sinclair. This was only one of many things she did not like about Sinclair. She had no cause for complaining, for it was her recommendation that they live here shortly after their marriage. Her decision was based primarily on the fact that Wayne Trent's family investments were here and Wayne was able to work in one of their offices with the Coal Company because of his family's influence, but more significant was her ultimate wish to move far away from Jason Snead.

What has happened to our relationship? I have tried my damnedest to make it work she thought. One morning, while sitting at the breakfast table, she had a sudden impulse to go and embrace Wayne. A quick look at his face was enough to suppress that impulse. After six months of marriage, Wayne had aged considerably. He was not enthusiastic, and he did not have the sparkle in his eyes now, no zeal, and no merriment. He looked at Edith now in a serious manner, his facial expression was that of a businessman who was having economic problems.

It was those love letters from Jason Snead, Edith recalled over and over again. Knowing the reason for his sadness was of no consequence when the knowing did not provide a solution. She could not approach Wayne and say, "Forget about those letters, my love, they don't mean a damn thing," she reiterated over and over again without any success. Wayne would have accepted her explanations, if he wanted to, but he did not. His affliction, a dreadful illness in any man, was for a man of his disposition hopeless. If he doesn't get over his resentment, it will bear on his mind, and he will more than likely commit suicide. Look at his sunken cheeks. He must be suffering from malnutrition, and lost a considerable amount of weight in a relatively short period of time.

He stared at the food untouched upon his plate.

"Why don't you eat the food that is on your plate?" Edith asked softly.

"My food," he responded quickly. "I'm sorry, Edith, but the sight of the food turns my stomach."

"You're always telling me that the food does not agree with you," Edith replied. "You must eat a decent amount of food, Wayne, for your own well being. Besides you have a problem with insomnia. There were many times that I have awakened and you were not in bed beside me. You were walking throughout the house, as if you were in a trance. Wayne, why can't you forget those letters I received from Jason Snead? Why can't you believe me when I tell you that Jason means nothing to me?"

"I do believe you, Edith, but I have lost faith in myself. It was a sudden shock to find out that you were receiving letters from Jason Snead."

"Wayne, please understand me," she said softly. "Do you know why I never told you? Yes, Jason wrote letters to me, but I never answered those letters. I thought he would get discouraged when he never heard from me, though I should have known that he is the type of person who does not give up very easily. I didn't want you to get upset and that is why I never told you about the letters. I remember the day when you walked into the house with one of his letters. I could tell by the expression on your face that there was something amiss, and I realized I was absolutely wrong for not telling you about the letters sooner. Was I really wrong, Wayne? Wouldn't you have been overwhelmed with anger even if I were to have told you sooner?"

"Yes, I would have been angry. There is only one way you could have prevented me from being concerned, Edith. Do you know what I'm referring to?"

Edith stood there and stared at him perplexingly. "No, I don't know," she said.

"All you had to say to him is, 'Jason stay away from me because I don't love you anymore, but you really must be sincere. I will be able to tell whether you are telling the truth.'" Wayne looked at her and his eyes were earnestly pleading for an opportunity to speak, simple respites of relief.

I should take some sort of action now, Edith thought. In reality, nothing is perfect, and the shame of lying would be exceeded by the kindness that inspired it. She lifted his chin with her hand and looked into his eyes. They were clear and very bright, but expressing something unusual now. Wayne would immediately know if she lied. She bowed her head as if she were worshipping. The stillness extended between them that seemed like a barricade. "I understand," Wayne said. "You're still infatuated with Jason Snead."

"Yes," Edith said meekly. "I pray that my attraction to Jason Snead will diminish in the very near future." Edith moved closer to Wayne, but he did not kiss her. Instead he merely stared into her gloomy eyes.

"Please don't make any promises, Edith? Promises should be based on honesty and integrity, not solely on the basis of a whim."

"Wayne," Edith sobbed. "Wayne."

"Be quiet," he replied. "Don't start crying?"

Edith tried to hold back her tears. "There is something I want to discuss with you. We have disrupted the entire day with nonsense. Our discussion will have to wait now."

"No, it won't have to," Wayne said. "It's better to discuss it now and get it over with."

"I guess you're right," Edith said. "It's just that I have an appointment with a medical specialist in Pellersville."

"No," Wayne said. "Do you really have to go?"

Edith's response was clear and composed. "Yes, I should go today, but I can call and try to change my appointment until another time."

"Don't?" He suddenly said. "I can drive you downtown to the bus terminal, and you can leave from there. They can spare me at the office for several hours. I'll call and tell them I'll be late today because of some urgent business that has to be taken care of as soon as possible."

"No, Wayne," Edith intervened. "It is not necessary for you to take me. I'll just call a taxicab. Besides, I don't want to jeopardize your position at the office."

"There won't be any problem," Wayne said. "There is a bus leaving for Pellersville at ten o'clock. I'll escort you to the bus after you purchase your ticket."

"Oh, well, I guess I'll accept your offer, but please don't stand around and constantly worry about me."

"I promise that I won't," Wayne said pleasantly. "Now I'll have to hurry to get you to the terminal on time."

After he kissed her and bid his wife a farewell, and watched the bus out of sight, Wayne stood for a considerable period of time on the pavement thinking about Edith. He tried to ignore the negative aspects of her life, but the annoying thoughts continued to prey upon his mind.

The first thing Edith noticed when she got back from Pellersville was the fact that Wayne was not at home from work. Poor Wayne, she thought, he has been mentally disturbed in recent days. I will try to comfort him. We can be happy together, if we don't permit our emotions to overcome us.

When the supper was ready, she called her daughter, Melissa and Helen Stringer, the sitter, to come to the table and eat their supper. Edith realized that Wayne was long overdue in coming home from the Coal Company office. She sat quietly in a rocking chair looking at the time on the wall clock. What has happened to him? Oh, my Lord, I wonder where he can be? She was up now and walking rapidly toward the telephone. She called the office manager at the Coal Company. "No, madam, Wayne Trent has not been in the office today," the office manager said. "I wondered about him myself seeing how he is always punctual."

"Where could he be?" Edith said sadly. "Don't you have any idea?"

"No madam. I will go and ask some of the other employees. They might know, and if anyone knows of his whereabouts, I'll call you back."

"Thank you," Edith said softly. Then she went back and sat in a rocking chair. There was nothing to do now but sit and wait patiently. She waited for a long time, but received no information regarding Wayne's whereabouts.

Melissa and Helen Stringer went into the living room and sat on a couch. It was a thing they did not often do. Yet, today there was a definite justification in sitting in the living room that was usually reserved for visitors. Today they sat on the couch in absence of noise awaiting the ring of the telephone.

Edith fell asleep in the rocking chair. Her sleep was interrupted by the sound of a whistle coming from the vicinity of the coal mine. She rose and walked to the front window. The morning was gloomy, and the rays of the rising sun could barely be seen through the smoke and haze that concealed the sky over Sinclair. Edith could not tolerate the scene any longer, and turned and walked slowly into the kitchen. She was aware of being hungry and thirsty, but when she tried to eat, she could not. "Wayne is dead!" She cried hysterically. "Oh, Lord, he is dead!" Then she ran up the stairs and threw herself across the bed.

After several hours, she became accustomed to waiting. She knew that she should have contacted the police, but somehow she could not bring herself to it because she would be ridiculed for reporting a missing person within a short period of time. What if they asked her questions regarding their relationship and if there were any specific reasons for him not coming home? How could she answer these questions except to exert to the truth?

Several days passed and the whereabouts of Wayne were still unknown until she heard the footsteps on the front porch. She rose and walked quickly into the living room and opened the door, her facial expressions displaying the signs of disappointment. "Oh, Wayne," Edith said. "I thought you were my husband, Wayne."

The mailman smiled gently and said, "Here is a letter for you." He turned and walked away.

When she looked at the envelope, she recognized that Wayne wrote the address. She became very excited and her hands began to tremble. After she regained her composure, she opened the envelope and withdrew the letter. Upon unfolding the letter, she began to read:

"Edith, I am in Pellersville. I arrived here shortly before you did just in time to see you leaving Doctor Swade's office in the company of Jason Snead. Sometime later you had lunch with Jason at Lombardi's Restaurant on Sixth Street. After viewing that incident, I became very angry that I didn't have the desire to follow you anymore. I am not going to play second fiddle to anyone."

"Oh my God, Wayne," she yelled out. "It's not what you're thinking. There's no intimate relationship with Jason Snead." She continued to read:

"This is my way of severing our marriage. I will make all the necessary arrangements for a divorce. I am certain that this action will be to your satisfaction. What can I really say to you? I had confidence and trust in you, but you lied to me. I honored you and you deceived me. I keep asking myself, should I give her another chance because there must be a good reason for her actions? I don't think so. I do want to take this opportunity to inform you that I love you very much and forgive you for your actions. Nevertheless, I can't exist in a life of doubt and deceit. Please give my regards to Melissa. Farewell, Edith."

Edith stood there in a state of shock holding the letter in her hand. She crumbled the letter into a small round ball and threw it on to the floor. Melissa, observing the actions of her mother in the living room merely asked, "What's wrong, mother?"

Twenty-Four

Wayne has left me. I am once again alone in the midst of these people in Sinclair, she thought.

Edith did not derive any satisfaction of freedom immediately, although she felt unattached and isolated. In that isolation she still had the responsibility of caring for herself and her daughter, Melissa.

Her wandering eyes focused elsewhere now, that she no longer was married. It is rather strange, she thought, how easy it is to understand now the meaning of freedom. I can do what I want, to date when I want, and to travel as I want. Yet, I am lonely.

Edith was sitting in the living room, and her hands moved nervously along the window ledge, but she was not conscious of it. She stared out into a torrential rain that had obscured her view of the street. She had been very lonely since the departure of Wayne Trent.

She did for a moment think of her relationship with Henry Shane. Henry is probably dead and buried somewhere in Korea, she thought. More importantly, she was thinking about the immoral life that she had been leading, and that is one of the reasons she didn't write to him.

In this respect she was right. Edith, by Christian standards was leading an immoral life. Since Andy's suicide she had been the mistress of Robert Heim and the wife of Wayne Trent and bedded with other men in succession, each wealthier than the last, and some of which she had spurned. She was at that moment contemplating having a relationship with Frank Torro, a man who could have been not only her father, but also her grandfather. The wrong of Edith's mental interpretation was the fact that being a Christian and a female, she thought she was not susceptible of being immoral. To her way of thinking, her behavior was not immoral, but merely essential for survival.

She had soon found, with the passing of time, that her desire of being a housewife was totally unacceptable. She despised meager tasks and housekeeping chores in general and preferred to be inactive. She soon found out that she could survive easier by taking advantage of her body assets that nature had bestowed to her. Edith's many perceptions of men made her a costly expenditure that she could only be a sugar daddy's companion, because a few young men did not have the financial means to afford her.

Some of the older men she permitted to bed with her. She deceived them invariably with a few young, potent men who pleasured her. Still, her subconscious thoughts of the heroic soldier image of Henry Shane made all other men seem like wimps, simpletons, and cowards to her. This very real problem was enlarged by the fact that being immeasurably strong herself, her feminine need for a man potent enough to satisfy her was almost always hindered by the strange mystery that certainly will attract men with a weaker character, or men seeking a mother image.

A man's perception of Edith often made him acknowledge: "All right I was a rotten son of a bitch to get involved with her, but she was a real sexy woman."

Edith regarded her promiscuity as a part of her quest for the great love of her life. She was incapable of taking a man and trying to turn him into an obedient companion, ignoring the positive attributes of his real character. She was not aware that her conduct was the same as that of a woman that she herself classified as a cheap little whore. The fact was that she was not reimbursed for her sexual favors—at least not by the sugar daddy's who kept her, and not at all by her active and potent gigolos. Why she behaved as she did, will forever remain incomprehensible.

Frank Torro was a very nice man, Edith thought. He was the only man that made her life pleasant since the death of Robert Heim. All the other men were only interested in one thing. Regardless, she still had dreams of luring Henry Shane back into her fold upon his return from the Korean War.

During all those days since her divorce from Wayne Trent, she was confronted with loneliness. Frank Torro was a regular visitor to her house, bringing her gifts and talked to her comfortingly.

It had been nice to have Frank Torro in her house. She had nothing to fear from him. He had been very gentle and considerate. Never by word or deed had he taken advantage of her. She often felt disappointed that he hadn't attempted anything. Of course she would have refused and reduced him to a state of apology. Then she would forgive him, but he hadn't given her the chance. She thought that a woman awaiting the return of her true love should make an effort to reform. Oh, but it has been so long since I have had any sexual satisfaction, she thought.

Why am I thinking this way? I loved Henry Shane. I'm going to wait for him, regardless of what he may think of me. Oh, God, give me the strength to control my emotions. I want to forgive Henry, I want to be his wife, and he was the only man that I truly loved.

Women are strange and unpredictable. Loneliness and lack of manly affection can cause them to behave in a strange way. Henry will understand when he returns and he will forgive my actions, she thought.

She had danced for many months in the arms of many men, thus neglecting to write to Henry Shane. Frank Torro and others who craved her attention took her to the best nightclubs in Jaystown. Still, she had danced, wined, and dined rejoicing in her beauty, in her effort to charm men after having been so long a victim of loneliness. She really did not defend herself against their attempts to kiss her, to fondle her, to have sexual relations. She laughed at her sure mastery over all the men she had met. Yet, there was a place in her heart for Henry Shane. There wasn't anything to write to Henry Shane about after he got married while he was stationed at Fort George, she thought. I told him once that he was the only man I ever loved, and will love. Still, she could have written to him. There is always something to say to the man she loved. She did not know what caused her to behave as she did, and was not concerned about what other people thought or said. She had been seeing a lot of Frank Torro, but recently business trips kept him out of town for days at a time.

Looking out the window, she saw that the rain had stopped, and the water had subsided along the curbing of the street. What had caused her sudden feeling of loneliness was the patter of the rain against the roof and windows. There was a slight breeze sweeping down on Sinclair from the mountains and driving the clouds to the east. In a matter of a few minutes, the sun broke through. The rays of the sun came down upon the town like a blaze of glory.

Her thoughts of loneliness were interrupted with the thought of being with a man who could comfort her, to ease her tension.

"I'll have to go out," she whispered. "I can't stand being here alone." She looked at herself in the mirror. Her face was pale and hungry looking, but other than that she looked pretty, she thought.

She picked up her purse from the table, and walked towards the door, opened it, then locked it. She went from the porch to the sidewalk, and as she had hoped, she saw Frank Torro's automobile coming down the street. He parked his automobile, got out, and walked towards her. Her eyes brightened at the sight of him.

"Thank God," she sighed.

"I see that you are glad to see me," Frank Torro said. "Is there any special place I can take you?"

"No," Edith replied. "I was just going to go for a walk."

Frank Torro placed his hand upon her shoulder.

"You have pleased me by coming," she said gently. "I guess I was a little lonely, Frank. Come on, let's go into the house. No one is at home. Melissa is staying with our relatives over in Aurora Springs."

"This place is making you lonely, isn't it?" Frank Torro said.

"I hate this place!" Edith burst out. "The people are nosey—being in this house without Melissa makes me feel lonely. I can't stand it." She paused. "Take me with you, Frank," she said quietly. "Please."

"All right, I'll call and make reservations up at Pine Ridge. We can spend the weekend together. I have a friend who manages the resort, and he will take care of us well. Do you mind if I use your telephone?"

"No, go right ahead," Edith replied.

After placing the call to Pine Ridge, Frank Torro and Edith decided to leave immediately.

It was dark when they arrived at Pine Ridge. When they entered the office, the manager approached them and smiled. "I have made arrangements for you, Mr. Torro, at the Lincoln Cabin," he said politely. "As you know, it is the best one we have here." He led them to the cabin set further back from the others.

"It has a certain attractiveness," she said to Frank Torro. "It's kind of romantic." Then seeing his eyes, she added quickly with a soft sigh, "too bad, Henry Shane isn't here."

Frank Torro did not answer her. They followed the manager into the cabin. He opened the door to the bedroom, paused and then smiled and said, "I hope you have a pleasant weekend at Pine Ridge." Then he departed.

Edith came into the room and looked around, seeing that it was somewhat attractive, better in fact, than being in her own lonely house. She wasn't afraid of Frank Torro. What she had been afraid of was herself, of her sudden response to him. She didn't have to be afraid of that anymore, not since she had catered to other male companions on other occasions.

At her side, Frank Torro, the gentleman, smiled down at her, his eyes confident and sure. Edith seldom thought of Henry Shane on occasions like this. She was only concerned about the pleasures at the moment, the sensational feeling of the relationship with the man available at the time of her desperate urge. Frank Torro had been successful on a few other occasions in making Edith forget all about Henry Shane and the other men in her life. He had made considerable progress with her, but in a different manner than her previous suitors. He sat on the edge of the bed, and slowly began to remove his clothes, and with deliberation, he assisted her with the removal of her lingerie.

It was very warm. Edith felt the perspiration gathering on the skin of her naked body. It made her very conscious of her immediate desire. The beautiful body she had cared for so well, bathing it, perfuming it, and attending to its sexual needs. Those kind of needs that men had turned so lavishly to at the sight of her throbbing breasts and wanting body. Her eyes always glaring and her mouth breath panting in her attempt to reach for the ultimate climax she craved.

She had been a married woman, and even with the husband she did not love, there had been times when she came close to liking sex, she admitted to herself with a sudden force of honesty. The time I kissed Henry Shane on the train platform things happened to me, she thought. I wanted him right there in front of all of those people. I always craved sex. I will like it, I will! If that makes me an immoral woman, then an immoral woman I will have to be. Funny, when I was married to Andy he always stopped in time—before it got to the point when I was about to have an orgasm. Oh, God, I don't know! What does happen to me? Why am I this way? I have to have a man all the time.

She turned and looked at Frank Torro, her eyes filled again with speculation. She didn't know how she looked at him, but Frank Torro did. Joy bubbled over his naked body, his veins throbbing. "Now!" he cried out.

"Frank!" she commanded. "Again, please again, —. Oh!"

Exhausted from the sexual activity, Frank Torro quickly fell asleep. Then it was morning.

They did not realize that they had overslept. Upon getting out of bed, they quickly took a shower, and then put on their formal clothes.

"I will call and make arrangements to have dinner in the Washington Room," Frank Torro said smoothly. "Of course, we may see some people from Sinclair, but you won't mind that. We will just ignore them, won't we, Edith?"

"Yes, my love," Edith said subconsciously. She was unaware that she had said that to many of her bed partners, out of the long experience

The Wailing Wind

of marriage and relationships with other men. Frank Torro liked the title bestowed upon him.

Edith had dressed very neatly for dinner. When she came into the dining room she saw men's eyes sparkle and women casting jealous eyes upon her. Frank Torro walked proudly beside her, his eyes glowing with pride. He was a tall, handsome man in spite of his age and very impressive with his manners. He escorted her to the reserved table.

"My dear," he said. "You are indeed a beautiful woman."

"Thank you," Edith replied. "And you are my handsome lover."

"What more could a man want?" He sighed. "I have ordered the drinks. You like to drink before dinner, don't you, Edith?"

"Of course," Edith said. How could she admit to such a man that her deceased husband had frowned upon her drinking? He had forbidden her to indulge in any type of alcohol after they were married, but ignored his request anyway.

The drink was good. One drink led to another. She realized that she was feeling tipsy, laughed easily long before the dinner was served. When the waiter arrived and placed the food on the table, she ate very little. Instead she preferred to drink, and listen to the compliments being bestowed upon her by her lover. She felt as if she was sitting on a cloud, floating endlessly into an unknown destination. What a wonderful, wonderful feeling, she thought.

Moments later, the waiter approached Frank Torro and informed him that there was a telephone call for him. He left with the waiter to the telephone booth. Edith sat there in her little world of make belief, smiling, and casting her eyes at other men sitting in the restaurant. She was utterly surprised when she saw Jason Snead enter the lodge and walk directly to the bar. What is he doing here? Edith thought.

When he recognized Edith sitting at the table, he motioned for her to come to the bar. She nodded her wobbly head and pointed to the empty chair across from her. At that moment, Frank Torro returned.

"Dear," he said. "I am going to have to go back to Sinclair. Some important business deal has come up that must be taken care of immediately. I will escort you back to the cabin, and I will come back as soon as possible." After escorting Edith back to the cabin, Frank Torro got into his automobile and drove off.

Edith was sitting in her cabin, weary and wobbly. She took off her dress and threw it on the floor, and lay on the bed with her slip and brassiere intact. The drinks were wonderful, but they were awfully strong, she thought. The room revolved in a slow and whirling dance before her eyes. She closed her weary eyes. In a matter of a few minutes she was asleep.

Later a pounding at the cabin door awakened her. She was startled and sprang from the bed, and seized her dress. She was still wobbly and in a state of confusion. She opened the door a crack. She recognized that it was Jason Snead who she had seen at the bar. He was holding a bottle of whiskey and soda and a bucket of ice in his hands.

"Do you mind having a drink with me?" He said. "I overheard the conversation while I was sitting at the bar, and saw your companion leave in his automobile. I thought you would enjoy some company in his absence. It has been a long time since I have been with you, Edith."

"Why—oh—yes!" Edith said. "I can't feel any worse. Do come in?"

Jason Snead walked into the room and went directly to the bathroom and returned with two glasses. "How do you like your drink?" He said. "Weak or strong."

"Well," Edith said. "Not too strong."

Jason dropped several ice cubes into the glasses. He opened the bottles and proceeded to pour whiskey and soda into the glasses.

"When is your companion going to return?" Jason asked.

"I don't know," Edith replied squeamishly.

It was very warm in the cabin. Edith discovered that she was, after all thirsty. She took the glass and drank the contents all at once. Almost immediately she felt better. The wildness of another adventure began seeping into her mind. She danced around the room. Jason poured her another drink. A craving sexual urge came over her at once. She hoped that Jason would seize her and sweep her onto the bed.

Outside, it was already dark. Jason Snead had respected her privacy upon his entrance to the cabin earlier in the evening and made no efforts to force himself upon her. Edith suddenly wondered what affect it would have on Jason if she were to dance around him in the nude. She proceeded to disrobe, and threw her dress on the floor and brassiere and lingerie on the bed. She hoped it would arouse his sexual appetite. This is one way she enjoyed to make men suffer, increasing their sexual desires for her. Jason looked at her in amazement. I have never seen her act like this in the past, he thought. His intention was to gradually seduce her into an affair, but not like this. He was startled. She was inducing him into an affair.

She threw herself upon the bed. She arched her beautiful slim body, feeling with curious warmth, her thrusting, pointed breasts, begging him to get into bed with her. Jason removed his clothes and got into bed with her.

"I am beautiful," Edith said. "All men want me. I like that." She laughed and then continued to talk. "Don't be shocked, Jason? I am giving you something you want, and something I want, and always will want."

"Come closer," she said. "Put your arms around me. Kiss me. That's it, that's it." Edith was having a difficult time watching Jason's face. Her eyes didn't behave properly anymore. He was close to her, much too close, but that is the way she liked it. She blinked at him and said, "What are you waiting for? This is what all men look forward too."

Then his mouth was on hers burning. Jason was a man of experience. His mouth moved on hers, slowly, charmingly and expertly. Her mouth parted under his seeking air, then he was kissing her in a way she had never been kissed before.

Her hands locked around his body. She found herself kissing him back in the same way. She was aware with part of her mind that she was doing these things to arouse another type of sensation in herself, and in Jason Snead. There was a burning sensation in her body. She felt inside of her a thrill that she had never witnessed before, a thrill not even Henry Shane, Andy Curtis, Robert Heim, Wayne Trent, Frank Torro, or any other man could arouse in her.

He released her. She opened her eyes and looked at him. "You are the best damn man I ever went to bed with. You are the type of man I have always had the need for."

"Come," he said, pulling her out of bed. "Let's have another drink."

She watched him with amazement in her eyes as he proceeded to fill the glasses. *I never remember Jason being so sexually active. I wonder what has changed him,* she thought. Now she was thinking of ways whereby she could hold on to this prize possession, a man she had known for sometime before, but spurned him in favor of Wayne Trent.

"To us," he said, as he raised his glass.

"To us," she echoed as they tipped their glasses.

He stood up after a time and took her glass from her hand. He drew her naked body upright. He was kissing her again, that special way. She was thrilled again beyond any woman's expectations.

Suddenly they heard the approaching sound of an automobile. "It must be Frank Torro!" she yelled. "Hurry, you must get the hell out of here!"

Quickly Jason Snead put on his underwear and grabbed the rest of his clothes and shoes and ran out of the back door into the darkness of the night.

"I'll never see him again," Edith whispered.

Jason had departed from the cabin in time, for now Frank Torro opened the door, slammed it, and then locked it. He came toward Edith. She saw his horrified eyes locking at her nude body, her brassiere and lingerie on the bed, and dress on the floor. She stood in the middle of the room trembling.

He saw her messed hair, her lips puffy and swollen, her eyes wild, and her body still panting from an affair that had occurred while he was gone.

"I don't care!" She screamed. "At last I found someone who gave

The Wailing Wind

me what I needed all my life. I know I look like a whore, like one of those girls that men pay to have an affair with."

She crossed the room, and sat on the bed. The tears stinging her eyes and gradually running down her cheeks. "To think," she said. "I found my happiness through Jason Snead. I'll probably never see him again."

Frank Torro did not utter a word, but merely looked at her in disgust.

"Oh, Frank!" she wept. "Henry, Henry Shane, I'm not good enough for you, now. I'm not! I'm not! Please Frank, she begged, don't tell anyone, please?"

"Don't worry, I won't!" he replied. "The only thing I have to say is that I feel sorry for you. You are a very weak woman. You must have a serious problem because it seems that you can't control your sexual needs. I wouldn't be surprised that you're a nymphomaniac. I thought there was a place for me in your heart, but I guess I was wrong."

Edith continued to weep.

Suddenly Frank Torro said, "Get dressed and I'll drive you back to Sinclair. Maybe it was my fault for bringing you here in the first place."

Back in Sinclair, Edith never heard from nor saw Frank Torro or Jason Snead again.

"I am an immoral woman," she sobbed. "I'm destined for hell. I had sexual intercourse with Frank Torro and deceived him. I did it with Jason Snead, a person who entered the cabin when I was inebriated. He satisfied in me something that I had been craving all my life. It was not a true love, it was a mysterious coincidence."

She shook her head and wept, but she couldn't stop the constant probing, the pounding in her head, the shrill sound as if Satin was rejoicing—calling her. They came down upon her heavier than death. Edith screamed, "With them, with anybody! I'm that kind of woman!"

Then she buried her face in her hands and wept, and attempted to surrender herself to the mercy of God. There she was found by Melissa's sitter, Helen Stringer, in an unconscious state with an empty bottle of sleeping pills and a picture of Henry Shane lying on the floor beside her.

Helen called for an ambulance, and Edith was rushed to the Sinclair Hospital where emergency medical personnel worked frantically to save her life. After many days in the intensive care unit, she made a remarkable recovery. Psychiatrists recommended that she be transported to the Forest Hill's Psychiatric Hospital in Woodville for extensive treatment in an attempt to enable her to resume a normal life in society.

It came to pass when Edith was making excellent progress towards a complete recovery at the Forest Hill's Psychiatric Hospital, a telegram was received by Lee Shane informing him that his brother, Henry Shane had been released from a North Korean prisoner of war camp.

Twenty-Five

Henry Shane was one of many American fighting men released from enemy prison camps in North Korea, and many of them were near death. He had detested that God forsaken war much more deeply than he had expected. The days between the high spirits of Camp Fuji to the tranquil mid summer days of Tachikawa, Japan there had been for almost all of them a painful emotion of fear tolerable only if the heart strengthened itself in opposition to kindliness, hope and existence itself. There had been moments of antipathy and animosity so deeply ingrained that to survive, he could do nothing except pray and go on and accept the pains of hell on earth. He had to forget everything that dishonored him and live without pride, without love, without faith and hope. Of the horrors of warfare, the things that he said can not be taken lightly.

With the prisoner exchanges of Operation Little Switch and Operation Big Switch and the end of the fighting, he expected these emotions to subside, and in a sense they did. Now they were succeeded for a brief period by a feeling he had never known before.

Immediately upon being released from the prisoner of war camp in North Korea, he was transported to a medical processing center near Seoul, South Korea. After the first week following his repatriation, he traveled by a C-47 aircraft from Seoul City Airbase to Tachikawa Air Base near Tokyo, Japan. Two young lieutenants whose names he did not know piloted the aircraft. They were in their early twenties. Their aerial navigation was casual and informal. They relied mainly on common sense methods of flying an aircraft. Anyone observing them could tell that the Korean landscape had become as familiar to them in terms of structured rice paddies, building ruins, as the pleasant mountains, the picturesque towns and the long scenic roads near home. The co-pilot, who also served as the navigator, with a map across his lap, followed the course with his forefinger and only glanced down now and then at the peaceful Han River, the shell craters nearby and the silent, deserted gun batteries of the ROK Army.

It was not peace. It was silence, and in the silence there was an eerie environment. When Henry arrived at Tachikawa the great flags of the United Nations swayed in the summer breeze near the entrance to the terminal. Overhead roared C-124 Globemasters, the pilots ferrying materials and supplies to the war ravaged South Korean capital city of Seoul. While he watched, one pilot, flying low over the terminal dipped his wings in thunderous salute as he passed overhead.

The Japanese on the streets below did not look up. They walked slowly and silently as though dazed and in a bewildered trance. The other repatriated American soldiers stood nearby and talked in subdued voices or did not talk at all. Everywhere there was strangeness in the air. In the occasional play and chatter of the little children, who had not yet recovered from the welcoming festivities, there was great excitement that day. The children still carried little American flags in their hands and in the sight of this childish joy there was something unmistakably out of place.

For this extraordinary state of mind that fell upon Henry for a little while after his repatriation and after the guns had been silenced was an uncertain sense of hopelessness. It was the indistinct, prolonging aftertaste of having accomplished something abnormal. The American forces unleashed their fury against the North Koreans and Chinese. Many Korean towns and hamlets lay in waste. It was of no advantage that to tell him that what the American and United Nation's forces had done was what they both had to do and the only thing they could have done. It was disheartening enough to remember the massive destruction caused by the war, and the American and United Nation's forces were involved in it. They had turned the savage evils of their enemies back upon them many times, and in so doing, something of their own integrity had been smeared.

The men who fought in this "Forgotten War" could feel no pride. Victors they were not—losers they were not—a stalemate. Now Henry was only a face in the crowd, lame and crippled moving sluggishly, silently along the streets of Tachikawa to the transient barrack to await his flight to the United States the following morning.

As he lay in bed staring at the ceiling, he painfully remembered the stench of death, the scorched and mangled bodies of his fellow Americans, the cold and blustery winter days of North Korea, the young, poverty stricken Korean children searching for food through the silent ruins of Seoul. He was deeply saddened seeing the dreadful, vacant eyes of hundreds of starving prisoners, and the shallow graves and crosses. They were all ensnared in one, and they all were the shocking horror of what he had known, of what he had been a part of.

Now he would be returning to the United States a broken man and eventually back to Sinclair where he would be confronted with a dismal and uncertain future.

Henry Shane's term of enlistment had expired when he was released from the army one fine day in September of 1953. He was going home to Sinclair laden with animosity that had saddened his heart and soul. An animosity that would continue to annoy and plague him for the remaining days of his life.

Early one bright morning he was able to garner the courage to board a train for home. He was dressed in his military uniform, and he had with him a duffel bag. Many people riding the train, recognizing that he had been wounded, and wearing campaign ribbons and medals on his blouse, came and talked to him about his ordeal in the war.

Traveling eastward from California, he knew at long last, and with certainty, that this journey was for him both an end and a beginning. He had damaged a part of himself over the years. Not only physically, but also morally.

Henry Shane was somehow distinct from other mortals. He had a worthy self-esteem, compassion and mercifulness for his colleagues, fought more intensely in the war, had sexual appetites in short that he was something special. He was one of the "golden boys," so that everything, including women and gratification was his by almost sacred right. More, having this feeling, he was far more anxious than most other people, and being what he was, a man of intricate involvement's, he could see nothing wrong with entrusting himself with the tasks of a superior person.

Now the thoughts of the deaths of his comrades in Korea had broken through the surface. They made an entrance through which the sensitivity he had all but killed in himself as a soldier, all the uncertainties, perplexities, inquiries that plague the lives of others, could from that day rise up to bewilder him. He was through with his old life style. He was prepared now to go back into the real world, to make peace with society, to surrender to anything, to the customs, mores, and legalities that governed others. It would be years before he would be able to comprehend the existence of theoretics much less to think in theoretical terms. The thoughts that meandered through his mind as the train rumbled eastward, muddled in their simplicity all the intricacies of life, but he did not know that then. He merely sat quietly, gazing out the window, thinking of the years that had drifted by him.

No more of that bullshit, he thought. I plan to die in bed, with my grandchildren congregating around me. I'm going to be a peaceful and upstanding citizen, owning my own land, with the golden wheat fluttering in the breeze as far as the eye can see. I haven't had a decent life, really. The money I had earned over the years was foolishly spent on booze and women, and catering to whorehouses. I want a woman now who isn't merely interested in any man who has money. I want to live where I can see green things growing and smell the earth soaking up the rain. I want to settle back in the peaceful Allegheny Mountains near home. After many weary hours of travel, he finally reached Jaystown where he would leave the train. In previous years it was possible for the train to stop in Sinclair, but poor economic conditions in railroading necessitated the closing of the station.

The train platform at Jaystown was crowded with many people as he got off of the train. There were other returning soldiers—some amputees, some with crutches, some bewildered, and others without a blemish.

A band at the farther end of the platform was playing John Philip Sousa's STARS AND STRIPES FOREVER and those nearest to him were singing patriotic songs. The crowd on the platform had gathered to welcome home the local boys who were returning from the war.

Somebody in the crowd had shouted his name. Then there rose a jubilant outburst of thunderous cheers. "It's some of the boys from the old neighborhood back in Sinclair," he whispered. He could see a number of them in the crowd. One he recognized immediately to be Richard Rand hurriedly walking toward him carrying a large, colorful plaque. He thought they were trying to make an ass out of him, but quickly reacted politely by merely saying, "thank you." Searching for words, Henry added, "What is this all about?"

"This isn't any bullshit," Richard Rand said. "It's to honor and welcome home a hero."

Henry was overcome with embarrassment and managed to say, "Did you want me to give this plaque to somebody else?"

"We hope you keep it yourself," Richard said. "It's the least thing we can do for a hero."

"A hero!" Henry shouted. "I'm no more a damn hero than what you are!"

"Cut the bullshit," Richard quickly interjected.

In accounts of the war in THE JAYSTOWN TRIBUNE the folks of the region had seen a news release about Henry Shane leading a charge in a battle in North Korea, but his fame had gone farther— much farther indeed —than he knew. He stood a moment laughing—an odd sort of laugh it was that had in it the silence of tears—and waving his hand to the many friends who now were calling his name.

In the uproar of the crowd and waving flags he could not see his brother for a moment. When he saw him in the breaking crowd he was shouting and waving his hand above his head. His enthusiasm increased when he stood before him, and then embraced him.

As he was greeting his brother, he heard a sweet, soft voice call his name. There beside him, stood the beautiful erect figure of Edith Curtis. Their eyes met and, before there was any thinking of propriety, he had her in his arms and was kissing her.

It thrilled him to see the brilliant luster of her beauty that day. Her eyes were wet with feeling as they looked at each other; to feel again the trembling touch of her lips. In a moment he turned to his brother.

"Lee," he said. "Where is Ruth and the children?"

"They are back in Sinclair," Lee replied. "They'll be more than happy to see you when you go to Sinclair."

"I thought that they would be here at the train station," Henry said. Then he stopped talking and reached for his duffel bag.

"Come on now," Lee responded as he snatched the duffel bag from the grasp of his brother's hand. "We're going to have a grand old time. I'm going to take you to the best drinking and eating establishment in Jaystown, and I'm not going to worry about the expenses either."

They crossed the street and headed in the direction of the parking lot that was a short distance from the terminal, while many questions were directed toward Henry. Upon reaching the parking lot they got into Lee's automobile and immediately drove to the Palace Hotel. Lee had made reservations in advance for a suite for all of them.

"It's pretty damn expensive," Lee grumbled as they left the reception desk. "It's kind of ridiculous to spend this much money, but I don't care. When a brother has been away so long fighting in a war, he is entitled to some comforts in life."

They were soon seated in the main dining room of the Palace Hotel. There was a great radiance of health and beauty in Edith's face. It was a bit fuller, but had nobler outlines and coloring as delicate as ever. She wore a navy-blue dress admirably fitted to the contour of her body. There was a similar but splendid dignity in her carriage, her big, dark eyes, and her nose with its little upward slant. She was, as she always had been, the well-groomed figure in the glory of womanhood.

When they had come back from dinner, Lee took off his shoes and sat comfortably in his stocking feet while Edith told of her trying experiences living in Sinclair and Henry of his ordeal in Korea.

Lee went away to his room in due time. Then Henry came and sat beside Edith on the bed. "Let's have a good and sensible discussion," he said. There was an awkward bit of silence.

"Well," she said, her finger upon her lip, "tell me more about the Korean War."

"I'm sick and tired of talking about that damn Korean War," he replied. "Love is a much better subject to discuss."

She rose and walked back and forth across the room, a troubled and bewildered look on her face. As he watched her closely, he thought he had never seen a woman who could carry her head so proudly.

"I don't think you really understand the meaning of love," she said suddenly as she returned to sit on the bed.

"How can you say such a thing?" he asked. "After all, I have loved you all these years in spite of the things you may have done."

"You told me that you have loved another woman once," she said, her hands resting on her lap, her eyes looking down soberly.

"When?" he asked. "Where?"

"In my bedroom, many years ago," she responded.

"Edith," he said. "You misunderstood me. I have always loved you."

She stood in front of him, then looking up into his eyes. He started to embrace her but she caught his hands and held them apart and came closer to his body.

"Did you say that you meant that you always loved me?" she asked in a whisper.

"I did mean you, Edith," he replied.

"Why didn't you tell me the night you were on military leave that you intended to go back to Fort George and marry another woman?"

"I was literally disgusted over your association with Robert Heim, and I got the impression that you were giving me a big line of bullshit," he answered quickly.

"Well, if you loved me as much as you have always indicated, then you would not have walked out on me after satisfying your beastly desires," she said.

"I would not have walked out on you, but I must confess that I was overcome with jealously thinking of sharing you with another man, and cuddled in the arms of Robert Heim—making love to him."

"You might at least have written and told me about your marriage," she suggested with a tone of sadness in her voice.

"I often thought about writing and telling you of my marriage to Faye Cooper while I was stationed at Fort George, but I felt guilty and foolish," he replied.

She looked very sober and thoughtful then. "Don't you remember our agreement that night at the Roxy Club?" she asked. "We parted with the genuine understanding that our love for each other would never cease regardless of what fate was in store for us. That was long, long, ago."

"I never loved any other woman—but you. I loved you then, and I still love you now, Edith, and that is enough. I love you in spite of all of your previous weaknesses and illicit activities. You are dearer than my life. It was the thought of you that gave me the hope and courage in the war and during my confinement in North Korea. I wish I could be as courageous here in this predicament. I am demanding that we start a new life together."

"I wish I knew if you were really serious," she said. "Whether you love me since you are aware of my immoral relationship with other men."

"Don't you believe me, Edith?" he quickly asked.

"Yes, I believe you. But you might not know your own heart. I'm afraid you will always bring up the subject of my immorality into the limelight when we are engaged in argument and disagreements."

"My love longs for you," he said. "It keeps me thinking of you always. Once it was so easy to be happy and carefree. Since you were out of my life it has seemed as if there were no longer any light in the world or any pleasure. I can not judge or condemn you because of your illicit behavior, because I am just as guilty as what you were for being involved in immoral activities. I did not know that love was such a mighty thing. Remember that I married a woman I really didn't love, and was involved in a divorce. To make matters worse, I got intimately involved with a Japanese girl while stationed in Japan. I impregnated her, and then the Korean War began. The last time I had seen her was when she was standing on the pier at Yokohama waving goodbye to me. It always seemed that when I was with Keiko that I loved her, but when I was in Korea, I seldom thought of her. I did not realize that my love for you was eternal."

"Love is a mysterious thing," she said, her voice trembling with emotion as his had trembled.

"I tried to forget about you, but I couldn't."

She was near to crying now, but she shut her lips firmly and kept back her tears. She came closer to him. Their lips touched and he put his arms around her tightly.

"I have waited long for this," he said. "This is one of the happiest moments of my life. I thought I had lost you."

"What a foolish man?" she whispered. "I have always loved you for years and years and you couldn't not see it. I know that you have endured pain and suffering, and my heart is saddened to see you come home from the war lame and crippled, but I still love you the way you are. Oh, if you would only believe it!"

She hesitated a moment, her eyes so close to his cheek he could feel the beat of their eyelashes. She continued to talk. "We were destined to be together," she added.

"I can thank God for that," he said. "He has made us for each other."

"I thank him for it too—I do love you so," she whispered.

When they sat down at length she told him what he had long suspected, that if they were to be married there would be complications with the church, and negative reactions from the community. Everybody in Sinclair was aware of Edith's immoral conduct while she was married to Andy Curtis, and shortly after his death. If they were to get married, then it would be necessary to have a private service before a justice of the peace.

"If it were not for your brother keeping me informed as to your whereabouts from time to time, I think I would have given up all hope of you," she added.

"Good for Lee!" he replied. "Let's go and tell him that we are going to have a reconciliation."

Lee was asleep when they entered his room, but he was startled when Henry put on the light.

"What the hell is going on?" he shouted, raising his head.

"Congratulate us," Henry said. "We're going to have a reconciliation."

"Have you finally decided after all these years?" Lee inquired smiling.

"Yes, love has conquered us both," Henry said.

"Well I'll be damn!" Lee answered. "This is the way it should have been years ago. I guess I won't waste anymore time lying here in bed. If you will be kind enough to step into the outer room, I'll put on my trousers and then we can talk about it more." He got out of bed and began to put on his trousers. "It beats the hell out of me!" He continued, entering the outer room, pulling up the zipper on his trousers. "I often thought more than likely you would get together someday. It isn't too often you will find a couple so well suited. Are you planning to get married?"

"We haven't decided on a definite date, as of yet," Henry said.

"The sooner the better," Lee said as he put on his shirt and sat down. "It used to be when a couple went out on a date a few times they were ready for the altar. If I were you, I wouldn't be disturbed over all the negative rumors that are going to be circulated by the people of Sinclair when they hear of your plans to get married. There will be some people who will condemn you both for the rest your life—yet there will be others who will forgive you and forget about the negative aspects of your past life."

Henry Shane and Edith Curtis returned to Sinclair where they lived in seclusion for several weeks. Then one day, unable to endure the thought of losing Edith, he got into his recently purchased pickup truck and drove to her house.

When Edith opened the door and saw him standing on the porch as if in a quandary, she did not say a word. Instead, she stood very still and looked at him while the silence between them extended out to the fringes of eternity. Then she slowly started to walk towards him, her footsteps creating a sound of emptiness on the porch. Henry watched her come, holding his breath firmly in his lungs. Then the tense calmness shattered and she was in his outstretched arms, leaning snugly, finally against his body.

Several days later they drove to Colby, Maryland to be married before a justice of the peace. She left her illegitimate daughter, Melissa, in the care of relatives in Aurora Springs. Though it saddened Edith once more to leave the child, she knew it was better that way.

After they returned to Sinclair, Henry purchased a plot of land and a clapboard house in the rural vicinity of Sinclair with hopes of fulfilling his dreams.

Edith reluctantly accepted the house. She was exhausted from always thinking of Henry Shane, and tired of constantly trying to oppose her love for him. Her capitulation now at long last was final, but she was unaware of the wailing wind that would continue to torment them for the remaining days of their life.

Epilogue

Nearly twenty-five years after the memorable experience of supervising the construction of a coal-fired electric power plant, coming from North Carolina to Sinclair one summer day, my thoughts went astray in the Coal Region. When the Greyhound bus neared Sinclair. I became joyous. I gazed at the green and succulent highlands with an elated sense of belonging and to the grazing lush pastures on the slopes, to the swift currents of the Stonycreek River, to the old football stadium, and the remembered bandstand. I grinned at them, happy thoughts in a swift passing of memories of Sinclair, anxious for the bus to stop, to be among them. When the bus stopped, the moment I alighted from the bus at the terminal, my joy ended. I was finally at home and the feelings of anxiety toward the uncertain had ceased. As the bus moved slowly out of the terminal, I stood on the concrete pavement, and part of me went with it, a state of meditative sadness, saying reluctantly goodbye. I watched the bus out of sight, then picked up my suitcases and strode off slowly. The journey to the site of my birthplace was over.

As I walked along the street, I noticed that the number of familiar faces and old scenes had dwindled, and that very day I became fully aware of the changes in Sinclair's environment. From the center of town at the bottom of the valley it is a climb to the top of the hill. When the air is quiet there is a fragrance of wild flowers, and up to the very last turn on Rosemore Avenue, the climber can hear the gurgling and rushing waters of the Stonycreek River below.

Set among the brush along the way is an old monument dedicated to the founder of Sinclair, and to the early settlers who migrated into the valley. Moss has grown over the stone base of the stained and weathered monument.

At the top of the hill the road forks. One way leads past an elaborate motel, recently constructed of regional mountain stone, and equipped with all the modern conveniences for lodging, recreation and entertainment. If you are thirsty after the climb you can stop there for a glass of cold draft beer or a can of a refreshing soft drink. In the summer, the drinks are served on a terrace, under colorful sun umbrellas, where in the evening, there is polka or rock concerts by the starlight, and one can watch the moon rise over the Allegheny Ridge five miles across the valley.

Follow the winding road to the left. It will take you by a small amusement park. There are scores of young teen-agers. Like their ancestors, the girls are stocky and well developed. The girls with long hair and shapely bodies are tanned from exposure to the sun that makes you think of the ripe grain fields in the summertime. They wear blue, skin-tight designer jeans and loose, lightweight blouses, and if you look at them directly they will meet your eye.

There is an assortment of small stores on the main street of the town. Where there are no stores, there are office buildings and high rises. Above the archway at the entrance to the ancient town hall is a fresco of a miner, and around him the figures of other common people: steel workers, farmers and soldiers. There is an elaborate memorial to the war dead in the town square—a statue of a soldier mourning his dead comrades—beneath it rows of bright red geraniums in full bloom.

The houses have been renovated with aluminum siding or brick veneer. Large picture windows face the wide, crowded streets. Everywhere there is a clatter of life: automobiles bringing families from the outlying areas, of bicycle and motorcycle riders, of shoes pounding on the concrete pavement. There are supermarkets, department stores, theaters, restaurants, nightclubs, taverns, arcades and service stations. In another part of town there is a large shopping mall under construction.

The mountain road leads out of town, past Saint Anthony's Catholic

Church and Cemetery, and overlooks the valley as in past generations. Below is the other half of the town. It stands by the junction of two main highways. The old railroad line from the west comes to an end at this point, but you can still follow with your eyes the remnants of the former railroad bed that ran out along the valley, adjoining the river. The high mountains are all around. The clouds that have been known to bring heavy, flooding rains to the valley only make the vegetation thrive more vigorously on the surrounding mountainside. On clear, sunny mornings the mountains are like glittering gold and in the evening they are a pinkish hue. By starlight they're as cool and remote as the firmament itself.

There is also an incline plane that moves noisily upward to the extreme top of the mountain carrying vehicles and passengers, while the old attendant dressed in steel-gray uniform, sounds a horn that echoes across the valley.

At the far end of town is a large tract of land that was once an abandoned coal stripping pit. It is now filled, and on it, a large church dedicated to Saint Michael. The silence by the altar is so deep that one can hear the vibrations of the incline plane two miles away.

We are the old folks, Mrs. Wheeling and I. Those others, with their rugged strength, their simple way of life, their undying youth are of the past. The younger generation is of a different breed. It gives me great comfort to think they will never have to go down into the depths of the earth to mine coal for a living. They are fine young men and women—pleasant and well mannered—but they will not be pathfinders of the future. What, with shopping malls, arcades, theaters and elaborate drinking and eating establishments, they find everything to be convenient.

Mrs. Wheeling was still living in the old estate with her widowed daughter, Deborah. It was Mrs. Wheeling's wish to live and die under that roof. She greeted me with enthusiasm and prepared a fine dinner with her own hands, and an inclination to please me as she had done many years ago.

"Come, Joe!" she said, as if I were still a young man again. "You go and sit in the family room and watch television and I'll clear the table. Deborah, go and keep him company?"

The bent, gray haired figure stood thoughtfully in the kitchen sorting dishes and silverware to be placed in the dishwasher. After the completion of her chores, she strolled into the family room and stood near me. I read to her some passages of the story that I had written about Henry Shane. There was an expression of great sadness on her face when I had barely read a few paragraphs. She walked slowly across the room and sat in a rocking chair near the window.

"It is a good account of his life," she said, wiping her eyes with the corner of her handkerchief.

"I'm delighted that you are pleased that I'm writing a story about Henry Shane's life."

"Oh, the story!" she answered, her elbow resting on the arm of the rocking chair, her hand supporting her head. "I like the idea of you writing a story about Henry Shane—but I was thinking of Sinclair in the days of my youth. How wonderful it was then?"

I was tired and weary after my day of travel and went to bed there in my old room in the Wheeling Estate. I left Mrs. Wheeling sitting in her rocking chair reminiscing about the dreams of her youth. I was aroused during the night, and I could hear the faint creak of her rocking chair intermingled with the steady, humming sound of the television set.

At sunrise, I went to Saint Anthony's Cemetery and scattered flowers on the graves of Henry and Edith Shane. There I go often since my retirement, to sit for a half summer day above those perished forms, and think of the old times, and those memorable tales of a venerable Korean War veteran.

AGMV
MARQUIS
Québec, Canada
1999